Beyond the Bottom Line

Beyond the Bottom Line:
The Producer in Film and Television Studies

Edited by

Andrew Spicer, A.T. McKenna and Christopher Meir

Bloomsbury Academic
An imprint of Bloomsbury Publishing Plc

B L O O M S B U R Y
NEW YORK · LONDON · OXFORD · NEW DELHI · SYDNEY

Bloomsbury Academic

An imprint of Bloomsbury Publishing Inc

1385 Broadway
New York
NY 10018
USA

50 Bedford Square
London
WC1B 3DP
UK

www.bloomsbury.com

BLOOMSBURY and the Diana logo are trademarks of Bloomsbury Publishing Plc

First published 2014
Paperback edition first published 2016

Library of Congress Cataloging-in-Publication Data
Beyond the bottom line : the producer in film and television studies /
edited by Andrew Spicer, A.T. McKenna, Christopher Meir.
pages cm
Includes bibliographical references and index.
ISBN 978-1-4411-7236-5 (hardback)
1. Motion pictures–Production and direction. 2. Television–Production and direction.
3. Motion picture industry. 4. Television broadcasting. I. Spicer, Andrew, 1953-
editor of compilation. II. McKenna, A. T. (Anthony T.), editor of compilation.
III. Meir, Christopher, editor of compilation.
PN1995.9.P7B49 2014
791.4302′32–dc23
2014004633

ISBN: HB: 978-1-4411-7236-5
PB: 978-1-5013-1777-4
ePub: 978-1-4411-6288-5
ePDF: 978-1-4411-2512-5

Typeset by Integra Software Services Pvt. Ltd

Contents

List of Illustrations

Contributors

Constanza Burucúa graduated from the University of Buenos Aires (Argentina) and having completed an MA in Latin American Audiovisual Industries from the International University of Andalusia (Spain), Constanza Burucúa obtained both an MA and a PhD in Film and Television Studies from the University of Warwick (UK). She then moved to Caracas (Venezuela), where she worked as an independent TV producer, while also preparing the manuscript of her book, *Confronting the 'Dirty War' in Argentine Cinema, 1983–1993* (2009). Since 2010, she has been working in the Department of Film Studies at Western University (Canada). Her research focuses on Latin American film cultures and, in particular, on Argentine cinema. She is also committed to the production of documentary films. *El Cerrito (2006), Reverón* (2009), *La reina del pueblo/The Queen of the People* (2010) and *Villanueva, el Diablo* (2012) are some of the titles that she has been involved with.

Stuart Cunningham is Distinguished Professor of Media and Communications, Queensland University of Technology, and Director of the Australian Research Council Centre of Excellence for Creative Industries and Innovation. He has played a leading role in the development of Australian film and television history and analysis; in the articulation of policy into media and cultural studies; and in shaping the debate and impact of the creative industries agenda in Australia and internationally. He was elected as an inaugural fellow in Cultural and Communication Studies in the Australian Academy of the Humanities, and has served in several leadership roles in advocacy, advice and governance in research and higher education, and in the screen and library sectors. His most recent books are *Digital Disruption: Cinema Moves Online* (edited with Dina Iordanova, 2012), *Key Concepts in Creative Industries* (with John Hartley, Jason Potts, Terry Flew, John Banks and Michael Keane, 2012), *Hidden Innovation: Policy, Industry and the Creative Sector* (2013) and *Screen Distribution Post-Hollywood: The New King Kongs of the Online World* (with Jon Silver, 2013).

Audun Engelstad has been Associate Professor at Lillehammer University College since 2006. He holds an MA in comparative literature and has gained a doctorate from the University of Oslo in 2005 for a thesis entitled *Losing Streak Stories: Mapping Norwegian Film Noir*. Engelstad teaches introductory classes in film history and film and television analysis, as well as special topic courses on subjects that include Nordic cinema, genre studies, film theory and research methodologies, and a recently established course on the film and television industries. His publications include articles on film genres and on television series; he is currently writing a book on film narratology. Engelstad is part of an international research project, Success in the Film and Television Industries (SiFTI), together with several of his colleagues as well as participants from the United Kingdom, Denmark and the Netherlands.

Sonia Friel is an AHRC-funded PhD candidate at Norwich University of the Arts, where she is currently completing a thesis that explores language and notation in relation to the creative practices of Jan Švankmajer and the Quay brothers. This doctoral research considers a diverse range of material created by these artist-animators – from their most famous animations to virtually undocumented drawings, sculptures, games and ephemera – and examines the role of concepts such as the visual metaphor or word-object in these works as alternatives to many of the conventions and devices frequently associated with linear narrative. Her research has benefited from the author's close contact with the contemporary Czech and Slovak surrealist group, based in Prague, and the British independent film producer Keith Griffiths, which has resulted in numerous conference papers as well as the chapter on Keith Griffiths for this publication.

Ben Goldsmith is Senior Research Fellow in the ARC Centre of Excellence for Creative Industries and Innovation, Queensland University of Technology. He previously worked as a lecturer and researcher in Screen Studies at the Australian Film, Television and Radio School. He is the co-editor (with Mark Ryan and Geoff Lealand) of the second volume of the *Directory of World Cinema: Australia and New Zealand* (2014), and co-editor (with Greg Hearn, Ruth Bridgstock and Jess Rodgers) of *Creative Work Beyond the Creative Industries: Innovation, Employment and Education* (2014).

Joe Kember is Senior Lecturer in Film at the University of Exeter. His research has focused on popular and visual culture throughout the nineteenth and early twentieth centuries, especially early and silent cinema. His book *Marketing Modernity: Victorian Popular Shows and Early Cinema* (2009) provides an analysis of the institutional development of early film in relation to emergent models of self-identity and personality at the turn of the century. Among his other recent books, articles and chapters are publications that have tackled spectatorship, performance and screening practices in exhibition sites such as Victorian freak shows, lecture theatres, public halls and the magic theatre. He is currently completing a co-authored book, *Picture Going: Popular Visual Media in the South-West, 1840–1914*.

Donna Kornhaber is Assistant Professor in the Department of English at the University of Texas at Austin, where she teaches film. She is the author of *Charlie Chaplin, Director* (2014). Her articles, on topics ranging from early animation and silent film to film noir and literary adaptation, have appeared or are forthcoming in publications including *Quarterly Review of Film and Video*, *Bright Lights Film Journal* and *Movie: A Journal of Film Criticism*, among others.

Paul Long is Reader in Media and Cultural History at Birmingham City University and Associate Director of the Birmingham Centre for Media and Cultural Research. He is the author of '*Only in the common people': The Aesthetics of Class in Post-War Britain* (2008). He has written widely on media history including studies of BBC4's *Britannia* series, Tony Palmer's TV series *All You Need Is Love* as well as the role of student unions in UK popular music cultures. His research on creative industries includes contributions to the EU-funded projects 'Creative Metropoles' and 'Cross-Innovation'. He is part of the AHRC-funded project 'Cultural Intermediation and the Creative Economy', where he researches the relationship of 'hard to reach' communities with the cultural sector (http://culturalintermediation.wordpress.com). He is currently developing research concerning the role of class, ethnicity and gender in creative industries work.

James Lyons is Senior Lecturer in Film Studies at the University of Exeter. He is the author of *Selling Seattle* (2004) and *Miami Vice* (2010) and co-editor of *Quality Popular Television* (2003), *Multimedia Histories: From the Magic Lantern to the Internet* (2007) and *The Rise of the American Comics Artist: Creators and Contexts* (2010). He is currently working on a new book on performance in documentary film.

A.T. McKenna teaches Media and International Communications at the University of Nottingham in Ningbo, China. He has published widely on American, British and Chinese cinema, and is co-author of *The Man Who Got Carter: Independent Production and the British Film Industry, 1960–1980* (2013) with Andrew Spicer. His next book, *The Boston Barnum*, about showman-producer Joseph E. Levine, will be published in 2015.

Christopher Meir is Lecturer in Film at the University of the West Indies, St. Augustine, in Trinidad and Tobago. He is the author of *Scottish Cinema: Texts and Contexts* (2014). He has also published articles on producers Jeremy Thomas, Ismail Merchant and Harry Alan Towers, as well as an interview with Andrea Calderwood.

Brett Mills is Senior Lecturer in the School of Film, Television and Media Studies, University of East Anglia. He is the author of *Television Sitcom* (2005) and *The Sitcom* (2009), and co-author of two editions of *Reading Media Theory: Thinkers, Approaches, Contexts* (2009/2012). He has written journal articles on comedy for *Screen, Television and New Media* and *Celebrity Studies*, and co-edited comedy-themed special editions of the journals *Participations* and *Comedy Studies*. He is the principal investigator on the three-year (2012–2014) AHRC-funded research project 'Make Me Laugh: Creativity in the British Television Comedy Industry' (www.makemelaugh.org.uk).

Jo Sondre Moseng is Associate Professor in Film and Television Studies at Lillehammer University College, Norway. His main research interests include contemporary

Contributors

Scandinavian film history, production studies, national cinema and youth films. He is a member of the core group in the research project SIFTI ('Success in film and television industries'), which has Norwegian, British, Dutch and Danish partners.

Sarah Ralph is Research Associate in the School of Film, Television and Media Studies at the University of East Anglia, working on the three-year (2012–2014) AHRC-funded research project 'Make Me Laugh: Creativity in the British Television Comedy industry' (www.makemelaugh.org.uk). She is the co-author (with Brett Mills) of two reports on the contemporary British television comedy industry submitted to the Department of Culture, Media and Sport. She is an editorial board member of *Participations*, is a part of the research team on the 'Remembering Alien' project and is co-editor of a forthcoming special edition of *Celebrity Studies* on audiences and celebrity.

Mark David Ryan is Lecturer in Film, Screen and Animation at the Queensland University of Technology in Brisbane, Australia. He is the co-editor (with Ben Goldsmith and Geoff Lealand) of the *Directory of World Cinema: Australia and New Zealand 2*. Mark has written extensively on Australian horror films, genre cinema, industry dynamics and movie production and cultural policy. His research has been published in *New Review of Film & Television Studies, Media International Australia: Incorporating Culture and Policy, Continuum: Journal of Media & Cultural Studies, Senses of Cinema* and *Studies in Australasian Cinema* among others.

Pauline Small is Senior Lecturer in Film Studies at Queen Mary, University of London. Her specialism is Italian cinema, where she has published in two main areas: a series of articles on contemporary Italian cinema, specifically the Mafia films of Matteo Garrone, Marco Tullio Giordana and Paolo Sorrentino, and the work of film-makers Mario Martone and Gianni Amelio; and on 1950s film-making, with a monograph, *Sophia Loren; Moulding the Star* (2009), an article on Gina Lollobrigida's Franco-Italian co-productions and a chapter on female stardom in the forthcoming *Italian Cinema Book* edited by Peter Bondanella (2013). She is at present researching Anglo-Italian productions of the same era, with particular emphasis on archive materials in Rome and London.

Andrew Spicer is Professor of Cultural Production at the University of the West of England. He has published widely on British cinema, cultural constructions of masculinity, *film noir* and production cultures. His books include *Film Noir* (2002), *Typical Men: The Representation of Masculinity in Popular British Cinema* (2003), *Sydney Box* (2006) and, with A. T. McKenna, *Get Carter: Michael Klinger, Independent Production and British Cinema, 1960–1980* (2013). He has edited or co-edited several special editions of journals, including *Journal of British Cinema* 9:1 ('The Producer'), as well as *European Film Noir* (2007) and *A Companion to Film Noir* (2013) with Helen Hanson. He is working on a monograph, *Sean Connery*, for publication in 2015. He is currently a member of a European project, 'Success in the Film and Television Industries' (SiFTI, 2013–2016).

Simon Spink is a film director and producer. He was the founder and Creative Director of Naski, an independent film production company based in Recife, Brazil. He has worked on a diverse range of productions, from documentaries and short films through to television series and online content. After an extensive career in Brazil working in a variety of creative roles, he is now based in the United Kingdom as a freelance film producer. He has recently completed postgraduate study in the creative industries and cultural policy at Birmingham City University. His research concerns digital distribution and markets for independent production.

Deb Verhoeven is Chair and Professor of Media and Communication at Deakin University in Melbourne, Deputy Director of the Centre for Memory, Imagination and Invention and a Chief Investigator in the ARC Centre of Excellence for Creative Industries & Innovation. She is the Director of the Humanities Networked Infrastructure (HuNI) project and Research My World, a university sector crowdfunding initiative.

Gertjan Willems is a PhD Fellow of the Research Foundation Flanders (FWO) in the Centre for Cinema and Media Studies (CIMS, Department of Communication Studies) at Ghent University. He holds an MA in Communication Studies (Ghent University, 2009) and an MA in Film Studies and Visual Culture (University of Antwerp, 2010). In his PhD thesis, Gertjan examines the relation between film, state and nation by focusing on Flanders. Recent publications have appeared in the *Journal of Belgian History* and (with K. Smets), 'Film policy and the emergence of the cross-cultural: Exploring crossover cinema in Flanders (Belgium)', in *Crossover Cinema: Cross-cultural Film from Production to Reception*, ed. Sukhmani Khorana (2013). For more information, see http://www.cims.ugent.be/members/gertjan-willems.

Acknowledgements

The editors would like to thank all the contributors. Their willingness to accept suggestions and respond to comments has made this collection a pleasure to work on and a valuable learning experience. We would also like to thank Katie Gallof at Bloomsbury for her initial interest in commissioning the collection and for her patience and advice during its preparation.

Christopher Meir wishes to thank Anna McLeish and Emile Sherman for agreeing to be interviewed for his piece, as well as the University of the West Indies, St. Augustine, for granting him research leave to work on this project.

Andrew Spicer wishes to thank the University of the West of England for some financial support towards the cost of the stills and to his partner, Joyce Woolridge, for her help in the final stages of preparing the manuscript and for compiling the index.

1

Introduction

Andrew Spicer, A.T. McKenna and Christopher Meir

The financial side of art has always proved problematic for academics and critics alike, as if fetish objects are somehow sullied by the profit motive. With the producer being so closely associated with bottom-line concerns, this apparent distaste for money matters within the academy could go some way to explaining the producer's relative absence from Screen Studies literature. However, although scholarly work on producers is remarkably sparse compared to, say, work on directors, depictions of producers in popular culture are plentiful. The producer, then, is not an unappealing figure. As a regular feature of movies, novels, cartoons, legends and anecdotes, the producer is often caricatured, but usually with a degree of affection. Nonetheless, while the grubbiness of bottom-line concerns may be attractive in tall tales and lampoon, they are still not adequately addressed by scholarship which often fallaciously dichotomizes art and finance. The producer, then, such an essential component of any *production*, remains a largely misunderstood and under-analysed figure.

It is not the purpose of this collection to romanticize the producer still further, nor is it merely to explode myths. Our purpose is to understand the role of the producer or, more precisely, the *roles* of the producers. The producer can define studios, genres, even national cinemas, but will also bring the artistic expressions of limited appeal from auteurs or boutique collectives to a screen. Given that the 'role' of the producer may comprise many different roles, in order to better understand producers, we feel that an edited collection, gathering together a range of different approaches and perspectives, is the ideal format to address this topic. Recent years have seen an increasing number of academic articles and monographs devoted to producers, yet this is the first collection devoted to the subject. Because this collection incorporates a wide variety of approaches and contexts, it is, we feel, a timely addition to this growing field of study. Moreover, this collection demonstrates how, by analysing the producer, these approaches and contexts can provide deeper insights into several of the dominant debates within Screen Studies, including those pertaining to authorship, creativity, media historiography, national and transnational media cultures as well as many others.

The producer is easy to caricature but the role is difficult to define. In the 1970s, Gore Vidal observed, 'It is curious … how entirely the idea of the working producer has vanished. He is no longer remembered except as the butt of familiar stories: fragile artist treated cruelly by insensitive cigar smoking producer.'[1] This volume seeks to remedy that 'vanishing', but first we must deal with the caricature identified by Vidal because it is so potent in the popular imagination. To this end, the first section of this Introduction, 'Unreliable histories and self-made scapegoats', provides a short historiographical account of the development of the familiar cliché of the producer and how this has contributed to their undervaluation. The second section, 'Media industry studies', places the producer within the broader field of media production studies and directly addresses the idea of the working producer through a broad definition of this most mysterious of roles. The third and final section, 'Contributors and contexts', provides a summary account of all chapters that comprise this volume, places them within wider academic discourse, and suggests some productive avenues for future work.

For this first edited collection of work devoted to the producer, we sought contributions with a wide variety of approaches and contexts in order that the reader has a rich resource to deepen their understanding of the producers' role. Given that much of the work published on producers in recent years has focused on Hollywood, we have deliberately chosen to downplay this field of study to provide an internationalist and pan-historical volume. Nonetheless, to address fully the enduring stereotype of the producer in a historiographical sense, it is to Hollywood that we must first journey.

Unreliable histories and self-made scapegoats

To find the root of Gore Vidal's familiar stories, the producer as cigar-smoking tyrant, we must look to Irving Thalberg. In 1922, Thalberg fired director Erich von Stroheim from *Merry-Go-Round*. It was a David and Goliath struggle, with the producer, not the director, in the David role. Thalberg had tried to fire von Stroheim from projects before but von Stroheim's starring roles in the films he directed made it impossible. However, von Stroheim's duties on *Merry-Go-Round* were entirely behind the camera and this made his dismissal less difficult, albeit, not easy. Thalberg, studio manager of Universal and barely 23 years old, went into battle with one of the most powerful directors in Hollywood and, by doing so, cemented his own reputation and made Hollywood movies a producers' medium for its Golden Age.[2] Producer power in the studio system was personified by Thalberg, a slight, slim non-smoker; the big cigar, the big desk and the big belly of caricature came later. The caricature came about as a result of many forces, including social, intellectual and cultural prejudices, but also from movies, the film industry and producers themselves (Figure 1.1).

Thalberg was the inspiration for Munro Stahr, F. Scott Fitzgerald's protagonist of *The Last Tycoon*, the mercurial genius who understood 'the whole equation' of movie-making. To understand an equation, it is useful to break it down into its component parts. In an ideal world, a capacity for compartmentalization allows the producer to be the overseer. They are the first in and the last out, and will maintain overall control of a project and carry the burden of 'real world' administrative and financial concerns. In

Figure 1.1 Portrait of Irving Thalberg in the 1920s. Courtesy of Photofest

performing this role, the producer creates space for the component creative personnel to focus on and fulfil their task more effectively. Michael Klinger, for example, once engaged in a lengthy correspondence to acquire rights to René Magritte's *L'Assassin Menace*, so that Mike Hodges could use the image for a fraction of a second in *Pulp* (1972).[3]

In a more cynical world, the producer is duplicitous, if not multiplicitous. This producer *confines* operatives to their component part, and so controls perception and restricts access to the 'whole equation'. The duplicitous producer profits from atomization of personnel and maintains overall control of 'real world' concerns such as money. Joseph E. Levine, for example, once summoned Mel Brooks into his office and explained, 'Mel, my job is to get the money for you to make the movie. Your job is to make the movie. My job is to steal the money from you. And your job is to find out how I do it.'[4]

Both idealist and cynical views of the producer have been true at different times, at the same time, and in the same person. Importantly, in both these anecdotes it is the producer who appears more capable, more competent and more adept at understanding the world than the sheltered director. A reductive analysis, perhaps, but it is one that informs producer historiography. To return to Vidal, it is not only the cruel producer that informs the familiar stories, but also the fragile artist. The dichotomy between art and commerce may be fallacious, but it is a stalwart of many of the portrayals that inform popular understanding of the producer.

In 1941, Hollywood produced one of the most widely quoted and best loved lampoons of film bosses in *Sullivan's Travels*, with its famous scene of studio money men repeatedly demanding assurances that successful but disillusioned screenwriter John Sullivan's proposed picture about the sufferings of the average man will have 'a little sex in it'. The producers try to convince Sullivan to stick with the escapist comedies that have proved so popular, and made 'a fortune', but Sullivan wants to make *O Brother Where Art Thou?* a 'commentary on modern conditions. Stark realism. The problems that confront the average man ... a canvas of the suffering of humanity!' As he pitches his movie to the studio executives, it becomes clear that Sullivan's background is one of wealth and privilege, while the studio men come from poverty and hardship. This realization causes Sullivan, crestfallen, to crumple into a chair and berate himself for having the temerity to imagine he could hope to understand the wider world. In pitching pecuniary street wisdom against artistic idealism, this deftly constructed routine finds a parallel in Leo C. Rosten's observations of the studio system. Noting the widespread prejudice against Hollywood's *nouveau riche* in the 1940s, Rosten suggests:

> When the name of a movie magnate is uttered, one of the first associations to spring into the mind of the listener is 'tailor' or 'button-hole maker'. The implicit assumption ... is that in one fell swoop a pants-presser jumped from a loft on West 37th Street to an office in Hollywood. This is an interesting stereotype (and a reflection upon Hollywood's publicity).[5]

Rosten's observations reveal not only a widespread prejudice against the self-made entrepreneur, but also that the stereotype of the unschooled interloper itself originated in, and was popularized by, Hollywood. This cliché of the producer was largely self-created, revelled in and travelled from popular culture mythology into serious discourse in the post-war era, most notably with the auteurist positioning of the producer as scapegoat in movies such as Jean-Luc Godard's *Le Mépris* (1963).

The *Nouvelle Vague's* attacks on producers were, however, more manifesto-driven affectation than sincerely held principle, and the producer Georges de Beauregard was as much an architect of the French New Wave as Truffaut or Godard. Championing the director in the name of artistic purity was both fashionable and marketable, and savvy producers made sound investments in auteurist confections, while the less savvy had their fingers burned. Indeed, the documentary *Henri Georges Clouzot's Inferno* (2009) provides a salutary lesson in placing too much faith in the genius auteur as Columbia, keen to capitalize on the Euro-art craze of the 1960s, gave Clouzot too much money and too much freedom to make *Inferno*. The film was never completed, though hours of beautiful but formless footage remain.

There is little doubt that the auteurists' elevation of the director led to an underrating of the producer. But this opportunistic and marketable attack on the producer bugaboo was taken up with almost evangelical zeal by auteurist critics in America in a charge led by Andrew Sarris. Notably, Sarris used the fashion for multi-director portmanteau films from the European arthouse as evidence of the primacy of the director.[6] However, others may have discerned a producer-led package of trendy directors as a cash-in on the auteurist superstitions of the arthouse audience.[7] Nonetheless, Hollywood absorbed auteur theory in the late 1960s as the cine-literate of the Hollywood Renaissance superseded the streetsmart Hollywood producer. One illustrative tale from this era sees Warren Beatty attempting to counter Jack Warner's negative reaction to *Bonnie and Clyde* (1967) by explaining that the film is an *homage* to the great Warner Bros. gangster movies of the 1930s. 'What the fuck's an *homage*?' was Warner's response.[8]

Whether apocryphal or not, the tale is revealing in many ways. Although Sarris had derided old Hollywood for recycling formulaic product, the key films of this apparently revolutionary era in American cinema were all genre formulas, production formulas, old and new: *Bonnie and Clyde* (gangster), *The Graduate* (1967, screwball comedy), *The Wild Bunch* (1969, western), *Easy Rider* (1969, biker exploitation). There is also the question of literacy. The so-called movie brats of the Hollywood Renaissance, like the doyens of the *Nouvelle Vague*, wore their erudition in matters cinematic proudly and indulged in homage, reference and intertextuality. The producers of Hollywood past would, by contrast, revel in their untutoredness, often pretending to be illiterate, valorizing a more intuitive approach to film-making based on almost magical concepts such as 'gut instinct' in a deliberate mystification of their own role.

As in Rosten's observations and *Sullivan's Travels*, the issue of social class is also again apparent. At the risk of over-generalizing, many of Hollywood's great producers were of immigrant stock and raised in ghettos. The auteur directors of the French New Wave were, by contrast, generally from more comfortable backgrounds, and while some of the movie-brat directors who dominated the Hollywood Renaissance may have had modest upbringings, none came from squalor. Indeed, as Hollywood absorbed auteurism in the late 1960s, few would deny that the industry was also being embourgeoised. Like Sullivan, the movie brats challenged the notion of the American Dream and, as they did, displaced a generation of Hollywood men who, with poverty-stricken backgrounds romanticized by press-agents and myth makers, laid claim to having lived it.

In late 1960s, Sarris, triumphantly convinced that the case for the director as author had been made and the argument won, wrote, 'Since producers and other studio satraps always took the lion's share of the loot, few tears have been shed for their downfall.'[9] But the news of the producers' demise was rather exaggerated as, concurrently, Robert Evans was turning Paramount into the most important studio of the early 1970s. Subsequent years saw the emergence of super producers, often working in pairs, such as Richard D. Zanuck and David Brown, Julia and Michael Phillips, and Don Simpson and Jerry Bruckheimer. Later, the flowering of auteurist American Indie cinema was galvanized by figures such as indie mogul Harvey Weinstein and low-budget pioneer Christine Vachon. Nonetheless, Sarris' comment about the 'lion's share of the loot' resonates, as the producer is so often associated with financial gain. Revealingly, Sarris does not use the word 'money', but rather 'loot', with its implication of gains ill-gotten.

That each project must begin with that most unappetizing task of pestering people for money to make the movie has undoubtedly added to the producer's venal public image. Subsequently, the producer must pester personnel to keep costs down and complete on time, then pester distributors for more money to circulate the movie, and then oversee the pestering of the public to pay to go and see the film. Indeed, sifting through a producer's archive one is often struck by the sheer volume of letters asking for money; and the volume of rejections calls to mind Winston Churchill's definition of success: 'stumbling from failure to failure without any loss of enthusiasm'. Whereas the producer could be seen as an enabler, on set the producer is often the one who says 'no'. But for every 'no' issued on-set, there will be a hundred 'nos' in a filing cabinet in the producer's office from potential investors, distributors, stars, directors and countless others.

It is often difficult to untangle disinterested observation, cultural prejudice and showman's bunkum, particularly as the image of the maverick serves all three inclinations so well. The producer as anti-hero, with a hide thickened by rejection and soul polluted by the corrupting indignities of the profit motive, has proved a durable archetype and popular culture provides ample renderings of the producer as lonely outsider. Fitzgerald's Munro Stahr is the high achiever fated to be outcast; Kirk Douglas' Jonathan Shields in *The Bad and the Beautiful* (1952) is brilliant but also a manipulative emotional cripple. In *Le Mépris* (Figure 1.2), Jack Palance's Jeremy Prokosch is a vulgar American moron who is excluded from conversations with his cultured, multi-lingual European colleagues, and in *ivansxtc* (2000) Danny Huston's Ivan Beckman contemplates his worthless existence following his cancer diagnosis.

Figure 1.2 Jack Palance as Jeremy Prokosch, in Jean-Luc Godard's *Le Mépris* (1963), a vulgar, philistine producer, who compares himself to the gods: 'I like gods. I like them very much. I know exactly how they feel. Exactly.' Courtesy of Photofest

It is now more than 20 years since Thomas Schatz wrote that auteur theory's influence had stalled 'film history and criticism in a prolonged state of adolescent romanticism'.[10] While we do not dispute this, we do feel that the time had come to stop blaming auteur theory for the producer's relative absence from scholarly discourse, especially as so many of the myths about the producer come from many other sources that often pre-date the earliest rumblings of auteur theory. While we acknowledge the shortcomings of auteur theory, we also acknowledge its strengths. What the auteurists did provide was a way of seeing and understanding by using the director as a vantage point when analysing texts. Similarly, the producer often provides a very useful vantage point for observation and interrogation of a much broader terrain. However, the producer is a figure shrouded in myth and mystery, and the subject of countless unreliable histories. The role of the producer is also often conflated with other roles and titles – such as, mogul, magnate, studio head, investor and showman. And all of the factors discussed thus far combine to create significant methodological problems within the field of media industry studies, some of which will be addressed in the next section.

Media industry studies

The collection's exploration of the role of the producer is a contribution to the debates emerging in the field of media industry studies, which has experienced a strong resurgence over the past five years.[11] In contradistinction to the paradigm characteristic of earlier studies – which focused on patterns of ownership and the 'almost omnipotent' control exercised by large corporations – production has been reconceived as a cultural practice involving professions, organizations and less regulated networks, and therefore a cultural rather than an exclusively economic phenomenon. In emphasizing 'cultural studies of production' with their own codes, meanings and rituals, media production studies has shifted from a Marxist orientation to a more anthropological and ethnographical approach.[12] However, in doing so, as Jennifer Holt and Alisa Perren argue, media industry studies does not abandon an attention to the wider forces of international capitalism but aims to synthesize the often competing claims of political economy studies and cultural studies and therefore to be equally attentive to economic, technological and political forces, to ownership, regulation and the marketplace, as well as to the activities of media workers and the production of specific texts. As they note, a cultural studies approach was always concerned with not just texts in themselves but also in the 'ways that cultural power is produced and reproduced, mediated and negotiated, circulated and consumed'.[13]

This theoretical shift has brought with it a welcome emphasis on *agency*, with detailed attention given, through empirically grounded studies, to the activities of media workers, and the varied interactions between agents and institutions. The focus has been on the ways in which 'media producers make culture, and, in so doing to make themselves into particular kinds of workers in modern, mediated societies ... how people work through professional organizations and informal networks to form shared communities of shared practices, languages, and cultural understandings of the world.[14] Scholars have investigated the nature of cultural labour, describing and analysing the lives, dispositions and *mentalités* of those who work in the cultural industries, which are becoming increasingly important economically and thus the focus of media and government attention as well as the academy.[15] An influential study has been John Thornton Caldwell's *Production Culture* (2008), which explores the discourses of the media themselves, the ways in which film and television workers construct their own cultural and interpretative frameworks, and thus the need to analyse their own self-representations and 'cultural self-performances' that are often neither logical nor systematic.[16] Caldwell's focus encourages an attention to the multifaceted nature of production practices and to their embedded nature within industry routines and cultures, including networking.

The film industry/the film producer

However, as media industries analysts recognize, although there are shared characteristics across the media spectrum, each particular industry has its own specific histories, traditions and practices that make it distinct. Although there have been studies of television producers – where the role is not subject to the same caricature discussed in the first section – and those working in other media, including contributions to this collection, the dominant paradigm has been created by accounts of the figure found in film theory and historiography. In his essay defining the approach of film industry studies within the broader field of media industries, Thomas Schatz argues that its key concerns are with film style, authorship and mode of production that are 'always and inevitably *in process*, co-existing in a state of constant change due to myriad external and internal forces'.[17] For Schatz, the mode of production encompasses both macro industry economics and the micro level of specific companies and individual producers and a concomitant attention to actual films. However, as a sub-set, film industry studies has been hindered by two major impediments. The first is a disabling split between studies of economic film history that have 'largely avoided confronting the movies as formal objects' and practices of textual analysis that have ignored production contexts.[18] The second, as discussed in the preceding section, is that, through its privileging of the director's role, Film Studies has conflated the notion of authorship with the thematic and visual signature of the auteur director.[19]

In order to circumvent these paradigms, it is necessary to return to an older tradition of film history, which, as Eric Smoodin notes in his essay, 'The History of Film History', 'stressed issues of industry and consumption' until these were displaced by the concept of the auteur-director and the decontextualized analysis of films from the mid-1950s onwards.[20] Earlier ethnographical/anthropological studies of the 'Hollywood colony' by Leo C. Rosten (1941), mentioned earlier, and Hortense Powdermaker (1950) have much to say about industry workers and the role of the film producer.[21] Rosten was the first analyst to cut through the myths surrounding film production and to amass a wealth of empirical data, conceiving Hollywood as a dynamic social and cultural entity that was geared to a mass market but which needed to treat each film as an individual product. He was keenly aware of the different labour hierarchies within the 'colony' and that cultural production was firmly situated within wider social and economic networks.[22]

Rosten and Powdermaker's pioneering work was followed, at some distance, by two seminal studies of the Hollywood studio system: Janet Staiger's work in *The Classical Hollywood Cinema* identifying the evolving 'modes of production' that have characterized the American film industry, and Thomas Schatz's *The Genius of the System*.[23] Staiger's concept of particular modes of production moved analysis away from a static view of a general film 'industry' towards an understanding of the particular combinations of finance, labour and the physical means of production that determined the nature of film-making at particular moments. Labour in Staiger's analysis refers to the total process that includes the hierarchical assignment of roles and the system of management controls. However, whereas Staiger's approach has little room for agency, Schatz's study emphasizes the cultural dimension in the creation of the studio system, thereby creating far more space for the activities of individual producers whom Schatz characterizes as 'the most misunderstood and undervalued figures in American film history'.[24] Schatz discusses in detail, for instance, the methods through which Irving Thalberg created the role of the studio production head, the ways in which Darryl F. Zanuck exerted his control over Twentieth Century-Fox's output or how David O. Selznick pioneered the role of the 'independent' producer, allowing him to take control of almost every facet of a film's construction, from inception to exhibition and promotion.

Schatz's study has been complemented by specific studies of these Hollywood titans, and there have been occasional studies of less celebrated producers including Matthew Bernstein's exemplary study of Walter Wanger, or Brian Taves' monograph on Thomas Ince.[25] Sheri Chinen Biesen's study of Joan Harrison and Virginia Van Upp was particularly welcome as it demonstrated that even within such a masculine culture as film-making, women could attain senior production positions.[26] Andrew Spicer has explored the importance of three producers – Jerry Wald, Adrian Scott and Mark Hellinger – in the development of *film noir*.[27] However, in this respect, as in Film Studies more generally, the dominant focus has been on Hollywood, which, as noted, we have deliberately downplayed in the current collection. On the contrary, we have sought to open out the field into different national cinemas across the globe and transnational cinemas, as discussed in the third section.

The producer: Roles and qualities

Although contributors to this collection argue quite rightly that producers need to be understood within the specific industrial and economic contexts in which they operated, it will be useful, because the role of the producer is so poorly understood, to try to define the role itself and the general qualities necessary in order to be successful.

This discussion both addresses the caricature adumbrated in the first section and acts as a useful corrective to cynical accounts such as William Fadiman's, which contends that 'any guy can be a producer' because there are no entrance requirements, possession of particular skills or professional training. Lack of talent is no bar to achievement because the producer can hire the necessary creative personnel.[28] What follows in this section is therefore an overview discussion of the *craft* of a producer – the skills, talents and competences that the role requires, without, however, attempting to define it in an absolute or normative sense.[29]

On a basic level, as recognized within the media industries themselves, a producer needs to be distinguished from an associate or line producer (or production manager), whose job is to control the logistics of an actual production. Alvarado and Stewart make a useful distinction between those who have allocative rather than operational control: between those who decide who does what and those who have to implement those strategic decisions.[30] A further distinction is between what Mervyn LeRoy called the 'creative producer' and the 'business administrator producer', the former dealing with the artistic aspects of a production (including scripting, casting and direction) and those who are primarily responsible for obtaining production finance and handling business matters.[31] The latter, in the film industry at least, are usually referred to as executive producers.

Although the distinction between an artistic and a business orientation might describe the difference between some producers, the labels actually obscure what most commentators consider to be the producer's key quality: to *combine* an artistic sensibility with financial nous and therefore act as a bridge between commerce and art – what Michael Balcon deftly called the producer's 'dual capacity as the creative man and the trustee of the moneybags'.[32] Eric Fellner argues that a producer needs a combination of 'creative insight to make the right choices' and 'business acumen to set out the whole [project] properly'.[33] Charlton Heston, who worked with many different producers, considered that a 'real producer' was 'a special combination, neither bird nor beast (or maybe both). He must have sound creative instincts about script, casting, design … about *film*. At the same time he must have an iron-clad grasp of logistics, scheduling, marketing, and costs … above all costs'.[34] This potent combination of apparently contradictory talents allows producers to perform what Pierre Bourdieu sees as an essentially intermediary role, mediating between the creative world of writers, directors, stars and cinematographers and the world of finance and business deals.[35] However, 'creativity' is a problematic term and separating it from 'commerce' is a difficult and even misleading task, as will be taken up in the next section of this introduction.

It is precisely this combination of art and commerce that allows the producer, usually, to take overall charge of a production. The British producer Michael Relph, who had a longstanding partnership with the director Basil Dearden at Ealing Studios and later as independents, makes a useful distinction between the more circumscribed role of the director – 'the tactical commander in control of the army in the field – the actors and technicians on the studio floor' – and the more capacious role of the producer, whom he saw as 'the strategical commander in control of the conception as a whole'. Although it is the producer's responsibility to ensure that the director is 'serviced with the money, personnel and equipment he needs', it is the producer who is in 'strategic command of the film from an artistic viewpoint' because the director may lose sense of the 'artistic proportions of the film as a whole. These will have been previously determined by the producer, director and writer, and the producer must see that the director brings their joint conception to the screen'.[36] For David Puttnam, the producer's overall control is essential because his experience led him to understand that the key personnel involved in a film's production may have divergent conceptions; thus the producer's prime role is to ensure 'that we're all making *exactly* the same movie'. Once Puttnam was convinced of that shared vision, his role was 'to protect the director and give him everything he needs'.[37]

The producer's overall control extends beyond the confines of the actual process of production to encompass a film's genesis through to its marketing and exhibition. Balcon considered that the producer must have 'that capability of looking at the film as an entity and be able to judge its progress and development from the point of view of the audience who [*sic*] will eventually view it'.[38] This ability to gauge public taste was central to Thalberg's conception of the producer's role because the film industry is 'a creative business dependent, as almost no other business is, on the emotional reaction of its customers. It should be conducted with budgets and cost sheets, but it cannot be conducted with blueprints and graphs'.[39] Producers often follow their instincts in this respect rather than conduct extensive market testing, but they are tenacious in trying to ensure that their films are distributed and screened in ways that are appropriate, often battling with agents, distributors and marketing departments long after the film has been completed, concerning themselves with the minutiae of publicity, release dates and sales.

In his pioneering study, Rosten understood the key role played by the producer in the organization of both the tangible and intangible elements in film production: attempting to control properties (studios, sets and equipment), finance and diverse, often volatile, artistic temperaments, as well as understanding the entertainment needs of a broad public.[40] Relph thought this quality involved an understanding of the strengths and limitations of the personnel involved: 'He must know the capabilities of his director, choosing a story that will exploit his talents and not expose his weakness. He must be constantly at hand to guide and advise yet must avoid interference with the director's creative freedom within the strategic concept.'[41] Of course, that estimation of competence extends to other personnel: to the screenwriter, cinematographer, set designer, actors and the editor. The producer needs to exercise her or his judgement as to whether the production has the right mix of talents.

There is also another, frequently overlooked, dimension to the producer's role: what Caldwell would call a cultural self-performance or, more simply, self-promotion and showmanship. This quality was recognized by Powdermaker, who noted that this entailed a strong reliance on instinct and a confident engagement with popular culture.[42] At its extreme, this showmanship becomes a producer's defining quality: as was the case with Joseph E. Levine.[43] Jerry Bruckheimer has successfully promoted himself as a brand that has a public presence and market value in both film and television.[44] This showmanship need not always be outright self-promotion but includes an ability to promote and hence sell the 'package'. Nor should it be necessarily associated with exploitation cinema or the lower end of the marketplace, but can include promoting a film's artistic credibility and cultural respectability. In his study of Jeremy Thomas, Christopher Meir identifies Thomas' principal skill as salesmanship, the promotion and marketing of his films – which might include the reputation of the auteur director working on the project – in order to sell them to potential financiers and distributors and so be able to remain in business in the new global marketplace.[45] A producer's showmanship often depends on building a 'reputation network', creating 'highly visible associations which give stature and publicity potential by providing opportunities for features and stories in the trade and popular press including announcing new "discoveries", highlighting awards and accolades and capitalizing on established or strongly emerging reputations'. In this way the promotion of the film becomes integral to the process of its production, with the producer operating as an 'industrial tactician'.[46] A producer's skills as a deal-maker, showman and promoter are difficult to quantify and assess, but nevertheless indispensable.

The importance of being creative

We can at this point return to the concept of creativity, often, as noted, taken as the marker of the genuine producer as opposed to the business administrator.[47] Hence Dino De Laurentiis' assertion that he has the requisite 'artistic feeling inside' that 'cannot be taught or learned', as opposed to his rival Carlo Ponti, who was a 'gifted lawyer with a nose for business, for deals'.[48] Producers themselves often argue that creativity is a pre-requisite for the role. David Lewis, who entitled his memoirs *The Creative Producer*, argued that the producer needs a 'sense of creativity … a sense of drama, a sense of character and character development, a sense of how far you can and can't go'; only in that way could the producer get the best out of those with whom he worked.[49] Larry Turman, producer of *The Graduate* (1967), thought 'the creativity of an artist' was the first quality demanded of a producer because being able to work with creative talents demands creativity'.[50] In the 'creative industries', which place a high cultural value on creativity, it is often essential for the producer to be seen as creative and thus, as Puttnam has observed, give the role a credibility it would otherwise lack, obviating its inherent unattractiveness and taint of commerce.[51]

However, in what ways are producers creative? Is it sufficient to identify those producers who are auteurs such as David O. Selznick, Darryl Zanuck or Val Lewton, ones whose personal vision informed the conception and execution of their films?[52] Many producers see themselves in this way. Sam Spiegel thought a producer should be able to 'conceive a picture, to dream it up, to have the first concept of what the film is going to be like when finished, before a word is written or the director cast'.[53] Hal Wallis opined: 'When you find a property, acquire it, work on it from the beginning to the end and deliver the finished product as you conceived it, then you're producing. A producer, to be worthy of the name, must be a creator'.[54] A more widely held view, alluded to in the previous section, is to understand the producer as a 'creative manager' who organizes the conditions under which creativity can take place but whose activities should be distinguished from 'primary creative personnel': writers, actors, directors, musicians and craft and technical workers who include editors, cinematographers and sound engineers.[55] Martin Dale distinguishes between 'true creators' who are originators (writers and directors) creating *ex nihilo* and the producer who is an 'enabling mechanism', practising 'secondary creation' by working on pre-existing material rather than originating it.[56]

We need also to understand a producer's creativity as having another dimension: the ability, so necessary for independent producers, of securing funds for a project by manipulating markets, negotiating deals, pre-selling and all the other elements of a complex financial package without which a film could not be made. Often producers derive creative satisfaction from piecing together the complex financial packaging necessary to make a film, balancing the different interests of the parties involved.[57] Producers can derive immense satisfaction from translating their financial acumen into a satisfying film or television production. Jim Goddard, a producer for Euston Films, a spin-off production company from Thames Television in the United Kingdom, opined:

> The kicks that people like myself get are in saying, 'What you've got up there was made for the amount of money the company allocated and doesn't it look great – I've helped pull all those factors together.' I take a terrific pride. My kicks are in looking at the bottom line figure at the end of the day and saying, 'We've brought it in OK.'[58]

The British producer Sydney Box, for instance, became more and more adept at putting together increasingly complex and ambitious deals, so much so that it has been argued that his bids for British Lion Films and London Weekend Television in 1964 constituted his most creative activity as a film producer.[59] In addition, we wish to argue that showmanship, skilfully and imaginatively deployed, is a creative activity, and often how a film is promoted and positioned is crucial to its eventual success.

We cannot define therefore 'creative' in any absolute sense, but nevertheless its possession is seen as desirable for the producer working in a creative industry. What is more important is to discern the nature and extent of a producer's *creative control* and how that is exercised. In order to understand that, we need to analyse the variable contexts in which that creativity occurs and what form it takes.[60] It is to those diverse contexts that we now need to turn as we survey the contributions to this volume.

Contributors and contexts

With such an overarching project in mind, we can turn to the individual contributions to this volume. The book is divided into three parts depending on the specific emphasis given to analysing and understanding producers. Part I,

'Theoretical and Historical Contexts', is concerned with some of the most general issues that need to be addressed in order to understand the work of any producer. Though rooted in specific national and historical contexts, the chapters in this part share an interest in locating the role of the producer within larger questions of history, industry and creativity, contexts which also shape many of the broader debates within Film and Television Studies.

The part begins with Joe Kember's chapter '"A Judge of Anything and Everything": Charles Urban and the Role of the "Producer-Collaborator" in Early British Film', which shows how the emergence of the producer as a recognized role in film-making has a specific history, dependent, in some senses, on particular national contexts, but one that grew and developed alongside film itself as an art form and as an industry. Beginning with an overview of the many roles that a 'producer' had to play in early cinema, roles that often overlapped especially with those performed by exhibitors, Kember argues that the specialization of the producer was a gradual process from the beginnings of cinema in the 1890s until the 1910s, by which time a figure which resembles that of the modern producer had emerged. Kember goes on to argue that historians have for too long used this lack of clear definition to underrate the producer's contribution to the development of early cinema, effectively conflating this figure with the fairground showman exhibitor. In so doing, Kember contends that historians have created a distorted understanding of early cinema history and of British cinema in particular. By examining the work of Charles Urban, a producer of nonfiction works who was active throughout the period, Kember demonstrates that a better understanding of Urban's work can reshape our understanding of the period as a whole.

By taking Norwegian cinema in the 1990s as their specific object in 'Mapping a Typology of the Film Producer – Or, Six Producers in Search of An Author', Audun Engelstad and Jo Sondre Moseng offer a typology of different types of producer. Their study focuses on the importance of the process of selecting properties for adaptation. Literary adaptation has long been conceived of as the province of writers and directors, but Engelstad and Moseng show that the producer plays a vital role in this process and that adaptation is one of the areas of media production in which the creative influence of the producer is most apparent. Assessing the different approaches that production companies take towards the creative and industrial process of film adaptation, Engelstad and Moseng discern six different types of producers that represent different nodes on the continuum between having a strictly commercial, business orientation and a wholly artistic one. Their typology refines Pierre Bourdieu's influential model of the role of producers as 'cultural intermediaries'.

Andrew Spicer's extended chapter, 'The Independent Producer and the State: Simon Relph, Government Policy and the British Film Industry, 1980–2005', engages with broad questions about the complex and shifting relationships between producers and governments that characterize European national film industries, all of which exist in the shadow of Hollywood's economic and cultural hegemony. As a case study through which to explore these issues in detail, Spicer focuses on the career of Simon Relph, an important figure in British cinema in the 1980s and 1990s, whose career was both shaped by British film policy as an independent producer and who, in turn, helped to shape those same policies as head of British Screen (1985–1990), a private-public body designed to support and promote a sustainable British film industry, before returning to independent production. By examining Relph's opportunities and difficulties in navigating the conflicted space between private enterprise and state support, Spicer not only demonstrates the importance of examining the relationship between producers and film policy but also illuminates how that relationship opens up broader questions regarding the development and trajectories of national film cultures.

Paul Long and Simon Spink also take up the question of government policy in their chapter 'Producing the Self: The Film Producer's Labor and Professional Identity in the UK Creative Economy'. Here, the writers consider the ways in which regional film policy in the United Kingdom constructs the 'work' of the producer and how working producers in turn relate to the institutions created by that policy during the period after 1997 in which the incoming Labour government promoted the importance of the 'creative industries' and in which the availability of Lottery funding altered the conditions of film production. Long and Spink's chapter focusing on the importance of regional film production acts as a complementary study to Spicer's, drawing on a range of interviews with working producers to analyse the ways in which they understand their own roles and careers in a changing industrial landscape.

Pauline Small's chapter 'Producer *and* Director? Or, "Authorship" in 1950s Italian Cinema' challenges the most influential way of thinking about creativity in cinema: the concept of the auteur director. She does this by examining two films directed by Luchino Visconti – one of the quintessential exemplars of the European auteur director – and the nature of his collaboration with two very powerful producers. In so doing, Small shows that even the most celebrated of auteur directors benefitted from such collaborations. *Senso* (1954), Small argues, could not have been completed or released without the assistance of Riccardo Gualino in getting the script approved by censors or forcing Visconti to abandon the idea of shooting an expensive and in the end unnecessary battle scene. Similarly, Small demonstrates that Titanus producer Goffredo Lombardo was vital to the development and production of the celebrated directorial triumph *Rocco and His Brothers* (1961). Small's findings offer a welcome corrective to the mythology of the auteur and pose a larger question about auteur directors generally and their relationship to the industrial realities of collaboration with producers.

Part I concludes with Mark David Ryan, Ben Goldsmith, Stuart Cunningham and Deb Verhoeven's 'The Australian Screen Producer in Transition', which focuses on the contemporary period. Their chapter assesses the profound impact that digital forms of production are beginning to have on the role of the producer, using data from a major survey to assess changes in producers' understanding of their work in the context of rapid technological change. Ryan and his co-authors attempt to measure the impact this development has had on the film and television industries, while looking for possible convergence across these distinct cultures. By interpreting the survey data, the writers give us insights into the feelings that producers in each field have towards their current working conditions and their views on their professional futures in a time of great uncertainty. Somewhat surprisingly, the writers find that it is television producers rather than film producers – who might be thought to be working in the most fragile end of the industry – who are the most uncertain about their futures. The writers also find that digital content production remains a very distinct production culture from its counterparts in film and television, even as academics routinely speak of media convergence.

Part II, 'Media and Genre Contexts', is concerned with exploring the work of the producer in different media, animation, film and television, and the ways in which the producer is shaped by and helps to shape different genres of media production. The producer's influence on Hollywood genre production has been documented by Rick Altman in his seminal study *Film/Genre* in relation to popular film genres.[61] Contributors to this part of the book also attempt to discern similar patterns of influence.

In 'The Producer in Animation: Creativity and Commerce from Bray Studios to Pixar', Donna Kornhaber engages with the role of the producer in commercial animation. For Kornhaber, such animation is a 'form of artistry ... that must be coordinated as much as it must be created' with 'administration and artistry being inseparable'. Within such a framework, she surveys the management styles and innovations of three of the most important and influential executive producers in American animation: Walt Disney, Leo Schlesinger of Warner Bros. and Pixar's Jonathan Lasseter. Examining their careers, Kornhaber argues that producers should be thought of as authors in animation as much as, if not more than, the animators themselves. She argues this case while also recognizing that the specific techniques used to manage creativity within the studio context is in itself a measure of the creativity of such producers. To support this claim, Kornhaber details the methods by which Disney dispersed authorship and labour so widely among his staff that only he knew how the whole of any given film came together. Schlesinger took a radically different approach, allowing his animators a great deal of control over their projects, creating in Warner Bros. an animation studio that was heralded for its diversity of output. Kornhaber positions Lasseter and Pixar as a hybrid of these two influential approaches to managing talent.

Brett Mills and Sarah Ralph's chapter, '"Trying to Ride a Naughty Horse": British Television Comedy Producers', combines questions of medium specificity with those of genre. Drawing on numerous interviews and ethnographic research, the authors offer a detailed and complex portrait of the working conditions of producers of television comedy in Britain. Within such a framework, their chapter engages with a number of key questions for producer research, including the differences and similarities between independent and 'in-house' producers, the motivations and aspirations of producers, the personal investment they make in their projects and the nature of the creative contributions to the projects they help to make.

Sonia Friel's chapter, 'Keith Griffiths' Poetics of Production', brings into focus the contribution that producers make to art cinema and experimental film-making, two areas often depicted as the preserve of visionary artist directors. Analysing the career of Griffiths – who is perhaps best known for his work with the Quay Brothers but who has also produced films directed by Patrick Kieller and Chris Petit among others – Friel shows how Griffiths' career demonstrates the vital contribution that producers in these seemingly non-commercial areas make by tending to the business of fundraising, logistical management and finding distribution outlets, thereby protecting and enabling the artists who go on to be recognized as auteurs. Friel's chapter also provides a bridge between Part II's concerns with medium and genre as she explores the ways in which Griffiths has turned to digital technologies for production and distribution because of their economic and artistic potential for the film-makers with whom he works.

In his 'The American Independent Producer and the Film Value Chain', James Lyons takes as his subject the producers of American 'independent (indie) cinema', a category of cinema that has changed from being a nationally specific grouping to an industrial and aesthetic transnational genre. As such, Lyons' analysis moves the producer to the centre of what, like the milieu analysed by Friel, is conventionally depicted as a director's enclave. Lyons argues for nuanced ways of appreciating the influence of the producer on all phases of a film's life in this particular environment, dependent as it is on entrepreneurial energy in putting together funding packages, exploiting the festival circuit and selling films internationally, often on a territory-by-territory basis. Crucially, Lyons argues that only the producer has such pervasive influence on these films and that without their management of that value chain, the economic model of independent cinema would not be viable. Lyons also demonstrates that indie producers must identify properties that have the ability to resonate with the audiences for this type of film-making. In short, Lyons demonstrates that indie producers are genre producers par excellence – equally understanding audience expectations and the industrial realities of the indie film scene.

Although many of the chapters up to this point have drawn upon nationally specific examples for their case studies, the chapters in Part III – 'National and Transnational Contexts' – foreground those contexts to explore the relationships between producers and industrial and cultural formations. As such, they demonstrate collectively the importance of the producer's role in creating and sustaining national cultures and transnational networks which are conventionally described through the work of auteur directors or famous stars. As a group, they also challenge the paradigm of the producer's role, which, as discussed in the first section of the Introduction, has been dominated by the figure of the Hollywood mogul, which, besides unfairly caricaturing the producer, also inscribes American cinema as the norm. By drawing attention to the specific issues that confront individual producers in different parts of the world, these chapters remind us of the fluidity of film and television production practices and the need to account for the specificities if we are to fully understand the producer, just as we must also appreciate the contributions made by producers if we are to understand national cinemas.

In the same way that producers have been left out of discussions of national cinema studies for the most part, they have also been conspicuously absent from discussions of transnationalism.[62] Apart from Tim Bergfelder's seminal study of European co-production in the 1950s and 1960s,[63] discussions of transnationalism have largely ignored producers and instead replicated Film and Television Studies' preoccupation with stars and directors. Yet the networks of production and distribution that characterize transnational industries are built and maintained by producers, while the content of specific film and television texts are often moulded by producers to meet international expectations. Leaving the producer out of discussions of transnationalism is thus disabling, as shown by the chapters in this part.

Constanza Burucúa's chapter, 'Lita Stantic: Auteur Producer/Producer of Auteurs', examines Stantic as a pioneering female producer whose work has left an indelible mark on Argentine and Latin American cinema. For Burucúa, Stantic's role as a collaborator with directors such as Fernando Solanas and Maria Luisa Bemberg and mentor to a younger generation of cineastes, including Lucrecia Martel and Pablo Trapero, make her the most important figure in Argentine cinema over the last 30 years. In so doing, Burucúa demonstrates that Stantic has a thematically cohesive and very personal oeuvre as a producer and has helped to give a number of auteur directors their start in the industry. Besides offering a welcome revision to Latin American film historiography – which has heretofore only discussed Stantic in relation to her solitary work as a director – Burucúa's chapter also offers a case study of the ways in which issues of gender can be explored in analysing the works and, more significantly for our purposes in this book, the specialized labour of the producer.

A.T. McKenna's chapter, 'Beyond National Humiliation: Han Sanping and China's Post-Olympic Historical Event Blockbusters', also attempts to inscribe the producer into national cinema historiography, despite using a markedly different figure working on the other side of the world from Stantic. Discussing the work of Han Sanping in contemporary Chinese cinema, McKenna argues that Han's career demonstrates that the producer shapes genres, with Han's particular favourite being the historical blockbuster. McKenna's case study reveals further dimensions to the producer's impact on national film cultures when he shows that the popularity of that genre can influence how the nation itself comes to imagine its history by capitalizing on moments of national celebration. McKenna's account also suggests that this influence is only one facet of Sanping's importance to film-making in China, where the true extent of his power is impossible to overestimate.

In his 'The Producer in Belgian Cinema(s): The Case of Jean (and Jan) Van Raemdonck', Gertjan Willems shows how the producer can be a key figure for understanding both the national and transnational dynamics of Belgian cinema. Van Raemdonck, who sometimes went by the name of 'Jan' to appeal to Flemish backers, is here shown to have deftly manoeuvred around Belgium's internal language divide and led the drive to Europeanize Belgian cinema by reaching out to co-production partners across the continent. Besides this skill as a dealmaker that understood and helped to shape the complex industrial landscape of Belgian cinema, Willems also shows the ways in which Van Raemdonck was influential in terms of popularizing genres, developing talent and generally professionalizing film production in the country during a career that spanned over 50 years from the 1950s until the early 2000s.

Transnational collaboration between producers is the central focus of Christopher Meir's 'Post-Imperial Co-Producers: Emile Sherman, Iain Canning and the

Contemporary Anglo-Australian Cinema'. Meir examines the careers of Australian producer Emile Sherman and British producer Iain Canning and particularly the output of their shared company See-Saw Pictures, founded in 2008 and which has already won a Best Picture Oscar for its first film *The King's Speech*. By doing so, Meir highlights the ways in which these producers have worked across a media network that has long existed between the two nations, despite significant challenges imposed by geography. By examining changes in the power dynamics inherent in the political and economic relationships between the two nations and the concomitant dynamics in the relationships between their respective film cultures, Meir argues that Canning and Sherman's collaboration typifies a new stage in this process.

The future of producer studies

While we hope this collection showcases the richness and diversity of producer-oriented research, the goal of this collection is not so much to provide a comprehensive survey of the field as it is to open out ways of approaching an understanding of the producer's role and thus to pose new questions for film and television theory and history. For that reason, we hope that future scholars will continue the explorations started in this volume and indeed take producer studies in different directions. Just as there remains much more to be said about the relationships between producers and directors, for instance, or the role of the producer in specific national cinema historiographies, we can also envision fruitful analyses of the producer within a range of generic contexts untouched here, or in relation to stars, cinematographers or the numerous other creative personnel with whom producers collaborate. Analysing and accounting for the contributions of producers can also lead to questions about other, related figures in the media industries, including casting directors, talent agents (many of whom, in contemporary cinema, eventually move into producing[64]), as well as distributors and sales agents, who are also often producers at some point in their careers, as shown by Meir's discussion of Iain Canning in this volume. Sales executives and agents, like producers, are viewed with varying degrees of contempt by media scholarship, which casts all three groups as tainted by their supposed commercial orientation, and yet their influence over production and audience tastes is extensive. It is time that theory and historiography accounted for these vital figures and the interrelationships among and between them, as well as with those who are traditionally defined as 'creatives'.

More research also needs to be conducted about how the work of producers is affected by contexts of race, class and gender. Burucúa's chapter in this volume offers a rich illustration of the value of this approach. Although most of the slender sheaf of work about producers concentrates on the film industry – and, to an extent, on their role within television as in Jeremy Tunstall's work[65] – several pieces here show the importance of exploring their role in other media, including animation. Ryan et al.'s chapter demonstrates the importance of engaging with the ways in which digital production is affecting how producers work as we move into an era of uncertainty and profound change. Such is the significance of the producer for film and television history and such is the dearth of scholarship that much work remains to be done. It is our hope that readers of this volume will be inspired to undertake further studies of the producer and in so doing begin to provide a fuller understanding of this figure who is vital to media cultures but who remains unfairly and misleadingly aligned with crass commercialism.

Notes

1   Gore Vidal, 'Who Makes The Movies?', in *United States: Essays 1952–1992* (New York: Random House, 1993), 1173.

2   Mark A. Vieira, *Irving Thalberg: Boy Wonder to Producer Prince* (Berkeley and Los Angeles: University of California Press, 2010), 13–15.

3   See Andrew Spicer and A. T. McKenna, *The Man Who Got Carter: Michael Klinger, Independent Production and the British Film Industry, 1960–1980* (London: I.B. Tauris, 2013), 86.

4   Anon., 'Joseph E. Levine: The Producers' Producer', *anecdotage.com*, accessed 5 November 2013, http://anecdotage.com/articles/19513/.

5   Leo C. Rosten, *Hollywood : The Movie Colony, The Movie Makers* (New York: Harcourt Brace and Co., 1941), 269.

6   Andrew Sarris, 'Notes on the Auteur Theory in 1962', in *Auteurs and Authorship: A Film Reader*, ed. Barry Keith Grant (Oxford: Blackwell Publishing, 2008), 45.

7   Mark Betz has argued that one reason for arthouse portmanteau movies being overlooked by historians is that they are so closely associated with the producer; Betz, *Beyond the Subtitle: Remapping European Art Cinema* (Minneapolis: University of Minnesota Press, 2009), 40.

8   Mark Harris, *Pictures From a Revolution: Five Movies and the Birth of the New Hollywood* (London: Penguin Press, 2008), 327.

9   Andrew Sarris, 'Directors, How Personal Can You Get?', *New York Times*, 12 May 1968, D19.

10   Thomas Schatz, *The Genius of the System: Hollywood Film-making in the Studio Era* (London: Faber and Faber, 1998), 5.

11   See David Hesmondhalgh, 'Media Industry Studies, Media Production Studies', in *Media and Society*, 5th edn. ed. James Curran, (London: Bloomsbury Academic, 2010), 145–63, at 145.

12   Hesmondhalgh, 'Media Industry Studies, Media Production Studies', 2–3, 151.

13   Jennifer Holt and Alisa Perren, *Media Industries: History, Theory, and Method* (Boston: Wiley-Blackwell, 2009), 8.

14   See Vicki Mayer, Miranda J. Banks and John T. Caldwell, 'Introduction – Production Studies: Roots and Routes', in *Production Studies: Cultural Studies of Media Industries*, ed. Mayer, Banks and Caldwell (New York and London: Routledge, 2009), 1–12.

15   An important recent study is David Hesmondhalgh and Sarah Baker, *Creative Labour: Media Work in Three Cultural Industries* (London: Routledge, 2013).

16   Caldwell, *Production Culture: Industrial Reflexivity and Critical Practice in Film and Television* (Durham, NC: Duke University Press, 2008), 5, 18 and *passim*.

17 Thomas Schatz, 'Film Industry Studies and Hollywood History', in *Media Industries: History, Theory and Method*, ed. Holt and Perren (Malden MA and Oxford: Wiley-Blackwell, 2009), 46, original emphasis.

18 Richard Maltby, ' "Nobody Knows Everything": Post-Classical Historiographies and Consolidated Entertainment', in *Contemporary Hollywood Cinema*, ed. Steve Neale and Murray Smith (London and New York: Routledge, 1998), 21–44, at 25–6.

19 Anthologies devoted to the question of authorship in film are overwhelmingly dominated by discussions of directors, see: John Caughie (ed.), *Theories of Authorship* (London: Routledge and Kegan Paul, 1981); Virginia Wright Wexman, *Film and Authorship* (New Brunswick: Rutgers University Press, 2003); David A. Gerstner and Janet Staiger (eds), *Authorship and Film* (New York and London: Routledge, 2003); C. Paul Sellors, *Film Authorship: Auteurs and Other Myths* (London: Wallflower, 2010). A partial exception is Barry Keith Grant (ed.), *Auteurs and Authorship: A Film Reader* (Oxford: Blackwell, 2008), which contains Matthew Bernstein's essay 'The Producer as Auteur'.

20 Eric Smoodin, 'The History of Film History', in *Looking Past the Screen: Case Studies in American Film History and Method*, ed. Jon Lewis and Eric Smoodin (Durham & London: Duke University Press, 2007), 1–33.

21 Rosten, *Hollywood: The Movie Colony, The Movie Makers*; Hortense Powdermaker, *Hollywood the Dream Factory* (New York: Little, Brown & Company, 1950).

22 John L. Sullivan, 'Leo C. Rosten's Hollywood: Power, Status, and the Primacy of Economic and Social Networks in Cultural Production', in *Production Studies*, ed. Mayer, Banks and Caldwell, 39–53.

23 David Bordwell, Kristin Thompson and Janet Staiger, *Classical Hollywood Cinema: Film Style and Mode of Production to 1960* (London: Routledge, 1988), 85–154; 309–38; Schatz, *The Genius of the System*.

24 Schatz, *The Genius of the System*, 8.

25 Matthew Bernstein, *Walter Wanger: Hollywood Independent* (Minneapolis and London: University of Minnesota Press, 2000); Brian Taves, *Thomas Ince: Hollywood's Independent Pioneer* (Lexington, KT: University Press of Kentucky, 2012). Mention should be made of George F. Custen, *Twentieth Century's Fox: Darryl F. Zanuck and the Culture of Hollywood* (New York: Basic Books, 1997), which has a strong emphasis on the production culture of Hollywood and how Zanuck worked within that framework.

26 Sheri Chinen Biesen, 'Joan Harrison, Virginia Van Upp and Women Behind-the-Scenes in Wartime Film Noir', *Quarterly Review of Film and Video*, 20 (2003): 125–44.

27 Andrew Spicer, 'Producing Noir: Wild, Scott, Hellinger', in *Kiss the Blood Off My Hands: Screening Classic Film Noir*, ed. Robert Miklitsch (Chicago: University of Illinois Press, 2014) 130–51.

28 William Fadiman, *Hollywood Now* (London: Thames & Hudson, 1973), 131–33.

29 For a useful collection of interviews see Steven Priggé, *Movie Moguls Speak: Interviews with Top Film Producers* (Jefferson, NC and London: McFarland, 2004).

30 Manuel Alvarado and John Stewart, *Made for Television: Euston Films Limited* (London: BFI Publishing, 1985), viii–ix.

31 Quoted in Alejandro Pardo, 'The Film Producer as Creative Force', *Wide Screen*, 2:2 (2010): 4.

32   Michael Balcon, *The Producer* (London: British Film Institute, 1945), 5.

33   Quoted in Pardo, 'The Film Producer', 7.

34   Charlton Heston, *In the Arena: An Autobiography* (New York: Simon & Schuster, 1995), 94.

35   Pierre Bourdieu, 'The Field of Cultural Production, or: The Economic World Reversed', in *The Field of Cultural Production: Essays on Art and Literature* (Cambridge: Polity Press, 1993), 29–73.

36   Alan Burton and Tim O'Sullivan, *The Cinema of Basil Dearden and Michael Relph* (Edinburgh: Edinburgh University Press, 2009), 6–7.

37   Andrew Yule, *Enigma: David Puttnam, the Story So Far…* (Edinburgh: Mainstream Publishing, 1988), 179.

38   Balcon, *The Producer*, 5.

39   Quoted in David Puttnam (with Neil Watson), *Movies and Money* (New York: Vintage Books, 2000), 4.

40   Rosten, *Hollywood: The Movie Colony*, 231, 239, 260–65.

41   Burton and O'Sullivan, *The Cinema of Basil Dearden and Michael Relph*, 7.

42   See Stephen Zafirau, 'Audience Knowledge and the Everyday Lives of Cultural Producers in Hollywood', in *Production Studies*, ed. Mayer, Banks and Caldwell, 190–202, at 196.

43   A.T. McKenna, *The Boston Barnum: Showmanship, Cinema and the Peculiar Talent of Joseph E. Levine* (Lexington: University of Kentucky, forthcoming 2014).

44   See Tom Steward, 'Making the Commercial Personal: The Authorial Value of Jerry Bruckheimer Television', *Continuum*, 24:5 (2010): 735–49.

45   Christopher Meir, 'The Producer as Salesman: Jeremy Thomas, Film Promotion and Contemporary Transnational Independent Cinema', *Historical Journal of Film, Radio and Television*, 29:4 (December 2009): 467–81, at 470–71.

46   A.T. McKenna, 'Independent Production and Industrial Tactics in Britain: Michael Klinger and *Baby Love*', *Historical Journal of Film, Radio and Television*, 32:4 (2012): 611–31.

47   For an informative overview see Pardo, 'The Film Producer as Creative Force', 1–23.

48   Quoted in Tim Adler, *The Producers: Money, Movies and Who Really Calls the Shots* (London: Methuen, 2006), 106; and in Tullio Kezich and Alessandra Levantesi, *Dino: The Films of Dino De Laurentiis*, trans. James Marcus (New York: Miramax Books, 2004), 81.

49   David Lewis, *The Creative Producer*, edited with an introduction by James Curtis (Metuchen, NJ & London: The Scarecrow Press, 1993).

50   Lawrence Turman, *So You Want to be A Producer* (New York: Three Rivers Press, 2005), 150.

51   Pardo, 'The Film Producer', 7.

52   Bernstein, 'The Producer as Auteur', in *Auteurs and Authorship*, ed. Barry Keith Grant, 180–89.

53   Quoted in Adler, *The Producers*, 16.

54   Quoted in Pardo, 'The Film Producer', 9.

55   Hesmondhalgh and Baker, *Creative Labour*, 9.

56   Martin Dale, *Europa, Europa: Developing the European Film Industry* (Paris: Académie Carat & Media Business School, 1991), 84.

57 See Martin Dale, *The Movie Game: The Film Business in Britain, Europe and America* (London and New York: Cassell, 1997), 96–97.

58 Quoted in Alvarado and Stewart, *Made for Television*, 186.

59 Andrew Spicer, *Sydney Box* (Manchester: Manchester University Press, 2006), 183–95, 207.

60 See Vincent Porter, *On Cinema* (London: Pluto Press, 1985), 63–76.

61 Tim Bergfelder, *International Adventures: German Popular Cinema and European Co-Productions in the 1960s* (New York and Oxford: Bergahn Books, 2005).

62 Two recent exceptions to this tendency are Tom Whittaker, *The Films of Elias Querejeta: A Producer of Landscapes* (Cardiff: University of Wales Press, 2011) and Tejaswini Ghanti, *Producing Bollywood: Inside the Hindi Film Industry* (Durham: Duke University Press, 2012), esp. 155–280.

63 Rick Altman, *Film/Genre* (London: BFI, 1999), 44–48.

64 See Turman, *So You Want to be A Producer*, to cite just one example, for the producer's own account of his transition from agent to producer, esp. 21–50.

65 See, for instance, *Television Producers* (London: Routledge, 1993).

Part One

Theoretical and Historical Contexts

2

'A Judge of Anything and Everything': Charles Urban and the Role of the 'Producer-Collaborator' in Early British Film

Joe Kember

As the variety of contributions to this volume demonstrates, the term 'producer' has always been relatively unstable, signalling a wide range of potential roles and functions within alternative film-making traditions. In early film studies, too, it has been used flexibly to refer not only to production companies and to the range of managers involved in operational and financial management of them, but also to individuals directly involved in film-making practice. In relation to the first five years of British cinema, this is hardly surprising, given that individuals such as Robert Paul, Cecil Hepworth, James Williamson and others frequently were responsible for both creative and management roles within their own production companies. A further complication is that these men were also routinely involved in film exhibition during their early careers – a fact which has supported the tendency within recent academic work on early film to emphasize the creative roles of exhibitors above and beyond those of film-makers.[1]

This chapter returns us to a consideration of the creative roles played by early British film producers, asking how such roles changed within production companies before 1914. However, raising this question brings us immediately to the heart of an apparent paradox that has troubled British film histories since at least Rachel Low and Roger Manvell's landmark 1948 account. Prefacing their list of 17 film production companies at work in Britain in the first decade of cinema, Low and Manvell caution, 'It should be remembered that even in 1906 anyone with the ingenuity to devise or adapt the elementary apparatus needed, and film a few hundred feet of "phantom ride", comic scene or news event, could claim to be a film producer.'[2] Comments such as these typify the paradox that during the first decade of cinema, British producers appear to have employed artisanal, *ad hoc*, or even amateurish methods, and yet this was also the period in which, unlike subsequent decades, they proved able to compete effectively in the national and international marketplace. By contrast, in her second volume, Low describes the period 1906–1914 as one in which the industry became both centralized and to some extent professionalized, with the 'days of the one-man show' superseded by a new 'specialization of technicians'; however, by now,

British film production was 'in a state of arrested development' in which 'the pioneer producing companies generally failed to meet the increasing needs of new art with either breadth of vision or commercial and artistic elasticity'.[3]

This pattern of regression married to rationalization runs counter to standard histories of film production in countries such as France and America during the same years in which the adoption of standardized production systems corresponded with a massive increase in the output and the ambition of these industries, and also in the sophistication of the films that they produced. At Pathé, for example, Richard Abel has shown that, following a period where production was governed by 'little more than a workshop of artisans', an early model of director-unit system came into operation under Ferdinand Zecca as early as 1905.[4] Charles Musser has argued that the central-producer system was established in America between 1907 and 1909.[5] Broader theorizations of early cinema have tended to reinforce this type of progressive model of film history, finding parallels between changes in film form, the activity of audiences and the transition from pioneership to institutional consolidation. For André Gaudreault, in what is probably the most provocative formulation of this periodization to date, it is even 'completely pointless to connect the terra incognita known as early cinema to the immense continent that is cinema itself': cinema was invented sometime between 1908 and 1914.[6]

These accounts are by no means equivalent, but they share with Low and Manvell a tendency to periodize stages of industrial and aesthetic development, distinguishing especially between the work of the 'pioneers' and the 'post-pioneer' industries that followed. The difference, of course, is that whereas Abel, Musser and others have sufficient cause to associate the rationalization of French and American cinemas with commercial and aesthetic progress in fiction film production, Low demonstrates that British fiction production followed an opposite trajectory, in which industrial developments accompanied a 'humiliating period of stagnation' – a problem that was noted in the otherwise optimistic trade press at the time.[7] Indeed, in his recent synoptic history of the producer in British film, Vincent Porter has substantially extended Low and Manvell's assessment, characterizing British film production, as 'essentially artisanal' until at least 1927, with American division of labour practices only appearing substantially following the emergence of standardized sound film.[8] Under these circumstances, one might justifiably question whether the term 'producer', as we have come to understand it, has any relevance to an account of British film before 1914 (if not before 1927), and whether we shouldn't simply regard British production of the period as stalled in an artisanal pioneer period, destined thereafter to play catch-up with more ambitious and imaginative industries overseas.

This assessment, which I will call the 'artisan thesis', makes two problematic assumptions, the first of which has been addressed by Simon Brown's recent reassessment of British film production in the 1908–1914 period. Challenging the relevance for the British context of what he calls the 'holistic relationship between industrial and stylistic development' suggested by Gaudreault and others, Brown's account reiterates that the industrial development of cinema in Britain was characterized by a shift from substantial domestic production to a period in which 'film manufacturing became secondary to a far larger and more complex model of business transactions, companies and cash flow'.[9] Importantly, Brown differs from Low in his diagnosis of the reasons for this weakening of the production sector: whereas Low assumes that the decline was evidence of a lack of ambition or creativity, Brown follows Michael Chanan's argument that the producers' difficulties had been created by complex commercial and industrial developments in the new era of fixed-venue cinema construction, and especially by the introduction of film rental.[10] Between 1898 and 1904, Walturdaw had been the sole rental company operating in Britain; by 1911 there were 48, and in spite of efforts made by British producers to restrict sales to these middlemen and continue selling large numbers of prints direct to exhibitors, by now several producers had ceased trading. Brown thus explains the paradox of increasing institutional complexity married to decline in production: while rental companies had become more numerous, sophisticated and dominant, British producers had largely failed to create their own distribution networks and were unable make sufficient profit from the relatively few prints they sold direct to the renters.

According to this account, although British producers could be accused of a lack of commercial savvy, the decline of British production did not necessarily reflect poorly upon their capabilities as film-makers, nor even upon the quality of their films; it was simply that as the 1900s and 1910s progressed, it became increasingly difficult to make a profit on any new releases. Meanwhile, as Chanan explains, 'The dealers who went over to rental and entered the import-export business built up an increasingly strong position: they had better control over the conditions of supply and demand than either producers or exhibitors.'[11] Indeed, the asymmetrical relationship between producers and distributors that would characterize British film history throughout the twentieth century arguably commenced in the years between 1904 and 1911, with the rise of film rental agencies willing to promote and distribute fiction films produced in Europe and the United States in order to make up for the growing shortfall in British production. Thus, while industrial models of film distribution and exhibition advanced rapidly in Britain during these years, the development of central-producer and other systems seen overseas (arguably, alongside some of the stylistic changes this introduced to fiction film), was stalled or weakened by changed market conditions.

Extending this line of argument, we can also address the second problematic assumption of the artisan thesis: that British film's earliest producers, and especially those that specialized in non-fiction and current events productions, were naïve or unambitious, little more than 'camera-pointers' whose initial commercial success might be regarded, at best, as serendipitous and whose eventual commercial come-uppance was therefore unsurprising. Drawing upon a case study of Charles Urban, one of few individuals who were prominently involved in non-fiction film production in Britain from 1897 beyond 1914, and making extensive use of the Charles Urban Papers held by the National Media Museum in Bradford, this chapter argues that terms such as 'artisan', 'pioneer' and 'inventor' tend to function reductively in such cases, obscuring the skill with which, from the beginning, men such as Urban identified their audiences, led public tastes for moving pictures and crafted a sophisticated production rationale that was tailored to this market. To see why this is the case, we need to gain a better understanding of the pivotal roles early producers played, distinguishing especially between producers who were principally involved in stage-management and direction of fiction film productions and those, like Urban, whose principal responsibility was to appraise market demand for both non-fiction and fiction film, and to foster fruitful collaborations with other creative personnel in order to meet it.

The 'producer-artist' and 'producer-collaborator'

The term 'producer' was actually a fairly familiar part of the discourse of the film industry in the teens, though it tended to describe a quite different set of roles than in later industrial formulations. 'The producer', according to Chas J.L. Clarke's 1912 account of Cecil Hepworth's production facilities in Walton-on-Thames, 'is the particular person who stage-manages and controls the whole show, has to be a judge of anything and everything and have many parts of the country mapped out in his head ready to be selected or rejected as they strike him as suitable or useless for the purpose he has in mind.'[12] Clarke's upbeat description for the readers of *Pall Mall Magazine* of 'How Cinematograph Pictures are Produced' offers an engaging glimpse into the energetic activity taking place at Walton within its 'several complete studios, each with its own producer and company', and also of the detailed organizational and stage management roles played by the figures usually known as producers at this site.[13] Similarly, in a fascinating 1911 report on the British Production Department of Pathé Frères at their studio in Great Portland Street, a correspondent for the *Morning Post* described the 'manager', Frank Powell, as 'constantly engaged in the work of rehearsal', sitting to the right of the camera operators and directing the action with the aid of a megaphone.[14] A 1909 cartoon in *The Bioscope*, which depicts the producer's frustration with staff as he attempts to film 'an important and expensive subject' during rain, reinforces this image of the producer as the on-set artistic manager of fictional productions (Figure 2.1).[15]

Representations of this kind confirm Frederick Talbot's assertion in his 1913 book, *Practical Cinematography and its Applications*, that the producer was effectively a new name for the stage manager, only one with a tighter schedule (and considerably less patience) than his theatrical counterpart.[16] At Hepworth's, indeed, film-makers such as Lewin Fitzhamon, who had joined the company in 1904, had begun with the title 'stage manager', and this persisted at Walton until at least 1912.[17]

These reports also emphasized the significance of the relationships between these autocratic figures and the new generation of professional film actors, camera operators and technicians they worked with. Indeed, according to one contributor to *The Bioscope*, the 'camera man' of dramatic and comedy pictures 'is more or less under the thumb of the producer – one could wish sometimes that he would give the producer his opinion, as an intelligent onlooker'.[18] Similarly, guidebooks for would-be film actors

Figure 2.1 The image of the film producer. *Bioscope*, 15 July 1909

during the teens and early twenties regularly advised that when it came to establishing a good working relationship with producers, 'The Producer can do all the talking that is necessary':

> As soon as you come before the camera commence to think. You will be told what you are expected to do and until you have done it don't stop thinking. Think of how you can best follow out the instructions given. Listen to the Producer when he explains the scene in which you are to take part. Turn his remarks over in your mind. Think, and by your subsequent actions demonstrate that you have THOUGHT. Above all don't ask the Producer questions. He gives instructions and you are expected to pay attention to them and follow them out.
>
> Nothing annoys a Producer more than to find that even two of his supernumeraries are disinterested in their work. People who are noticed laughing and talking will not receive another 'call' for work at that studio.[19]

One might easily dispute the schoolboyish quality of interaction suggested here, in a publication chiefly intended to target those with no prior experience of the film industry or perhaps looking to diversify from the stage. However, these varied accounts of the role of the producer on set, especially insofar as they described working relationships with screen actors, cumulatively suggest a genealogy connecting more obviously with later practices of film direction than production.

For example, probably the most regularly repeated theme of such writing was the assertion of the producer's absolute control over actors' performances, and especially the claim that 'the rapid expression which will be thoroughly right and effective behind the footlights, becomes thoroughly wrong and ineffective in the second case [of film]'.[20] Though standardized roles for film directors in relation to acting performance emerged much later than this, producers such as Powell were regularly credited with precise control of acting performance and celebrated for their ability 'to get the utmost out of each movement, and to give it a special, and, as it were, a permanent value'.[21] Porter's assertion that 'The producer and the director were originally both the same person, and there was no clear division of labor between them', therefore points us irresistibly towards a much longer history connecting the longstanding theatrical practices of stage-management and stage-direction with the role accredited to the producer during the teens, and ultimately with later forms of creative directorial work.[22] Echoing research concerning much later practices in British film and television, we might legitimately describe such figures in the teens as 'producer-artists', acknowledging that they played roles we are now more likely to associate with artistic directorial control.[23] I am not suggesting here that the functions of stage managers, producer-artists and directors across the decades were identical, and certainly not that the producer-artist might qualify in any recognizable or useful sense as some form of producer-auteur; rather, my argument is that as fiction film production companies developed, the technical and creative personnel they employed both drew upon continuities of practice, sometimes derived from theatrical institutions, and also introduced incremental changes to these practices.

Such institutional linkages are evidenced by the biographies of many British producer-artists of the teens, who are now most often described interchangeably as producers, directors or producer-directors. Frank Powell, for example, had begun his career as a stage director in the United States and Europe for such luminaries as Ellen Terry before adopting a producer-artist role at British Pathé studios; and he is now best remembered for his numerous directorial credits for Biograph, Pathé and Fox. Similarly, Percy Nash, a prominent producer for numerous British companies between the early teens and mid-twenties, had spent much of his early career as a jobbing actor, provincial manager and finally as a stage director at His Majesty's Theatre for Sir Beerbohm Tree. His recently discovered memoirs make a passionate case for cinema as a form of 'Theatrical Art'.[24] According to Gerry Turvey, Ethyle and Ernest Batley, along with their daughter Dorothy Audrey, were 'an established theatrical family' on the British provincial circuit, before their respective debuts as film producers in 1910 and 1912; between them, Ethyle and Ernest produced 109 films for six separate companies before 1917, and Ethyle was lauded in the press as a pioneering female producer.[25]

Of course, within different national cinemas, commercial contexts and even in different studios, the distinct roles of producers emerged at different times, and would often fulfil quite different tasks of management, collaboration and creative work. For example, the theatrical associations with producer-artist roles discussed thus far had a specific commercial significance in the British industry of the early teens: several production companies at this time, including Hepworth's, were seeking to promote aspects of legitimate, home-grown, 'quality' entertainment in order to court wealthier domestic audiences, and to distinguish their productions from the bulk of material now being imported from France, America, Italy and elsewhere. In this context, with the British industry now seeking to adjust to changing market conditions by providing its own, elevated, spin on fictional, dramatic film-making, individuals with Powell's, Nash's or the Batleys' experience became extremely useful.

However, significant though this type of theatrical pedigree quickly became, it is not the only relevant genealogy to consider in relation to the early British fiction film producer. Some of the first generation of British film-makers had worked within alternative fictional and dramatic traditions of visual storytelling. For example, the early showman/film-maker William Haggar, whose family theatrical troupe had travelled across Welsh fairgrounds for decades, produced a number of dramatic productions, albeit with relatively informal production roles taken on by himself and other family members. James Bamforth diversified into film production from his successful lantern slide business, borrowing both popular narratives and production processes from an industry that had already reached industrial maturity. Hepworth himself famously entered the film industry from a background in his father's lantern business, recalling of his earliest fictional productions that 'First we thought of a story; then we painted the scenery if it wasn't all open air, as it usually was. Then we acted and photographed it.'[26] Though depending upon the collaboration of smaller numbers of people and requiring substantially lower levels of capital investment than in later years, such processes did not depend on perpetual invention, whimsy or artistic intuition as the artisan thesis tends to assume; rather, they drew from existing institutions, which had fully developed and often highly sophisticated production strategies of their own.

However, more significant in terms of the development of production strategies before 1910 was the substantial non-fiction output of early British film. Indeed, as Luke McKernan has shown, until this date, non-fiction British productions outnumbered fiction productions and they would remain very significant for some years to come, even though imported American and European titles had been supplying the fiction shortfall in theatres for some time prior to this date.[27] As late as 1912, one disgruntled observer complained that 'To frequent the picture shows is to gain the impression that England is a land in which nothing happens but an occasional horse race or Royal review.'[28] In this light, Low and Manvell's claim that pre-1906 British film production consisted of little more than a capacity to understand and exploit the 'elementary apparatus', could perhaps be read as a simple reminder that varied non-fiction genres dominated British film at this time and that, in some cases, the footage of passing events might indeed be all that was needed to secure the interest of audiences. One might consider, here, the multitude of street scenes and other 'local views' shot at this time, in which passers-by were encouraged to visit the film show in order to catch a glimpse of themselves, their families, friends or neighbours on the screen. The success of films such as these was governed largely by their topicality and localities, meaning that it was more important that copies could be produced and distributed quickly to the appropriate audiences than that they were precisely staged, or subjected to detailed, creative post-production. Under such conditions, the role of the producer-artist, at least insofar as it would come to be defined during the early 1910s at studios such as Hepworth's, had little relevance.

However, as before, we should not conclude that the formal simplicity of many of these films, or their apparently minimal processes of filming and post-production, implied an unsophisticated or unskilled production process overall. Even the production of local films presented substantial logistical difficulties for central production companies, whose chief function was to coordinate the demands of hundreds of individual exhibitors in as many locales with the timely provision of operators and equipment and thus to generate large numbers of up-to-date, single-copy, tailor-made films. Moreover, conventions for discriminating between fiction and non-fiction films had not yet fully emerged, with some genre categories, such as those depicting newsworthy conflicts, incorporating what Stephen Bottomore has described as 'arranged ', 'reconstructed' or 'staged' scenes.[29] In such productions, the camera operators, often working alone in foreign countries on behalf of production companies at home, might be required to co-ordinate their filming with significant military actions, or to negotiate with locals in order to reconstruct or invent actions the camera had been unable to witness. Meanwhile, in Britain, the production company had the crucial tasks of assessing the public mood for topical pictures; of coordinating these requirements with the creative skills of operators, editors and other technicians; and of arranging for effective publicity, sales and distribution.

Examples such as these suggest the existence of a series of widely variant but routine and effective systems of production in operation from before 1900, each of which required monitoring and adjustment. This was the primary function of the figure I am calling the 'producer-collaborator': an individual who was also required to be 'a judge of anything and everything', but whose field of action was much wider than the producer-artist's, extending into management of other creative personnel throughout the production process. Charles Urban, predominantly a manufacturer of non-fiction, provides a striking example of such a figure, whose principal aptitude was to bring key creative talents into dialogue and then to marshal these forces into an effective response to public demand, or to attempt to reconfigure that demand. In doing so, Urban was not altogether unique in the British film trade at this time: the early industry provided a wealth of entrepreneurial opportunities for foreign and domestic investors and managers, some of whom were already involved in the business of entertainment. But Brown is surely correct in his assessment that Urban's background as a salesman set him apart from many other early British producers – a proposition evidenced by Luke McKernan, whose writings on Urban have also emphasized the significance of his American upbringing and commercial training.[30] As a former salesman of phonographs and kinetoscopes, Urban was already highly skilled in identifying, addressing and leading new markets.

'One happy family': Producer-collaboration in Urban's British production companies, 1897–1915

Fortunately, Urban also showed a propensity to record his working practices for posterity. The collection now known as the Charles Urban Papers was assembled by Urban himself, comprising not only a career's worth of international press clippings, publicity material, catalogues, film schedules and contracts, but also an unusual wealth of correspondence with creative personnel and with various competitors, peers and external authorities. Unlike so many subsequent influential producers, his papers did not end up dumped into a skip, but preserve a varied account of Urban's transactions with other organizations and creative personnel. The Papers are supplemented, too, by Urban's *Memoirs*, which recount his life and business dealings until 1903.[31] His British career, as chronicled by McKernan, lasted from 1897 – when he began work at the London offices of Maguire and Baucus (soon to be renamed, under Urban's guidance, the 'Warwick Trading Company') – until the First World War, at which point his operations on behalf of the British War Office initiated a largely unsuccessful post-war venture into the American film business.[32]

The archive collectively paints an unusually detailed picture of the production rationale Urban inaugurated and, to a large extent, persisted with throughout his career in Britain and America. This rationale probably found its most coherent expression after 1903, when Urban left Warwick and founded the Charles Urban Trading Company, but it persisted into the early teens, at which point Urban had his greatest commercial success with the Natural Colour Kinematograph Company. However, even his recollections of his early career tend to emphasize the genius for organization, which would subsequently characterize his entire approach to the industry. Urban had first spent three months at the New York office of Maguire and Baucus 'in order that they might test my ability before I took over in London':

> This also had its advantage for me. I would learn about New York City and its business methods – I would get a closer insight into the Edison film and machine production work, could study the trading methods with American distribution and how the requirements from London were being dealt with by the home office.[33]

Equipped with this invaluable knowledge of the production operations of the early film industry in New York, Urban's first impressions of the London operation were less flattering:

> During the week, I got a very good idea of how this office was run, its go-as-you-please methods and the remedies (according to my ideas) which must be applied if this business was to survive or expand. To Mr. Baucus, whom I met the afternoon of my first day at the office, I suggested many things which I believed essential to observe and changes I would insist upon making, if I was to take over the managerial part of this work. Unless I could have full sway, I would not take over the responsibility.[34]

The *Memoirs* persist in this celebration of Urban's bravura command over an unfamiliar business in a foreign country, detailing his rapid rise to the managing directorship of the newly registered Warwick Trading Company and his rescue of its failing fortunes. This account is no doubt substantially coloured by Urban's habitual practices of self-promotion, but the tone of informed self-assurance, coupled with a confident understanding of the managerial strategies that were likely to succeed in the film business, also characterizes his subsequent enterprises as they are detailed in surviving papers.

Whereas Urban's assertive personality and desire to lead the marketplace can be traced through the multi-faceted accumulation of publicity within the Urban papers, his talents for organization and collaboration are better revealed by surviving correspondence and other records of his management techniques. For example, a routine part of Urban's role as a producer of topical films was communication and negotiation with an extraordinarily wide range of external agencies and authorities. Initially, Urban's most regular communications were probably with the Commissioners of Her Majesty's Works and Public Buildings, alongside local authorities, whose responsibility it was to grant permissions to film at certain British locations or during certain events. Some of these letters reveal Urban's persistence with what could prove reluctant or bureaucratic authorities, and they also demonstrate that Urban had a good eye for forthcoming news stories likely to fascinate the picture-going public. Letters received in the days before Victoria's funeral, for example, reveal Urban busily negotiating with the Commissioners on behalf of Warwick in order to gain permissions to film in particular prized spots along the route. More generally, Urban regularly corresponded with representatives of the Royal family, most often, again, seeking permission to film, but also attempting to build closer, more personal (and practical) ongoing working relationships with the Royal publicity machine. Other correspondence reveals Urban managing camera operators, technical personnel and transportation in order to ensure that topicals arrived in theatres quickly– a prime consideration because exhibitors benefited directly when they could be the first in their area to exhibit footage of newsworthy events. He subsequently claimed a record of two hours and 31 minutes between receipt of the exposed negative and screening to the public.[35]

Urban's direct overall management of these logistical matters – from securing permissions, to working with operators, to arranging for efficient distribution – remained an important feature of his expansive role during the 1900s and early teens. Unflagging energy also characterized his communications with various military and propaganda organizations during the First World War, the details of which reveal something of Urban's dynamism and ability to coordinate with external agencies. Indeed, less than four weeks after Britain had entered the conflict, Urban wrote to Field Marshall Earl Roberts proposing that he should attend the new colour programme, 'With the Fighting Forces in Europe', then being screened at Kinemacolor's flagship venue, London's Scala Theatre, and offered to run this programme as part of a recruiting campaign in provincial theatres across the country.[36]

Though this proposal was abruptly turned down (recruitment was already 'brisk'), Urban persisted, with uneven success, in his attempts to negotiate with various units and personnel within the War Office.[37] In April 1915, Urban wrote to Earl Kitchener, proposing to secure additional Kinemacolor films 'of the different stages in training the soldier from the raw recruit through all the phases of transport and different branches of the army and the work in the camps and trenches of France and Belgium', and offering both to defray the costs of filming and to submit to strict War Office supervision.[38] During the next three months, this proposal, presumably along with numerous others from different companies, was considered by the Under-Secretary of State for War, Sir Reginald Brade, who ultimately appointed Edmund Maddick as the Intelligence Department's Director of Kinematography.[39] With typical perspicacity, Urban immediately wrote to congratulate Maddick, who had been a long-time associate of Urban's at the Scala, arranging to meet him – presumably in advance of any meeting with the wider Association.[40] Whether this private meeting with Maddick actually took place is unclear, but by the end of September 1915 Urban was under contract with Sir Claude Schuster of the Lord Chancellor's Office to film, 'for the purposes of cinematograph reproduction in monochrome and colour certain portions of the British Fleet and the British Army within the United Kingdom'.[41] On 9 October, Urban received the command to join the Grand Fleet under Admiral Jellicoe and departed, along with three other camera operators, in order to capture the footage that would be released in December as the highly successful propaganda film, *Britain Prepared*.[42] During filming and post-production, Urban recounted that negotiations with officers continued: the cameras needed to occupy safe positions and to depict the forces in a flattering light, but were not permitted to capture recognizable landmarks; the editing, which he frequently undertook himself, 'called for much patience and tact to satisfy all of the War Office people, and the Officers in command of the various contingents'.[43] Nonetheless, Urban ensured that he remained on friendly, businesslike terms with the officers involved, later exchanging a number of good-natured letters, and providing copies of the films to be screened on board.

Not all of Urban's enterprises were so productive, but the minute, incisive work of persuasion and coordination he undertook during this episode typifies his resourcefulness and resolve when pursuing a production opportunity, even under trying circumstances. His precise control of each step of the production process was equally evident in his management of his own staff, most notably in relation to his camera operators, upon whose judgement, technical expertise and professional savvy the entire enterprise of topical film-making depended. In the *Memoirs*, Urban described the 'training of a cameraman', from the cumulative acquisition of knowledge and experience, to the point at which he could be trusted to ' "handle" events' in distant locations:

If it is in him, he soon becomes a reliable man, whom you can send to a foreign country and trust his discretion as to securing worthwhile pictures. In many instances however, once the camera-man is no longer under the direct supervision of the home office, he is apt to make this a sort of holiday trip at the company's expense, sending in only enough passable negatives to 'get away with it.'[44]

In response to this type of problem, Urban claimed that he would himself revisit some of the countries filmed by his operators as a 'sort of check up on their results'; he was an accomplished camera operator and editor in his own right. However, given the far-flung locations that the Charles Urban Trading Company operators visited, covering events from mountaineering in the Alps to the Russo-Japanese War, it seems unlikely that Urban found much time for this type of paternalistic quality control, and he certainly appears to have trusted his experienced operators, as surviving information on these men tends to reveal.[45] In fact, during most of his career, his publicity probably traded on the expertise of camera operators more heavily than any other feature. Urban's catalogues are loaded with potent and unusually lengthy descriptions of the ingenuity of operators, and especially of the perils undergone in the quest to secure the best pictures, partly on behalf of the exhibitors, who might construct a stimulating dramatic lecture for their audiences from such material.[46]

However, operators were not the only employees whose skill and ingenuity Urban saw fit to advertise, nor were they the only ones to be subject to his particular brand of industrial paternalism. This became especially evident in the publicity that accompanied the opening of new production facilities at 'Urbanora House' in Wardour Street in 1908. With typical hyperbole, Urban described the exacting division of labour he had set in place at this site, proclaiming that 'For the first time in the history of Kinematography the many complex and delicate processes indispensable to the artistic production of the perfect motion-picture have been combined and brought together under one roof.'[47] In two booklets, presumably intended for distribution to customers and friends in the press, Urban detailed each step of this highly mechanized and efficient production process, making especially grand claims for the organization and effectiveness of his staff:

> The most casual reader will readily realise the paramount value of this concentration of forces, the obvious advantages of having the advanced scientist and the skilled machinist in that direct and sympathetic association...; it is organization *in excelsis*.
>
> At the battle of Liao-Yang a Japanese regiment lost all its officers, so that a colour-sergeant took command and maintained the advance of the battalion until relieved by a commissioned officer from another division; similarly every Urban artificer is skilled not only in his own departmental work but in the many intricate processes allied and accessory to it; he is the craftsman grown artist by training and instruction; he is an enthusiastic atom in the great mosaic and is at all times capable, like the Japanese colour-sergeant, of extending his general duties to promote the general success.[48]

Urban's metaphor, as ever, is immoderate, but his reference to the Russo-Japanese War (which neatly referred back to previous films by the Charles Urban Trading Company) was intended to convey not only a high degree of operational precision, but also a sense of the 'life or death' levels of commitment, coupled with refined expertise expected from each 'artificer'. The overall impression intended was one of collective, almost systemic mastery, in which the 'great mosaic', presumably, was ultimately to be regarded as Urban's own creative masterpiece.

A few years later, Urban would apply the same principles of division of labour at 'Kinemacolor House', which he opened a few doors away from Urbanora House, in what was now becoming an important centre for the British film industry on Wardour Street. In an internal notice delivered to staff on 22 July 1912, Urban wrote that the success of Kinemacolor now necessitated the division of the business into separate departments with 'capable and energetic men' in charge of each. While all employees, the notice made quite clear, were under the hire and fire of Urban, they were also engaged in a great and collective enterprise and could expect rewards for unwavering commitment to the cause:

> Bearing in mind the fact that the industry is of such a fascinating and lucrative character, and that the company undoubtedly holds the most exalted position in the trade, it is felt that the staff should be proud of their association with a firm of our records and stability. Obviously, the success of the business depends upon the loyal working and co-operation of all members of the staff, and their promotion is accordingly governed by the energy, amount of interest, and intelligence with which they discharge their duties to the firm.
>
> It is with men as with machines – the best obtainable only are required and valued. No favours will be shown, and we want to see the staffs of all departments co-operating as one happy family, each member honestly striving to bring the work in that portion of the business for which he is responsible as near perfection as possible.[49]

Urban's stirring prose, delivered only to his employees in this instance, highlighted the work of all technicians and labourers in a collective effort of production, drawing directly upon Taylorist discourses of scientific management in order to promote a positive analogy between men and machines. At the same time, Urban was advancing a deeply paternalistic version of this type of division of labour, requiring his 'happy family' to engage in mutually beneficial efforts of problem solving, innovation and collaboration. It was clear that Urban regarded film production as an intrinsically collaborative operation, though one which functioned best under the creative, supervisory roles he had repeatedly created for himself, according to his own account, from his first week at Maguire and Baucus.

Thus, in publicity generated for audiences, exhibitors, rental companies and the press in general, and even in communications with his own employees, Urban consistently emphasized the significance of creative work at each stage of the production process. Urban was early to recognize the commercial value of publicizing such forms of work, demonstrating a salesman's understanding of the crucial part that discourses of creativity might play in targeting old audiences and creating new ones. But he also suggested that ultimately the vision that unified the whole enterprise was his. This meant that his role as a producer-collaborator was highly visible, becoming especially prominent in the personal vision he espoused in film catalogues for his various companies, and in the flagship shows he established at London theatres such as The Scala in order to showcase his films. Repeatedly, publicity of these kinds laid claim to an unsurpassed tradition of quality, with the businesslike, forthright Mr Urban serving as guarantor: 'We do not cater to degenerate tastes', he pointedly advised in a 1906 Charles Urban Trading Company Catalogue, several years before British fiction producers had begun in earnest with their own bid for legitimacy.

Urban's popular persona, coupled with his perpetual clamour for quality film-making, provided a figure and a theme which the popular and trade presses were always able to support. This was most apparent following the success of Kinemacolor, when Urban acquired some small measure of celebrity.[50] Such popular recognition was by no means unwelcome, but it had been acquired as part of a longstanding and deliberate strategy to foster brand identity for his productions within different companies. In carving out this popular niche, creating small but efficient and collaborative bodies of staff, and seeking to develop an audience around his brand, Urban arguably helped to set in place what Porter, discussing the later activities of film production at Ealing and Hammer, has called an effective 'context of creativity'.[51]

Film producers in early British film history

Urban faced a British marketplace that was radically different to the one established in the 1920s and beyond, and he specialized in factual rather than dramatic productions. But the types of roles he performed, enabling creative work to take place within an efficient, innovative, collaborative environment, and seeking to identify and create new audiences for his own brand of film-making, suggest surprisingly direct connections with the careers of subsequent generations of British producers, which have been considered regularly in terms of creative collaboration, professional negotiation and market leadership. Indeed, Andrew Spicer's definition of the role of the British producer, drawing on both Michael Balcon's 1945 account and a 1948 *Kinematograph Weekly* article by Sydney Box, provides a description which might be applied with equal felicity to Urban's role between 1897 and 1915: 'the producer is the mediator between commerce and creativity ... whose key function is to have an overview of the whole filmmaking process'; an individual 'who can both satisfy commercial imperatives (make films that are profitable) and lead public opinion rather than merely pandering to existing tastes'.[52]

This linkage between producers working across over four decades may seem provocative, even ahistorical, especially in the context of the periodization which continues to characterize international early film as a 'terra incognita' – a body of work somehow divorced from the industries and cinematic forms that were to follow. It might also seem to confirm the alternative contention of some historians of British cinema, that across the first three decades of film production in Britain, very little had changed. One might even speculate that the careers of men such as Urban and Box were linked less by national genealogies of film style or commerce than by simple institutional similarities: both worked principally within niche domestic markets in the context of powerful competition, often from overseas; both sought to establish small but efficient creative teams within mid-sized businesses in order to cater for such markets, or to create new demand. In both cases, too, the models of film production that evolved remained viable for a number of years but ultimately proved vulnerable to competition, hostile legislation and changing public tastes.

However, having drawn this comparison, we should also acknowledge that the roles of British producers had also undergone substantial changes during these years. Moreover, in contrast with the assumptions of the artisan thesis, we should recognize that from the beginning, British producers were not unsophisticated in their approach to film-making, nor naïve in relation to national and global markets. Although conditions were unpropitious in Britain for the development of central-producer systems during this period, the producer-collaborator emerged early, embodying professional mastery of the production process and of the developing market, but within different commercial and institutional circumstances than were at work in France or the United States. In this context, the changing collaborative roles of figures such as Hepworth, especially in relation to the production of fiction films at Walton – which one commentator described as 'a model factory', equal in efficiency if not size with production facilities overseas – require further investigation.[53] The case of Urban demonstrates more clearly that the business of non-fiction film-making, too, though evidently a different type of enterprise, was equally dependent upon a rationalized process of creative collaboration, one carefully tailored to address a target market within specific commercial conditions. Urban's omnipresent control of this process, though far from infallible, extended across a wide range of professional contexts, from staff management to external publicity, providing a consistency of vision that permitted him, even in times of commercial volatility, to maintain some measure of stability and command. Explanations currently offered for the relative commercial failure of British producers during the teens must therefore be qualified further by acknowledging the expertise demonstrated from the beginning of the film industry by individuals such as Urban.

Notes

1   For an early and definitive account of the creative exhibitor, see Charles Musser, 'The Eden Musee in 1898: The Exhibitor as Creator', *Film and History: An International Journal of Film and Television Studies*, 11:4 (1981): 73–96.

2   Rachel Low and Roger Manvell, *The History of the British Film, 1896–1906* (London: George Allen and Unwin, 1948), 15.

3   Rachel Low, *The History of the British Film, 1906–1914* (London: George Allen and Unwin, 1949), 92.

4   Richard Abel, *The Ciné Goes to Town: French Cinema: 1896–1914* (Berkeley: University of California Press, 1998), 20.

5   Charles Musser, 'Pre-Classical American Cinema: Its Changing Modes of Production', *Persistence of Vision* 9 (1991): 46–65.

6   André Gaudreault, *Film and Attraction: From Kinematography to Cinema* (Chicago: University of Illinois Press, 2011), 8.
7   Low, *The History of the British Film, 1906–1914*, 92. For a contemporary acknowledgement of the slump in domestic production, see, for example, 'The Cinematograph and the Actor', *The Bioscope*, 5 September 1912, 705; and 'The British Film', *The Bioscope*, 1 August 1912, 337.
8   Vincent Porter, 'Making and Meaning: The Role of the Producer in British Films', *Journal of British Film and Television* 9:1 (2012): 9.
9   Simon Brown, 'From Inventor to Renter: The Middleman, the Production Crisis and the Formation of the British Film Industry', *Early Popular Visual Culture* 11:2 (2013): 103.
10 Michael Chanan, *The Dream that Kicks: The Prehistory and Early Years of Cinema in Britain*, 2nd edn. (London: Routledge, 1996), 190–94.
11 Chanan, *The Dream that Kicks*, 192.
12 Chas. J.L. Clarke, 'Filming Laughter and Tears. How Cinematograph Pictures are Produced', *Pall Mall Magazine* 50 (1912): 852–53.
13 Clarke, 'Filming Laughter', 856.
14 The report was republished in the showman's journal, *The World's Fair*. 'Behind the Scenes: A Cinematograph Rehearsal', *The World's Fair*, 18 November 1911, 11.
15 A. Glossop, 'The Troubles of the Film Producer', *The Bioscope*, 15 July 1909, 47.
16 Frederick Talbot, *Practical Cinematography and its Applications* (London: Heinemann, 1913), 242.
17 See 'Pictures in the Making: A Visit to the Hepworth Factory', *The Bioscope*, 28 March 1912, 943–47.
18 'Britannicus', 'The Moving Picture Photographer', *The Bioscope*, 4 April 1912, 39.
19 Aurele Sydney, *Cinema: Practical Course in Cinema Acting in Ten Complete Lessons, Lesson 4* (London: Standard Art Book Co. ltd, 1920).
20 'Behind the Scenes', 11.
21 'Behind the Scenes', 11.
22 Porter, 'Making and Meaning', 8.
23 In using this term, Andrew Spicer draws especially on John Caughie, 'Broadcasting and Cinema 1: Converging Histories', *All Our Yesterdays: 90 Years of British Cinema*, ed. Charles Barr (London: British Film Institute, 1986), 189–205. Andrew Spicer, 'The Production Line: Reflections on the Role of the Producer in British Cinema', *Journal of British Cinema and Television*, 1 (2004): 35.
24 Bernard Ince, ' "For the Love of the Art": The Life and Work of Percy Nash, Film Producer and Director of the Silent Era', *Film History: An International Journal*, 19:3 (2007): 298.
25 Gerry Turvey, 'Constrained Emancipation: The Career of Ethyle Batley, Britain's Pioneering Woman Film Director', *Film History: An International Journal*, 21:4 (2009): 360.
26 Cecil Hepworth, 'Those Were the Days', in *Film Makers on Film Making: Statements on their Art by Thirty Directors*, ed. Harry M. Geduld (Bloomington: Indiana University Press, 1967), 29.
27 Luke McKernan, ' "Something More than a Mere Picture Show": Charles Urban and the Early Non-Fiction Film in Great Britain and America, 1897–1925' (PhD diss., University of London, 2003), 110.
28 'The British Film', 337.

29   Stephen Bottomore, 'From Theatre Manager to Globetrotting Cameraman: The
     Strange Career of Charles Rider Noble (1854–1914)', *Film History: An International
     Journal*, 24:3 (2012): 290.

30   Brown, 'From Inventor to Renter': 104. On Urban's American training, see Luke
     McKernan, 'The American Invasion and the British Film Industry', in *Crossing the
     Pond: Anglo-American Film Relations before 1930*, ed. Alan Burton and Laraine Porter
     (Trowbridge: Flicks Books, 2002), 7–15.

31   Charles Urban, *A Yank in Britain: The Lost Memoirs of Charles Urban*, ed. Luke
     McKernan (Hastings: The Projection Box, 1999).

32   McKernan, 'Something More.'

33   Urban, *A Yank in Britain*, 38.

34   Urban, *A Yank in Britain*, 43.

35   'Urbanora House: The Home of Kinematography', booklet (URB 3/1), 1.

36   Urban to Field Marshall Earl Roberts (31 August 1914) (URB4/1, 1–3).

37   R. J. K. Mott (secretary) to Urban (2 September 1914) (URB4/1, 4).

38   Urban to Earl Kitchener (27 April 1915) (URB4/1, 5–6).

39   Sir Reginald Brade to Urban (1 July 1915) (URB4/1, 12); Urban to Sir Gilbert Parker
     (10 August 1915) (URB4/1, 14); H.C. Gordon to Charles Urban (9 August 1915)
     (URB4/1, 15).

40   Urban to Edmund Maddick (10 August 1915) (URB 4/1, 17).

41   Contract between Sir Claude Schuster and Charles Urban (23 September 1915). (URB
     4/1, 23).

42   Charles Urban, 'How the Somme Battle was Photographed' (URB4/1-106).

43   Charles Urban, 'How the Somme Battle was Photographed' (URB4/1-106).

44   Urban, *A Yank in Britain*, 55.

45   See especially Bottomore, 'From Theatre Manager.'

46   Joe Kember, *Marketing Modernity: Victorian Popular Shows and Early Cinema*
     (Exeter: University of Exeter Press, 2009), 193–202.

47   'Urbanora House: The Home of Kinematography', booklet (URB 3/1).

48   'The Home of Kinematography', booklet (URB 3/1).

49   Typescript notice to staff (22 July 1912) (URB 3/1).

50   See, for example, 'Mayfair Gallery. Men of the Day. No. 163. Mr. Charles Urban',
     Mayfair, 14 August 1912, 996.

51   Vincent Porter, 'The Context of Creativity: Ealing Studios and Hammer Films', in
     British Cinema History, ed. James Curran and Vincent Porter (London: Weidenfeld
     and Nicholson, 1983).

52   Spicer, 'The Production Line', 34.

53   'Pictures in the Making', 947.

3

Mapping a Typology of the Film Producer – Or, Six Producers in Search of an Author

Audun Engelstad and Jo Sondre Moseng

The cult of the director, particularly in relation to European cinema, has meant that academic attempts to analyse and discuss other types of talent involved in film-making have been virtually non-existent. The film producer has generally been thought of as a project manager or an employer whose main responsibility is to package the film and control the finances, supervise the production and eventually exploit the movie's market potential. Such broad descriptions indicate a multitude of different ways of producing films, and not all of these descriptions are accurate with respect to the impact the producer has on the film.

In order to grasp the role of the producer, this chapter will offer a profile analysis of six Norwegian film production companies. The material of this study is based on in-depth interviews with producers from six different production companies. One production company is commercially oriented; one is art-house oriented; and the other four, in various ways, occupy intermediate positions between these two poles. Analysing these production companies revealed some striking differences in their profiles, to the extent that it makes sense to distinguish between different *types* of producers.

Being more than simply the entrepreneurial project manager or businessperson that stereotyped images of the producer often imply, we will put forward a typology of the film producer based on how the professionals work in a mid-range European film nation such as Norway. In order to grasp the role of the producer, we have analysed the top film companies in relation to, among other things, their size and their scale of production, as well as the kinds of films they produce. Their different strategies as film producers, and their engagement in the creative process, will be uncovered by analysing their approach to film adaptations.

Over the past ten years, approximately 40 per cent of Norwegian fiction films were based on a literary source, a figure consistent with previous decades. Moreover, the general trend of adapting literary sources for film production is similar to trends found in a number of other Western countries. According to Peter Bloore, close to 40 per cent of the films developed in the United Kingdom are adaptations, while in Hollywood, the numbers are around 50 per cent of the projects developed.[1]

The context of current film production in Norway

Despite the international acclaim achieved by films such as *Insomnia* (Skjoldbjærg, 1997) and *Junk Mail* (Sletaune, 1997) – both of which featured at the Cannes International Film Festival's Critics' Week programme – and *The Other Side of Sunday* (Nesheim, 1996), which was nominated for an Oscar in the Best Foreign Film category, Norwegian film in the 1990s did not prove popular with domestic filmgoers; the market share dropped to as low as 5 per cent in 1997. The Ministry of Culture grew increasingly concerned about the lack of viability in the independent production sector and the low audience for Norwegian films. In order to meet these pressing challenges, the Ministry hired the firm Ernst & Young Management Consulting (EYMC) in 1998 to evaluate the Norwegian film industry and the funding system.[2]

The main problem with the Norwegian film industry that the report identified was a fragile sector of independent production companies, most of which were short-lived and had a meagre catalogue of feature films on their lists. The EYMC report led to a major reform in Norwegian film policies. The government increased its allocations to film production, but in order to invigorate the independent sector and to secure a more viable industry, the state-owned production company Norsk Film AS (Norwegian Film, Ltd.) was terminated in 2001. The funding was redirected into the newly established Norwegian Film Fund, to which only independent producers could apply. The public broadcaster NRK – formerly a major player in the field – withdrew from film production, since it was barred from applying to the fund.

The termination of Norsk Film AS and the withdrawal from film production by NRK created a void in the film production sector. A handful of film production companies were already operating in the market at the time, but several newcomers, of various sizes, arrived within few years – some as a result of the recently established Norwegian Film School. The competition for funding changed radically.

In order to survive in a restructured industry, production companies have devised new strategies. They seek out film projects of a particular kind to produce, since they have well-founded strategies as to how they engage with creative talent. In order to succeed in the sector, the production companies need to identify a niche to occupy, and make sure that this niche is large enough to meet the demands of the market as well as to satisfy the representatives of the funding system.

By 2012, it had become evident that the Norwegian film industry had reconsolidated, with a group of ten top players accounting for 60 per cent of the total feature film production between 2003 and 2012. Popular genre films have drawn the domestic audience back to the cinemas, reaching an exceptional market share of 24 per cent in 2011. In addition, since 2010, private investments exceed 50 per cent of the total production costs of feature films.[3] The industry and its output have been commercialized to an unanticipated degree. In this current situation, the film producer – as opposed to the director or screenwriter – has become the dominant player in the industry.

Outlining a producer-oriented approach to adaptation studies

Adaptation studies in the academy have been, until recently, chiefly dominated by aesthetic approaches. Adaptation studies take an interest in teasing out various stylistic and narrative strategies that are at play within literature and film. It is striking that in so many of these analyses, the penchant is to make claims about aesthetic choices regarding style or narrative devices, and these choices are directly connected to the film director in question. With respect to artistic agency and intentionality, the result – that is, what we see on the screen – could just as well come across accidentally or spontaneously in the artistic process, or other people in the process could be responsible, such as the screenwriter, the film editor, the cinematographer, the actor or the producer.

However, the recent turn in adaptation studies, what Simone Murray has identified as 'the third wave of adaptation studies', comes with a call for new approaches and perspectives.[4] At the centre of Murray's study is what she regards as the material phenomenon of the adaptation industry, and the cultural production involved therein. What tends to be overlooked, according to Murray, is an examination of the how and why, from the perspectives of those responsible for making adaptations happen: authors, agents, publishers, editors, book-prize committees, screenwriters, directors and producers. While Murray gives a rather cursory depiction of the role of the producer, this chapter will attempt to examine how these producers' various strategies towards adaptations are reflected by their general approach to film production.

Rick Altman has proposed a model for studying the relationship between different key agents within the film industry with respect to film genres. Among the conceptual tools offered by Altman is what he calls playing the producer's game, which he views as being in contrast to the critic's game.[5] While the critic looks for specific traits in a list of existing films, the producer tries to identify and anticipate the elements to which an audience will respond positively. The games proposed by Altman are applicable to studying adaptations.

The critic's game would run something like this: (i) Define the merits of the source text with respect to style, theme, conflicts, characters, setting, etc. (ii) Establish through textual analysis to what extent these merits are materialized in the film version. (iii) Draw conclusions about the achievements of the film versus the source text. (iv) Look into similar adaptations and make claims about what kinds of source texts will either make artistically challenging films or commercially successful films, or will run the risk of being a failure in both respects.

While the critic's game by nature consists of making theoretical assessments drawn from an existing catalogue of films, the producer's game concerns examining possible properties for future film productions. It might run something like this: (i) Study the art section of the newspaper for interviews, book reviews and sales charts, and arrange meetings with editors and literary agents. (ii) Find a title that can appeal to a broad audience. (iii) Estimate production costs. (iv) Assign a screenwriter and a director with the desired artistic qualities to develop the production. (v) Start marketing the film, emphasizing its most potent selling points – which are not always the book or its author. (vi) Start all over again and repeat the process.

This approach works to illustrate that the producer is usually not concerned with making aesthetic evaluations based on a thorough analysis of the text. The key interest in playing the producer's game is to discuss how the film producer engages with the literary field, and the processes and strategies that are in play when a book is optioned and turned into a feature film. The producer-oriented approach is followed in our study of Norwegian film production, covering the last decade, and focusing on how the film producer engages with the literary field.

A brief summary of Norwegian adaptations

In the 1990s, a number of Norwegian heritage films – based on literary classics (Knut Hamsun was particularly favoured) – were produced by Norsk Film and by NRK, as these firms had a cultural responsibility to keep the literary heritage alive and available for a new audience. The situation changed significantly from 2000 to 2011. Of the 62 films based on a literary source, more than two-thirds of all the adapted films were based on novels by contemporary authors who are well known to a broad reading public. Although stylistically different, they belong to the Norwegian storytelling tradition, which features a clearly focused plot and somewhat enigmatic characters. Most of the literary texts are characterized by a straightforward style of writing, which has been transposed to a conventional style of classical storytelling for film. Although nearly all of the literary texts are written by contemporary authors, only a handful of the novels and short stories can be related to a modernist tradition of aesthetically or thematically challenging literature. With few exceptions, the adapted films from these artistically ambitious texts correspond to what Robert Stam has called aesthetic mainstreaming, in which 'the novel is "cleansed" of moral ambiguity, narrative interruption and reflexive mediation'.[6]

However, some modifications can be made to this approach. First, the adaptations made from children's and youth novels usually do not have an author with a well-known name outside of their target reading audiences. This means that for the producer, the novel can seldom be seen as an established commodity in the market place on which the film can draw. Second, the Norwegian literary industry is successful by almost any measure, and several authors who write what we might perceive as artistic novels in terms of content and style are very popular among the reading public. A fair amount of these novels are optioned for film adaptations, although only a few of these projects are realized. However, most of these films gravitate towards what Stam describes as mainstreaming – although to a lesser degree than the Hollywood films Stam had in mind.

Adaptation as a key to a producer profile

The kinds of literature most of these novels represent are usually seen as easily adaptable to the film medium, where the adaptation process merely requires transposition of characters, events and setting from one medium to another. In addition, the cultural item can be seen as pre-sold, as it is already well-known among the anticipated audience. Thus, as a general rule, one can easily get the impression that for the film producer optioning novels for film production is guided by risk avoidance, and that there exists some kind of sure-fire formula for making adaptations. Yet, this notion is at best only partially true, since adaptations always demand considerable changes and choices with respect to style and narrative scope. Thus, when the producers discuss their strategies and priorities, their explanations point to several other determining factors.

One of the striking facts the interviews uncovered was the lack of what we might term conventional trade wisdom. That is, the companies do not seem to have a common approach to film adaptations, and they all go by their own rules of thumb. At no point in the conversations did they say anything indicating that their guidelines were informed by the success or failure of other adapted films in the market. This does not necessarily mean that they do not study what their competitors do, but if they do, they keep quiet about it. This is somewhat surprising, because they could easily have expressed this with general phrases such as 'everybody knows', or 'history has shown' or 'years in the trade have taught us' that so-and-so novels are likely to make successful films. Late in the conversation, and usually as a response to a probing question, they would admit that a well-known author was of importance, but this hardly ever seemed to be a key factor. The producers reported that they do not generally search for bestsellers, but the fact that an interesting book might also be a bestseller, or in other ways had a reputation, could help get the film project off the ground.

The interviews also confirmed that adapting novels is seen as a necessity, although not in a particularly negative way. Of the many developed manuscripts the production companies received every year, written on spec by newcomers as well as established screenwriters or directors, very few of the screenplays had the desired qualities – in the producer's mind – for further involvement in the project. The lack of interesting original material forced the producers to look elsewhere for projects to be developed. Optioning books for adaptation is one of the means the producers have in order to develop sufficient projects.

Adaptations have the advantage that the basic story already exists; thereby risk can be reduced at the development stage. In Norway, in particular, where state funding constitutes a major source of film production financing, an already existing story means that resources – finances and creative attention – can be channelled into other parts of development in order to optimize the project, before pitching it to the national film board and other investors. Moreover, adaptations enable the producer to stay in control of the project for a longer period of time, and to intervene in creative decisions without undermining the egos of the creative personnel involved. In this sense, adaptations can be argued to be the producers' game.

The production of adaptations can be divided into different stages. The first stage concerns examining the literary field, and more generally relates to the production companies' supply of story material; assessments of ideas and their potential value; and issues of optioning. At the second stage, the optioned novel is developed. A team is put together in order to develop the project from the treatment stage to a finished screenplay, after which the producers must secure the finances and sales in advance. If the project is green-lit, the next steps are production (including pre- and post-production) and marketing prior to its theatrical release.

Sketching out the various steps in working with an adaptation enables us to see how the producer is involved at different stages in the development process, from the inception to the decisions regarding the kind of film that is envisioned, and with respect to how, when and why the different creative collaborators (i.e. screenwriter and director) are brought in to the film project. In accordance with the aims of this chapter, we will concentrate on the first two of these stages, as this is where the producer influences the production most directly. In the following stages, parts of the responsibility are handed over to line producers, crew and distributors, among others. However, it is important to recognize that issues of adaptations can be raised and discussed at every stage of production.

Business decisions as exercising creativity

As is the case with most European nations, Norwegian film-making is executed at the intersecting point of art and commerce, dependent on public funding in order to get the production process started, yet at the same time in need of a market in which to sell the finished product. Finding the right balance between originality and familiarity in any given project is therefore one of the most important tasks of the producer. This is the case even when faced with an already existing story, as is the case with adaptations. In order to understand the decision-making process of film adaptations, it is helpful to draw on the four criteria of creativity in a product that Teresa Amabile has identified.[7] These criteria can shed light on the choices and decisions made by the producers in the initial phases of an adaptation project, for example, the acquisition and development phases. The first criterion is originality – the impression of the product as novel in some way. The second criterion is that the product resonates with the public and has a certain commercial appeal. The third criterion is the critical acclaim that the product receives. Applied to film producer's work, these three criteria are closely connected.

As for the third criterion, critical acclaim, it is important to stress that the producers do not seem to bother about whether the literary source received favourable reviews or not. While focusing on contemporary subjects, the novels acquired are nevertheless written by authors that in one way or another have a resonance with the reading community. The producers' approaches vary in this respect, some preferring best-selling authors promoted through major book clubs, while others follow their taste and sense of quality, and select credible, though not always commercially popular, names and titles. Most of them, however, seem to engage in the field somewhat haphazardly. But as all of the producers stress the increasing importance of making adaptations, it is not so much the public reception of a given book that guides their choices, as much as it is their own assessment of the idea of the book-as-transferred-to-film.

Amabile's fourth criterion of creativity is that the product must help the organization – which in this case means the production company – to meet its strategic objectives and work within available timeframes and budgets. Before deciding whether to initiate the project or not, the producer has to imagine the creative potential in the finished film and, at the same time, assess its commercial prospects. This typically implies business considerations – for example, of target groups, financing options and marketability.

Adaptations are thought of as desirable because, as M. Bjørn von Rimscha has pointed out, their literary sources minimize the time-consuming activity of developing new story ideas, and this therefore reduces the financial as well as creative risks.[8] However, the average costs of the adaptations considered in this study were not less than those found in movies with original scripts. This suggests that financial considerations cannot alone explain the high number of adaptations, even if they are judged easier to pitch. Rather, adaptations allow producers, in most cases, to exercise their creative proclivities in ways that original scripts cannot.

Our study shows that the approach of different producers to filmed literature is not identical. By looking into the processes that inform the decisions related to making adaptations, we can identify more general distinctions between different types of producers. In the following section, we will elaborate on the considerations and strategies involved when a film producer decides to turn a book into a feature film.

The archetypes: The blockbuster producer and the art cinema producer

The Norwegian blockbuster production company Filmkameratene is characterized by a strong orientation towards the domestic commercial market. One of their most recent blockbuster hits is *Max Manus – Man of War* (Sandberg & Rønning, 2008), based on the biography of the legendary Norwegian Second World War resistance hero, Max Manus. Filmkameratene was formed by John M. Jacobsen in the mid-1980s, and is one of the longest-running Norwegian film companies operating today. Jacobsen is an experienced CEO and is regarded as a rather sly fox in the industry. He is well known for picking projects with an appeal to the broadest possible audience. His partner, Sveinung Golimo, is known as one of the most talented and hardworking producers to have come out of the Norwegian Film School.

The blockbuster producer confirms the stereotyped, public image of the profession, as a powerful but rather low-profile businessman who explains his many successes by referring to gut feeling and well-developed intuition. What counts for the blockbuster producer is whether a certain project has a high concept potential and a wide reach in order for it to be commercially exploitable. As such, the blockbuster producer is particularly careful about which projects to concentrate on, and he bases his decisions on somewhat idiosyncratic criteria – expressed by vague phrases such as 'the well-told story' or 'original concepts'– and is not concerned about the source of the adaptation. Golimo sums up Filmkameratene's strategy in the following way:

> We keep in contact with a few authors. But just as we are not committed to any director, in the sense that we will produce a specific director's next film, the same goes with the authors. We try to pick something unique every time. If that means we will continue with an author, fine. And if it can work out with the same director once again, we will do that. But we are always on the lookout for the unique stories and the unique projects, more than we are concerned about developing or maintaining talent. That is our goal.[9]

Filmkameratene's latest project is an adaptation of Knut Hamsun's *Victoria* (1898) – still in production at the time of the interview – a story about a young couple's illicit love that is probably the most accessible of Hamsun's novels. According to the producer, the timing is right for releasing a period film once again, given the time that has passed since the cycle of heritage films in the 1990s. He hopes the story of overwhelming love will resonate with a younger audience that does not necessarily relate to Hamsun, as well as an older audience that would be curious about seeing a Hamsun novel on the screen.

At the other end of the spectrum, we find the art cinema producer, represented by Motlys – a name that translates as 'backlight'. Motlys, too, dates back to the mid-1980s, and for more than a decade the company predominately produced documentaries. Among the company's latest feature films, we find the internationally critically acclaimed *Oslo, 31 August* (Trier, 2011) and *Turn Me On, Dammit* (Jacobsen, 2011).

The stereotype of the European art cinema producer is someone drawn to the profession by a passion for art. Art cinema producers tend to be somewhat fastidiously selective in their orientation, making their discriminating taste guide the kinds of projects they choose. As for the producer we interviewed at Motlys, Yngve Sæther, previously in his career, when working as a programme director at a repertoire cinema, would regularly give lectures to publishers and aspiring authors on the topic of writing for film. Before turning to film production, Sæther was trained in literature and film studies, and for several years held the position as a head of the national association for art cinema theatres. While expressing disappointment with the standard of Norwegian screenwriters in general, Sæther regarded authors of fiction to be more artistically dedicated and focused. On several projects, he collaborated with fiction authors he found distinctive and exciting, either asking them to adapt one of their own stories or inviting them to develop an original idea for the screen. During the interview, he repeated several times that he regarded literary adaptation as more than mere transposition. 'I do not see the point of being faithful to the literary source. In my mind, the film is the king. And the film has to be good. You need to do what it takes to make it good. That is my belief' (Figure 3.1).[10]

Emphasizing that the story in itself was not the only thing that matters, this producer pointed to the importance of attitude, mood, temper and sensation as

Figure 3.1 Yngve Sæther, producer at Motlys, in front of a movie poster of one of his successful film adaptations. Photo, Siv Dolmen, with his kind permission

qualities represented in the text. Of all the producers interviewed, he was the only one to list specific narrative traits that could be easily transposed in an adaptation, such as 'a short narrative time-span', 'a breach between the protagonist's desire and his capabilities', 'interesting supporting characters' and 'comic relief that takes the edge off of the serious treatment of the main plot'. He also referred to his literary preferences as a kind of 'pop cultural sensibility', which he explained as a story that combines universal, existential themes with the spirit of the age.

The blockbuster producer and the art cinema producer constitute contrasting archetypes. However, these polar categories in themselves do not do justice to the variations that actually exist between film producers nor to the fact that most European film production operates in between these two extremes. Indeed, in most national European film industries, there is little room for more than a few companies with a clear-cut production profile. As domestic markets in Europe are quite limited, and because most producers are heavily dependent on state funding and hence vulnerable to shifting conditions surrounding film production, it is risky business to compete in the film market by solely cultivating either a blockbuster or an art cinema profile. In effect, most European film production companies are intermediates – somewhere between the two poles, balancing their output and assessing new projects according to the way in which the wind is blowing in the industry in order to secure funding and stay ahead of competitors.

The intermediates

The four remaining production companies in our study do not easily fit into the either-or model based on the blockbuster/art cinema dichotomy. These companies were established during the period 1997–2002, when the Norwegian film reforms were clarified and implemented, yet none of the producers in question were inexperienced newcomers at the time. Clearly, their strategy and timing were favourable, as all of them became dominant players in the industry within the first decade of the new millennium. At first glance, these companies appear quite similar, both in terms of size and scale of production. Moreover, it might be hard to tell them apart by analysing their filmographies, as their projects vary considerably and no single, distinct profile can easily be detected. The Norwegian film companies by and large compete for the same projects, the same audience and, consequently, might be hard to distinguish one from the other. Yet, to perceive these companies as an indistinguishable mass by simply looking at their completed projects is jumping to conclusions. In fact, by studying their approaches to adaptations, and more generally, the strategies involved in developing new projects, we found that the intermediate Norwegian film companies differ considerably. Prominent disparities relate to the producers' conception of creativity, as well as their cultivation of talent. These dissimilarities relate not only to the types of movies they made, but also to the producers' working strategies.

Nurturing producers

The production companies' search for source material for new films varied. Three of the intermediate companies – Maipo, Paradox and 4½ (Fourandahalf) – can be recognized by their having a nurturing manner, in which the producers maintain long-term relationships with creative personnel and seek to cultivate the creative talent of their partners. Nurturing producers regard themselves as initiators, who start out with a more or less personal vision of the final product, and then build the project step by step. They invest time and resources in people and in creative teams in whom they believe, perceiving themselves just as much as personal mentors as employers. Still, nurturing producers are cautious about developing stories if they have not taken part in the inception of its idea. In their minds, adaptations are seen as a particularly safe mode of production, and they anticipate that such projects would continue to be important to them in the future.

The producer at Paradox, Finn Gjerdrum, claimed that he found it crucial to conceptualize the film project before even negotiating an option with the publisher. This process involves finding the parts of the book that are 'filmic', sketching out interesting characters, visualizing the story-world, writing the first drafts of the synopsis, assessing the production value and possible audience reach, as well as the possibility of bringing the right constellations of creative talent together. He referred to this process as 'putting the package together', pointing to an alternative understanding of the Hollywood term 'packaging' when applied to a European context.

In line with his nurturing attitude, Gjerdrum particularly stressed the role played by building a team that can deliver his own vision of the film. In some cases, this implies selecting a director associated with the style or 'temper' that he desires for the adaptation, or a screenwriter who can bring forth a new and appealing quality to the optioned novel. At other times, putting the right teams together is conceived of as vital in order to secure goodwill among rights-owners, investors, and the National Film Board. For example, at the time of the interview, he had recently optioned a novel from an internationally acclaimed Norwegian author, and in order to show him respect, the producer immediately hired another acclaimed author-screenwriter to adapt the book.

> It helps to have a name with some standing. We try to combine one well-known author with another well-known author. Two names, that could be exciting, to see how that match works out. We think of it as a comedy. Then we will bring in a director the actors enjoy working with. At that point, you have a package you can present to someone. You have already moved up the ladder. I think it will be hard for the consultant at the National Film Board to say: 'No, damned if I believe in that project'. And you can go to a distributor and say: 'Here is this and that person, and they have won such and such prize', and so on. 'We'd like that', they're gonna say.[11]

To the producer at Paradox, these packaging strategies are essential to adaptations. Strange as it might seem, in his mind it is important that the film can offer something its source text cannot provide. One approach might be to appoint directors, photographers and VFX artists with distinct ideas of what the visual concept should be like. Another approach is to steer the project in a certain preferred direction. Gjerdrum often starts out by focusing on parts of the book, a specific situation, a character or a perceived mood that caught his interest at the time of reading, in advance of writing the first draft of the treatment, as he sometimes does. For example, Gjerdrum emphasized several times during the interview that he often makes an effort to turn the grave and difficult situations he finds in these books into audience-friendly, dark humour. After all, as he pointed out, it is easier to attract an audience if the film is somewhat upbeat in its tone. These innovations, however, were always offered for approval by the author.

Synnøve Hørsdal at the production company Maipo shared the Paradox producer's interest in cultivating talent, but she was less engaged in attracting aspiring artists in order to test their artistic potential. Instead, to minimize risk, the producer chose to work with affiliated and trusted screenwriters and directors. As a company, Maipo is renowned for its success with a large number of adaptations, such as the popular *Elling* series. As Maipo's lead producer, Hørsdal seemed to bet on safe horses, as she tended to select either popular children's books or novels from authors with an established resonance with a general audience. As was the case with the Paradox producer, she engaged only in immensely popular children's stories, with animated characters, in order to take commercial advantage of an already familiar brand:

> We have acquired the rights to several well-known children's books. They are regarded as established brands that the audience is aware of. There is no coincidence that these stories address the family segment. This segment constitutes an extremely difficult audience to reach, unless they are already familiar with the story-world and basic characters. This is how the business works. Yet, we also base our choices on what we want to do, what we like, and what we wish our company to take part in.[12]

This producer's rationale is to increase equity capital before engaging in other, artistically ambitious projects with less appeal. In contrast to the Paradox producer, however, the Maipo producer does not see children's films as a playground for up-and-coming talent or as a chance for directors with a recent career setback to recover. She prefers the sense of control provided by working with old acquaintances, be they directors or screenwriters. In fact, she has been cultivating collaborations with a few, top-selling contemporary authors for several years, in order to select stories from their back catalogue and, at times, and with mixed results, make use of them as screenwriters.

The third of the intermediate companies, 4½, has not yet pitched itself into the market of children's films. The company is the largest in the Norwegian film industry, recognized for internationally acclaimed films at film festivals, as well as for being partners in several critically acclaimed Scandinavian co-productions, such as *Flame and Citron* (Madsen, 2008) and *You, the Living* (Andersson, 2007). As part of its expanding strategy, the company has taken an increased interest in adaptations in the latter part of the 2000s.

4½ is a joint venture in which a team of writer-directors and creative producers are equal partners. Having directors as associates, the company preferred to originate and develop story ideas in-house in its early years of existence. However, as the company grew, they saw adaptations as a method to keep affiliated talent busy, as well the mechanism through which to test exciting graduates from the National Film School. This strategy has so far only been partially successful, in critical and commercial terms, compared to the numerous highly acclaimed films for which 4½ has otherwise been recognized, such as *Reprise* (Trier, 2006), and *King of Devil's Island* (Holst, 2010). Nevertheless, CEO Karin Julsrud reports that she does not intend to avoid adaptations in the future; at the time of the interview, 4½ had no less than four different projects in development. Julsrud – who has her background as a television producer at NRK, as well as a consultant at the National Film Board – claimed that she and her partners would base their project investment decisions on artistic qualities alone, and has optioned several books by critically distinguished authors that resonate with the educated, literary public:

> Things differ from one project to another. As for two of the adaptations we have in development, if we make them, we know that we will have a film that targets

a specific audience: women twenty-five years and older. This means our primary audience will be women aged between thirty and fifty years, the main body of the book club members – and they are many. It is not the sexiest audience for a film, really, but it is a large group of people. So if we can get them to go to the movies, we know quite a bit of what we are dealing with. We would not have touched such a project if we had not known that this author and that book have a large audience.[13]

Of particular interest in this present context is the fact that story ideas were the subject of staff meetings. In line with the nurturing profile of the company, the partners and other creative employees meet every week for brainstorming and discussions. Developing new ideas, including those based on literary sources, was part of the in-house team spirit that characterizes the company.

Of the three nurturing producers, 4½ is the one with the most diversified strategy towards adaptation. Their interest spans from lesser-known youth novels to internationally acclaimed authors, from critically acclaimed literature aimed at a female reading audience, to historical biographies about a glamorous actress with a secret past as a spy, and an author well-seasoned in crime. Perhaps this diversity is the result of their having engaged in these projects more or less by coincidence. Rather than being a necessity for keeping the wheels turning, adaptations were one of several means to develop interesting film projects, involving both new talent and seasoned film-makers.

The accommodating producers

The fourth intermediate company, Friland, stands out from the rest. A partnership of two producers, Asle Vatn and Christian Fredrik 'Kifrik' Martin, runs the company. Vatn was formerly a commissioning editor for the National Film Fund, Martin the first producer to graduate from the National Film School. The two set up the company in 2002, and throughout the following decade the company had a remarkable output. Today Friland is recognized as one of the most successful in the business. The attitude of the company can be regarded as offbeat and somewhat reckless, as they produce everything from high concept thrillers and gross-out high school comedies, to art-house movies and risky projects. The working principles of the company, however, reveal a quite distinctly *accommodating* profile, as evident in the company's adaptations.

The two producers of Friland have no formalized contact with publishers, despite repeated attempts to initiate business relationships with editors and sales agents in the book trade. Even if the two producers claim that from the company's inception they already had a plan to incorporate interesting novels into their portfolio as a clear strategy, they feel that they have not succeeded until recently because of the lack of literary objects that suited their taste. At the time of the interview, the company had recently released their first two adaptations, both of which had been brought to their attention by coincidence. Having released a film based on the Nicolaj Frobenius' novel *Theory and Practice* (2004) the week before the interview, the producers repeatedly used the phrase 'theory and practice' to describe their approach to adaptations:

> We have discussed and theorized how we should approach the literary field, and how to make contact with publishers. Our orientation in the literary landscape consists of reading some reviews, by monitoring the sales charts, and, of course, by drawing on our own tastes. Those are the three criteria we run Friland by, with respect to adaptations. Good sales numbers, good reviews, and a match with our own taste; that is the ideal combination. However, each project has a unique prehistory that has less to do with the actual novel, than with actual people and business opportunities. What the theory is missing, then, is that we need directors and screenwriters who are willing to do adaptations. Someone has to be interested in doing the projects.[14]

The producers' accommodative attitude to film-making implies that for their collaborations they intentionally seek out strong talent. The company's track record suggests that they prefer either well-established names or acquaintances that they believe are about to make a breakthrough in the industry, or in popular culture. As accommodating producers, they regard themselves more as background figures than initiators, whose main task is to facilitate favourable conditions for artistic talent to flourish. As such, they are comfortable with leaving the creative decisions in the hands of others. Their accommodative manner is clearly tied to the company's strategy about its position in the industry. As an up-and-coming enterprise, they wanted to be associated with newsworthy names and projects.

The wish to be associated with talented artists and craftspeople might explain the wide variety of their films. Frobenius, the author of *Theory and Practice*, is not only a distinguished novelist but also a prominent screenwriter, best known for his screenwriting credit on *Insomnia*. He approached the producers with the idea of making an adaptation of his novel, which he had already started to develop together with a celebrated director. The combination of screenwriter and director, along with the possibility of bringing the punk scene to the screen (an important theme of the novel), was impossible to resist. The interview left the impression that the screenwriter and the director were given more or less a *carte blanche* to take the movie in any desired direction. Parts of the story depart considerably from the novel. The film, entitled *Sons of Norway* (Lien, 2011), has an art-house feel to it, and reached a medium-sized audience (approximately 80,000), with which the producers seemed fairly content.

The other adaptation, *Headhunters* (Tyldum, 2011), based on a novel by the internationally famed crime writer Jo Nesbø, worked out quite differently. For years, the producer had been on the lookout for material for an international thriller, but took little interest in the output of crime novels that were primarily police procedurals. Jo Nesbø's success meant that he had been on the radar of nearly every producer, but he had so far been uninterested in making film versions of his novels. With *Headhunters*, it was different, and Friland, almost by chance, inherited the project from the Swedish-Danish company Yellow Bird, which did not manage to raise the necessary finances.[15] The producers then invited a screenwriter who was highly experienced in a variety of genres to transform the novel into an action feature. He was teamed with a talented director the producers believed would be able to deliver the darkly humorous side of the story, as well as carry a blockbuster feature of those proportions.

As is clear, Friland is focused on attracting talent that will help build its reputation in the industry. The idea is that gifted employees will supply the company with original material to exploit. This does not mean that Friland's producers leave every creative decision in the hands of others. Like all producers, Vatn and Martin intervene in the development of projects. However, they make it clear that they regard film as the director's medium, in the sense that the director must have a sense of ownership in the film and be able to let his or her personal vision shape the project. Otherwise, as they see it, the film would suffer from the director's lack of artistic energy.

The producer profile grid: Mapping a typology of the film producer

Based on the interviews and analysis of these six Norwegian production companies and their producers, we have so far identified various positions with respect to the strategies involved when film adaptations are produced. Even though all of the interviewees considered adaptations to be a particular mode of production, several of them claimed that the basic principles were not completely different from initiating and developing new projects based on an original idea.

This inquiry into the producers' approach to adaptations has revealed a multitude of practices that, even if some might be perceived as having insignificant differences, are carefully carried out as part of the companies' specific routines and working procedures. Moreover, these practices are part of their attempt to attract and maintain creative talent, on which the companies are dependent in order to build their reputations, as well as to entice investors and obtain public funding. This work of positioning is essential to stay in business.

Our study relates to that of Pierre Bourdieu's discussion of the field of cultural production, in the sense that the focus is on the production of cultural artifacts and the logic that governs this production, rather than the internal qualities of the artifact itself.[16] However, whereas a Bourdieusian study such as Simone Murray's analyses the various ways film adaptations become distinguished from other films, our study reveals that the film producers cite different reasons when they turn to adaptions. As well, unlike Bourdieu, our model is not concerned about hierarchical positions and the struggle for dominance. Although our model accords with Bourdieu's theory in that their practice as producers define their position within the market place – as most potently demonstrated by the difference between the blockbuster producer and the art cinema producer – this seems to have less to do with competing for legitimacy, which would be the traditionally Bourdieusian understanding. The successful and long-running production companies have each managed to occupy a niche within the film sector, where their particular assets come to the fore. This allows them to operate *alongside* their competitors, where, to a certain extent, the market is shared between the different companies.[17]

The six companies that we have examined are all top players that continue to dominate the contemporary Norwegian film industry. We find it useful to analyse the relations between production companies (and hence between producers) by placing them along two axes: one horizontal and one vertical. The model shows how the production companies differ from each other, while still competing in the same market, with respect to attracting talent, projects, funding and audience attendance. We have named the resulting model the 'producer profile grid' (Figure 3.2).

The horizontal axis of the model describes the company's perceived profile and standing in the industry. The position on the axis is determined most of all by the company's filmography. In addition, extra-textual material surrounding the company (promotion, web presentations, trade press interviews, etc.) and documents, such as public funds applications and balance sheets, might be included as well. The terminal points of the first axis are the purely commercial and the purely artistic (Filmkameratene and Motlys, respectively). As we have seen, however, most film companies operate near the middle of this axis (Maipo, Paradox, 4½, Friland).

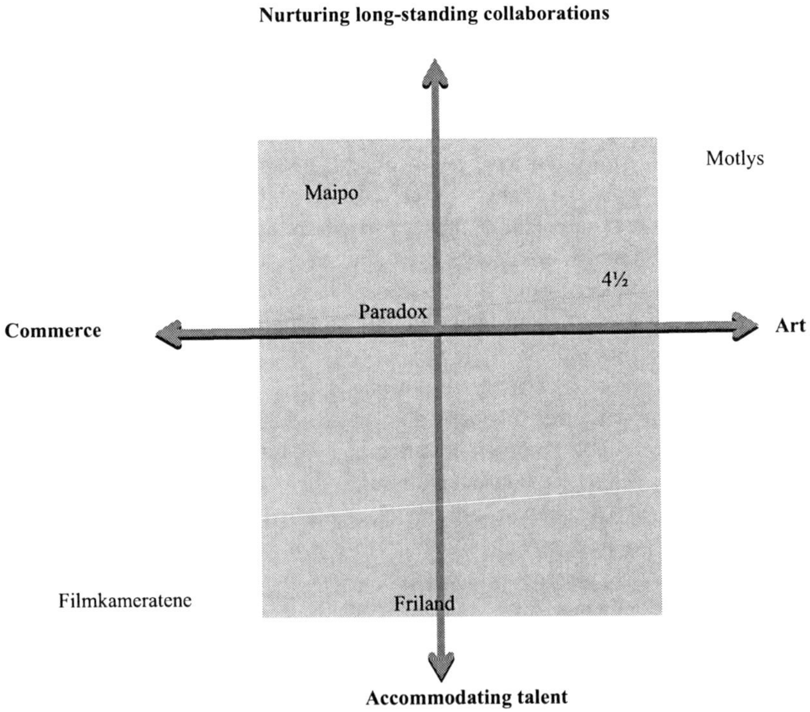

Figure 3.2 The producer profile grid
Note: The grey area in the model indicates the space occupied by the intermediates

The vertical axis relates to the producers' specific working procedures. This designates the degree to which they initiate projects and intercede in further creative decisions. For example, does the producer envision a particular mood, a visual concept, or other features of the planned film? Is she involved in the writing of treatments and scripts, or does she conceive herself mostly as a supportive reader? What attitude does the producer have towards the creative personnel on whom he is dependent, and by extension, how does he understand his role as a film producer? At the one end of the axis, some producers tend to use the benefits of forming and maintaining long-term relationships with creative talent such as screenwriters, directors and authors. At the other end of the axis, producers seek out exciting talent in the hope of fostering outstanding collaborations and a heightened reputation in the industry.

In our study, the nurturing producer at Maipo and the art cinema producer at Motlys seem to concentrate on forming long-standing collaborations with creative talent. While this strategy might reduce risk, it also seems to imply less intervention in the creative process from the producer. The most clear-cut example of bringing in new talent to the production house is the accommodative producers at Friland. Interestingly, this position seems to imply less intervention in the creative process as well, since the desire to be associated with the right talent leads to a slightly more permissive attitude. We can place the three other companies in our study in between these terminal points. Closest in their relation to the exploring producers at Friland are the blockbuster producers at Filmkameratene. However, the blockbuster producer intercedes in creative decisions insofar as he initiates projects and operates with specific guidelines of what he wants out of his high concept films. The nurturing producers at 4½ are slightly closer to Motlys than to Friland. Finally, the nurturing producer at Paradox works to cultivate long-lasting relationships with attractive talent, but gives equal amounts of attention to both established personas in the industry and newcomers with potential for a breakthrough. While it is evident that his creative involvement varies depending on his collaborators, being placed at the point of intersection of the two axes constituting the producer profile grid suggests a producer type with considerable room for manoeuvre and, thus, a more varied filmography compared to the other companies.

It should be stressed that the positions the producers hold in the profile grid are not set once and for all. The model is flexible as the positions can shift, over time, according to the kinds of projects they produce. Any given film can, potentially, dramatically change the producer's future strategies. The benefit of the grid is that it illustrates some of the issues that concern the producers, and that there are a multitude of ways of being a producer. Further, the grid also shows how the producers have occupied a niche within the Norwegian film industry after its restructuring. Occupying such a niche successfully is one of the explanations for why these production companies have managed to become top players in the film industry.

Given the number of adaptations made in Norway over the past decade, looking into how this practice is carried out gives a fairly clear-cut picture as to how the productions will be organized. To study the history of an original film is more ephemeral, since ownership of an idea can be contested. This tendency is not as strong with adaptations, where the steps of the production history can be traced more easily.

Thus, it is beneficial to look at adaptations in order to study the producer. And vice versa, production studies can bring new insights to adaptation studies. James Naremore has famously called for importing sociology into adaptation studies, accounting for, among other things, its commercial apparatus, and thereby moving adaptation studies towards the centre of media studies.[18] Too often, however, the producer's point of view has been left out of adaptation studies, even in Murray's penetrating investigation of the different players and arenas of the adaptation industry. Our study shows that taking the producer's approach is important in order to understand the consistently significant output of film adaptations. This trend is not only Norwegian, but replicated in many European countries as well as in America.

How generally applicable are our conclusions to other European film industries? Certainly, Norway is a small film nation with quite a different industry structure from, say, the British or the German systems. However, even if the European film industries vary considerably in terms of size, reach and film policies, it is possible to identify some general characteristics. For one thing, there has always been the threat of Hollywood dominance in domestic markets. In order to nurture national film production, there is also a long tradition for state support for the film industry in Europe, where the subsidies are geared towards development and production rather than distribution. Nevertheless, there is an increasing dependence on private investment in production, as well as an increasing incidence of pan-European collaborations. It is therefore reasonable to believe that most European film industries share some basic characteristics in terms of structure and power relations. The producer profile grid presented earlier could, we hope, prove useful as a point of departure for inquiries into any European film industry. This will give valuable insight into how the many small- and medium-scaled production companies that populate the European film sector operate strategically in a rapidly changing and economically volatile market.

List of interviews

1. Sveinung Golimo   Filmkameratene   12 September 2011
2. Finn Gjerdrum   Paradox   12 September 2011
3. Asle Vatn & Kifrik Martin Friland   14 September 2011
4. Synnøve Hørsdal   Maipo   24 May 2012
5. Yngve Sæther   Motlys   24 May 2012
6. Karin Julsrud   4½   5 October 2012

Notes

1 Peter Bloore, *The Screenplay Business: Managing Creativity and Script Development in the Film Industry* (London: Routledge, 2013), 11.
2 Ernst & Young Management Consulting (EYMC), *Gjennomgang av støtteordningene til norsk spillefilm* (Kulturdepartementet: Oslo, 1999).

3   According to the annual reports from The Norwegian Film Institute, the amount of private investments in feature films have increased from an average of 33 per cent of the total budget in 2002, to an average of 61.5 per cent of the total budget in 2012.

4   Simone Murray, *The Adaptation Industry: The Cultural Economy of Contemporary Literary Adaptation* (London: Routledge, 2012), 11.

5   Rick Altman, *Film/Genre* (London: BFI Press, 1999), 38ff.

6   Robert Stam, 'Introduction', in *Literature and Film. A Guide to the Theory and Practice of Film Adaptation*, ed. Robert Stam and Alessandra Raengo (Malden, Mass: Blackwell, 2005), 43.

7   Teresa Amabile, *Creativity in Context* (Boulder, CO: Westview Press, 1996).

8   M. Bjørn von Rimscha, 'Handling Financial and Creative Risk in German Film Production', *Wide Screen*, 3 (2011): 6.

9   Sveinung Golimo, interview with authors, 12 September 2011.

10 Yngve Sæther, interview with authors, 24 May 2012.

11 Finn Gjerdrum, interview with authors, 12 September 2011.

12 Synnøve Hørsdal, interview with authors, 24 May 2012.

13 Karin Julsrud, interview with authors, 5 October 2012.

14 Asle Vatn and Kifrik Martin, interview with authors, 14 September 2011.

15 Yellow Bird was established in 2003 and specializes in adapting Scandinavian – mostly Swedish and Danish – crime fiction for film and television, such as Henning Mankell, Stieg Larsson and Liza Marklund. In 2009, they acquired the rights for *Headhunters*, but did not manage to develop the project. Instead, they became co-producers with Friland. This kind of inter-Scandinavian cooperation is quite common, and helps to secure funding from various national funds.

16 Pierre Bourdieu, *The Field of Cultural Production* (Cambridge: Polity Press, 1993).

17 The producers regard themselves as colleagues, rather than competitors, after years of meetings at conventions, markets and festivals. One of the producers even mentioned that they used to joke about joining forces to establish a big company together.

18 James Naremore, 'Introduction: Film and the Reign of Adaptation', in *Film Adaptation*, ed. James Naremore (New Brunswick, NJ: Rutgers University Press, 2000).

4

The Independent Producer and the State: Simon Relph, Government Policy and the British Film Industry, 1980–2005

Andrew Spicer

We are crofters over here. We have the technology and we have the brains but we don't have the money.

Stephen Woolley[1]

What kind of industry should Britain aspire to have? For me, that's always been about an industry which is reinvesting in itself much more than it does ... I wish for an industry which would require that at least part of what is generated here is reinvested in new production. Not new production that is simply offshore production from Hollywood, but indigenous production. This is what we have lacked.

Simon Relph[2]

Introduction

Government policies set the broad framework within which independent producers – those who have no direct financial links with major companies or conglomerates – have to operate and the actions of the state frequently play a crucial role in the fortunes of individual film-makers. Nearly all nation states implement various mechanisms to support and protect their film industries, judging them too economically and culturally important to be left solely to market forces – which would mean, in practice, their domination by American-based transnational corporations.[3] Some mechanisms are non-selective – quotas, levies, tax incentives and co-production agreements – designed, primarily, to try to ensure the film industry's economic viability; others are selective whereby the state, working through councils, commissions and other institutions, identifies particular categories of films that deserve some form of subsidy, usually in the form of production finance. These subsidies, used to encourage independent production, are almost always predicated on cultural or social criteria – such as cultural diversity, traditions and histories – that place a value on film beyond the economic, as exemplified in the provisions of the European Union's Maastricht Treaty (1992).

However, the production and distribution of feature films is an international industry whose global operations lie beyond the control of any individual nation state. Although governments can influence production mechanisms, they are far less able to alter the pattern of international distribution, which, since the 1920s, has been controlled by Hollywood studios pursuing an aggressive and highly co-ordinated system for 'exporting entertainment'.[4] Because most national domestic markets are normally too small to support higher-budgeted productions that can compete in the international marketplace, independent producers need access to these global distribution networks that offer guaranteed distribution as part of a film financing package. Most national governments recognize these economic realities and collude with Uncle Sam by offering various inducements that will encourage American majors to make films in their territories (rather than elsewhere) because these productions generate inward investment, providing the finance capital and employment that has become critical to the sustainability of their film industries, as well as generating ancillary revenues. Indeed, the tax incentives that are officially established to protect indigenous production often work more powerfully in favour of American media corporations.[5] Thus national film policies characteristically seek two contradictory outcomes. On the one hand they attempt to sustain a culturally diverse industry that will contribute meaningfully to the nation's history and its cultural concerns. On the other, they try to provide the conditions for their country to become an attractive location for international productions.

In order to explore these tensions and their impact on independent producers in some detail, this chapter will focus on one particular national cinema, Great Britain. Britain, it has been argued, is positioned distinctively 'between' Europe and America, its film industry, in the words of Labour's first Culture Secretary, Chris Smith, being able to function 'as a bridge, geographically, culturally and economically, between Europe and the United States'.[6] Although this positioning might be seen by politicians as an opportunity to exploit two markets, Lindsay Anderson, writing in 1949, argued that British cinema has oscillated inconsistently between these two 'opposite poles', lacking the Europeans' 'courage to tackle, in an adult manner, the completely adult subject' and also 'the flair for popular showmanship that is characteristic of the American cinema'.[7] John Hill has argued that this liminality has made British film policy uncertain in its direction, neither consistently encouraging a distribution-led, market-driven system on American lines nor following a European model of generous state subsidy that would nurture a culturally valuable art cinema, but usually falling somewhere between these two stools.[8]

For the most part, the gravitational pull of Hollywood has been far stronger than that of Europe. The abiding political and cultural ties between Britain and America (the 'special relationship') and a shared language have made Britain's film industry peculiarly prone to Hollywood domination; in the resonant words of independent producer Leon Clore, 'If the United States spoke Spanish, we would have a film industry'.[9] The films of the Hollywood studios have filled British screens and shaped audience expectations and tastes since the end of the First World War, and the industry has been heavily reliant on American capital, which has penetrated deeply through a network of British subsidiaries.[10] The most important consequence of this dependence has been a fracturing of the British film industry itself – divided between distribution and exhibition sectors that have been consistently profitable through handling American films and were opposed to any form of state regulation, and a much weaker production sector that looked to the state for some form of support.

The other factor that operated against independent indigenous production in the United Kingdom was internal monopolistic practices. The two most powerful and long-lasting British film companies – the Rank Organization and the Associated British Picture Corporation (ABPC) – had fixed links with the American majors and operated a cosy duopoly to control exhibition in the United Kingdom through their ownership of the two main cinema circuits, Odeon and ABC, respectively. Unless a film obtained a release on one of these chains, it could not hope to be profitable. Distribution was controlled by Rank and ABPC operating alongside the American majors. Thus a domestic duopoly and American competition were inextricably linked and rival independent exhibitors or distributors forced to compete for a tiny fraction of the market.[11] Because profits were generated through exhibition and distribution, neither the American companies nor Rank and ABPC had a compelling economic incentive to create or sustain a varied indigenous film production ecology. Thus outside the two main companies, British film production was highly fragmented consisting of myriad small companies, a 'cottage industry' populated by 'crofters', to adopt Stephen Woolley's term. There were repeated calls for the government to intervene to curb the power of the domestic corporations and their restrictive practices; and successive reports – in 1944, 1966, 1983 and 1994 – warned of the deleterious effects of monopolistic practices on the domestic film industry and highlighted the major problems that independents faced. However, here too the British state was reluctant to intervene to curb corporate power.[12]

The acute instability and precariousness of British film production created by this collusion between British and American corporations have, as Duncan Petrie notes, emphasized the importance of producers.[13] John Caughie argues that these conditions have created both a 'desire for independence' and an imperative need for that independence to be carefully protected and safeguarded by being well-organized. Hence the need for what Caughie calls the 'producer-artist', whose importance 'seems to be a specific feature of British cinema, an effect of the need continually to start again in the organisation of independence'.[14] It has been these enterprising, imaginative producers, passionate about film, who have been best placed to exploit the confined spaces that have occasionally opened up in the British film industry. In doing so, they have often looked to the state to provide some measure of support.

In this chapter, I shall be focusing on one 'producer-artist', Simon Relph, whose interactions with the state were varied: independent producer; film commissioner as head of British Screen, a quasi-autonomous non-governmental organization (quango); member of a film consortium funded by National Lottery money; and author of a report on low-budget film-making. Although Relph has been largely overlooked in existing histories despite his importance to the development of the British film industry – illustrative of the neglect of producers – my concern is not to provide a comprehensive assessment of his career.[15] My interest is to examine the ways in which successive changes in government policy from the 1980s onwards have shaped Relph's activities, and how he, in turn, helped to fashion new policies. By concentrating on Relph's work, it becomes possible to understand how state policies influenced the actual nature of film production, whilst simultaneously acknowledging the importance of the producer's role and the active agency of film-makers, nearly always ignored in accounts of film policy.[16] Concentrating on the vicissitudes of a particular career, especially one as multifaceted as Relph's, permits an understanding of how patterns of film-making changed over time, and reveals that film policies themselves are processes, shaped by the varied economic, social and political forces in play at any particular historical moment.[17]

Becoming an independent producer: Skreba and Greenpoint

Simon Relph was born, in April 1940, into a film family. His grandfather, George (1888–1960), was a distinguished stage actor who also made a number of films; his father, Michael (1914–2005), was a successful production designer, writer and producer, who worked at Ealing Studios before becoming an independent in tandem with his long-term business partner, the director Basil Dearden.[18] Simon Relph's apprenticeship in the industry during the 1960s came through a lengthy stint as an assistant director, working frequently for the long-standing producer-director partnership of Betty Box and Ralph Thomas. Box became his first mentor, guiding and promoting his career and encouraging Relph to be involved in pre- and post-production work and thus become familiar with all aspects of the craft of film-making. Relph continued as an assistant director on numerous prestigious productions including two directed by Charles Jarrott, *Anne of the Thousand Days* (1969) and *Mary, Queen of Scots* (1971), Roman Polanski's *The Tragedy of Macbeth* (1971), John Boorman's *Zardoz* (1974) and John Schlesinger's *Yanks* (1979). Relph recalls being most strongly influenced by the work of Schlesinger – and in particular by the practices of his long-term producer Joseph Janni (a second mentor) – whose films, notably *Sunday Bloody Sunday* (1971), represented the kind of intelligent, probing, 'character-driven productions with a political background' that Relph aspired to make.

Relph gravitated towards becoming a producer because he recognized that he lacked the single-minded ruthlessness that characterized top directors. Relph considered that his own talents lay in the 'organisation of the creative process', cultivating the 'highly developed powers of persuasion' he judged to be the most important attribute of a successful producer. He saw the producer's role as 'build[ing] a bridge between the artistic side of film-making and the logistical'.[19] However, in making the transition from assistant director to producer, Relph was determined to remain close to the production process itself, running the film 'from the floor' rather than taking an office-based executive role. Relph's opportunity to make that transition came whilst working on Warren Beatty's *Reds* (1981), a major

Hollywood production that interweaves the chequered love affair between radical feminist Louise Bryant (Diane Keaton) and radical journalist John Reed (Beatty) with the events of the Russian Revolution and the struggles of the American Left; Beatty argued that *Reds* 'reclaimed an era of American history that every school child should see'.[20] Relph was hired as assistant director, but when Charles MacGuire, the assistant producer Beatty had brought with him, returned to America quite early in the production, Relph assumed that role as well, working closely with Beatty on location and at Twickenham Studios. Beatty became a third mentor, remaining a life-long friend (Figure 4.1).

Relph's transition to the role of producer was completed by the formation of Skreba, a partnership (reflected in its name) between Anne Skinner, Relph and Zelda Barron. Skinner, whose idea the company was, had worked in the industry since the 1950s as a production secretary, then continuity script supervisor, working closely with numerous distinguished directors – in particular Boorman, Joseph Losey, Ken Russell and Schlesinger – and had worked with Relph on several films. Barron had followed a similar path and worked with Relph on *Yanks* and *Reds*. She had also co-produced *The Triple Echo* (1972), Michael Apted's first film. Each partner was thus highly experienced and formed Skreba in order to afford themselves greater creative control, both in choice of project and in its execution; Barron was looking for the opportunity to direct.

Figure 4.1 Simon Relph and Warren Beatty on location in Helsinki for *Reds* (1981). Courtesy of Simon Relph

Skreba's first project was an adaptation of Rebecca West's 1918 novel *The Return of the Soldier*, the story of a shell-shocked amnesiac veteran that opens out into a powerful study of class tensions. Although the respect in which the company partners were held enabled them to attract three celebrated actors – Alan Bates, Julie Christie and Glenda Jackson – in the principal roles within a budget of £1.8 million, no British finance could be obtained. Skreba managed to secure finance from an unorthodox source, a wealthy Los Angeles orthodontist, Barry R. Cooper, keen to become involved in the film industry. Despite the prestigious leads, an American name was now needed. Skinner had worked with Ann-Margaret, who was a fine actor and had a natural gift for picking up accents. Both Skinner and Relph felt that she would be able to play against type as the soldier's demure cousin and recommended her to the director Alan Bridges. Skinner and Bridges travelled to LA to meet Ann-Margaret, but finally it fell to Relph, in an agonising long-distance telephone call, to persuade Bridges that she would be successful.

Thus *The Return of the Soldier* went ahead, only for the money to run out two weeks into shooting. It was salvaged by an unlikely source, George Walker, ex-boxer and gangland minder, who had made a fortune in property speculation, enabling him to dabble in film financing, including the two Joan Collins' vehicles, *The Stud* (1978) and *The Bitch* (1979).[21] Relph recalled that Walker, an ardent admirer of Christie, was desperate to go to Cannes with a 'respectable' film that would give him the cultural cachet to secure invitations to the prestige screenings and 'walk the red carpet'. Indeed, Walker had been interested in part-financing the film before Cooper stepped in and was prepared to rescue the production, though he was now able to extract extremely tough terms for his involvement. It was through such contingent and haphazard circumstances – so characteristic of the British 'cottage industry' – that *The Return of the Soldier* was finally released in 1982 after an 18-month production in which the partners had had to defer their salaries. Skinner recalled that they received no encouragement from within the British film industry after its release, resulting in ham-fisted distribution, promotion and exhibition. Compounded by the litigation that delayed its American release, *The Return of the Soldier* was only modestly successful.[22] The production was thus a baptism of fire from which the company's partners learned several lessons, the most important being the necessity to secure guaranteed finance.

Relph characterizes Skreba, born from the industry itself, as a 'technicians' grouping'. At the same time, he formed a second, contrasting company. Greenpoint, a partnership between Relph and Ann Scott, was a 'creative conglomerate ... a coming together of creative people from other fields rather than film business people'.[23] The conglomerate was composed of the writers and directors – Richard Eyre, Stephen Frears, David Hare, John Mackenzie and the oldest and most influential, Christopher Morahan – for whom Scott had acted as in-house producer at the BBC in its *Play for Today* slot.[24] Their connection with Relph came through the four years he spent at the National Theatre (1974–1978), where, under Peter Hall's guidance, Relph was responsible for the whole backstage operation and for the move to the South Bank. It afforded Relph the opportunity to get to know these writers and directors whose productions he admired and with whom he wanted to continue to work. Morahan et al. were anxious to make films where they would enjoy greater freedom, higher production values and more extended shooting schedules, as well as having the opportunity to garner the critical acclaim and cultural status that, at this point, was reserved for films rather than television productions.[25] Films were also much more widely shown; television plays had one, possibly two, screenings. Other writers and directors, including Christopher Hampton and Mike Newell, joined as the company expanded.

Greenpoint had a straightforward rationale: 'to enable the talent within it to do what they wanted to do'. Each member had an absolute right to make whatever film they chose, which the others were pledged to support. Although these usually consisted of work by the conglomerate's writers and directors, Greenpoint, as did Skreba, also cultivated new talent in key roles including cinematography, editing and set design.[26] In contrast to Skreba's first two films – *The Return of the Soldier*, and also *Secret Places* (1984) about a Jewish refugee in a girls school during the Second World War – that were carefully crafted period adaptations, Greenpoint's films, based on original screenplays, were both contemporary and political, as typified by its inaugural production *The Ploughman's Lunch* (1983). This was conceived and executed by its writer Ian McEwan (not part of Greenpoint) and director Richard Eyre as a 'state of the nation' film – portraying the restless anomie and competitiveness of 1980s Britain – in the manner of European art films such as *The German Sisters* or *Man of Iron*, both released in 1981.[27] It was followed by *Singleton's Pluck* (1984) (Figure 4.2), an Ealingesque comedy directed by Eyre, and the much more hard-edged *Wetherby* (1985), a bleak, enigmatic, character-based melodrama, written and directed by David Hare. Vanessa Redgrave was outstanding as a provincial schoolteacher whose life is overturned by the suicide of a disaffected young man she hardly knew. *Wetherby* was also seen as a comment on the nation, on a 'Britain in desperate disrepair ... where passion is dying'.[28]

Figure 4.2 Lindy Hemming, Simon Relph, Richard Hope and Ann Scott during the filming of *Singleton's Pluck* (1984). Courtesy of Simon Relph

Although distinct, both companies' films were, in different degrees, art house, and intended to make an important contribution to European cinema.[29] (*Wetherby* won the Golden Bear at Berlin). This artistic aspiration was underpinned by Relph's pragmatic financial acumen. His guiding principles were to 'squeeze the most juice out of the orange' by ensuring that the director and crew had the maximum possible resources at their disposal within the constraints of the budget, and to determine budgets in relation to the anticipated returns in the marketplace. Neither Skreba's nor Greenpoint's films were aimed at the mainstream American market, but could hope for sales in the United Kingdom, Australia, Canada and in Europe, where television companies were regularly buying films from smaller distributors, which guaranteed an income from all the major European territories and attracted finance from European partners. In the longer term, both companies benefited from the growth of the 'classics' divisions of the Hollywood majors that provided specialized distribution in North America. Thus, despite only modest returns in the domestic market, these outlets allowed Greenpoint to increase the budget for its films – rising from £599,000 for *The Ploughman's Lunch* to £1,125,000 for *Wetherby* (1985) –thereby enabling shooting schedules to be extended modestly, allowing a more creative use of studio sets and camerawork, and the use of 35mm rather than 16mm.[30] However, the profit margins were always relatively modest and neither company had resources beyond those that were raised for each individual film.

Relph had to be imaginative in the ways that these companies operated because there was virtually no support from within the British film industry, except Channel 4, discussed later. Production of indigenous films had dwindled to a meagre 24 in 1981, and cinema admissions had slumped to a mere 54 million in 1984.[31] There was virtually no private finance available and, as noted, the major combines, Rank and Thorn-EMI (which had acquired ABPC in 1969 and was itself taken over by Cannon in 1986), showed no inclination to invest in most British films, or screen them on their cinema circuits, preferring American product.[32] Although 'big budget popular' British films were generally able to secure a circuit release, 'cheaper films with a smaller but still clearly identifiable audience' had much greater 'difficulty in getting sufficient access to the market place'.[33] Relph argued that although Rank and Thorn-EMI had virtually withdrawn from production, the internal financing arrangements that had been a feature of a vertically integrated industry remained, ensuring that independent producers were last in the queue to receive any revenue from their films.[34] He further contended that British producers were being stifled not through lack of creativity, or obscure, dull or parochial subject matter but because of this constricted and inequitable marketplace: 'We've been doing quite interesting and varied work, which is true to ourselves and at the same time consistently appealing, but we're not getting a fair return financially. Although the films actually turn over considerable sums of money, they don't return significantly to the producers.'[35] Relph's observations were borne out in a contemporaneous survey, which revealed that the returns from the UK market did not reflect its size, forcing British producers to raise approximately 70 per cent of production costs from overseas sales.[36] In addition, the survey noted that with the small independent distribution sector contracting, British film-makers often had to relinquish virtually all the rights in their films in order to obtain a distribution deal, thus making it very difficult to show a profit, even if their films were successful commercially.[37]

Thus, Skreba and Greenpoint looked for a measure of state support to help sustain production. *Secret Places* received a subsidy of £500,000 from the National Film Finance Corporation (NFFC) – a state 'film bank' established in April 1949 to provide limited production finance for independent British producers. However, a more important source emerged in the form of a new television company, Channel 4, launched in November 1982. Channel 4 was required, under its public service remit enshrined in the 1981 Broadcasting Act, to act as an alternative to the existing ITV channels. It was therefore expected to 'encourage innovation and experiment in the form and content of its programmes' and to appeal to tastes and interests 'not generally catered for'. In the eyes of its first chief executive, Jeremy Isaacs, Channel 4 was committed to playing an actively interventionist role in the British film industry along the lines of the television industries in France and Germany.[38] Channel 4 deployed a 'publishing model' of production, commissioning outside companies to produce its programmes and films, which Isaacs believed should have a 'socio-cultural provenance and purpose' that went beyond their financial returns or their importance to ratings.[39] This policy was implemented by David Rose, Senior Commissioning Editor for Fiction, who ensured that Channel 4 funded films were socially and politically astringent and often visually experimental, based on original screenplays and produced both by established film-makers and emerging talent.[40]

Channel 4 initially invested £6 million in commissioning 20 films a year, which rose to over £10 million by the end of the decade.[41] Relph recalled that Channel 4 was 'a great white hope for us' because it provided the financial, distribution and exhibition facilities (able to secure a cinema screening as well as being broadcast on the channel itself) for exactly the kind of films he and his fellow 'cultural collaborators' at Greenpoint wished to make, 'It was a big change moment.' Relph therefore cultivated a close relationship with Isaacs and Rose. *The Ploughman's Lunch* received £300,000 (50 per cent) and *Wetherby* £750,000 (67 per cent) of their funding from Channel 4; overseas distribution came through Film Four International.[42]

It was through Rose's influence that Relph took over as the producer of Bill Douglas' *Comrades* (1985), after Ismail Merchant had left the production because he was preoccupied with other projects but also because he and Douglas were incompatible personalities.[43] *Comrades* had been commissioned and part funded by the NFFC as it exemplified the ambitious and experimental films that its managing director, Mamoun Hassan, judged were worthy of support despite being risky at the box-office. *Comrades* was a three-hour Brechtian epic about the Tolpuddle Martyrs – a group of six Dorset farm workers who formed a union in the 1830s in an attempt to win a fair wage for a fair day's work, but were sentenced to transportation to Australia for seven years. *Comrades* was co-funded by Channel 4, which provided £1 million of its £3 million budget.[44] It was the least commercial of Skreba's films, taken up by Relph because of his admiration for Douglas' artistic ambition – 'Bill, in my view, is a cinema genius. He's incredible and exceptional' – and his sympathy for its subject matter: the powerful political dimensions of a story that has become central to British trades union history.

During the final stages of producing *Comrades*, Relph accepted the appointment as the first chief executive of a new organization, British Screen, and thus changed from independent producer to film commissioner, having agreed to give up producing his own films for three years. In many ways this was a logical move for Relph, given his experience in the industry; his criticism of the existing structures of the British film industry; his support for films that were not obvious box-office; and his enthusiasm for the efforts of Isaacs and Rose at Channel 4 to reshape the ways in which films were commissioned, financed and supported. The establishment of British Screen represented a new phase in the relationship between independent producers and the state.

British Screen: Market stimulation, not subsidy

The Conservative administration led by Margaret Thatcher, which came to power in 1979, was determined to end state support for the film industry as part of its policy of media deregulation. It therefore abolished the requirement for exhibitors to show a variable quota of British films that had been established in 1927 as a way of preventing a complete American domination of British Screens.[45] Also scrapped was the film levy, created by the Labour government in 1950 (known as the Eady levy after the civil servant, Wilfrid Eady, who introduced the measure) that required exhibitors to pay a tiny fraction of the price of each cinema admission into the British Film Production Fund administered by the NFFC, which was also terminated. The 1984 white paper, *Film Policy*, argued that both the quota and the levy were 'outmoded in modern conditions' and 'an unwarranted intrusion into business decisions'; therefore 'the paraphernalia of Government intervention and an intrusive regulatory framework dating from the era of silent films' should be cleared away: 'the Government intends to shift its approach to the film industry away from the statutory intervention of the last 30 years and toward the creation of the right business environment'.[46]

This was a highly significant change in British film policy, not only ending long-term measures for state support but reversing the policy of the Labour governments in the 1970s under Harold Wilson's premiership, which advocated that film should be understood as having cultural as well as economic value. A 1976 working party, chaired by Sir John Terry, the Managing Director of the NFFC, had argued that film was important to British cultural and social life, and proposed that the government should invest more money in the British film industry, strengthen the NFFC and establish a British Film Authority.[47] The Conservatives' stance was a reversion to an earlier period, when attitudes towards the film industry had been shaped by the Board of Trade that had a negative attitude to any claims about the cultural value of film.[48]

However, as John Hill argues, the Tories were not prepared simply to abandon film to the dictates of the marketplace, recognizing that this would mean an uninterrupted flow of American films on British screens.[49] Thus although the NFFC was abolished in 1984, it was replaced by a quango, the British Screen Finance Corporation, inaugurated in March 1985, swiftly rechristened British Screen Finance Limited. Its function had been outlined in the 1984 white paper: 'the new company will preserve the positive functions of the NFFC, whilst at the same time being enhanced by the dynamic of private enterprise'.[50] British Screen was funded by a government grant of £1.5 million for four years, supplemented by donations of £300,000 from Thorn-EMI and £250,000 from Rank – the major beneficiaries of the abolition of the Eady levy as they enjoyed increased revenue from their cinema circuits. An additional £300,000 was provided by Channel 4, £250,000 from the British Videogram Association and a further £600,000 was accrued from the value of residual rights in NFFC films.

Although his politics were different, Relph endorsed the concept of British Screen as a public-private partnership whose role was to invigorate the market for films, encouraging others, including foreign companies, to invest in the British film industry. Relph commented, 'what the State can and should do is stimulate the business', declaring emphatically that British Screen was 'not a subsidising body and all investment decisions are taken with a view to the best possible commercial return'.[51] British Screen's initial (1986) report stated, 'Despite the fact that we have some Government support, the company is run on wholly commercial lines. Our first concern in making an investment is to recoup the investment as quickly as possible and reinvest it in new production. We are equally concerned that all these investments should eventually prove profitable.'[52]

In order to achieve this, Relph argued that the films funded by British Screen would need to demonstrate a 'considered relationship' between their costs and the anticipated returns. This financial prudence was one that, as noted, Relph had exercised in his own productions; indeed he saw an essential continuity between his new role at British Screen and his previous activities as an independent producer, describing the organization as 'fertilizing the patch in which I have been ploughing for the past five years'.[53] British Screen thus supported medium-budget British films (up to £3 million) and its financial investment ranged from £350,000 to £750,000; films budgeted at over £1.5 million had to have a finalized American distribution deal. Relph's overall objective was for British Screen to become financially self-supporting by the time government money was withdrawn at the end of four years. In addition, British Screen administered the National Film Development Fund (NFDF), a tiny direct government grant of £500,000 per annum to support low-budget films made by British producers, with a maximum loan of £24,000 per project. The NFDF was a separate organization with its own CEO, Adrian Hodges, and later Colin Vaines.

An important commercial consideration for Relph was to obtain a good return from overseas markets. In partnership with Zenith (a subsidiary of Central Television) and Palace Pictures, Relph set up The Sales Company 'as both a profit centre ... and a means of obtaining low cost foreign sales for those projects in which British Screen is a principal investor'.[54] Carol Myer, who had been head of sales at Film Four International, ran the company, which reduced costs by negotiating pre-sales and offering distribution guarantees in selected areas, which meant that more of the rights to the film could be retained by the independent producer. Typically, The Sales Company paid the distributor 5–7.5 per cent rather than the customary 15–20 per cent for distribution rights. It thus became a key instrument to improve recoupment from existing investments and to keep 'in touch with direct revenues from distribution in as many territories as possible'.[55] He also lobbied for the industry to cease regarding a theatrical release as the absolute and make far better use of secondary markets, including video sales of back catalogues. He wanted to create a British Screen video label to exploit attractive titles in the NFFC catalogue. In addition, Relph wished to see an expansion of independent cinemas and thus increase the opportunities for British films to reach the public.

However, commercial considerations and industrial *nous* were to be balanced by a commitment to cultural diversity and experimentation. In Relph's view, British Screen was a 'halfway house' between the British Film Institute's continuing Production Fund that had a 'specifically cultural mission' to support experimental and avant-garde film irrespective of its market value, and commercial investments motivated solely by the expectation of profit. Thus British Screen's role was to support films that were 'individual, original and not trying to repeat a pattern'. The demands for profitability were to be tempered by encouraging 'original high quality British film work, especially from younger less established producers and directors'.[56] It was for this reason that British Screen supported the production of short films as a training ground for emerging talent. Relph summed up this tightrope act when he stated that British Screen was 'pledged to invest in projects that should be commercial, but they may well be more risky than others which would find support elsewhere. There's going to be a bit of bravery about British Screen which is protected by the Government's contribution.'[57]

Relph's insistence on the potential economic viability of films that British Screen invested in was in marked contrast to the practices of the NFFC under Hassan's leadership. Relph was wary of initiating projects as Hassan had done, 'either by commissioning scripts or by being the first investor to commit itself unconditionally to a film, regardless of whether anyone else is likely to follow'.[58] This policy meant that at the time it was abolished, the NFFC had committed £5 million to films that had not yet been produced. (*Comrades*, thanks to the support of Channel 4 and Curzon Distribution, was an exception). Relph invested a lower proportion of a film's budget than the NFFC had done, as well as making finance conditional on a sales agreement. He also insisted upon faster returns on British Screen's investments, determined that they should be recouped *pari passu* with other equity investors; British Screen was not to be the last in the queue, providing 'end money' as the NFFC had done.

Unlike Hassan, Relph had the considerable advantage of not being answerable to an external board in order to greenlight projects; Relph commented, 'I don't think committees tend to make the best kinds of decisions'.[59] He was obliged to confer with his chairman (Lord Barnett, a Labour Peer) if British Screen's investment exceeded £500,000. But Barnett had no power to intervene in the initial decision and made his judgement on strictly commercial criteria.[60] British Screen's board could only act retrospectively by removing Relph as chief executive or by imposing new restrictions.

Relph's authority to implement his own judgements meant he could act 'quickly and firmly according to consistent and identifiable criteria', and thus react much more swiftly than the NFFC had done to opportunities that arose in a volatile, fast-changing industry.[61] There was an internal management board, chaired by Relph as Chief Executive, which consisted of the Managing Director, Lyn Goleby (succeeded by Kate Wilson), Jane Headland, Head of Finance, and Annette Caulkin who was in charge of assessing the scripts that were submitted. Thus although Relph had the final say, this team would all consider projects that were submitted and decisions on which ones to fund were reached collectively (Figure 4.3).

Another clear difference from the NFFC as it had evolved under Hassan's direction was the breadth and variety of British Screen's investments. Relph was clear that British Screen was not 'just a vehicle for the making of films which happen to fit my own particular tastes' but was committed to supporting film production 'in an even-handed way ... I've tried to get that balance, nurturing every corner'.[62] In addition to the internal board, Relph sought advice from outside opinion if he felt he might have been unreasonably prejudiced against a project. Relph insisted that British Screen was not 'a studio under my control' but was 'here to support the producer, not to be the producer'.[63] He thus invited young producers, writers and directors to come and talk about ideas and scripts: 'I can only respond to what is out in front of me ... My job is to choose the best possible projects that the film community brings to me, provided there is a balance between cost and potential revenue. It is not to go out and make things

Figure 4.3 Colin Vaines, Simon Relph, Lord Barnett and Lyn Goleby relaxing at the Cannes Film Festival in 1986. Courtesy of Simon Relph

happen.'⁶⁴ However, as with Rose at Channel 4, Relph had approval of the schedule and budget, the key personnel involved and the cast, as well as the production cash-flow and insurance arrangements. In addition, he paid close attention to the first few days' rushes until he was convinced that the production team could be left to get on with the filming. If the producer was inexperienced then British Screen would recommend the guidance of an experienced executive producer. However, Relph insisted that his role was to 'help assist' film-makers 'not to tell [them] what to do'.⁶⁵

In Relph's view, British Screen's role was not simply to decide which films to invest in but also to work 'between' companies. Relph often acted as an informal broker organizing financial packages and becoming involved in encouraging, advising or raising support for producers even when not directly investing in their films and ensuring all the financial sources were pulling in the same direction – as with Initial's *Pascali's Island* (1988). Relph recalled that he 'spent most of my time helping producers to piece together the finance, which is usually in several parts'.⁶⁶ However, he 'derive[ed] considerable creative fulfilment from the executive producer/impresario role' that he occupied, as a film's 'grandfather rather than father'.⁶⁷

The achievements of British Screen

The establishment of British Screen as a new form of state intervention in the film industry was highly contentious. Although the *Financial Times* reported that '[f]ilm-makers have welcomed the choice of Mr Relph, who is one himself' as its CEO, many were highly sceptical about how far British Screen would be able to make any difference to the manifest weaknesses of the British film industry.⁶⁸ One, unnamed, producer was quoted as regarding the whole exercise as a 'gigantic waste of time'; some felt that Relph had been 'handed the tiller with the iceberg already in sight', – appointed merely to preside over the last rites of public support for film in Britain.⁶⁹ Hassan, unsurprisingly, objected to British Screen 'making investment conditional on a sales agreement being reached – since this passes the decision about the creative value of the film to distributors'.⁷⁰ There was some justice in this criticism as Relph admitted that at British Screen he would not have backed *Comrades* had it not come with UK distribution, a foreign sales agent and Channel 4 attached. Relph was also hampered by the lack of support from either Rank or Cannon, which invested only in *The Kitchen Toto* (1987). British Screen's films were not accorded any priority on either's cinema circuits, and neither company renewed its commitment after the initial period of three years had expired. By contrast, Channel 4, which had committed for five years, remained fully supportive and co-produced a large number of films with British Screen.⁷¹ Rose, who had initially thought that both organizations would remain entirely separate, found himself in 'almost a daily dialogue' with Relph.⁷²

Despite this support, Relph was fully aware of the precariousness of his situation and made considerable attempts to attract new investors. In particular, he was looking to the major ITV companies to support British Screen in a way that ran parallel to

Channel 4 but investing in more mainstream films that could attract a broader audience. In 1989, he persuaded Granada's enlightened Chairman, David Plowright, to provide £750,000 over a three-year period. However, the wider scheme was stymied by the opposition of Greg Dyke, Director of Programmes at London Weekend Television who, like his predecessor John Birt, thought that television had no responsibility to support the film industry. Relph also considered that British films earned very low returns from television screenings and, as part of his drive to increase the revenue from NFFC and British Screen films, attempted to persuade television companies to pay more for broadcasting rights, with limited success.[73] Overall, Relph's achievements in attracting new sources of capital funding in British Screen was limited.

In its formative phase, British Screen benefited from the American box-office success of several residual NFFC films, notably the E. M. Forster adaptation *A Room with a View* (1985) – what *Variety* described as a 'boomlet of classy budgeters'.[74] Overall, the commercial performance of British Screen's films was patchy. The crime thriller *Empire State* (1987), for instance, was a major disappointment at the box-office. However, its careful harbouring of resources, the effectiveness of The Sales Company and British Screen's ability to recoup investment money quickly meant that it was able to increase the money that could be invested in making British films year on year. During Relph's five-year tenure, British Screen supported 57 films – over three times as many as the 17 films supported by the NFFC in the previous five years – with a total production cost of over £95 million, a 13-fold increase on the government's grant of £7.5 million, returning £28.5 million in taxation; by 1990, British Screen's films had earned £50 million in overseas sales.[75] Without British Screen's support, the vast majority of these films would not have been made. At the time, Isaacs made a public declaration of his enthusiasm, praising Relph for having 'done wonders' with a tiny subsidy and providing a 'climate of opportunity'.[76] In retrospect, David Hancock considered that the company's rate of returns on its investments made British Screen 'probably the most successful public funder of films in the world'.[77]

If British Screen proved to be economically successful, it also contributed to cultural diversity and aesthetic experimentation, funding a wide variety of films that covered a far broader spectrum of taste than Relph's own, though British Screen drew the line in not funding films that were 'pure exploitation where there is no redeeming content' or in 'films designed solely for television transmission'.[78] At one end of the spectrum were the art-house films such as Derek Jarman's *The Last of England* (1988), a more experimental and controversial film than anything the NFFC had funded, but which was, as Relph commented, 'within the limits of its budget [£90,000] perfectly commercial'.[79] There were auteur pieces, including David Hare's mordant political thriller, *Paris by Night* (1988), made by Greenpoint Productions, an offshoot of the parent company in which Relph had no stake, therefore avoiding a conflict of interest. There was a core of politically progressive social realist melodramas notably *A World Apart* (1988), an anti-apartheid film set in Johannesburg in 1963, that was nominated for the *Palme d'Or* at the 1988 Cannes Festival where director Chris Menges received the Grand Jury award. More obviously commercial fare included the horror film *Dream Demon* (1988), several comedies, for instance, the Comic Strip's *Eat the Rich*

(1987), and a number of thrillers, including *Stormy Monday* (1988) and *Scandal* (1989), British Screen's most commercially successful film. Thus British Screen not only funded many more films than the NFFC had in the preceding five years, but its range was broader. It also nurtured the first steps in feature film-making of numerous British film-makers, including Michael Caton-Jones, Mike Figgis, Paul Greengrass and Beeban Kidron. By the end of decade, showing 'more resilience than most believed possible',[80] British Screen had become the main source of production finance for British independent producers aside from Channel 4, and its imprimatur had become an 'essential ingredient' in getting films funded.[81]

However, although British Screen was able to intervene effectively in promoting indigenous production, it was subject to the vicissitudes of the international marketplace over which Relph had no control. The upsurge of interest in British films in America from which British Screen had benefited in its first years waned; American independent distributors became much more selective about which films they supported and the market for small British films has virtually disappeared. In a move to improve British Screen's economic viability, he announced a shift in direction, funding films, such as the sci-fi thriller *Hardware* (1990), which were 'more popular and accessible, capable of being exploited through mainstream distribution rather than arthouses'.[82] Despite Relph's best efforts, British Screen had failed to become self-sufficient and he had to renegotiate an extension of the government grant. Having done this, Relph considered that the time was right for a change of leadership at British Screen and resigned in June 1990, having been in post for five years, two years longer than his original commitment: 'I thought there ought to be another mind making the choices...It was not a good thing for one person to go on occupying such a key role...So I stepped aside.'

Overall, British Screen was only able, in Relph's words, to 'mitigate the effects of the market' not to change its fundamental characteristics. Thus British Screen was a typically lukewarm and tentative state intervention in the British film industry whose scale was something of a joke internationally – *Variety* commented that Relph worked with 'loose change'.[83] In *The View from Downing Street* (1991), a monograph written in response to the vaunted 'Downing Street Summit' chaired by Thatcher in June 1990 that he attended, Relph and his co-author Jane Headland argued that the British film industry continued to suffer from the deleterious divorce of production from distribution and exhibition and of the residual internal pricing structures that starved producers of funds. It advocated a continued role for British Screen together with the need for a disciplined commercial approach to film-making, thus taking advantage of the rise in cinema admissions and the increasing value of the video market, which had, so far, lined the capacious pockets of the American majors. In this way, they suggested, Britain might indeed become the 'Hollywood of Europe', a 'unique bridge' between the two markets and cultures, the slogan, coined by Lew Wasserman the head of Universal, which had animated the Downing Street discussions.

Returning to independent production, Relph's companies, Skreba and Greenpoint, had mixed fortunes in their attempts to exploit both the European and North American markets. Both were able to draw upon some state support from British Screen,

Channel 4, and also the European Co-Production Fund, the most tangible result of the Downing Street Summit. *Damage* (1992), an Anglo-French co-production between Skreba, Nouvelles Éditions de Films and Studio Canal, demonstrated the benefits of the Co-Production Fund. Adapted by David Hare from Josephine Hart's bestselling novel and directed by Louis Malle, it depicts the sexual obsession of a British cabinet minister (Jeremy Irons) for the French girlfriend (Juliette Binoche) of his son, played out against the rootless world of Euro-politics. Relph worked for six months with the director's brother Vincent to put together a complex financial package.[84] In a reversal of orientation, Greenpoint enjoyed a major hit with the *Enchanted April* (1992) – a period adaptation, set in the aftermath of the First World War, which celebrated women's independence and right to happiness – because it had exactly the cultural caché and 'feelgood factor' that appealed to Harvey Weinstein, head of Miramax, which distributed the picture in North America. Relph, in the role of executive producer, was responsible for negotiating the film's finances, with Scott producing and Mike Newell directing. Relph was the producer for Greenpoint's *The Secret Rapture* (1993), directed by Howard Davies from Hare's 1988 play, which portrays the desperate attempts of two estranged sisters (Penelope Wilton and Juliet Stevenson) to cope with the unpredictable actions of their young, alcoholic and unstable stepmother (Joanne Whalley-Kilmer) after their father's death (Figure 4.4).

Relph pursued his encouragement of young talent by supporting low-budget indigenous production through the British Film Partnership Plan, a scheme devised

Figure 4.4 Juliet Stevenson, Simon Relph and Joanne Whalley-Kilmer on the set of *The Secret Rapture* (1993). Courtesy of Simon Relph

by a working party of ten independent producers chaired by Relph. In an effort to cut costs and accelerate recoupment, the scheme required cast, crew and facility suppliers to reduce their fees and agree to a less intensive shoot over a longer period of time that eliminated overtime in return for a half share in the revenues. The other half went to British Screen and Channel 4, which each contributed half of an agreed £1 million funding at 30 per cent below the market rate. Because significant savings were made on the production costs, the investment could be recovered more rapidly. Relph commented, 'the scheme will protect indigenous films ... The idea is to reinstate good, small films which in the past did not justify their cost.'[85] Two by writer-director Nick Ward, *Dakota Road* (1992) and *Look Me in the Eye* (1994), were made in this way. The first was a complex melodrama about repressed emotions and the taboo of incest, set in a tiny farming community in Norfolk near an American air base. The second, made by Skreba and produced by Relph, was an innovative erotic melodrama about a suburban schoolteacher's sexual fantasies and her encounter with a duplicitous photographer. Both *Blue Juice* (1995) – Britain's first (and only?) surfing movie set in Cornwall starring Ewan McGregor and Catherine Zeta-Jones – was another low-budget Skreba film, providing an opportunity for director Carl Prechezer and writer Peter Salmi to make their first film under Relph's experienced tutelage. However, in 1995, the funding landscape for British films was about to change significantly through the distribution of money from the National Lottery – its introduction another watershed that decisively altered the relationship between the independent producer and the state.

National Lottery money and the film franchises

A National Lottery was introduced by Thatcher's successor, John Major, in 1994. Relph was a member of the industry body, the Producers Alliance for Cinema and Television (PACT), founded in 1991, which lobbied vigorously and successfully to win Lottery funding for film. Persuaded that the industry deserved a form of indirect state assistance, over a five-year period, 1995–2000, the government, through the four UK Arts Councils, poured £135 million of Lottery money into the UK film industry, part-funding through loans over 400 films and videos.[86] These sums dwarfed those made previously available from public sources, though the allocation for any individual film was not huge. In addition, channelling money through the Arts Councils represented a significant cultural shift: for the first time film was treated as having the same status as 'fine art' activities such as opera and ballet.[87]

Even so, the Arts Council of England (ACE) had to walk the customary tightrope between art and commerce – funding a broad array of films, from high-end commercial features to avant-garde shorts, all of which were designed to 'enhance the quality, range and number of British films', but also, as equity investments, to recoup their costs, if not show a profit. In words that echoed Relph at British Screen, Peter Gunner, Chairman of the Lottery Panel, argued that Lottery money would stimulate the industry, 'lever in additional money, attract new investors and encourage investment in high-quality projects previously considered too risky'.[88] Applicants for any award had to demonstrate the financial viability of their organization and access to other sources of funding and make a case for the 'public benefit' that would result from their film. Skreba's *The Slab Boys* (1997) – a quirky, off-beat melodrama set in Paisley, West Scotland, in the 1950s about three working-class lads looking forward to the staff dance at the carpet factory where they work, adapted from John Byrne's successful play – was part-Lottery funded: by the English and Scottish councils together with Channel 4 Films, Granada and the European Script Fund. Greenpoint's Anglo-French co-production *The Land Girls* (1998), produced by Relph and directed by David Leland, was adapted from Angela Huth's best-selling novel about three young women sent to work on a farm during the Second World War. It received £1.5 million of its £6 million budget from the Greenlight Fund, which made up to £5 million of Lottery money available to producers of higher-budgeted films and was administered by British Screen. *The Land Girls* was critically lambasted: 'bland' and 'wishy-washy', an 'amiable, predictable and eminently forgettable cop-out'.[89] However, *The Land Girls* was very popular with UK cinemagoers, and is screened regularly on Channel 4 attracting large audiences.

Although his expertise had been called upon by ACE to evaluate individual applications, Relph, like many others, considered that allocating funds on a case-by-case basis was unsatisfactory. He therefore supported PACT's contention that the government should act more strategically by creating a number of British studios that would be capable of developing, producing and distributing films. A feasibility study commissioned by ACE recommended granting film franchises to substantial, vertically integrated companies that would be able to develop a portfolio of films.[90] Responding to its findings, Charles Denton, the chair of ACE's film advisory panel, argued that such companies would place producers in a stronger bargaining position in their negotiations with American corporations and would offer a long-term solution to the endemic problems of the British film industry.[91]

Following the victory of the Labour Party in May 1997, the franchise scheme was adopted as the central plank of the new administration's policy towards the film industry. Labour had consistently adopted a more sympathetic attitude towards the film industry than their Conservative counterparts and was eager to offer support. Chris Smith, the new head of the renamed Department of Culture, Media and Sport (DCMS), who, as noted, thought Britain might become a 'Hollywood of Europe', used the Cannes Film Festival, only three weeks after Labour's election success, to announce that the government would grant three film franchises, each running for an initial six years. The three successful applicants were: Pathé Pictures, the UK production wing of the French media giant; DNA, a joint venture between Duncan Kenworthy and Andrew Macdonald; and The Film Consortium (TFC) consisting of Scala Productions (Nik Powell and Stephen Woolley), the successor to Palace Pictures; Parallax Pictures, the company run by Sally Hibbin that had produced Ken Loach's films since the late 1980s; and the two Relph partnerships, Skreba and Greenpoint. TFC received £30 million to make 39 films over its six-year tenure.

The franchise scheme was highly controversial but represented an ambitious attempt to establish a sustainable film industry by enabling the three winners to develop, produce and exploit a continuous slate of feature films. It formed part of New Labour's vision of 'Creative Britain' in which the cultural industries (with film as key component) would become a central economic driver.[92] Although the franchise scheme was designed to stimulate indigenous production, it also saw the economic viability of the British film industry being derived from a popular, commercially competitive cinema that could achieve major success in the international marketplace and compete with American companies. Labour's film policy, delineated in *A Bigger Picture* (1998), argued that preference should be shown to films that had the potential to secure international distribution. The report also emphasized that it was the government's responsibility to attract foreign investment, which meant, of course, a continued dependency on American funding and off-shore productions.[93]

The Film Consortium

The Film Consortium (TFC) was, as Relph recalls, a loose confederation yoked together to win the franchise, though Relph enjoyed good relations with the other companies. TFC's assets were a quarter share in The Sales Company, whose role was to place TFC titles with distributors on a film-by-film basis for sales of international rights, according to where the film fitted most comfortably; an exhibition outlet, Virgin Cinemas; and a 'revolving credit facility' with the Paris-based finance house Cofiloisirs to part-fund individual films.[94] As the partners had to sit in judgement on each other's films, TFC was run by a board of executives appointed from outside any of the component companies: Kate Wilson, formerly of British Screen, was CEO in charge of finances and making deals, with Colin Vaines – who, as noted, had previously run the National Film Development Fund working under Relph at British Screen – as head of production, receiving and assessing scripts. Vaines emphasized that the 'companies involved in the consortium will operate at arm's length'; although they could express their views, the board would take the final decision. Conscious of the frustration and resentment felt by independent producers who were not part of any of the franchises, Vaines emphasized that TFC was a porous organization: 'the whole point is to keep it open and have a lot of good possibilities available'; therefore, it could be used by producers outside the named 'in house' companies.[95] The role of Wilson and Vaines was not so much to support the individual component companies but to find the best product and thereby build a strong organization with a revolving fund that could be reinvested in further films.

Thus, the ability of Relph and his partners in Greenpoint and Skreba to determine TFC's overall policy was limited. Although the high expectations and aspirations were genuine, Relph acknowledges that TFC tended to get the second best of each company's products: the ones for which other sources of finance could not be found. He recalled that although the idea was that the franchises would attract other funding, 'investors actually saw this Lottery money as a freebie and not an inducement that you were a company with which to invest'. Thus being part of TFC did nothing to assist any of the individual companies in their efforts to leverage other monies, which went against the intentions of the scheme. In its first year of operations, TFC only completed one film, *Hideous Kinky* (1998), an intelligent adaptation of Esther Freud's episodic, semi-autobiographical novel about her 'alternative' childhood in Morocco with her sister and mother, directed by Gilles MacKinnon and starring Kate Winslet as the hippie mother. It was a project already in advanced stages of development by Greenpoint. Ann Scott had optioned the novel in 1993 and had originally approached the BBC for funding. The BBC remained as part of a complex production that included French partners (L Films and AMLF), thus drawing money from the European Script Fund, and £1.07 million of Lottery funding via TFC, representing a third of its overall budget of £3.2 million. Scott co-produced with her French counterparts (Annabel Karouby and Marina Gefter), with Relph acting as executive producer. Wilson described *Hideous Kinky* as 'exactly the kind of film we want to be involved with', arguing that it was 'essentially British – a British director with a growing international reputation and an actress who is recognized worldwide as one of the United Kingdom's genuine film stars', a British story with 'universal appeal'.[96] However, although modestly successful, the film did not recoup its costs.[97] Several TFC films were far less successful and TFC's poor commercial performance led to the departure of Wilson and Vaines in May 1999. Chris Auty, who had run Jeremy Thomas' Recorded Picture Company throughout the 1990s, was brought in as CEO, with Julie Baines as head of production.

The changes in management were part of TFC's chronic instability. Although Carlton (the company that had bought out Rank's film interests) had agreed to handle TFC's UK distribution with BMG Video managing publicity and advertizing, both companies went their separate ways shortly after the franchise was granted. In January 2000, Virgin sold its cinemas to the French group UGC. In an attempt to stabilize the consortium, Auty brokered a deal with WhiteCliff Film and Television, run by Richard Thompson, heir to the Hillsdown food empire. There was intense criticism that a company which had made its major profits in the meat-packing industry should now be in control of one of the film franchises. However, Auty argued that with TFC's constituent partners pushing forward their own projects, the new arrangement gave him 'the opportunity to pursue strategic growth within a private-public partnership in exactly the fashion envisaged by the original Lottery franchise policy'.[98] In April 2000 came the announcement that WhiteCliff had bought out the major portion of Scala, Parallax, Greenpoint and Skreba's shares, thereby ending Relph's involvement in this ill-fated enterprise.

As Robert Murphy argues, Auty's longer term objective was to convert TFC into a production finance company, moving away from developing its own projects to investing in films it could sell to distributors round the world. This was the exact opposite of what the franchises were supposed to do, which was to create stability by retaining assets in films and thereby retaining their worldwide returns.[99] By the end of its six years, TFC had made 16 films, just over half of the promised total, and recouped $54 million less than the figure in its original business plans.[100] Relph, who thought TFC could build a lasting business from its Lottery-funded base, was deeply disappointed by the outcome: 'what I dreamed would work, didn't come off'. Seen in a broader context, the whole franchise scheme fell disastrously between two stools. Although the sums available seemed huge in comparison to previous state funding of films, they were, in reality, far too small to create and sustain companies that could compete successfully in the international marketplace.[101]

Supporting indigenous production:
The Relph Report and trying to establish a studio

After the failure of TFC, Relph continued to play a role in the British film industry, but as an advisor and elder statesman – he was a governor of the BFI and the National Film School – rather than as an active producer.[102] He was commissioned by the UK Film Council (UKFC) – another quango, created by the Labour administration in 2000 as the single body that would oversee all the activities of the British film industry – to make a report on how low-budget film production might be strengthened by becoming more competitive, and to make recommendations for a code of practice, including production guidelines. The 2002 Relph Report was based on a survey of the financing, production costs and practices of 26 British films made over the previous five years compared with five films made outside the United Kingdom. It argued that the increased costs of making 'lower-budget' (£2–4 million) British films created by the inflated salaries and expectations that had arisen as the result of Lottery funding often exceeded their earning potential in the domestic and international marketplace. The high cost of production 'has forced producers to dispose of all value in their films simply to get them made'. [103]

Espousing the methods implemented by the earlier British Film Partnership, the Report proposed a series of practical measures that would bring down the costs of low-budget films to a sustainable level. This would create greater opportunities for film-makers (and more work for crews and suppliers) thereby enabling producers to build lasting businesses that would sustain the industry. The key to achieving this objective was to balance costs against anticipated revenue and to keep salaries down in order to ensure that all participants – producer, director, main cast and crew – were partners in the production thus having access to a 'revenue corridor' as the film was sold in various markets. Adopting an argument that was consistent with everything Relph stood for, the Report urged the UKFC to 'protect a sector which is vital for the development of home grown talent, providing opportunities for culturally marginal as well as mainstream subjects'.[104] Consistent with Relph's principles at British Screen, the Report advocated that low-budget films should be 'more experimental, more risky' than their higher-budgeted counterparts.[105]

Although the Report was recognized as valuable, there was considerable opposition from the film unions anxious about the potential risk to jobs that the Report's proposals seemed to imply and thus very wary about its recommendations.[106] Concerned to avoid controversy, the UKFC did not ensure that the provisos of the

Report were adopted, which disappointed Relph who also wanted to modify and update its findings as digital production became more widely used. However, Relph was pleased that it has proved helpful to numerous producers: 'which I suppose is the most important thing'. Seen in context, the Report was swimming against the tide. Although the UKFC offered limited support to less profitable forms of film-making and opportunities for emerging talent, including the New Cinema Fund and the Low Budget Film Scheme (discussed later) designed to support low-budget production, the major thrust of its policies was to improve the British film industry's commercial viability. Under the direction of its chairman, Alan Parker – a well-known advocate of high-budget international films involving partnerships with American companies and a scathing critic of parochial British film-making – the UKFC gave larger amounts of funding to high-end productions and to encouraging inward investment. An assessment of the UKFC's activities lies beyond the scope of this chapter, but it has been widely criticized for adopting policies that were too supportive of trade interests, thus failing to curb the power of the American multinationals that continue to dominate the British film industry and consequently offering limited support for indigenous independent producers.[107]

Relph's commitment to low-budget indigenous film-making was also evident in his struggle to create a small studio that would nurture burgeoning film-making talent, a conception shaped by his father's experiences at Ealing Studios. Relph's idea was to create a collective that would harness the 'energy and passion' of a group of film-makers united in their commitment to making interesting and challenging films but who wanted the security of being able to make a living in the industry. The collective's members would be paid a salary and have complete creative freedom within a budgetary ceiling of £1 million. By producing a slate of films each year, both full-length features and short films, the studio could hope to balance its overall costs with any revenues reinvested for future productions. Relph, as the new Michael Balcon, was to oversee production and nurture the efforts of the collective's directors, writers and producers. The prime objectives of the studio were therefore to provide a bridge between film training and the industry as a whole and to create a sustainable production base.[108] Relph secured financial support from British Screen, the BFI and ACE in 1997 for a feasibility study to create a small studio at Freshford Mill, near Bath in South West England. However, the scheme faltered because Relph was unable to raise the private equity capital, estimated as £10 million, which he felt would be necessary to establish the collective.

In 2005 Relph revived the studio idea and entered into a partnership with Michael Kuhn's Qwerty Films. Together they approached the UKFC with the project, whose response was that it could not finance a scheme such as this without inviting tenders from the industry as a whole for such a low budget film initiative. Eighteen companies submitted schemes and finally two were awarded £3 million support – Warp X, together with Relph and Kuhn. The latter's partners were the UKFC itself, FilmFour, Screen Yorkshire (one of nine film agencies created by the UKFC to help stimulate and support regional film making) and Vertigo Films, which was to provide UK distribution.[109] However, no sooner had this award been made than it became apparent that there was an increasing mismatch between the partners' objectives and Relph reluctantly withdrew from the scheme. Eventually it faltered when Screen Yorkshire withdrew their support for reasons that were never entirely clear, though they gave out that Vertigo and Qwerty were determined that the studio would be run from London rather than Leeds, thus negating any direct benefit to the region.[110]

Conclusion

The focus on Relph's career as both independent film producer and film commissioner has afforded numerous insights into not only the fluctuations of the British film industry and of the state's shifting policy towards it, but also several fundamental continuities. Reviewing the industry in 1952, Political and Economic Planning noted that the fundamental issue for government was whether the state should co-operate with the industry or 'refashion' it.[111] The closest the British government ever came to refashioning the film industry occurred when Harold Wilson, then President of the Board of Trade, toyed with the idea of 'busting up the circuits', in a post-war Labour administration that had nationalized several key industries and created the health service. In the end Wilson left the industry largely untouched, palliating the effects of a marketplace dominated by a duopoly and by American international corporations by setting up a limited form of state intervention through a levy on cinema admissions that paid for the NFFC. Wilson's actions typify a British film policy that has been far less interventionist than on Continental Europe.[112] When even these limited concessions were abandoned by the Conservative administration in 1985, Relph was chosen as the person who could forge a different form of private-public partnership. Although successful, Relph had neither the resources nor the mechanism to change the basic structures of the industry that continued to be dominated by American interests.

Lottery money and the film franchises, in Relph's case The Film Consortium, offered the promise of creating entities that might enable British cinema to compete more successfully against American competitors. But in the event, their dismal failure demonstrated the difficulties that nation states have in intervening at this level. The most recent survey, at time of writing, details how American-owned companies continue to take the lion's share, 84.2 per cent, of the profits.[113] In a highly fragmented industry, independent producers continue to struggle, competing for a small share of the market and fighting to secure exhibition for their films, the majority of which are low or even micro-budget, with an average production spend of £200,000, as opposed to the American-financed films that averaged £9.7 million.[114] The considerable amount of public funding now available has not remedied these enduring structural imbalances. Stephen Woolley's comment, made in 1988, seems as resonant as ever: British producers remain 'crofters', part of what seems to be a perpetually unstable independent sector scrabbling for a tiny share of the cake. The problem faced by the British film industry – common, in different degrees to all national cinemas – is in trying to balance two opposing forces: nurturing strong and diverse indigenous film-making practices that can contribute to a healthy culture whilst at the same time attracting American capital and 'runaway' productions that will sustain what is an economically highly attractive service industry but one whose major profits go to multinational conglomerates, rather than into indigenous production, as Relph lamented in the second epigraph.

However, this chapter's focus on Relph has not been an inconsequential story of futility and disappointment. The 20 films for which Relph was responsible as either producer or executive producer, together with many of the films he nurtured through British Screen, represent a considerable achievement. And to this we must add the number of writers and directors who owed their first chance of working on a feature film to Relph. As a producer-artist, Relph's logistical knowledge was allied to cultural aspirations and by shrewdly blending a commercial strategy – aligning budgets to what the market would support – with artistic ambition, Relph produced films that were intelligent and challenging, as well as engaging for audiences: *Reds, The Return of the Soldier, The Ploughman's Lunch, Wetherby, Comrades, Damage* and *Look Me in the Eye.* He was also the 'grandfather' to the 57 films produced during his tenure at British Screen, including *Scandal, Stormy Monday* and *A World Apart.* If these films reflect the creative talent of their writers and directors, it was Relph's passionate commitment, understanding of their artistry, and organizational flair that ensured they actually reached the screen. They exemplify what Christopher Williams has aptly characterized as a 'social art cinema', distinctively British in its determination to say something meaningful about indigenous social issues, but also European in its aesthetic orientation, part of a broader challenge to the hegemony of the Hollywood genre movie built around fast-paced action and stereotyped characterization.[115] Analysing Relph's career is therefore instructive as it takes us to the heart, not only of the dilemmas faced by the independent film-maker, and of the vexed and complex relationship that exists between the film producer and the state, but also of the imaginative and varied ways in which the producer-artist can, despite the difficulties, make a difference and create rewarding films.

Acknowledgements

I should like to thank Professor Vincent Porter for his detailed comments on an earlier version of this piece that helped improve its focus. I also wish to thank Simon Relph for his kindness in agreeing to be interviewed, for his help in locating material on British Screen and for the loan of illustrative stills.

Notes

1   Quoted in Duncan J. Petrie, *Creativity and Constraint in the British Film Industry* (Basingstoke: Macmillan, 1991), 50.
2   Simon Relph, extended interview with the author, Bradford-on-Avon, 19 April 2013. Subsequent unattributed quotations by Relph are from this source.

3 See Albert Moran, 'Terms for a Reader: Film, Hollywood, National Cinema and Film Policy', in *Film Policy: International, National and Regional Perspectives*, ed. Moran (London: Routledge, 1996), 1–19; see also Geoffrey Nowell-Smith, 'Introduction', in *Hollywood and Europe: Economics, Culture and National Identity 1945–95*, ed. Nowell-Smith and Steven Ricci (London: BFI Publishing, 1998), 1–16.

4 Anne Jäckel, *European Film Industries* (London: BFI Publishing, 2003), 12. See Kristin Thompson, *Exporting Entertainment: America in the World Film Market 1907–1934* (London: BFI Publishing, 1985).

5 See Mette Hjort and Duncan J. Petrie, 'Introduction', in *The Cinema of Small Nations*, ed. Hjort and Petrie (Edinburgh: Edinburgh University Press), 1–22.

6 Chris Smith, *Creative Britain* (London: Faber and Faber, 1998), 87.

7 Lindsay Anderson, 'Alfred Hitchcock', *Sequence* 9 (1949): 113–24 at 113.

8 See John Hill, 'British Film Policy', in *Film Policy*, ed. Moran, 101–13, at 111.

9 Quoted in Nick Roddick, 'If the United States Spoke Spanish, we would have a Film Industry . . .', in *British Cinema Now*, ed. Martyn Auty and Roddick (London: BFI Publishing, 1985), 3–18, at 3.

10 For a useful overview see Tom Ryall, *Britain and the American Cinema* (London: Sage, 2001).

11 See Margaret Dickinson, 'The State and the Consolidation of Monopoly', in *British Cinema History*, ed. James Curran and Vincent Porter (London: Weidenfeld and Nicolson, 1983), 74–95.

12 See Sarah Street, *British National Cinema* (Abingdon, Oxon.: Routledge, 2009), 20–22.

13 Petrie, *Creativity and Constraint*, 177–84.

14 John Caughie, 'Broadcasting and Cinema 1: Converging Histories', in *All Our Yesterdays: 90 Years of British Cinema*, ed. Charles Barr (London: BFI Publishing), 189–205, at 200.

15 For further details of Relph's career, a filmography, and an edited version of the extended interview that informs this chapter, see Andrew Spicer, 'Interview with Simon Relph', *Journal of British Cinema and Television* (forthcoming, 2014).

16 See, for instance, Dickinson and Street's seminal *Cinema and State: The Film Industry and the British Government 1927–84* (London: BFI Publishing, 1985).

17 See Maggie Magor and Philip Schlesinger, ' "For This Relief much Thanks": Taxation, Film Policy and the UK Government', *Screen*, 50:3 (2009): 299–317.

18 For an informative overview see Alan Burton and Tim O'Sullivan, *The Cinema of Basil Dearden and Michael Relph* (Edinburgh: Edinburgh University Press, 2009).

19 Phillip Bergson, 'The Europeans', *What's On*, 7 March 1985, 34.

20 Carolyn Porter, 'Reds', *Film Quarterly*, 35:3 (Spring 1982): 43–48, at 44.

21 For a more detailed account of the production, see Leslie Geddes-Brown, 'The Real-life Drama Behind the Film', *Sunday Times*, 16 May 1982, 23.

22 See John Walker, *The Once and Future Film: British Cinema in the Seventies and Eighties* (London: Methuen, 1985), 147–50.

23 Quotation from Greenpoint's production notes included in the BFI microfiche for *Wetherby*.

24 Morahan had been Head of Drama for the BBC (1972–76) and was responsible for the *Play for Today* series.

25 See the recollections of producer Mark Shivas, 'Little Big Screen', in *Cinema: The Beginnings and the Future*, ed. Christopher Williams (London: University of Westminster Press, 1996), 185.

26 Bergson, 'The Europeans'.
27 See Sheila Johnson, 'Charioteers and Ploughmen', in *British Cinema Now*, ed. Auty and Roddick, 99–110, at 105.
28 Nigel Andrews, 'Review of *Wetherby*', *Financial Times*, 8 March 1985, 21.
29 In Jill Forbes, 'The Dark Side of the Landscape', [interview with Relph] *Sight and Sound*, 55:1 (Winter 1985/86): 36.
30 'Greenpoint Raises Pic Budgets Despite Limited U.K. Returns', *Variety*, 25 July 1984, 27.
31 Eddie Dyja, *BFI Film and Television Handbook 2004* (London: BFI Publishing, 2003), 32, 39.
32 For a useful overview see John Hill, *British Cinema in the 1980s: Issues and Themes* (Oxford: Clarendon Press, 1999), 39–51.
33 Relph, *A Review of UK Production: For the Prime Minister's Seminar*, 15 June 1990 (London: mimeo, 1990), 5; quoted in Hill, *British Cinema in the 1980s*, 51.
34 Forbes, 'The Dark Side', 36.
35 Quoted in Guy Phelps, 'A Degree of Freedom: Simon Relph at British Screen', *Sight and Sound*, 56:4 (Autumn 1987): 268.
36 Richard Lewis, *Review of the UK Film Industry: Report to BSAC* (London: British Screen Advisory Council, 1990), 52.
37 Lewis, *Review of the UK Film Industry*, 70–71.
38 John Hill, 'British Television and Film: The Making of a Relationship', in *Big Picture, Small Screen: The Relations Between Film and Television*, ed. John Hill and Martin McLoone (Luton: John Libbey/University of Luton Press, 1996), 151–76, at 156, 158.
39 Hill, 'British Television and Film', 164. Channel 4's pattern of production was complex. Sometimes it only purchased the UK television rights; in most cases it co-funded with other film or television organizations; only in exceptional cases did it provide full funding.
40 Nigel Willmott, 'The Senior of the Silver Screen', *Broadcast*, 28 October 1983, 13–14.
41 Hill, 'British Television and Film', 157.
42 John Pym, *Film on Four 1982/1991: A Survey* (London: BFI Publishing, 1992), 177, 202.
43 Sheila Rowbotham, 'A New Moral World', *Guardian Weekend*, 18 July 2009, 16–17.
44 Pym, *Film on Four 1982/1991*, 134.
45 There was also originally a renters (distributors) quota; this was abolished in 1947 as part of the first General Agreement on Tariffs and Trades (GATT) treaty.
46 Anon. *Film Policy*, Cmnd. 9319, July 1984, 5, 13, 18, 12.
47 *The Future of the British Film Industry: Report of the Prime Minister's Working Party*, Cmnd. 6372, January 1976.
48 Dickinson and Street, *Cinema and State*, 50–52.
49 John Hill, 'British Film Policy', in *Film Policy*, ed. Moran, 105.
50 *Film Policy*, 15.
51 Forbes, 'The Dark Side of the Landscape', 49.
52 British Screen Finance Limited, 'Chief Executive's Report', in *Accounts for the Year Ending December 1986*, 2.
53 Phelps, 'A Degree of Freedom', 268.
54 British Screen Finance Limited, 'Chief Executive's Report' (1986), 3.
55 British Screen Finance Limited, 'Chief Executive's Report' (1986), 3.
56 British Screen Finance Limited, 'Chief Executive's Report' (1987), 2.

57   Forbes, 'The Dark Side', 36.
58   Phelps, 'A Degree of Freedom', 268.
59   Forbes, 'The Dark Side', 36.
60   Barnett had been chief secretary to the Treasury and Chair of the Public Accounts
     Committee (1979–83). Relph recalled that he was 'tremendously supportive'.
61   Phelps, 'A Degree of Freedom', 267.
62   Phelps, 'A Degree of Freedom', 270.
63   Phelps, 'A Degree of Freedom', 270.
64   Phelps, 'A Degree of Freedom', 270.
65   Quoted in Petrie, *Creativity and Constraint*, 89.
66   Adam Dawtrey, *Screen Finance*, 26 July 1989, 3.
67   Phelps, 'A Degree of Freedom', 270.
68   Dawtrey, *Screen Finance*, 26 July 1989, 2.
69   Dawtrey, *Screen Finance*, 26 July 1989, 2.
70   Dawtrey, *Screen Finance*, 26 July 1989, 2.
71   See *Screen Finance*, 6 October 1993, 13–14.
72   Nicholas Kent, 'Commissioning Editor', *Sight and Sound*, 56:4 (Autumn 1987): 263.
73   This was a widespread concern in the industry and the issue had been highlighted in
     the Terry Report; see Hill, 'British Television and Film', 154.
74   'Non-U.K. Click For Native Pics Aids British Screen', *Variety*, 14 May 1986, 6, 43.
75   Jane Headland and Simon Relph, *The View from Downing Street* (London: BFI
     Publishing, 1991).
76   Haroly Myers, 'Cannes Sesh Tackles Indie Prod'n Problems In Britain', *Variety*, 18 May
     1982, 2.
77   David Hancock, 'Profile of the Film Industry', in *The UK Cultural Sector: Profile and
     Policy Issues*, ed. Sara Selwood (London: PSI, 2001), 302.
78   British Screen, 'Forty Four Films in Four Years', (1989).
79   Phelps, 'A Degree of Freedom', 271.
80   Alexander Walker, *Icons in the Fire: The Decline and Fall of Almost Everybody in the
     British Film Industry 1984–2000* (London: Orion, 2004), 97.
81   Don Groves, 'British Screen Gets Coin Injections, Sez 10–15 Pix Possible', *Variety*, 16
     November 1988, 5.
82   Don Groves, 'British Screen Finance Changes Direction, Output', *Variety*, 25 April
     1990, 3, 13.
83   Roger Watkins, '"View" Sets British Screen Ltd. On A Multiple-Financing Streak',
     Variety, 12 May 1987, 10.
84   'Production Notes', BFI microfiche for *Damage*.
85   Don Groves, 'British Film Finance Group Fights to Save Small Prod'ns', *Variety*, 25
     April 1990, 5, 26.
86   James Caterer, *The People's Pictures: National Lottery Funding and British Cinema*
     (Newcastle: Cambridge Scholars Publishing, 2011), 1.
87   Caterer, *The People's Pictures*, 2.
88   Quoted in Caterer, *The People's Pictures*, 53.
89   Martin Doyle, 'Review of *The Land Girls*', *Financial Times*, 3 September 1998, 22.
90   Arts Council of England, *Lottery Film Franchising: A Feasibility Study* [The Spectrum
     Report] (London: ACE, 1996).
91   Caterer, *The People's Pictures*, 63.
92   Smith, *Creative Britain*.

93   Department of Culture, Media and Sport, *A Bigger Picture: The Report of the Film Policy Review Group* (London: DCMS, 1998).

94   Stuart Kemp, 'UK Lottery: Sweet Hereafter?', *Screen International*, 23 May 1997, 12.

95   Adam Dawtrey, '3 Players Win U.K. Lottery', *Variety*, 16 May 1997, 1, 52.

96   'Production Notes', BFI microfiche for *Hideous Kinky*.

97   Caterer, *The People's Pictures*, 90.

98   *Screen Finance*, 20 January 2000, 3.

99   Robert Murphy, 'Another False Dawn? The Film Consortium and the Franchise Scheme', *Journal of Popular British Cinema*, 5 (2002): 31–35, at 34.

100   Adam Dawtrey, 'Franchises Get Overtime', *Variety*, 21–27 July 2003, 16.

101   Terry Ilott, 'UK Film, Television and Video Overview', in *BFI Film and Television Handbook 1997*, ed. Eddie Dyja (London: BFI Publishing, 1996), 19.

102   There were occasional projects for which Relph acted as an executive producer, notably two episodes of the prestigious television series *Birdsong* (2012), based on Sebastian Faulks' celebrated novel.

103   Simon Relph (with Jane Headland and Anita Overland), *The Relph Report: A study for the Film Council Examining the Costs of Lower Budget UK Films and their Value in the World Market* (UKFC, March 2002), 8.

104   Relph, *The Relph Report*, 3.

105   Relph, *The Relph Report*, 3.

106   See 'Low budget feature film production – a view from BECTU [Broadcasting, Entertainment, Cinematograph and Theatre Union]', 28 February 2003; accessed 14 June 2013, http://www.imago.org/images/pdfs/727377e386e1128969b1cd5241a b839e.pdf.

107   See Margaret Dickinson and Sylvia Harvey, 'British Film Policy in the United Kingdom: New Labour at the Movies', *Political Quarterly*, 76:3 (July 2005): 420–29; Jack Newsinger, 'British Film Policy in an Age of Austerity', *Journal of British Cinema and Television*, 9:1 (2012): 133–44; and John Hill, ' "This is for the *Batmans* as well as the *Vera Drakes*": Economics, Culture and the UK Government Film Production Policy in the 2000s', *Journal of British Cinema and Television*, 9:3 (2012): 333–56; see also Andrew Higson, *Film England: Culturally English Filmmaking since the 1990s* (London: I.B. Tauris, 2011).

108   Adam Dawtrey, 'Brit Pix to Build a Country Camp', *Variety*, 28 July–3 August, 1997, 9, 14.

109   Adam Dawtrey, 'Polygram Alum Kuhn gears up Qwerty Pix with Fox Deal', *Variety*, 18–24 October 2004, 8.

110   Adam Dawtrey, 'Yorkshire Nixes Kuhn Studio', *Variety*, 6–12 November 2006, 8.

111   Political and Economic Planning, *The British Film Industry* (London: PEP, 1952), 219.

112   Dickinson, 'The State and the Consolidation of Monopoly', 91.

113   BFI, *Statistical Yearbook 2013* (London: BFI Publishing 2013), 17.

114   BFI, *Statistical Yearbook 2013*, 188.

115   Christopher Williams, 'The Social Art Cinema: A Moment in the History of British Film and Television Culture', in *Cinema: The Beginnings and the Future*, ed. Williams, 190–200.

5

Producing the Self: The Film Producer's Labour and Professional Identity in the UK Creative Economy

Paul Long and Simon Spink

Introduction

This chapter explores accounts of the working lives of film producers. Drawing on a series of interviews with individual producers based in the West Midlands region of the United Kingdom, we seek to understand the role of the producer as a form of cultural labour within the framework of national policies for the creative economy.

The context for this study was the establishment of the Department of Culture Media and Sport (DCMS) by the New Labour Government in 1997 – a move that inaugurated what is described in hindsight by some commentators as a 'Golden Age' for cultural policy.[1] Whatever its legacy, a key aspect of the efflorescence of policy in this moment was the recognition of the value of 'creative industries' for economic growth; the branding of UK Plc.; as well as culture's role in urban regeneration and social inclusion.[2]

The economic, social and cultural objectives of DCMS policy were implemented by organizations such as the UK Film Council, established in 2000 to oversee the British film industry. In turn, this body devolved aspects of its work to the non-metropolitan regions in the form of nine screen agencies, each 'charged with encouraging public access to film culture and building vibrant and sustainable media sectors across Great Britain'.[3] As a result of budget cuts by the Conservative/Liberal Democrat coalition, the Film Council was closed down in 2011, along with many of the regional agencies that were unable to survive without the support of public funding. Screen West Midlands (Screen WM) was the body that provided a centre of gravity for participants in this research, while its successor Creative England provided some continuity and a reference point for understanding the role of the producer and the possibilities for screen culture in the United Kingdom.

The experience of the producers studied here speaks of a specific historical milieu of UK policy orientations and support structures that were designed to develop a sustainable film industry and which have been characterized by discourses in which creativity, enterprise and economic value are entwined. Whatever sustainability means, it has pertinence here for the questions we ask about the quality of working lives, of the nature and meaning of work for individuals who have felt that opportunities exist to make films as a means of making a living and to plan, maybe *hope* for, a career as a producer. We thus offer the kind of empirical detail of cultural labour and the contexts in which it takes place that scholars such as Andrew Beck and David Hesmondhalgh have suggested is lacking in comprehending the media industries.[4] In so doing, we explore how the nature of the producer's work involves a mode of *self*-production as a creative professional as much as it does the making of films. Our attention is to the management of reputation, the articulation of ideas about creativity, competence and industry knowledge. Our approach echoes that of John Thornton Caldwell, who suggests that film-makers constantly reflect on and negotiate their cultural identities in a mode of embodied theoretical discussion. His interest in 'very local forms of knowledge and expression' resonates here, for its consideration of how producers fit with the contemporary economic realities of work, of what might be revealed about broad trends in the cultural industries by 'examining very local work, critical practices, and aesthetic "theories" employed and debated throughout the production chain'.[5]

Hereafter we describe some of the background issues in the contemporary creative economy in which our interviewees have been nurtured. We outline the character of their portfolios and experiences as film-makers, exploring their understanding of what a producer does and indeed *is*. We go on to examine how these producers developed their roles and contemporary working conditions. Finally, we discuss the way in which producers negotiate the push and pull of creativity and commerce in the attempt to get films made and to forge a professional reputation.

UK cultural policy and the cultivation of production

While cultural production has, in many ways, *always* been about the economy, the prioritization of income generation, of orientations to export and return on investment, have been integral to the idea of 'creative industries' at the core of DCMS policies and its authorization of bodies such as the UK Film Council. Such priorities accord with wider and longer-term trends noted by Beck, who suggests that one of the most significant developments in recent years has been the governing role of marketizing and corporatizing dynamics. In the United Kingdom, this has meant that previously existing state-sponsored or state-sanctioned monopolistic or duopolistic structures in which cultural work has taken place have been increasingly privatized and commercialized.[6] Certainly, the character of agencies such as Screen WM is captured by such a description. Such bodies were in receipt of public funding but also charged with the pursuit of other sources of finance and the development of 'private' projects as part of an overall contribution to boosting the economic role of the creative sector. The marketizing dynamic is continued by Creative England, which conceives of cultural organizations in primarily business terms, aiming to inculcate in them strategies for growth and sustainability. Its mission is to encourage them 'to learn from their peers and develop new business partnerships. And by developing links with other business sectors we help creative content businesses recognize that their products and services now have value across almost every part of the UK economy.'[7]

When it closed in 2011, the Chair of Screen WM reported that during its ten-year existence, Screen WM had co-financed 17 feature films and had attracted co-investment worth nearly £40 million.[8] This record can be considered in the context of national production with data from Skillset, the UK's Creative Industries' Sector Skills Council. In 2010, Skillset reported that a total of 30,200 people work in the UK film industry: 59 per cent in exhibition, 37 per cent in production and 4 per cent in distribution. 58 per cent of workers were London-based, while a mere 1 per cent were located in the West Midlands.[9] In addition, a 2008 assessment from The Northern Alliance of 'Low & Micro-Budget Film Production' reported that from 2002 to 2007 a total of 357 films were made in the United Kingdom, of which 50 per cent originated in London with 2 per cent – a mere seven films – made in the West Midlands.[10] Such figures are evidence of the challenging space in which our participants have sought to make films and to build reputations and livelihoods. As Simon, an interviewee with stridently commercial objectives, stated rather dismissively: 'I don't think you can call something an industry when there is no money being made.' What then, does it mean to be a film producer in this context? Indeed, what claim to this title have those who contributed to this research?

While the authors have established relationships with several of the interviewees represented here, the majority had been recruited via individual recommendations and an appeal via a local Producers' Forum, itself a legacy of Screen WM support. We conducted semi-structured interviews with ten individuals – here anonymized – who were self-identified as 'film producers'. In each case, the respondents were able to speak of careers and histories of production that varied between the long-established – one has over 30 years' experience – or emergent: Simon has completed one feature, albeit with a £300k budget and a cast and crew of over one hundred. Our approach was guided by the kinds of provisos noted by Caldwell, who cautions that reference to film and video production workers cannot represent 'the industry' in any unified manner.[11] This translates here into the plural manner in which the role of film producer is understood and indeed, the distinctive nature of relationships each has with the sector.

Most of those interviewed have several short films in their portfolio, inclusive of 'no-budget' productions and those funded through a mixture of public and private sources. Their work has been exhibited nationally and at international festivals, where several have been entered into competition, with some success. Six of them have produced one or more features or are in the process of developing large-scale projects. All had experience of other types of production – mainly in television – as well as freelancing roles in film work of all descriptions. And, all of them balanced film projects with employment in other sectors, with three interviewees holding roles in secondary and higher education. Whether announcing themselves as film producers or in more general terms as a film-maker or 'creative worker', each maintained some kind of professional 'brand', whether in the form of a registered production company or online site advertising their experience and forthcoming work. Such features are important to the credentials and claims to the title of producer. While we did not ourselves seek to make qualitative judgements about the status of individuals *qua* producers, issues of integrity, authenticity and credibility are important dimensions of occupational identity. Indeed, a number of the more experienced interviewees noted encounters with individuals claiming the title producer, albeit with dubious credentials. Luke, who had established himself first in radio and as a successful scriptwriter, commented of producers, if not a wider group of would-be creatives, that 'there seem to be a lot of them in this industry, continually flitting about and talking about things that never happen'. Such judgements were rarely based in assessments of budgets or box-office, but concerned evidence of how individuals have overcome the struggle to get films made and the kinds of production values each individual evinces and embodies in their work and reputation – a key issue that we return to later.

Understanding the producer's role

It is logical to proceed with a consideration of how interviewees defined the producer's role and articulated its place in the film-making process. A useful context is provided here in the account of a David, a former Screen WM executive. His role in supporting many shorts and features merited credit as Executive Producer and close involvement in a range of projects. David outlined the strategy developed by the agency as it sought to 'pump prime' the foundations of local industry in anticipation of the inevitable day when public funding would dry up. While the agency's remit was to nurture a broad production base of television and film craft workers, directors and writers, its 'smart move', as he put it, was to pinpoint 'producers as engines' for the screen economy who would discover the 'Holy Grail' of sustainability.

David's experience is one that immediately serves to identify the amorphous dimensions of this role, reflecting that: 'it's one of those jobs that most people don't know that they want to do it. Most people don't know what it is. But very few have a working definition of what is really involved in being a producer'. Certainly, pinpointing a definition of the producer proved difficult for most interviewees, even though they have articulated it in practical ways in their very productions, insisting nonetheless upon its indispensability in the creation of a film. Luke outlined the variety of the role: 'you are a kind of project manager who is holding together enormously complicated enterprises which at the same time have to succeed on a financial level, on a writing and conceptual level, they have to be marketed, pitched'. Alongside business acumen and creative sensibilities, there was a need too for the kind of affective work and emotional skills characteristic of contemporary labour that is typical of the cultural sector.[12] Pete described a job that required a range of skills involving project management, sales ability, therapy and counselling; as Luke put it, 'you have to be entirely responsive to the fact that one of your crew may have a crisis'. Simon considered that the producer required a diplomat's skill in presenting different personas to different agents, involving the management of a variety of discourses: 'my job is to speak in other people's language all the time'. For Ewan, the most experienced of our producers, the role he took in the film crew originated in a sense that while he understood creative work, he was 'technically inept'. As a result he had always been the person who had functioned as producer – a role that meant identifying talent and bringing people together, organizing shoots and of course obtaining finance to underwrite such ventures or finding ways of making things work without it.

In descriptions of the role, there is a sense that it is a certain 'type' of person who becomes the producer rather than an ability to learn and master a set of rationalized skills and tasks. Some of these ideas as well as the pragmatic acceptance of the plural dimensions of the producer's role are explained in part by the often accidental and sometime circuitous route that the interviewees have followed in building experience. Janet, for instance, was originally recruited as an office administrator for a charity that developed professional productions aimed at involving and training disadvantaged children in film-making skills. She went on to take a major production role in the company and is now a self-employed consultant with a wider purview of cultural projects. Screen WM's David had originally studied film at university and, while exploring the possibilities of cultural work in advance of graduation, he obtained a placement in local television and, in his words 'got the bug' for the sector. It might be a comment on the focus of the film studies curriculum but for David, the idea of working in film at all, let alone being a producer was not an obvious option; he recalls that 'I didn't think you could really do it as a job.'

Geoffrey, whose primary employment is in the care sector, views his route into film-making as prompted by his undergraduate studies in fine art. Geoffrey considers that his skills emerged from an artistic 'common sense' allowing him to manage his first film production, which was made under DIY principles, 'literally with scissors and sticky tape'. He recalled how he had made further no-budget shorts, feeling his way through production and the myriad roles it entailed: 'There was no money for this. At this point I didn't even know I was making a film.' The realization of what it meant to make a film and an understanding that he had begun to achieve something came when he entered one of his shorts into a local film festival. He recalled that the award of a prize was an important moment where he could tell himself: 'Oh! I'm a film-maker.' The authorization of his identity as a producer (and writer, director, camera operator, etc.) came through the recognition of festival audiences, 'confirmation that something you've done is good'. For all interviewees, the engagement with an audience was one of the palpable rewards of film work and was a measure of what it meant to be a professionally oriented producer.

Pete's career in film began in youth work at a moment when it became possible to employ video technology in project development as an aid in cultivating media literacy and thereby facilitate his charges' ability to express themselves. He found a 'natural role' in such media work and 'just evolved into the role of a producer'. Wryly hinting at the indistinct definition of a producer's role, its self-directed parameters and entrepreneurial quality he remarked, 'I didn't apply for the job.' Instead he had 'made' the job for himself by establishing a video production company and learning much of his trade in a Hollywood venture with an overseas production that formed the basis of his first feature.

Echoing Pete's experience is Danny's development: a young animator, he has recently established his own studio, lately gaining a prestigious commission from a digital TV channel. He recalled that in spite of studying in a practice-based animation degree, 'nobody's there with a lead: you just have to find your own way'. Organizing fellow students in a studio situation was all very well, but when it came to the practicalities of developing a professional project from scratch *outside* the classroom, that was a different matter: 'I didn't know what I was getting into.' Creative decisions were the least of Danny's concerns as he listed the pressures of dealing with 'reports, accounts and so on' in order to understand the managerial and economic demands of locating his work in an industrial context.

Moira's narrative captures a conscious and conscientious approach to professionalization as a producer in response to the realities of discovering the demands of the film industry. She established herself in television in a variety of roles and had ventured into film by producing a short supported by funding from Channel 4's Film Four strand 'Ideas Factory'. The film was in turn submitted for exhibition at Cannes. Attending the festival, she recalls how 'I came back, very excited by the business of film.' There, she discovered that in spite of her considerable creative credentials, she was such a novice that she did not even understand how to conduct a meeting or distinguish herself from the many other equally talented individuals present: 'You might have a script but so what? So do thousands of other people.' While Cannes might have a reputation for red carpet receptions, of canapés and champagne, 'It's a trade fair. It's hard work if you go with serious intent.' Nowadays, she attends Cannes annually and with that serious intent, having gained an understanding that film production entails much more than a concentration on the shooting schedule, set and editing room: 'there was a whole world I didn't know about […] the role of the sales agent, the booker […] financing plans, co-production'. Having been nurtured amidst TV crews and studio conditions, and having taken on the multiple roles possible in shorts, she noted how, in orienting her ambitions to feature development, that 'at some point reality kicks in and you have to think like a business'.

Making a living

These narratives of professional development illuminate the nature of the working life of interviewees – one in which an identity as a producer is constructed. Positioning themselves as cultural entrepreneurs, their responsibility is for the creation of the conditions in which their productions can be realized, even if the possibility of making a living from their efforts is uncertain. As Barney says of his attempt to recruit crew for no-budget productions: 'we get would-be runners ringing up and asking whether they'll be paid and I just laugh: there are twenty or thirty asking for that role'. Such conditions are accepted as an aesthetic prerequisite in John's practice when he suggests that 'there's an element of filmmaking which keeps the culture of filmmaking exciting, which has never made money and you have to accept that you are a glorious amateur'.

Nonetheless, he was critical of schemes such as social media sites that film-makers use for recruiting crews, which perpetuate these conditions. He was critical of one site, which sources crews for low-budget film, for presenting a professional face 'in an old Hollywood division of labour idea' while often stipulating that volunteers should expect to receive no pay for the work they do.

These conditions are familiar enough to appear unexceptional. For instance, Skillset estimates that 44 per cent of those working in media industries – 37 per cent of those in film – had to undertake a period of unpaid labour before being in a position to expect to be paid.[13] While not suggestive of a rule, it is those at the 'bottom-end' of the professional ladder who, like Barney, find themselves amidst the endless pool of talent that creates the competition in which such conditions seem inevitable. As Banks and Hesmondhalgh suggest, the highly individualized nature of cultural labour leads to a fatalistic acceptance of such iniquities.[14] However, for more established and successful producers, the very idea of free work was treated with resistance. Pete said of his production work that 'I've been very fortunate [...] it has always earned me a living.' Yet for him, the suggestion of working for free on a movie was 'utter bullshit'. Whether shooting a short film, and especially on a feature, the implications for crew members of working for free represented an ethical issue for Pete: 'That's probably two months of their lives [...] when they can't pay their bills, their rent, their mortgage: they can't feed their kids.' To ask people to work for free meant that 'the producer hasn't done their job'. According to him, 'you've got to honour people [...] it's not the way the industry should be working'. For Luke, pay was also a moral issue, suggesting that the industry is bedevilled by 'too many cowboy producers'; unscrupulous individuals look for workers who can be exploited because 'everyone wants a credit'. The ultimately unproductive nature of this situation is summed up in Luke's observation that, in his experience, 'working unpaid for things rarely ever results in your ending up getting paid for things'.

Unpaid labour had been a cause for concern for David in his role at Screen WM, and he took an interest in the well-being of the workers on the films and projects it generated. Whether focusing on producers or other members of film production culture, he noted how he had dealt with lots of people with 'day jobs' or who were 'doing it for thin air'. For those trying to make a living as a producer, any reward was always in jeopardy thanks to what he described as the perverse nature of how the film industry is structured. Experience suggested that the producer's fee is the first to be squeezed when a budget needed to be reduced. Ultimately, the burden of the role is that the producer is the person who is 'usually first in on a project and then invests the most time of anyone [over] the lifetime and will be the last to be paid: if they are ever paid'.

David's reflections draw attention to the nature of the working week this role may entail. Producers often invest their own money in their projects or, if employed for the most part outside film, they invest of their valuable 'spare' time. This involves a great deal of *self*-investment in creative work which is highly personalized in nature and often involves dissolving the boundaries between work and other aspects of an individual's life.[15] This is evidenced in the accounts of all of our interviewees. Pete, for instance, works across his social media platforms in order to engage friends, partners and others in cultivating an audience for his films and finding new modes of delivery. He starts work when he logs on to his computer, engaging directly with the 50 or more new contacts he makes every day. In launching his operations, Danny related how he had been the beneficiary of sponsorship from a Midland-based media centre, which offered studio space under the auspices of Screen WM funds. He recalled the exceptionally long hours worked, sometimes commencing before and staying way past the official opening hours of the centre, and that 'whatever I was earning […] went straight into the business'. Even with current commissions, growing recognition and sense of success, this kind of pattern continues to describe aspects of his working life. Danny tagged a recent photograph of himself taking lunch in a local pub which he posted on a social media site: 'This is photoshopped – I'm too busy to eat.'

Moira maintains a freelance career in film and has lately taken to investing her own money in the development of feature projects. These involve considerable attention to detail as well as maintaining her patience and nerve over long periods of time. As she noted, as one plans ahead for a shooting schedule while sourcing finance, everything is dependent upon enlisting actors and crew for some future point that may never materialize and, each of them is, in turn, planning for their own living. Actors offered a script may take months to read it and give a commitment while it takes further time to formulate and secure a contract. Moira posed a rhetorical question when describing her circumstances: how does one plan for an income amidst this process? Of necessity, she balances free and paid labour – sometimes manifest in deferred future payments – over a working week of 70 hours or more. Typically, this week involves researching funding and budgets for any one of the projects she has in development. It may take weeks to develop a feature budget that entails preparing several variants based on a sliding scale in which each will involve different schedules and ideas about the production value of the resulting film. Each of these tasks impacts upon the working week, meriting further discussions with agents that take place alongside other duties. These duties include reading scripts: she serves as a consultant to other writers and has to review versions of work she has commissioned, giving and taking notes and commenting on various drafts for each project. She'll also be planning a schedule of necessary visits to film fairs and festivals at home and abroad. Such travel involves the investment of personal resources – financial, temporal and professional; as for Moira, each environment involves endless networking. For her, this is an activity to be dreaded, although for any creative worker it is an unavoidable aspect of the never-ending quality of the nature of their labour and where they nurture their sense of a professional self and public reputation.[16]

Ultimately, Moira's recognition that this work 'has become my lifestyle' was characteristic of the status of interviewees. A pertinent response to such accounts would be to ask why pursue *this* form of work at all? Given the entrepreneurial, project-based nature of production, this work is after all elective in nature and its challenges are well known; most film-makers recognize from the outset that the glamour often associated with the industry is a myth. Barney, for one, recalled that in the presentations from film-makers in his first screenwriting course at a local college, producers had warned of the long hours, low pay and the hardships of production. As Luke commented: 'I'm not sure there's a single job in the world that is quite so demanding simultaneously on so many different levels as being a producer of quality content.'

Geoffrey, who holds down full-time employment outside his film production, maintained that 'I can stop tomorrow if I want to.' However, it is hard to imagine that he, or any other interviewee, would be able to make such a break given the personal investment that they have made in film in terms of their social and cultural capital, their finances, well-being and emotions. As Moira stated, 'it is very much a heart-driven industry [...] a lot of us work on passion projects'. Certainly, theorists of creative labour suggest that workers tolerate precariousness, insecurity and (self-) exploitation for the reasons expressed in Danny's heartfelt statement that summarized the position of the majority: 'I love my job.'[17]

Tensions between commerce and creativity in the producer's role

As Graham Murdock notes, a key reason why creative work appeals and how producers manage the apparent contradictions of their situation 'are rooted in deeply romantic conceptions of the artist's expressive capacities and rights'.[18] Creative work offers potential autonomy, self-actualization and 'the chance for non-alienating employment conducive to self-expression'.[19] Such ideas have been described as motivating 'self-exploitation'.[20] The kind of experiences described earlier are those in which work and social life become indistinguishable, and where insecure or 'bulimic'[21] work patterns become accepted, naturalized even, alongside poor pay and even significant bouts of unpaid work. Certainly, it is the ineffable qualities of creativity that are key to understanding the narratives of our interviewees, the commitment they show to their work and indeed the wider context in which they have sought to make a living and how they think about their roles.

Robert Hewison, for instance, has summarized the contemporary significance of creativity, observing the frequency with which the word and permutations thereof appeared in the titles of documents from the Blair-Brown years of government. He concludes: 'The rhetoric of "creativity" was New Labour's binding cultural theme.'[22] In tandem with the lauding of entrepreneurial skills and market optimization at the core of the 'creative industries' policy, the role of producer thus offers a potentially totemic figure in this milieu.[23] To analysts such as Peter McCullen and Steve Harding looking for examples of the optimization of the creative sector, film producers straddle the 'art' and 'business' of moving images.[24] As such, they are crucial to the effective integration of cultural and economic knowledge – an analysis manifest in the discourse of our interviewees, which evinces what Hesmondhalgh calls the 'commerce-creativity dialectic'.[25]

The question of the creative aspects of the producer's role was voiced in rhetorical fashion by interviewees themselves, suggesting that this was the core of its definition.

Pete articulated it thus: 'what type of producer are you? Are you a creative producer or a money producer?' Either way, the two poles were indivisible and he suggested that if one was overly interested in the aesthetic execution of the film one should maybe concentrate on being a director: 'If you have not got your eye on the business then you should not be producer'. As David suggested, it was the role of agencies like Screen WM in dealing with producers in need of its structural and financial support to remind them of this relationship that 'this is a business transaction'.

For Simon, production is by its nature entrepreneurial. As a confident businessman, he was rather critical of what he had encountered in the film world – particularly the expectation of support from public money – suggesting that many producers could learn a lesson from other industries and 'should all go on MBA courses'. For him, this position was not at odds with a devotion to artistic creativity, which had its right and proper place in the producer's duties. His passionate belief was that something overlooked in UK film was a sense of 'creativity in business' which meant a problem-solving approach to realizing projects and a vision for success in the marketplace. Simon said of conventional film-makers that 'they see commerce as a dirty word. They understand commerce via a Hollywood example, which I do not advocate at all, which is deeply boring and uninteresting'. While mindful of business priorities, he had seen it as his job to ensure that the set was 'a reserved space' for the production of the comedy at the heart of his feature film. Likewise, Janet described herself as a creative manager, 'there to support the creation of a beautiful piece of work'.

Pete also reflected how our participants were, on the whole, well practised in thinking of an 'end product' and its reception in the market. In a producer's role, he works very hard to let others achieve their creative potential but sees himself offering a caution against the potential *cul-de-sac* of imaginative indulgence – a reality check in warning that 'no-one will want to see the film' if it veers too far from what the *market* wants. For David, the producer's indispensible creative input is evinced from the very start of a project in the fact that everyone involved has no definitive idea of how the finished film will appear. In bringing together mock-ups, trailers, cast shots, budgets and a sense of how all contributions will manifest themselves in the production values of the shoot, the producer is key to representing a vision of the project to financiers, distributors and, indeed, to many of the cast and crew too. The producer's role involves balancing the demands of budget and creative vision, a need to 'make it add up'; showing the possibilities of film from its planning to its realization; and to the challenge of 'constantly trying to do the impossible' by ignoring what money says can and cannot be done. As Luke puts it, 'there's the film you write, the film you make and the film you find in the end'.

For all the producers here, the films they made embodied their sense of creativity, professionalism and success, both personal and collective. A sense of success is most clearly manifest in perceptions of quality and, for this group, its synonym 'production values'. For Moira, her engagement with the culture of Cannes illuminated ideas of professionalism, ambition and achievement: 'what I noticed at that time there were a lot of people calling themselves filmmakers and they'd just come out of college or school but they hadn't had experience of the real industry and the quality of work was really suffering [...] they didn't have the industry knowledge of how to achieve a certain quality'. Moira's own approach to production was predicated on honestly answering through her practice the question of 'how do I make films of quality?' The realization of production values on screen was itself a manifestation of one's achievement – of the marshalling of talent, management of logistics and, in many of the films produced by our interviewees, achieving something beyond the apparent limits of the budget.

Pondering the way in which financial limitations impact upon one's creative ambition, Danny commented that the producer has to be pragmatic about what can be achieved, accepting 'I'll have to try and make it do'. For him, there was enormous personal and professional satisfaction in discovering how peers imagined that his short promotional pieces cost £45k, when in reality they cost a quarter of that figure. In Janet's practice, the use of film to empower young people to develop skills and find a voice – described by her as a typical New Labour project – was one that pursued quality. She recognized the way in which such projects might entail an approach that was 'all process no product'. She was critical of schemes that lacked a professional focus and meaningful objective, and which offered a form of busy work for idle hands; to her 'it was really important to us to make an end product that was high quality'. Such objectives were vital in aiding the motivation of the young people with whom her company had worked. In this way, participants were encouraged to express themselves and gained investment in and ownership of their work and, indeed, were able to envision how this might translate into a future in production work as measured by such quality. Just as Janet aimed to manifest value in her film work, she sought to inculcate her values in her trainees, to reproduce in them her own aspirations and professional qualities as a producer.

Conclusion

Simon told us of how on a publicly funded production training course that he had attended, he had heard it said that 'a film is the producer's. That's what I've been led to believe and I believe it firmly.' Without the producer, the film would never have been made. In the generous accounts provided by our ten interviewees, we have encountered many assertions of this kind. Balancing managerial skills, diplomacy, emotional labour, business *nous* and creative zeal, these producers have all worked hard in difficult circumstances to get their films made. In so doing, they have sought to build their reputations and status, thereby insinuating themselves into a field which, when seen from a number of perspectives, may not look much like an industry at all – at least not one that brings the stability and security found in the other types of employment many of these individuals have felt it necessary to maintain. Ultimately however, each has forged a meaningful identity as a film producer where the definition of the role is manifest in their experience and shared ideas about its creativity and value.

While these accounts bear consideration in relation to the economics of the UK film sector, it is the empirical detail of the producers' work and position as creative workers that are focused on and analysed here. We have sought to place this work in the context of a discourse of the creative economy and the legacy of screen policy and development involving the prioritization of film as business – an orientation that is evidenced strongly here in what interviewees say about their work and position. But, as in many observations about creative labour, the attachment to their work that these producers articulate is of a nature that seems to be of a different order to the cliché of the rapacious entrepreneur interested only in profitable return on investment. As Moira said of her role, after weighing up her taxing work schedule, 'Look, it is a privilege, ridiculously given the amount of hours, the things I have to juggle and the lack of income, I still consider it a real privilege.' Such is the ambivalence of the producer's role.

Further research might ask pointed questions of the actual films produced by these interviewees and how they have fared in the industry as a whole. Did they reach their audience? How were they received critically? How did they fare as commodities? What kinds of legacy have they created for these producers as creative figures? What kinds of aesthetic assessment can be made of the 'production values' and 'vision' that each has aimed for? In the end, each has at least got the job done of producing films that would bear such questions. In doing so, they have defined one sector of the film business and what it means to be a producer.

Notes

1   For a summary see: John Newbigin, 'A Golden Age for the Arts?' *Cultural Trends*, 20:3–4 (2011): 231–34.
2   See: Tessa Jowell, *Government and the Value of Culture* (London: DCMS, 2004).
3   'UK Screen Agencies', Creative Skillset, accessed 1 June 2013, http://www. creativeskillset.org/film/knowledge/links/article_2495_1.asp.
4   Andrew Beck, 'Introduction: Cultural Work, Cultural Workplace – Looking at the Cultural Industries', in *Cultural Work: Understanding the Cultural Industries*, ed. Andrew Beck (London: Taylor & Francis, 2003), 1–12. David Hesmondhalgh, 'Cultural and Creative Industries', in *The Sage Handbook of Cultural Analysis*, ed. John Frow and Tony Bennett (London: Sage Publications, 2008), 563.
5   John Thornton Caldwell, 'Cultures of Production: Studying Industry's Deep Texts, Reflexive Rituals, and Managed Self-Disclosures', in *Media Industries: History, Theory and Method*, ed. Jennifer Holt and Alisa Perren (Malden, MA and Oxford: Wiley-Blackwell, 2009), 209. See also the same author's *Production Culture: Industrial Reflexivity and Critical Practice in Film and Television* (London: Duke University Press, 2008).
6   Beck, *Cultural Work*, 2.
7   Creative England, *Our First Year. Review 2011–2012* (Birmingham, Borehamwood, Bristol, Leeds, Nottingham, Salford: Creative England, 2012), 11.
8   Alan Thorne, 'Abolition of Screen WM could Boost Creative Industries, says chairman', *Birmingham Post*, 30 September 2011, accessed 1 June 2013, http://

www.birminghampost.co.uk/business/creative/abolition-screen-wm-could-boost-3918508. The *Internet Movie Data Base* lists 41 productions, a figure which by no means accounts for the entirety of Screen WM's output, as several works produced by our participants that were in receipt of funding support are unlisted.

9   'Film Sector – Labour Market Intelligence Digest 2010', accessed 1 June 2013, http://www.creativeskillset.org/uploads/pdf/asset_15385.pdf?1.

10   Northern Alliance, *Low and Micro-Budget Film Production in the UK* (UK Film Council, 2008). Low-budget films are listed as £1 million to £250k, micro-budget as £250k to £50k, 'no-budget' as £50k to £0. Of an average of 100 films produced per year, 40 per cent were reported to be no-budget, 28 per cent micro-budget and 22 per cent low-budget.

11   Caldwell, *Production Culture*, 7.

12   For a discussion see: Rosalind Gill and Andrew Pratt, 'In the Social Factory?: Immaterial Labour, Precariousness and Cultural Work', *Theory, Culture and Society*, 25:7–8 (2008): 15–17.

13   Creative Skillset/UK Film Council, 'Feature Film Workforce Survey 2008', accessed 1 June 2013, http://publications.skillset.org/index.php?id=9.

14   Mark Banks and David Hesmondhalgh, 'Looking for Work in Creative Industries Policy', *International Journal of Cultural Policy*, 15:4 (2009): 420.

15   As summarized in Rosalind Gill, 'Life is a Pitch: Managing the Self in New Media Work', in *Managing Media Work*, ed. Mark Deuze (London: Sage, 2010), 255.

16   See, for instance: Chris Bilton, *Management and Creativity: From Creative Industries to Creative Management* (Oxford: Blackwell, 2007); David Lee, 'Networks, Cultural Capital and Creative Labour in the British Independent Television Industry', *Media, Culture and Society*, 33:4 (2011): 549–66.

17   E.g. Angela McRobbie, *British Fashion Design: Rag Trade or Image Industry?* (London: Routledge, 1998); Mark Banks, *The Politics of Cultural Work* (London: Palgrave, 2007).

18   Graham Murdock, 'Back To Work: Cultural Labor in Altered Times', in ed. Beck, *Cultural Work*, 32.

19   Banks and Hesmondhalgh, 'Looking for Work', 417.

20   McRobbie, *British Fashion Design*, 1998.

21   Andy Pratt, 'Hot Jobs in Cool Places. The Material Cultures of New Media Product Spaces: The Case of the South of Market, San Francisco', *Information, Communication And Society*, 5:1 (2002): 27–50.

22   Robert Hewison, ' "Creative Britain": Myth or monument?', *Cultural Trends*, 20: 3–4 (2011). 235.

23   E.g. Charles Leadbeater and Kate Oakley, *The Independents* (London: Demos, 2009).

24   Peter McCullen and Steve Harding, 'Independent Moving Image Producers and Their Networks', in *Art & Design and… Business, Innovation and Management*, eds. E. Findlay and I. Creed (Brighton: University of Brighton, 2012), Kindle Edition.

25   David Hesmondhalgh, *The Cultural Industries* (London: Sage, 2007), 20–21.

6

Producer *and* Director? Or, 'Authorship' in 1950s Italian Cinema

Pauline Small

Narratives of post-war Italian cinema have consistently excluded the role of the producer in their analysis of this important era of Italian film-making. They subscribe instead to the perspective of the *politique des auteurs* initiated by the *Cahiers du Cinema* group in the late 1950s, an approach which asserts the centrality of the auteur to the film-making process. Although Peter Bondanella, in his overview of Italian cinema first published in 1983, recognizes 'the pitfalls of overemphasis on the director', he nevertheless acknowledges that his book remains 'primarily about Italian cinema as an art form, with the director playing the key role'.[1] Mira Liehm's analysis of the post-war period, also dating from the 1980s, appears to offer a chronological approach, but subheadings within the individual chapters again show the persistence of the director as the key analytical focus. Chapter Five, for example, ('The Difficult Years, 1950–1959') presents a section entitled 'The Loners: Rossellini, Antonioni, Fellini', and the whole of Chapter Nine ('Highlights of the Sixties') is subdivided through the names of directors Fellini, Antonioni, Visconti and Pasolini.[2] It is tempting to consider these views as being a product of their time, but in fact the argument that 'the director is the lynchpin of the film [...] who has invented the project, written the script and raised the finance' clearly persists in more recent publications.[3]

Much less prominence, indeed, hardly any at all, is afforded to the part producers played in bringing films such as *Ladri di biciclette/Bicycle Thieves* (Vittorio De Sica, 1946), *La strada* (Federico Fellini, 1954) and *L'avventura* (Michelangelo Antonioni, 1960) to the screen. Recent critical perspectives have shifted attention towards investigating the detail of the production process, in the belief that film-making is essentially collaborative, with multiple creative contributions to the final product, the film. To give further clarity to this collective process, research is now being undertaken to uncover evidence of 'the struggles which took place during a film's production'.[4] As this chapter will show, the Italian film industry was in this period almost entirely without the financial stability of American or multi-national conglomerate funding; consequently these 'struggles' in the production process were considerable, and exerted particular pressure on the relationship between producer and director. In particular, this chapter seeks to establish the significance of the producer within Italian film-making – a role which remains little acknowledged and considerably under-researched. In doing so, it will challenge the dominance of the auteur-director perspective on Italian cinema. Drawing on materials from film archives[5] and historical accounts of the relevant period,[6] it will consider the work of two major production companies, Lux and Titanus, headed respectively by Riccardo Gualino and Goffredo Lombardo, with the aim of demonstrating the extent to which they were instrumental in shaping post-war Italian film-making.

The general production context

If we are to understand the significance of the role of Lux and Titanus more fully, it is important to contextualize their activities within the general framework of the industry in the early 1950s, when post-war film-making began to gather momentum. The relevant data is somewhat scattered, but useful statistics are found in the journal of the trade organization *Unitalia*, set up in 1950 to promote Italian cinema on the international front. In April 1954, *Unitalia* published a survey of the facilities available to film-makers who might consider Italy as a shooting location. It stated that, nationally, there were 13 production lots with a total of 56 sound stages, of which 44 were based in Rome, and the remaining 12 in 'various locations' outside Rome. The survey goes on to show that a substantial part of the entire production capacity of the industry was held in three locations in Rome. The state-owned Cinecittà had 13 sound stages; Titanus and Ponti-De Laurentiis each had five.[7] In the pre-war period, the industry had been much more diversified. Turin and Naples were important centres for silent film-making, while in the latter years of the Fascist regime studios were created in Venice by two major production companies, Scalera and Cines, and there were facilities also at the Tirrenia studios in Tuscany.

The figures from *Unitalia* show the extent to which the industry had become increasingly Rome-based. This was consistent with the more general centralizing policy of the 1930s Fascist regime; but it has to be noted that the regime was in any case renowned for its efforts to stimulate film-making within Italy, founding the Venice Film Festival in 1932, the film-making school, the Centro Sperimentale, in 1935 and finally bringing the Cinecittà studio complex to completion in 1938. These initiatives bore fruit in the 1950s when the phenomenon of 'Hollywood by the Tiber' emerged, privileging Rome locations and utilizing the Cinecittà complex in US-funded productions, including the highly successful *Quo Vadis* (Mervyn Le Roy, 1951) and *Roman Holiday* (William Wyler, 1953). The benefits of these so-called runaway productions to national film-making are debatable, especially since many non-Italian cast and crew were simply brought in for the duration of the shooting, but one can nevertheless say that they enhanced the image of Italy internationally, and at the same time stimulated the industry both financially and in terms of its capacity to provide equipment and technical expertise.

This pattern of centralization is clearly seen in the history of Lux and Titanus, the focus of this study. However, before progressing to examine the individual companies it is useful to reference a second set of data in order to demonstrate their status within the production activity of the post-war period. Lorenzo Quaglietti assembled figures showing that in the period 1945 to 1957 Lux produced the highest number of films (78), followed by Excelsa (57) and Titanus (48); he states that in the same period 287 production companies 'came and went', having only produced a single film.[8] Aldo Bernardini's summary, covering the period 1930 to 1995, lists Titanus (144 productions), and Lux (141) as the leading companies, figures surpassed only by the 155 productions of Reteitalia, a multimedia company that entered the field in the 1980s; production companies making a single film numbered 1,851.[9] Both critics point out that the same producers would frequently form a company, dissolve it and re-group under another title. The figures demonstrate that, in keeping with other European cinematic enterprises, the Italian film production was fragmented, lacking in stability and characterized by production groupings of a distinctly transient nature.

This scenario throws into sharp relief the profile of Lux and Titanus, which, in contrast, provided a much more stable framework that was fundamental to the artistic achievements of the industry, its directors and actors as well as a range of highly skilled scriptwriters, costume and set designers and cinematographers. As we have seen, the *Unitalia* overview of the industry lists Cinecittà, Titanus and Ponti-De Laurentiis as the three leading studios for shooting in 1954. Manifestly absent from the list is Lux which, despite its role as a major production company, owned neither plant nor film-making equipment. This was not, however, untypical because, as we shall see, the entire industry operated the package-unit system, a term employed by Janet Staiger in her analysis of changes in the Hollywood industry during the 1950s.[10] In this sense the profile which will emerge shows that, in its ownership of studio space and dubbing facilities, Titanus is in fact the exception. We will now consider the very different ways in which Riccardo Gualino and Goffredo Lombardo operated their business, firstly in general terms and then in detailed case studies of two films directed by Luchino Visconti: *Senso* (1954) produced by Lux Film and *Rocco e i suoi fratelli/Rocco and His Brothers* (1960) produced by Titanus. These case studies offer the opportunity to assess the balance between the respective roles of director and producer that underpins this chapter.

Lux: General characteristics and mode of operation

Riccardo Gualino founded the Compagnia Italiana Cinematografica Lux in 1934 and his personal history is closely linked to the evolution of the company. He was born in the small Piedmont town of Biella in 1879, rising to prominence in the 1920s as a major industrialist in Turin as head of an international conglomerate, SNIA (Società di Navigazione Italo-americano). His commercial activities were based largely on shipping and textiles, and not at all on film production. Gualino, however, had strong interests in art collecting, theatre and music, and at this time Turin was renowned for its film-making, especially at the long-running FERT studios (Fiori Enrico Roma Torino) established by Enrico Fiori and Stefano Pittaluga, where one of the great silent films *Cabiria* (Giovanni Pastrone, 1919) was made. The power of Gualino's empire brought him into conflict with the ruling Fascist regime; he was arrested for financial irregularities in January 1931, sentenced to two years of *confino* (a form of internal exile), and banned from involvement in business for 10 years. On his release, however, it seems that the regime nevertheless permitted him to set up a film company which, during its time in Turin, operated largely as a distribution company listing only three productions for the 1930s. The company's relationship with Fascism remains unclear. Alberto Farassino suggests Mussolini may in fact have sanctioned Lux's beginnings as part of the more general Fascist agenda to promote the film industry.[11] From 1932 the industrial conglomerate formerly headed by Gualino re-directed its activities into a multinational grouping entitled Rumaniaca, which transferred in its entirety to Rome in 1940. In this way Gualino's film company, a minor holding of the Rumaniaca empire, moved to the capital. It was renamed Lux Film. After the war, it entered vigorously into the production business in conjunction with its Paris-based sister company Lux CCF (Compagnia Cinematografica Francese).

It is essential to understand that throughout its period of operation in Rome, Lux remained a group of offices, in short a studio without studios, far removed from the Hollywood model with its ownership of extensive facilities – plant, technical equipment, sound stages – and employment of a highly structured, comprehensive workforce. Lux, like many other lesser companies that set up, often briefly, simply hired the space for interior shooting (often at Cinecittà or indeed at Titanus) and equipment such as cameras and lighting, from a central source, Mole Richardson, the Rome-based outlet of the US company. Lux treated all employees as freelance, contracting them for the duration of the film; it provided funding to make the film and on completion generally acted also as distributor through its extensive national and international networks. It invited individual producers to propose, cost and present a package for approval and financial support on a basis termed *prezzo bloccato* or fixed price: if the project over-shot, the additional costs were borne by the named producer and not Lux. Indeed, the company was renowned for nurturing production talent by way of its financial rigour, while at the same time allowing considerable independence in creating and operating individual projects. In the early 1950s, producers who capitalized on the Lux system of operation included Carlo Ponti and Dino De Laurentiis, who later went on to run their own independent enterprises at international level, as well as producers such as Antonio Mambretti, Luigi Rovere and Valentino Brosio, whose work remained within the ambit of the national industry.

By the early 1950s, Riccardo Gualino, whose dynamism had long guided operations, became an increasingly distant, autocratic figure who delegated much of the day-to-day business to the firm's second-in-command Guido Gatti, and also to his son Renato Gualino, later a major figure in the various national and international film bodies with which Lux interacted. Despite the fact that the package-unit system remained central to its mode of operation, it is nevertheless true that certain figures concentrated their activity at Lux, which presents an impressively diverse production profile at this time. Key films were those starring Silvana Mangano, produced by Dino de Laurentiis, especially the much-publicized and highly successful *Riso Amaro/Bitter*

Rice (Giuseppe De Santis, 1949), and investigative films such as the Mafia exposé *In nome della legge/In the Name of the Law* (Pietro Germi, 1949). Most importantly for this study, Lux consistently funded a range of literary adaptations from *Piccolo mondo antico/The Old Fashioned World* (Mario Soldati, 1941) to *Il mulino del Po/The Mill on the Po* (Alberto Lattuada, 1949), thereby establishing a reputation as a company intent on artistic film-making, a policy of major importance to its role in the making of *Senso* in 1954.

Titanus: General characteristics and mode of operation

The character of Goffredo Lombardo and the mode of operation of Titanus contrast strongly with Lux. While Lux appears as the antithesis of the Hollywood system, Titanus was, apart from the state-run Cinecittà, the only Italian business that was vertically integrated. The company was started by Gustavo Lombardo under the title 'Lombardo Film' in Naples in 1908. It set up business during the period of silent cinema when Naples was a particularly important centre of film-making, with early masterpieces such as *Assunta Spina* (1915), produced by director Gustavo Serena's company Caesar Film, and starring the renowned actress Francesca Bertini. Another prominent actress of the period, Leda Gys, married Gustavo Lombardo and their son Goffredo, born in 1920, eventually inherited the family business. The company also ran a much smaller outlet in Rome, and in 1928 the entire business transferred to the capital, where it set up the beginnings of the Farnesina complex of studios on the north-west bank of the Tiber. By 1939 there were five sound stages, one of which was requisitioned by Allied troops during the liberation of Italy necessitating the arduous task of re-establishing the complex after they had left. Gustavo Lombardo died in 1951, and thus in the 1950s, the focus of this chapter, it was his son Goffredo whose activities definitively shaped the company.

Our understanding of the workings of Titanus under Goffredo Lombardo is greatly enhanced by a brochure published by the company's own press department, sections of which are reproduced in Aldo Bernardini's history of the studio. They present the structure of the company in a set of simple graphics fanning out from a central administration into subdivisions of production, distribution and exhibition.[12] We can see from these details that in production terms Titanus became an increasingly strong presence in Rome, expanding its domain across the city. In late 1954, it purchased the site of the former Scalera production company, labelled Titanus-Appia on Rome's southern outskirts, thereby adding five more sound stages and additional dubbing facilities to its capacity. The original studio location, now termed Titanus-Farnesina, remained the main site for shooting and post-production work, and the centrally located dubbing facilities already established in Via Margutta were retained. As well as facilitating its own film-making ventures, Titanus' facilities were of critical importance to the national industry. Its extensive studio space and equipment was hired out and intensively used by a whole range of small-scale production companies that, to repeat Quaglietti's term, 'came and went' throughout the post-war period. In addition, American film-makers made use of the studio's sophisticated dubbing and copying facilities to adapt their films for the Italian market. The company also offered a national distribution network for its own films and those of other film-makers, national and international. To this end it operated offices at local level in 13 cities of the Italian peninsula, as well as an International Office, based in Rome, that linked up with designated agents in Europe and Latin America. Titanus was also part of the Italian Film Export company formed in the 1950s to facilitate the distribution of Italian films in the United States. Finally, the Titanus documents list a chain of 12 Titanus-owned cinemas, 10 in the Naples area, evidence that the exhibition division was a minor element of company business.

In contrast to Riccardo Gualino, who increasingly relied on his son Renato to operate as the public face of Lux, Goffredo Lombardo was very active at national and international level, organizing an extensive range of promotional events within Italy and undertaking frequent trips to America and within Europe. Broadly speaking, Titanus also operated the package-unit system, as far as the employment of personnel was concerned. Director Dino Risi testifies that while working at Titanus, 'no-one had a contract, but often the crew of a successful film would simply transfer in its entirety to the next production'.[13] The point holds true for those who worked in both popular cinema and art house film-making: even the production history of established directors such as Vittorio De Sica and Federico Fellini is consistent with a film-by-film pattern of production. A studio policy of sorts may be identified from the wide-ranging list of Titanus productions: the tenor of productions was largely populist and of considerable importance to a number of national stars. Amedeo Nazzari and Yvonne Sanson sustained their careers in a run of popular melodramas such as *I figli di nessuno/ Nobody's Children* (Raffaello Matarazzo, 1953), while the comedy series that began with *Pane amore e fantasia/Bread Love and Dreams* (Luigi Comencini, 1953) launched the star careers of Gina Lollobrigida and Sophia Loren. This list clearly presents a strain of film-making that was very different from the more refined reputation of Lux. However, in their dealings with Luchino Visconti, both producers reveal the complexity of their own and Italy's film-making endeavours in the 1950s. We will now consider how their role as producers intersected with that of a major auteur.

The making of *Senso*: Producer and auteur

The origins of *Senso* can be traced to an earlier agreement between Visconti and Lux for a film entitled *Marcia nuziale/Wedding March*, which was never made. The film laws of 1949 required that all papers relevant to the proposed film including costings, contracts and script were submitted ahead of shooting for government approval to the designated 'Revisione Cinematografica' (henceforth translated as the 'Censorship Office'), a section within the Ministry of Arts. Approval at this stage also opened up possibilities of a range of government subsidies and preferential loans. The script of *Marcia nuziale* is episodic, with material drawn from contemporary newspaper reports, and it was clearly aimed at exposing the contradictions and at times the hypocrisy of the institution of marriage. Permission to start shooting was refused. Suso Cecchi d'Amico, who co-scripted the film with Visconti, observes that the Censorship Office considered it as tantamount to a 'manifesto for divorce'. As a result Gualino took the decision to abandon the project, delivering the message to her and Visconti 'through gritted teeth'.[14] The chronology of subsequent events is important because it enables us to understand the cultural and political context within which the producer–director relationship operated. Submission of the script of *Marcia nuziale* is dated 7 March 1952 in the ACS file. The timing could hardly have been less opportune. On 28 February 1952 the Minister for Culture Giulio Andreotti, whose ministry oversaw the Censorship Office, had launched a public attack on the recent film *Umberto D*, directed by Vittorio De Sica, which tells the story of a retired schoolteacher struggling against poverty and social indifference to his plight. The content of Andreotti's attack on De Sica, published in *Libertas*, the organ of the ruling Christian Democrat party, was revealing, to say the least. He wrote, 'De Sica is an international director, and if the world believes that the Italy he shows [in his films] is the real Italy of today, he will have done his country a great disservice.'[15]

These arguments bear close resemblance to the detailed judgement on the script of *Marcia nuziale*, which states that the entire film is 'intrinsically immoral', and replete with 'far too many real-life stories being made by so-called leftist directors intent on creating scandal'. Viewed together, the comments make clear that the independence of film-making was itself under threat, with particular directors singled out for attack. More generally, the Cold War climate of the early 1950s resulted in a whole range of film-making ventures being vetoed by the ruling Christian Democrat government.[16] Nevertheless, Gualino appeared utterly resolved to continue his collaboration with Visconti. Cecchi d'Amico recalls he suggested that 'if we [Cecchi d'Amico and Visconti] could speedily pull together a suitable alternative proposal, Gualino promised to authorise its production forthwith'.[17] Cecchi d'Amico and Visconti duly identified *Senso*, a short story by Arrigo Boito first published in 1891 and, true to his word, Gualino sanctioned the production of *Senso*, which began shooting the following year, in September 1953.

Ahead of shooting, the papers for *Senso* were presented and duly passed by the Censorship Office. The subject matter was clearly perceived to be less controversial than the contemporary narrative of *Marcia nuziale*. The film recounts the love affair between Livia, a Venetian noblewoman, and Franz, an army officer, played out during the Austrian occupation of Venice in the 1860s, the period of the Risorgimento in which Italy struggled to gain its independence. Through the character of Franz, the film expresses a deep cynicism, emphasizing the needless destruction of war; as such it offers a perspective that does little to glorify what was traditionally presented as a period of great Italian patriotism leading towards the Unification of 1870. In this sense the film was in fact decidedly controversial, and received very mixed reactions when it was premiered. The quality of those working behind the camera was exceptional. It included Francesco Rosi and Franco Zeffirelli as aides to the director, cinematographer Giuseppe Rotunno and costume designer Piero Tosi, all of whom went on to establish major reputations within the industry. The level of expertise is particularly apparent in the scenes at the opera house, a rich and visually stunning opening sequence, which distils beautifully the political and historical thrust of the film, depicting the Austrian officers (in the stalls) and rebel Italian nationalists (in the gods) watching a performance of *Il trovatore* by Giuseppe Verdi, the composer closely associated with the nationalist cause. Gualino, on seeing the early stills from the film, is recorded as asserting, 'this is not a film, it is a work of art'.[18] The work of art was, however, to cost Lux very dear, as we can see how its budget eventually far outstripped the earlier project (Figure 6.1).

The papers for *Marcia nuziale* proposed a budget of 222,000,000 lire which was to be shared between the Italian Lux Film and its French sister company Lux CCF. Lux was instead the sole producer of *Senso*. The original archive budget proposal of 529,478,000 lire (termed *preventivo*) dated 22 August 1953 was revised, and the final account of actual costs incurred (termed *consuntivo*) dated 11 March 1954 was 868,956,930 lire, showing how far costs had spiralled out of control. The production file also gives evidence of the astonishing scope of the shooting: Visconti sought absolute authenticity of costume and props, hiring everything from boots to flags purpose-made for the film. Location shooting, largely in Venice and Verona, was extensive; it included the hire of the Venice Opera House for three days, where the opening sequence was actually shot, as well as the now-vacant Scalera studios in Venice for much of the interior shooting. *Senso* is a film that boldly addresses questions of Italy's own mythology regarding the process of Unification, a creative tour-de-force of great visual and technical splendour surpassed perhaps only by Visconti's own achievement in *Il gattopardo/The Leopard* (1963).

Figure 6.1 Alida Valli as Livia and Farley Granger as Franz in *Senso* (1954). Courtesy of Photofest

With its literary origins and intense attention to the detail of set and costume design, the aesthetics of *Senso* correspond precisely to the Lux ethos of film-making. Materials showing the interaction between Lux and Visconti during the making of the film are not comprehensive, but they nevertheless offer valuable insight into their respective roles. Although the task of producer is formally entered in the credits as being carried out by Domenico Forges Davanzati (also listed as producer for the aborted project on *Marcia nuziale*), we can be clear that in the case of this film Lux did not apply its usual rules, mapped out earlier in the chapter, regarding financial responsibility for a production. Forges Davanzati did not set up and control the budget, nor did he retain ultimate responsibility when costs mounted. The key budget decisions were instead taken by the owner's son, Renato Gualino, whose name is on both sets of papers in the ACS file. The first application for government monies is signed by him, and explicitly states that all other costs for *Senso* 'will be met from our own resources'. As we have seen, by the time the final budget is lodged some six months later, Lux had incurred 'from its own resources' a bill that was ruinously high, and far in excess of the original estimation. In contrast, Visconti's papers show that he worked on decisions regarding the detail of shooting and editing with Riccardo Gualino to whom he refers in a later interview as 'the old Gualino, my producer, a really good man'.[19] They consist of three A4 pages, two typewritten and one handwritten with the explicit heading 'from the hand of Riccardo Gualino' ('di pugno avvocato Gualino').

Page one consists of Gualino's views on the use of voiceover, specifically the voice of the Countess Livia, at various points in the film. On page two, cuts requested by Gualino to a range of numbered scenes, 10 in all, are listed. As a number of versions of the script were developed it is difficult to identify precisely which scenes are referred to, save for the one Visconti terms 'the most important', the night-time walk of Livia and Franz through the alleyways of Venice. The director states that, in response to Gualino's suggestion to reduce this long sequence, he has developed a 'new version' which makes it 'about half its original length'. On all other counts it appears Visconti simply complies, acknowledging that overall the proposals will 'reduce the number of set changes required', thereby easing pressure on cast and crew and, in a comment that proves particularly ironic, that the cuts will serve to 'reduce costs'. Page three on the other hand reveals less harmonious exchanges. Gualino's handwritten suggestions, in note form, elicit equally brief responses from Visconti. To the producer's request to give attention again to the duration of the night-time walk, already mooted, Visconti responds 'I will not accept any further cuts to this'. To Gualino's terse request to 'review the shooting of Custoza', Visconti writes 'suggested', which might be amplified to convey the response, 'you are suggesting this, but I am unwilling to accept your suggestion'.

The Battle of Custoza took place in 1866, and was an early, humiliating defeat of the Italians by the Austrians who controlled Venice during the Risorgimento, the period which eventually concluded with the unification of Italy. It was an important part of what Visconti called his 'original plan' for the film, which he initially wished to entitle 'Custoza'. The battle scenes of Custoza were to form a major part of the grand narrative of the film, fundamentally linked to the individual narrative of the Italian countess and Austrian officer, the occupied and the occupier, a love affair that presents in distilled form the complex tensions of the era. In this respect the finished film shows how drastically the ambitions of the director were scaled down: the battle scenes eventually make up only 15 minutes of a film approximately two hours in duration.

The final version of the film was not, however, attributable solely to the efforts of the director and the producer. As Giovanni Cavallaro shows, there were at least three versions of the film script which was modified during shooting, and debates persisted about the title of the film, which shifted from 'Custoza' to 'Urugano d'estate/Summer Tempest' and finally back to the original plan to call it 'Senso'.[20] We can be clear nevertheless that while Renato Gualino signed off the original budget papers and the request for further funding support, it was his father Riccardo who followed closely, though in the end not closely enough, the film's progress during shooting, and finally stepped in to curtail production. *Senso* performed creditably at the national box-office, but it failed to secure major international distribution. It is only in more recent years that film-makers such as Martin Scorsese have prompted a re-evaluation of its qualities. In its time, as Carlo Ponti asserts, 'Visconti's film ruined Lux'.[21] It prompted the company's subsequent, complete withdrawal from the production field. However, to the question, 'To what extent was Lux crucial to the making of *Senso*?', one can surely answer that Gualino and Visconti were collaborators in bringing this remarkable film to the screen, at the same time each holding to their own particular vision of Italian film-making.

The making of *Rocco and His Brothers*: Producer and auteur

Senso was forged in a difficult political climate, and the same is true of *Rocco and His Brothers*. However, the detail of the acrimonious debate generated by *Rocco* differs from that of *Senso* in a number of ways. The film recounts the struggles of a Southern family transferring to the industrial North in the early years of Italy's economic boom. The idea of the script again emanated from a collaboration between Visconti and Cecchi d'Amico, the entire project proposal was approved by the Censorship Office and shooting began in Milan in February 1960. *Rocco* was in fact initially intended as a film to be produced by Vides, the production company owned by Franco Cristaldi, with whom Visconti had recently worked on *Le notti bianche/White Nights* (1957). Cristaldi's company first issued contracts for *Rocco*: the original contract of Alain Delon dated 3 November 1958 was with Vides, though on 28 February 1959 it transferred to Titanus. ACS documentation for the film also shows that Titanus paid Vides for rights to the *Rocco* script, which was thus already in development before Titanus took on the project. *Le notti bianche* is a low-budget, highly experimental production, shot entirely within a series of constructed sets at Cinecittà. It was funded primarily by Cinematografica Associati (abbreviated in the titles to CI.AS), a short-lived company that listed Franco Cristaldi, Luchino Visconti, Suso Cecchi d'Amico and Marcello Mastroianni (the film's male lead) as joint-partners; budget documents dated

19 January 1957 show that they each contributed the sum of 100,000 lire to set up this one-off venture. Why production of *Rocco* then shifted to Titanus is not entirely clear. Cristaldi records that it resulted from a bitter personal dispute between himself and Visconti.[22] At the same time, the question of funding may have played a part. Cristaldi was in the early stages of his career and the film may well, quite simply, have been too costly an undertaking for him to contemplate at this time. It is also fair to say that, once the full scope of the proposal became clear, perhaps only a well-established company with the industrial 'muscle' of Titanus could take it on (Figure 6.2).

If one compares the budgets, it is quite clear that the plans for *Le notti bianche* were on a much more modest scale than those envisaged for *Rocco*. For *Le notti bianche*, co-funded jointly by the Italian companies CI.AS and Vides, costs were 286,071,342 lire. *Rocco* was a Franco-Italian co-production by Titanus and Les Films Marceau that proposed initial expenditure of 533, 430,000 lire. Like *Senso*, *Rocco* was conceived as having a long location shoot, this time a six-week spell in Milan, with the Titanus studios in Rome to be used for interiors. ACS records do not present final budget figures for *Rocco*, but the remarkable crisis that came about late in the Milanese shooting schedule makes it certain that extra costs were incurred. In the first instance these events do not appear driven by central government, which

Figure 6.2 Annie Girardot as Nadia and Alain Delon as Rocco Parondi in *Rocco and His Brothers* (1960). Courtesy of Photofest

had, as already noted, given the film full approval. Filming of the death of the film's female lead, Nadia, due to be shot at a location on the outskirts of the city called the Idroscalo, was halted by the Milanese authorities on the grounds that 'the murder of a whore' (as some of the more vitriolic press accounts termed it) would present a negative image of the city. Gaetano Carancini's notes on the film encapsulate well the impact on cast and crew: 'the situation was incredibly dramatic because the entire cast and crew numbering 150 people were left high and dry, robbed of these final days to enable them to complete the schedule'.[23] Whatever the motivation of the local authority, the matter was raised and debated in Parliament. Visconti himself wrote open letters to the government and censorship issues dragged on, well beyond the film's premiere. Even though critics have given extensive coverage to these events,[24] the role of Goffredo Lombardo in the proceedings has been somewhat overlooked.

The film was completed and accepted for its first public viewing at the Venice Film Festival in September 1960. After further filming in Rome, the cast and production team had transferred to Lake Fogliano, south of Rome, where they shot the sequence of Nadia's death without changes, thereby conceding nothing to the pressures exerted on the entire team. What is more, for the Festival presentation, Lombardo took the quite exceptional step of supporting its bid for an award (and, one can surmise fairly, for its more general reception) by circulating a booklet to all the major figures attending the festival, including the jury, which set out the remarkable history of the making of the film. *Rocco* did not win the Grand Jury Prize, in itself a source of further controversy, but the booklet contains crucial evidence of the part the producer played in the film's fortunes. Lombardo's own authored entry, entitled 'Dovevo farlo', may fairly be termed an act of faith in that it was published while the public debates continued, and well before the enormous commercial success of the film became manifest.[25] The title of Lombardo's article translates literally as, 'I had to make this film.' With the very hostile climate in mind, the phrase surely takes on further meaning conveyed by the statement, 'this was a film that I was committed to, that I believed I had to see through to the very end'. Carancini's aforementioned account of the final stages of the film-making makes clear that the ensuing censorship battle had put the whole project in jeopardy. The threat that it could not be finished, and/or would never be given the final government approval necessary to reach the screen (the so-called *nulla osta*) constituted a very great risk for all involved, but especially for the finances of Titanus. From the profile of the industry presented earlier in the chapter, we can be clear that this was not a production framework where *any* company could sustain the losses that the collapse of a venture such as *Rocco* would engender.

The efforts of Lombardo to promote *Rocco* did not conclude here. The film was screened on the last night of the Festival and, while participants awaited the jury's decision, Titanus organized an off-shore celebration on a luxury yacht at the Lido, hosted jointly by Lombardo and Visconti and attended by all major figures in the cast, including Alain Delon, Annie Girardot, Renato Salvatori and Claudia Cardinale. The event can surely be read as both a bid to secure the main Festival prize and, additionally, a show of solidarity against establishment intrusion into the film-making process. Despite the outcome on the following day, when the jury failed to award *Rocco* the main Festival prize, Lombardo appeared undaunted. He organized another lavish post-screening event for the following month on 14 October, when the film had its commercial premiere in Milan. John Foot views this as an ill-advised gesture 'designed to provoke further intervention of the censor'.[26] Alternatively one could argue that, by demonstrating so publicly his support for the film, Lombardo was effectively challenging the authorities to respond in kind, obliging them to reflect on the wisdom of making an equally open attack on a film studio and its owner who at that time played such an important role in the national industry.

The *Rocco* debate reverberated also on the international stage. The film was first screened at the London Film Festival in November 1960. In early 1961, *Films and Filming* dedicated an entire issue to Italian cinema, and chose Lombardo as their 'personality of the month', with the producer's photo and an accompanying full-page report drawing the conclusion that as a result of the *Rocco* saga, 'Lombardo has become a martyr in the cause of freedom of Italian cinema'.[27] For the film's commercial premiere in Britain on 14 September later that year, Titanus produced a press book full of information about the making of the film, its stars and what might be termed another 'declaration of faith' by Lombardo where he speaks of Rocco as 'the first film I entrusted to the direction of Luchino Visconti, a film which I decided to produce personally. [It is] the fruit of a fervent and intense understanding between myself and this brilliant director'. One year on from Venice, it is clear that Lombardo continued to figure prominently in debates surrounding the film, unstinting in his support.

As with *Senso*, *Rocco* remains a major film in the canon of Italian film-making: unlike *Senso*, it was a national and international success, greatly enhancing the reputation of the company and of the industry in general at all levels, and preparing the way for the second great collaboration of Lombardo and Visconti, *The Leopard*. Subsequent film history shows that by the early 1960s, Lux and Titanus were no longer the key production companies in the national industry. Riccardo Gualino died in 1964, but by then in any case the company worked purely in the distribution sector. The productions *Sodom and Gomorrah* (Robert Aldrich, 1962) and *The Leopard* effectively bankrupted Titanus, but despite this, as the data in the early part of the chapter has shown, their central place in Italian production history remains unchallenged.

Conclusion

The stated aim of the chapter was to assess the role of two leading Italian producers. As such it forms part of the perspective fostered by the 'new film history' which seeks to uncover evidence of the 'distinctive voices' contributing to the production of a film, and to 'locate those which were most influential'.[28] We have seen that Riccardo Gualino and Goffredo Lombardo were two very different personalities, heading production companies with radically different structures. This is in keeping with the broadly unstructured, artisanal nature of Italian film-making identified within the chapter. Though in many ways exceptional in their details, these case studies give focus to general questions of authorship in Italian cinema and beyond: one might usefully consider also the contribution of producer Franco Cristaldi's company Vides to the directorial career of Francesco Rosi in the 1960s, the collaboration between Pier Paolo Pasolini and Arco Film, led by Alfredo Bini and, potentially, many other producer–director relationships in the domain of European cinema, so long conceived as purely auteur-led. Gaps inevitably remain in the scenario presented in this chapter, as decisions on production details are not always faithfully recorded. However, the evidence here nevertheless substantiates the conclusion that the 'voices' of Riccardo Gualino and Goffredo Lombardo were important to the case studies analysed, to the film-making of a major auteur, Luchino Visconti, and to the Italian film industry in general. This surely validates the importance of revising notions of 'authorship' in the creation of a film. What this chapter has shown may be rightly termed a process of successful collaboration between producer and auteur-director, who jointly negotiated a successful route through the artistic, commercial and political challenges of this exceptional period of Italian film-making.

Archive sources

1) Production files in the Archivio Centrale dello Stato (ACS), Rome
Marcia nuziale, Box 50, file CF1368
Senso Box 93, file CF1794
Le notti bianche Box 172, file CF2598
Rocco e i suoi fratelli Box 263, file CF3282
2) Film files in the Archivio Visconti, Istituto Gramsci, Rome Series 7, Cinema
Marcia Nuziale UA21
Senso UA 24
Le notti bianche UA25
Rocco e i suoi fratelli UA26

Notes

1 Peter Bondanella, *Italian Cinema from Neorealism to the Present* (New York: Continuum, 1983), vi.
2 Mira Liehm, *Passion and Defiance: Film in Italy from 1942 to the Present* (Berkeley, Los Angeles and London: University of California Press, 1984), 151–59, 218–47.
3 Jill Forbes and Sarah Street, *European Cinema: An Introduction* (Basingstoke: Palgrave MacMillan, 2000), 38.
4 James Chapman, Mark Glancy, and Sue Harper (eds), *The New Film History: Sources, Methods, Approaches* (Basingstoke: Palgrave MacMillan, 2007), 69.
5 Two main archives are used: the production files lodged at the Archivio Centrale dello Stato, Rome (henceforth ACS) and personal papers of Luchino Visconti, termed the Archivio Visconti, lodged at the Istituto Gramsci, Rome. Archive references for individual files are listed earlier. All budget details cited from these files are in Italian lire.

6   The chapter draws on Italian-language histories of Lux and Titanus, which mix factual information and the personal recollections of a wide range of industry professionals: Guido Barlozzetti, *Modi di produzione del cinema italiano: la Titanus* (Ancona: Di Giacomo, 1980), Aldo Bernardini and Vittorio Martinelli, *La storia di Titanus: tutti i film* (Milan: Coliseum, 1986), and Alberto Farassino, *Lux Film* (Pesaro: Fondazione Pesaro/Il Castoro, 2000). In addition, I have drawn on the personal testimonies collected in Franca Faldini and Goffredo Fofi, *L'avventurosa storia del cinema italiano raccontata dai suoi protagonisti* (Milan: Feltrinelli, 1981) and the individual recollections of Visconti's creative collaborator in Suso Cecchi d'Amico, *Storie di cinema (e d'altro) raccontate a Margherita d'Amico* (Milan: Bompiani, 2002). Where possible, I have cited additional sources in order to supplement these individual, inevitably partly subjective, accounts. English-language versions of the material are not available, and all translations are my own.

7   Paolo Uccello, 'Industrial Equipment', *Unitalia*, 5:2 (December 1954): 54.

8   Lorenzo Quaglietti, *Il cinema italiano del dopoguerra* (Pesaro: Mostra del Cinema, 1974), 47–8.

9   Aldo Bernardini, *Le imprese di produzione* (Rome: Anica, 2000), xii.

10   Janet Staiger, 'The Hollywood Mode of Production', in *The Classical Hollywood Cinema: Film Style and Mode of Production to 1960*, ed. David Bordwell, Janet Staiger, and Kirstin Thompson (London and New York: Routledge 1960), 330.

11   Farassino, *Lux Film*, 82.

12   Bernardini and Martinelli, *La storia di Titanus*, 143–45.

13   Bernardini and Martinelli, *La storia di Titanus*, 41.

14   Cecchi d'Amico, *Storie di cinema*, 105.

15   Giulio Andreotti, 'Piaghe sociali e necessità di redenzione', in Quaglietti, *Storia del cinema*, 159.

16   For a fuller account of this subject, see David Forgacs and Stephen Gundle, *Mass Culture and Italian Society from Fascism to the Cold War* (Bloomingfield: Indiana University Press, 2007).

17   Cecchi d'Amico, *Storie di cinema*, 106.

18   Ponti, quoted in Farassino, *Lux Film*, 118.

19   Jacques Doniol-Valcoze and Jean Domarchi, 'Entretien avec Luchino Visconti', *Cahiers du Cinema* XVI: 93 (March 1959): 10.

20   Luchino Visconti, *Senso*, ed. Giovanni Cavallaro (Bologna: Cappelli, 1960), 58.

21   Ponti, quoted in Farassino, *Lux Film*, 118.

22   Cristaldi, quoted in Faldini and Fofi, *L'avventurosa storia*, 27.

23   Luchino Visconti, *Rocco e i suoi fratelli*, ed. Guido Aristarco and Gaetano Carancini (Florence: Cappelli, 1960), 248.

24   See especially the detailed account in John Foot, 'Luchino Visconti's *Rocco e i suoi fratelli*: Censorship and the Left in Italy 1960–1961', in *Reflexivity: Critical Themes in the Italian Cultural Tradition*, ed. Prue Shaw and John Took (Longo: Ravenna, 2000), 9–36.

25   Goffredo Lombardo, 'Dovevo farlo', in Visconti, *Rocco e i suoi fratelli*, 68–70.

26   Foot, 'Luchino Visconti's *Rocco e i suoi fratelli*', 16.

27   Anon, 'Goffredo Lombardo: Paying His Debts', *Films and Filming* 7:4 (January 1961): 5.

28   Chapman, Glancy, and Harper (eds.), *New Film History*, 70.

7

The Australian Screen Producer in Transition

Mark David Ryan, Ben Goldsmith,
Stuart Cunningham and Deb Verhoeven

… the term 'producer' covers a broad range of roles. It includes both entrepreneurs and employees. It spans the hands-on role of the line producer and the financing role of the executive producer. It extends across a wide variety of screen-based media, from film and television to corporate videos, computer games and new media.[1]

The role of the screen producer is ramifying. Not only are there numerous producer categories, but the screen producer function is also found on a continuum across film, television, advertising, corporate video and the burgeoning digital media sector. In recent years, fundamental changes to distribution and consumption practices and technologies should have had a correlate impact on screen production practices and on the role of existing screen producers. At the same time, new and recent producers are learning and practising their craft in a field that has already been transformed by digitization and media convergence. Our analysis of the work, experience and outlook of screen producers in this chapter is based on data collected in the Australian Screen Producer Survey (ASPS), a nationwide survey conducted by the ARC Centre of Excellence for Creative Industries and Innovation, the media marketing firm Bergent Research and the Centre for Screen Business at the Australian Film, Television and Radio School (AFTRS) in 2008/2009 and 2011.[2] We analyse the results to better understand the practice of screen production in a period of industry transition, and to recognize the persistence of established production cultures that serve to distinguish different industry sectors.

Theoretical background

The ASPS project was initiated in 2008 to address a deficit in screen producer research which has typically relied on either analysing *observed* workflows and industry cultures or on personally *experienced* (e.g. 'knowledge in practice', 'participant observation') approaches. Instead, the ASPS is built on reported data gathered from a broad sample of producers in order to map the culture and motivations of this influential sector of the Australian screen industries. Three strands of academic work are of particular relevance here: studies of creative labour and work in the media industries; production studies; and creative industries research.

In his book *Media Work*, Mark Deuze identifies four elements that 'tend to get mixed up' in analyses of what is involved in work in media industries: content, connectivity, creativity and commerce.[3] The producer is 'a uniquely "in between" figure' who spans and mediates all four of these elements through their finance, creative and practical production work.[4] While Deuze's focus is not restricted to screen producers, his arguments around the precariousness of media work (defined as 'the financial and existential insecurity arising from the flexibilization of labor'[5]), the management of creativity and media convergence are highly relevant to our study. There are many other contributions to critical analysis of precarious media work; the 'consistent findings' of which, Mark Banks and David Hesmondhalgh say, include that

> creative work is project-based and irregular, contracts tend to be short-term, and there is little job protection; that there is a predominance of self-employed or freelance workers; that career prospects are uncertain and often foreshortened; that earnings are usually slim and unequally distributed, and that insurance, health protection and pension benefits are limited; that creatives are younger than other workers, and tend to hold second or multiple jobs; and that women, ethnic and other minorities are under-represented and disadvantaged in creative employment. All in all, there is an oversupply of labor to the creative industries with much of it working for free or on subsistence wages.[6]

The tendency to paint a particularly bleak picture of media labour is emphasized by some writers' focus on 'below the line' media workers, that is, those with less industrial power than producers.[7] David Lee, in his work on British independent television production, describes this as a focus on '"ordinary" cultural workers'.[8] This work characterizes media labour as primarily project based, freelance and insecure. But the 'uniquely in-between' producer figure could hardly be described as 'ordinary' given the combined creative and managerial roles they often occupy. Producers, as 'above-the-line' workers, are not as easily substitutable as below-the-line workers, particularly, for example, on runaway or footloose projects that 'destination shop' around the world to take advantage of tax incentives or exchange rate differentials in order to lower production costs. What can also distinguish the attitudes of the producer cohort (and other key creative roles) from 'ordinary' media workers is their adherence to the notion of 'good work' that creative labour represents in the modern economy and the undeniable attraction of (relatively) autonomous labour that it promises.[9]

Closely related to work on cultural labour is a contemporary field that has come to be known as 'production studies'. Emerging from cultural studies first in the work of John Thornton Caldwell on film and video production workers in Los Angeles, production studies adopts ethnographic methods to examine the 'cultural practices and belief systems' and 'industrial reflexivity' of media workers.[10] In common with some of the work on media labour discussed earlier, production studies tend to focus on 'below-the-line' workers. This is made explicit in the title of Vicki Mayer's book *Below the Line: Producers and Production Studies in the New Television Economy.*[11] Mayer broadens the definition of 'television producer' to include workers whose labour is essential to television production and whose identities are constructed in and through media work, but who are largely invisible in both academic and industry discourse. Through case studies of television set assemblers in Brazil, soft-core cameramen at the annual New Orleans Mardi Gras, casters or talent scouts for reality television shows and volunteer advocates and regulators of local cable television in America, Mayer deconstructs academic deployments of (and limits on) the terms 'creative', 'professional' and 'producer'. Rather than referring to those in creative, managerial or financial control, Mayer uses 'producer' in a deliberately broad sense to mean, essentially, anyone 'whose labor, however small, contributes to [television] production'.[12] However, in pushing a 'laborist' line of approach this far, Mayer risks losing the distinctions between the levels of risk and precariousness carried by the employee or contracted worker and those carried by those who are responsible for leading and/or coordinating production projects. In order to specifically address these distinctions, the ASPS defines a producer as 'someone who manages the financial, creative, technical and/or logistical challenges of making screen content'.[13]

The third area of relevant scholarship is creative industries research. The ASPS was commissioned by the ARC Centre of Excellence for Creative Industries and Innovation (CCI), whose focus is on an enterprise or entrepreneurial approach to cultural and media production and consumption with an emphasis on the transformations that digital affordance effects in the field. The CCI has conducted theoretical work on structural change in cultural and media markets,[14] strategies of 'born digital' games firms under conditions of rapid global change[15] and the skills needs and gaps in Australia's digital games industry.[16] The CCI has also worked extensively with national statistics, including trends in the relation between the broad creative class and key creative roles such as the producer.[17] Analysis of this kind has shown that, for example, while there had been record growth in internal migration into Queensland and its capital, Brisbane, and corresponding growth in the professional and creative workforces, there has not been a commensurate increase in producer and key creative capacity in the region.[18] With the ASPS, the CCI has engaged directly in analysing the Australian screen producer in a period of industrial transition.

Surveying the producer

The ASPS arose from the observation that very little independent scholarly research focused on the screen producer, and that the field of producer studies needed more systematic empirical grounding across all subfields of screen production (not only film and television but also commercial/corporate and new media/digital). A targeted national survey was deemed necessary to avoid 'glossing over the important role played by producers, owing to the gap between "top-down" analyses that scope the industry at the sectoral level and "bottom up" analyses that focus on the work lives of creative practitioners'.[19] The surveys provided the opportunity to interrogate several issues around the culture of producing in Australia from the perspective of producers themselves. These included the relationship between a producer's experience and education, and their sources of project funding; the levels of business expertise in the different sectors; the impacts of media convergence, digitization and industry change; and most recently, the transitional pathways of established media producers into digital media production. The objective was to produce findings that would have value for policy makers and industry bodies, as well as giving screen producers themselves a clearer picture of their own professional context. The period between the two surveys was dynamic. Changes in the policy environment included the establishment of a new national funding agency and the introduction of new financing mechanisms, in particular the Australian Screen Production Incentive (which includes a Producer Offset). The finance environment was also characterized by fluctuations in the value of the Australian dollar, and the overall industry ecology was marked by significant changes to production and consumption technologies.

The first ASPS, conducted between November 2008 and June 2009, established a comprehensive list of over 4,000 individuals with at least one producer credit – a surprisingly large number. Focus groups in Melbourne and Sydney were consulted to ensure that the survey questions were acceptably framed. A senior statistician was consulted to verify the project methodology. A random sample of 2,000 was then invited by e-mail to participate in the ASPS, with the incentive of a prize draw (five iPods were won by participating producers). Approximately 12 per cent of invitees (n = 227) completed the online survey. The ASPS established baseline statistics on the demographics of the producer cohort, as well as data on their industry experience, education, professional development and funding sources for their work. Producers' sentiments towards their work and profession were also assessed. Producers were divided into one of four sectors – television, film, commercial/corporate and new media (referred to as digital media in 2011 survey) – based on respondents' self-identification of which sector was their main income source. A key finding of the first survey was that producers in each of these sectors demonstrated distinctive attitudes, motivations and backgrounds.

A second ASPS was conducted between November and December 2011 and emulated the methodology of the first survey to produce a reliable basis for comparison. An updated database of approximately 5,000 screen producers was prepared. A focus group with a small representative sample of film, television, digital media and commercial producers was held in Melbourne to develop and refine the original questionnaire in light of more recent industry practices and vocabularies. In order to increase the response rate from the first survey, a cash prize of $2,000 was offered, with the winner selected from randomized results of a voluntary game of skill. Every twentieth participant also received a free cinema ticket. A modified stratified sample method was used to ensure sampling of an adequate, diverse range of screen producers. E-mails soliciting participation were sent to 4,872 producers, with an 8 per cent overall response rate (n = 407). Due in part to the larger initial population and in part to the revised approach to sampling, this produced an 80 per cent increase over the 2008 response rate (n = 227). Despite the adjusted sampling method, the spread of film, television and commercial producers in the second ASPS was similar to that in the first; however, there was a large increase in the number who identified as digital producers (from 8 per cent of the total in 2008 to 14 per cent in 2011), which may be explained by the growth in this sector over the period. The 2011 ASPS also received significantly more responses from producers in all sectors aged 20–24, and from television producers aged 35–39. The second ASPS asked the same questions as the first, but several questions were added: on international partnerships, tax incentives, levels of debt and attitudes to government support and industry leadership.

Television producers

Producers who identified television as their main source of income made up the largest group in both ASPSs: 47 per cent of respondents in 2008, and 37 per cent in 2011 (Figure 7.1). Across the two surveys there is surprising consistency in this category (particularly given fluctuations in the national television production slate in this period). In both ASPSs, 56 per cent of television producers were men, and the cohort overall averaged 17 years of experience in the industry. Given the option of self-identifying in one of ten producer roles,[20] in 2011, none identified as a digital producer, indicating that this is not a common job title in television, and/or that at this stage of the transition to digital, such a role is typically outsourced. In terms of the types of content produced, the majority of television producers in both ASPSs worked in multiple genres, but documentary was the most common genre in 2008 and 2011, nominated by 66 per cent in both surveys.

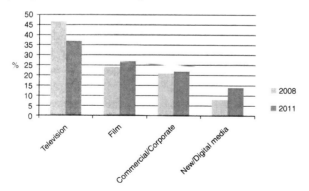

Figure 7.1 Graph showing responses to the Australian screen producers survey question: Which one of these industries is your main source of income?

Some differences between the surveys were apparent. In the second ASPS, television producers were the oldest sector on average, with 57 per cent aged 50 or over compared to 47 per cent in 2008. The 'aging' of producers in this sector (or put another way, the failure of younger producers to enter this sector) may vindicate the poor performance expectations held by TV producers in the earlier survey (only 4 per cent were optimistic about growth). The overall television production sector (by number of projects, total dollar value of production and hours produced) shrank during the period under study. However, other explanations were provided by those surveyed. For one producer the key barrier to entry lay with the design of funding schemes; 'Too much reliance on Government funding by very experienced companies means it is too hard for people making their first or second production.' Another provided commentary on how the aging of the sector underlined a sense of precariousness: 'Age is an issue. As you get older, people are more inclined to go with younger people who are less expensive to employ.' The poor performance of the national television slate may also explain other distinctions between the two survey results. For example, one significant difference between the two ASPSs came in response to the question posed to all producers: 'In which sector have you previously produced?' In 2008, 68 per cent of all producers had previously worked in television. In 2011, this figure had dropped to 60 per cent.

In terms of their working arrangements, the most significant change among television producers between the two surveys was the proportion of those employed on a permanent, full-time basis: 29 per cent in 2008, falling to 17 per cent in 2011. The reason for this may perhaps be, at least in part, the increasing tendency for the major networks to outsource production to independent companies, although this is contradicted somewhat by the proportion of television producers working directly for the largest media companies (i.e. those with over 200 employees, likely to be the major networks), which increased from 29 per cent in 2008 to 46 per cent in 2011. Taken at face value, and given that television producers constitute the largest grouping in both ASPSs, these statistics might appear to tell us something about the precariousness of employment conditions among screen producers in general. As we will discuss later, however, the shift away from permanent full-time employment is not exactly mirrored in the other sectors. In 2011, television producers were least likely to have another job either within or outside the industry, with only 27 per cent reporting additional employment, compared with 55 per cent of film producers, 48 per cent of digital media producers and 42 per cent of commercial producers.

The second survey found TV producers to be the most negative about their own future role, with the highest percentage of all sectors nominating to retire (14 per cent) and the lowest number believing they will be in the same industry doing better (only 54 per cent) over the next three years. An overall sentiment index calculated across several survey questions revealed TV producers to be the least optimistic sector surveyed (see Figure 7.2). If they have any optimism, it is reserved for the belief that others will achieve success before they do (a negative sentiment that is revealed across the survey as more likely to rise with age).

Producer sectors	Calculated score (overall sentiment out of 100)
TV	36
Commercials	37
Film	46
Digital media	54
TOTAL	41

Figure 7.2　Producer sentiment index by sector

Film producers

Film producers were remarkably constant as a distinct industry cohort across the two surveys. Producers whose main source of income was from work in film made up a quarter of respondents in both ASPSs (24 per cent in 2008, 27 per cent in 2011) (Figure 7.1). Almost half in both 2008 and 2011 were aged over 50 (43 per cent in 2008, 46 per cent in 2011), with an average age of 47. The gender balance was consistent, with 53 per cent male in 2008 and 54 per cent in 2011. Most film producers worked in multiple genres, although drama was decisively the principal genre in both surveys (78 per cent in 2008, 81 per cent in 2011). Among all respondents, film producers were more likely to run their own company either as an employer or sole trader (75 per cent in 2008, 65 per cent in 2011), with the main difference in employment status being the rise in freelance employment (9 per cent in 2008 to 17 per cent in 2011). Film producers (consistently across both surveys) were more highly educated but reported the least security of employment and steady income. Despite this strong sense of precariousness, they were also (again consistently across surveys) the most positive about their future prospects, with three-quarters believing they would be working in the same industry in 10 years' time and doing better (perhaps because they couldn't do worse?). Reinforcing this positive outlook, the sentiment index recorded film producers as the most optimistic in terms of their personal prospects over the next 3–10 years (although not in the shorter term of 12–24 months).

In part this optimism can be explained by the low value placed by film producers on financial success. Neither was being well known to the public a motivator for film producers. Instead, their prime incentive is satisfying creative vision. However, the area of motivation did produce one of the few distinctions between the first and second survey of film producers. Winning the respect of peers leapt from 4 per cent in 2008 to 31 per cent in 2011 ('drives me a lot'). Of the four producer groups, film producers were most likely to own a share of their work (97 per cent owned at least 1 per cent of the rights, compared with 86 per cent of digital, 69 per cent of television and 47 per cent of commercial producers). Film producers were also most likely to own at least a 50 per cent share in their work (67 per cent, compared with 52 per cent digital, 47 per cent television and 26 per cent commercial producers). And yet film producers also indicated their frustrations with financial settings and their impact on business sustainability: 'The regulatory and tax incentive environment for private investment in films has become so prohibitive and difficult that it is almost impossible to attract reasonable amounts of private investment to sustain it.' They also commented: 'The biggest problem is business sustainability. Working on low budget films with low fees and overheads and how time-consuming it is to apply for development funds when trying to keep the momentum going on the projects.'

Commercial/corporate producers

The proportion of commercial/corporate producers (hereafter 'commercial') also remained steady across the two ASPSs: 21 per cent in 2008, 22 per cent in 2011. Commercial producers were on average slightly younger than their counterparts in television and film, with a substantial proportion aged under 40 (44 per cent in 2008, 40 per cent in 2011). Among all respondents, commercial producers were most likely to have worked in multiple genres, with advertising (85 per cent in 2008, 74 per cent in 2011) and corporate communications (64 per cent in 2008, 70 per cent in 2011) being the main genres of production. Commercial producers were more likely to be freelancers than their counterparts (21 per cent in 2008, 25 per cent in 2011), although in both ASPSs most ran their own company either as an employer or sole trader (64 per cent in 2008, 56 per cent in 2011).

A very considerable difference between the 2008 and 2011 cohorts of commercial producers is that while the gender balance of commercial producers in the 2008 ASPS was consistent with the overall average (53 per cent male, 47 per cent female), there was a significant disparity in 2011, in which 64 per cent of respondents were male and 36 per cent female (see Figure 7.3). The sharp decline of women's participation in this sector warrants further investigation.

Significantly, in the 2008 ASPS, commercial producers were already more engaged with new media production than their counterparts in film and television. In 2008, more producers reported either having previously produced new media content (40 per cent, compared with 23 per cent of television and 25 per cent of film producers) or to be currently producing new media content at the time of the ASPS (40 per cent, compared with 15 per cent of television and 11 per cent of film producers). In this regard commercial producers were an industry bellwether. Taken together, the proportion of traditional media producers (commercial, film and TV) with digital production experience rose significantly between the two ASPSs. In 2008, 28 per cent of traditional media producers stated that they had 'previously

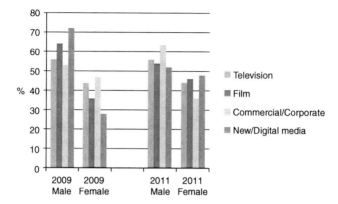

Figure 7.3 Graph comparing gender profiles of 2009 and 2011 ASPS cohorts

produced' digital content. In 2011, this figure rose to 39 per cent. In 2008, 20 per cent of traditional media producers were producing digital content at the time of the ASPS. By 2011, that figure rose to 32 per cent.

Other indicators point to the growing importance of digital media production. Growth was also registered in the time spent by all producers in digital production (up from 9 per cent to 16 per cent) and in the proportion who rated digital production 'most important to me' (up from 9 per cent to 13 per cent). These figures are broadly in line with the overall rise in the proportion of producers earning their principal source of income from digital (up from 8 per cent to 14 per cent). Most interestingly, however, the proportion of traditional producers *intending* to produce digital content in the future rose only marginally over the two surveys, from 43 per cent in 2008 to 45 per cent in 2011. Coupled with the clear persistence of production cultures in the 'traditional' media sectors across the two surveys, this could indicate that traditional producers are outsourcing some digital work to a cohort of specialized digital media producers, rather than taking on this work themselves and transforming their practice as a result.

New media/digital producers

The proportion of new media (8 per cent in 2008) or digital producers (14 per cent in 2011) increased substantially across the surveys, which may have been due to the increased digital media sample size in 2011. Regardless of the reasons, this cohort clearly formed a distinctive professional culture compared to other producer types. The highest proportion of women were working as digital producers in 2011 (48 per cent) (see Figure 7.3). What especially distinguishes this cohort of producers is its youth and relative inexperience. Fifty-one per cent were aged under 40 in 2008, and 46 per cent in 2011. The equivalent figures for traditional media producers were 26 per cent in 2008 and 28 per cent in 2011. Digital producers claimed an average of only ten years' experience in the industry (compared to 17 years for the other cohorts), although given the relatively recent emergence of digital media production, it was no surprise that these producers were less experienced than their counterparts.

Among the four producer groups, digital producers were more likely to be freelancing. While the proportion of freelancers increased across the board from 2008 to 2011, the largest jump was in digital media, where the figure rose from 6 per cent to 18 per cent. A considerably higher proportion of digital producers felt that it was easy to enter the industry than their traditional media counterparts – 40 per cent compared with 23 per cent of film, and 28 per cent of traditional media producers overall – although digital producers were also most likely to work in another industry in 2011 (36 per cent, compared with just 18 per cent of television, and 26 per cent of traditional media producers overall).

In terms of education and professional training, digital producers again differed from the other producer groups. While creative arts was by some distance the principal field in which all producers across both surveys reported having completed a course of study, in 2011 digital producers were much more likely than traditional producers to have completed degrees in information technology, education, management/commerce and natural and physical sciences. Digital producers were also more likely to have postgraduate qualifications. IT was considered by those with qualifications in that field to be most important in gaining their current position. The importance placed on IT suggests that these producers already know what a recent study of creative intensity across the British workforce concluded: 'creative talent has its greatest economic impact when working in tandem with ICT', while the combination of IT and creative labour is now clearly a 'distinctive feature' of the creative industries.[21] In both ASPSs, the majority of new media/digital producers were creating content for personal computers (72 per cent in 2008, 82 per cent in 2011), with a substantial proportion also producing for mobile devices (44 per cent in 2008, 57 per cent in 2011).

Further differences between digital and traditional producers were evident in the sources of project funding, ownership of intellectual property and levels of debt carried. Digital producers recorded the highest proportion of self-funding (28 per cent) of projects in 2011, and tended to own more projects outright – 38 per cent of digital producers reported owning 100 per cent of IP in their work, compared with just 22 per cent of traditional producers. Nearly three-quarters of digital producers carried less than $50,000 in debt, and only 2 per cent carried more than $250,000. The equivalent figures for traditional producers were 65 per cent with less than $50,000 debt, and 5 per cent with over $250,000.

In terms of sentiment and outlook, digital producers were considerably more optimistic than their peers. 81 per cent were confident about the potential for growth in their industry, compared with 55 per cent of film, 45 per cent of television and just 42 per cent of commercial producers. In fact, more digital producers expressed a positive outlook than their counterparts on every measure. On their own short-(12–24 months) and long-term prospects (3–10 years), 80 per cent and 84 per cent of digital producers expressed positive sentiments, compared with 68 per cent and 70 per cent of traditional producers. 64 per cent of digital producers expressed confidence in the positive short-term performance of their industry, compared with 53 per cent of traditional producers. While levels of confidence in the positive effects of state and federal governments' policies were low among all cohorts, digital producers were more optimistic than their peers. Similarly, when asked about their prospects of achieving their professional goals, digital producers were considerably more positive than their counterparts (38 per cent to 22 per cent). Digital producers also expressed greater confidence in the strength of industry leadership (32 per cent to 15 per cent).

Differences and consistency

The two surveys register strong continuity, but there were notable differences between 2008 and 2011:

- Average industry experience for all producers increased by five years.
- Participation in TV production fell from 68 per cent to 60 per cent.
- Strong growth in digital media projects in development and production.
- Reported revenue earned from digital media almost doubled in 2011.
- Responses suggest that this is a trend which is likely to continue.
- Fewer traditional producers (all sectors other than digital media) were permanent full-time employees.
- Traditional producers relied less on their industry financially and more on other incomes.
- Perception of earning a high income declined dramatically.
- Producers with a creative arts degree increased.
- Producers with a management background increased.

Most notable is the rise in digital production amongst producers in all segments. The percentage of film, TV and commercial/corporate producers who are currently producing, or have previously produced digital content increased exponentially from 48 per cent to 73 per cent. The proportion of producers who spent most time in digital rose from 9 per cent to 16 per cent. 'Most time spent in TV' fell from 43 per cent to 34 per cent. The proportion saying digital was 'most important to me' rose from 9 per cent to 13 per cent, although film also rose from 43 per cent to 47 per cent. TV was down from 40 per cent to 32 per cent.

Despite these evident differences, the 2011 results confirm the key original finding of distinct production cultures. While digitization has made an evident impact (more identify as digital producers and more nominate digital production as an area of future interest and employment), the 2011 findings remain consistent with the 2008 findings. There are also several common issues across cohorts. All producers identified the development of quality creative ideas as a primary concern; finding people to share critical knowledge; and a lack of confidence in their own essential producing skills such as dealing with the marketing and legal aspects of production. And yet one of the striking observations when comparing the surveys is the lack of convergence between producing cultures. While there are many commonalities, especially among television, film and commercial producers, there are also clear differences between the four producer groups.

Emerging themes

Precariousness, flexibility, the 'Portfolio Career'

The ASPSs provide insights into some of the principal concerns of the academic literature on media labour, particularly precariousness, the 'portfolio career' and flexible working conditions. The ASPSs demonstrate that conditions of precariousness are endemic to the sector, but producers are also in quite different positions than their below-the-line colleagues. Producers often play significant roles in the initiation, creative control and/or management of media projects. As project initiators, they create or facilitate work for other media professionals. Through the creative control they can exert over projects via, for example, the negotiation and control of rights, and contracting the project team and services, their decisions determine the conditions of other media workers.

In both surveys, a significant proportion of producers ran their own companies. Sixty-six per cent in 2008 and 48 per cent in 2011 were small businesses or microenterprises – firms with fewer than five employees. This is common in media industries around the world,[22] although critical studies of the management of media firms tend to focus on the largest firms rather than those that are typical[23] – which is also a reason why there is a strong focus on below-the-line employees. The ASPSs show that microenterprises were (by some margin) most common in film, with 78 per cent of film producers in 2008 and 85 per cent in 2011 working either as a sole trader or as a microenterprise employing between two and four people.

Other findings lend some support to arguments advanced in the media labour literature about precariousness and flexible employment conditions. While the numbers of producers identifying as freelancers were relatively low – 12 per cent in 2008 and 16 per cent in 2011 – so too were the numbers employed on a permanent full-time basis (16 per cent /11 per cent). In addition, 11 per cent of producers in 2008 and 9 per cent in 2011 were employed on either fixed-term, open-ended or project contracts. Overall, in 2008 only 3 per cent of respondents said that they had 'never' experienced flexible working arrangements, with 34 per cent saying that they did 'always' or 'most of the time'.[24] In 2011, the corresponding figures were 4 per cent and 57 per cent. 40 per cent of all producers in 2008 said they were 'very' or 'slightly' driven by flexible working arrangements, while in 2011, 66 per cent of traditional producers stated that flexible working arrangements drive them 'a lot' or 'a bit'.

During their careers, media workers are likely to have several employers, and to experience 'periods of salaried employment interspersed with contract employment, self-employment, and unemployment'.[25] Mark Deuze argues that 'people building their careers in the media…are typical examples' of the trend labelled by Charles Handy (1989) as the 'portfolio worklife'.[26] To some extent this is not new; the project-based character of much media production ensures that media workers are likely to be employed by or work with many different companies over their careers. While the concern of below-the-line media workers – particularly over the typicality in their industry of the 'portfolio' or 'boundaryless career' – is well documented,[27] Deuze acknowledges that 'many in the higher skilled knowledge-based areas of the labor market seem to prefer such precarious working conditions, associating this with greater individual autonomy, the acquisition of a wide variety of skills and experiences, and a reduced dependency on a single employer'.[28] This latter attitude appears to be borne out in the ASPSs. In response to the question, 'Why did you choose to work as a freelancer or run your own company?', 51 per cent of all respondents in 2008 and 55 per cent in 2011 answered 'greater freedom', with 'better quality of work' and 'better earning power' also scoring highly. This correlates with other attitudinal postures discussed later.

The ASPSs' findings on respondents' work outside media production lend further weight to the argument that portfolio careers are common in this industry. In 2008, 65 per cent of respondents had previously worked in another industry, with 31 per cent reporting that they were doing so at the time of taking the ASPS. In 2011, 27 per cent of all producers were working in another industry at the time of taking the survey, while a further 15 per cent had another job in the media in addition to their work as a producer. Interestingly, while in 2011 digital producers were more likely than their counterparts to be working in another industry, they were also the most optimistic about the prospects of their chosen field.

Outlook

Digital producers' optimism correlates to the perception of industry growth. More than 80 per cent of digital producers believed their industry would grow over the next three years. Digital and younger producers were most positive about their prospects of 'having a big hit' over the next three years. Given that digital producers tended to be younger and less experienced than their traditional media counterparts, and less indebted, their optimism could be the product of their relatively recent entry into the field. And yet this does not explain the fact that film producers – who on average were much older and more experienced – were most optimistic about their own long-term prospects, with 75 per cent seeing themselves working in the same industry in 2021 and doing better than they were in 2011, compared with 71 per cent of digital, 55 per cent of commercial and 54 per cent of television producers. Again, film producers had a high expectation of growth in their sector, with more than half predicting expansion over the next three years. Rapid generational leadership change in this sector may be harder to achieve due precisely to the extremely flexible nature of its firm structure and project-based production dynamics.

'Psychic income'

Another distinctive and related feature of the screen industry is the importance placed on non-monetary motivations and rewards. This 'psychic income' 'consists of the myriad intangible benefits that together compensate for the loss of financial income'.[29] In response to a series of questions on their principal motivations, 94 per cent in 2008 and 100 per cent in 2011 rated 'satisfying my creative vision' as their primary driver. Only 48 per cent in both ASPSs were either 'very driven' or 'slightly driven' by the prospect of 'making a lot of money'. Slightly larger proportions – 72 per cent in 2008, 78 per cent in 2011 – were either 'very driven' or 'slightly driven' by 'steady income stream', but in both surveys this rated lower than 'contributing to the art form' (77 per cent /78 per cent) and 'achieving critical success' (77 per cent /87 per cent). These results are also borne out in a major survey of AFTRS alumni conducted in 2011.[30] Producers place a lower emphasis on financial sustainability than on their pursuit of creative expression. As Cameron, Verhoeven and Court observe in their discussion of the first ASPS, 'On the one hand "psychic income" might be holding the industry back. On the other, it might be the very element holding it together.' That is, it may be a drawback (because it may make financially unsustainable businesses more likely) or a benefit (because it facilitates the initiation and production of projects that might be rejected as unviable if assessed on commercial grounds alone).[31]

The propensity of producers to take on projects that either may produce no or little income or may appear to have little chance of financial success is another reason for the levels of work outside the screen industry. Over the two surveys, producing has provided 67 per cent of television producers' income (64 per cent for commercial, 55 per cent new media/digital, 41 per cent film). As well as having the lowest proportion of income from producing, film producers had the highest proportion of income from other occupations (32 per cent, compared with 22 per cent for new media/digital, 15 per cent commercial, 14 per cent television), and the highest level of reliance on family support (6 per cent, compared with 3 per cent for new media /digital, 2 per cent commercial, 2 per cent television) and on private income (9 per cent, compared with 5 per cent for commercial, 3 per cent television, 2 per cent new media/digital). Television showed a classic employee skew in 'total personal income from producing' in the 2008 ASPS, composed of solid salary-wage earning. Film showed a classic arts skew, with a large proportion of unsustainably low-income earners (45 per cent earned less than $25,000 from producing in 2008) and a very small number of high-income earners (7 per cent earned over $150,000). This correlates with a strong sense of earnings foregone (opportunity cost), which is highest in film, and also with the finding on producers' motivation: the creative vision is more powerful than the money.

Geography

Not surprisingly, the majority of respondents in both surveys were based in the two most populous states, New South Wales (NSW) (46 per cent in 2008, 49 per cent in 2011) and Victoria (29 per cent in 2008, 26 per cent in 2011). The vast majority of these producers were based in either Sydney or Melbourne. In the 2011 ASPS, 60 per cent of television producers were based in NSW, reflecting the fact that all five free-to-air television networks, the largest pay-television provider and most pay-television channels are headquartered in Sydney. That said, it is worth noting that the figure of

60 per cent of television producers based in NSW is considerably higher than the last recorded total of commercial free-to-air television employees based there (42.6 per cent in 2006).[32] While there will undoubtedly have been change in the sector since 2006, this discrepancy is likely to remain, with higher ratios of technical and on-screen employees to producers in other locations due to the concentration of creative decision-making in Sydney (and, to a lesser extent, Melbourne). This is an intrinsic part of the screen ecology; geography underscores differences between above and below the line labour.

The landscape is somewhat different in new/digital media. In 2008, 39 per cent of new media producers were based in Melbourne, and only 33 per cent in Sydney. Although the figures shifted in 2011 to 34 per cent for each city, the prominence of Melbourne (and to a lesser extent Brisbane) in new/digital media is noteworthy. Melbourne has been the centre of computer game development in Australia since the early 1980s. In 2008, the Australian Bureau of Statistics produced a report on *Digital Game Development Services* which found that three-quarters of games development businesses then operating in Australia were in NSW, Victoria or Queensland.[33] Although most were based in Victoria (16), Queensland's firms were larger; 48.6 per cent of the total games development workforce was located in Queensland. In 2009, another report identified 62 game development and related companies, with 22 in Victoria, and 18 in Queensland.[34] Despite the closure of several major studios, most foreign-owned, between 2008 and 2011, several major developers remain based in Melbourne, including EA Games' Firemonkeys, whose game *Real Racing 3* was showcased at the iPhone 5 and iPad Mini global launch in 2012. The resilience of game production in Melbourne is due in part to the policies of successive state governments – at least until recently – which have included subsidizing access to software development kits (SDKs), providing funding to establish the national headquarters of the Game Developers Association of Australia in Melbourne and to build a motion capture laboratory, as well as investing in game development and marketing.

Conclusion

The Australian Screen Producer Surveys paint a multi-hued picture of contemporary screen producers in a specific national market. The main findings of the two ASPSs tell two stories. First, digitization and media convergence continue to impact on production practices and outlooks, and digital production is increasingly important to all producers. The surveys demonstrate that cross-media mobility is not simply a characteristic of media consumption; it is also a fact of life in production. And yet, while digitization and the popularity of new distribution platforms have had a range of impacts on screen production, including facilitating the emergence of a distinct cohort of digital producers, change or transition has been unevenly felt and experienced across the various production sectors. For example, commercial producers showed considerably higher rates of involvement in digital production than their counterparts in film and television.

Second, we can clearly identify the persistence of different production cultures, particularly between traditional and digital producers, but also among the traditional production sectors of television, film and commercial. While there is evidence of increased engagement by traditional producers in digital projects, we are not (yet) seeing correlated changes between the previous and current practices of these culturally discrete cohorts. Despite the willingness of proven producers to engage in emerging online, transmedia and cross-media production, distinct production cultures persist.

The ASPSs set out to explore the practices, attitudes and aspirations of producers as they adjust to working in an increasingly convergent digital media marketplace. The first survey confirmed some assumptions about production cultures and producers' attitudes, but also provided a range of new insights. The second survey enabled us to compare the impact of digitization and media convergence change over time, and to appreciate the continuities of producer practice in a period of unsettling technological change.

Notes

1   Allan Cameron, Deb Verhoeven and David Court, 'Above the Bottom Line: Understanding Australian Screen Content Producers', *Media International Australia*, 136 (2010): 93.
2   A detailed report can be found at http://www.cci.edu.au/producersurvey2012.
3   Mark Deuze, *Media Work* (Cambridge: Polity Press, 2007), 57.
4   Cameron, Verhoeven and Court, 'Above the Bottom Line', 94.
5   Enda Brophy and Greig de Peuter, 'Immaterial Labor, Precarity, and Recomposition', in *Knowledge Workers in the Information Society*, ed. Catherine McKercher and Vincent Mosco (Lanham, MD: Lexington Books, 2007), 180.
6   Mark Banks and David Hesmondhalgh, 'Looking for Work in Creative Industries Policy', *International Journal of Cultural Policy*, 15:4 (2009): 420.
7   For example: Susan Christopherson, 'Beyond the Self-Expressive Creative Worker: An Industry Perspective on Entertainment Media', *Theory, Culture and Society*, 25:7–8 (2008): 73–95; Rosalind Gill, '"Life is a Pitch": Managing the Self in New Media Work', in *Managing Media Work*, ed. Mark Deuze (Thousand Oaks, CA: Sage, 2011), 249–62; David Hesmondhalgh and Sarah Baker, *Creative Labour: Media Work in Three Cultural Industries* (London: Routledge, 2011); Vincent Mosco and Catherine McKercher, *The Laboring of Communication: Will Knowledge Workers of the World Unite?* (Lanham, MD: Lexington Books, 2008).
8   David Lee, 'The Ethics of Insecurity: Risk, Individualization and Value in British Independent Television Production', *Television and New Media*, 13:6 (2012): 481.
9   See Banks and Hesmondhalgh, 'Looking for Work in Creative Industries Policy', 415–30; Mark Banks, 'Autonomy Guarantee? Cultural Work in the "Art–Commerce Relation"', *Journal for Cultural Research*, 14:3 (2010): 251–69; David Hesmondhalgh and Sarah Baker, '"A Very Complicated Version of Freedom": Conditions and Experiences of Creative Labour in Three Cultural Industries', *Poetics*, 38:1 (2010): 4–20; Adam Arvidsson, Giannino Malossi and Serpica Naro, 'Passionate Work? Labour Conditions in the Milan Fashion Industry', *Journal for Cultural Research*, 14:3 (2010): 295–309.

10 John Thornton Caldwell, *Production Culture: Industrial Reflexivity and Critical Practice in Film and Television* (Durham: Duke University Press, 2008), 1.

11 Vicki Mayer, *Below the Line: Producers and Production Studies in the New Television Economy* (Durham: Duke University Press, 2011).

12 Mayer, *Below the Line*, 179.

13 Australian Screen Producer Survey Questionnaire, 2011.

14 Jason Potts and Stuart Cunningham, 'Four Models of the Creative Industries', *International Journal of Cultural Policy*, 14:3 (2008): 233–247.

15 John Banks, 'The iPhone as Innovation Platform: Reimagining the Videogames Developer', in *Studying Mobile Media: Cultural Technologies, Mobile Communication, and the iPhone*, ed. Larissa Hjorth, Jean Burgess and Ingrid Richardson (London: Routledge, 2012), 155–172; John Banks and Stuart Cunningham, 'Games/ entertainment Software', in *Handbook of the Digital Creative Economy*, ed. Ruth Towse and Christian Handke (London: Edward Elgar, forthcoming).

16 Sandra Haukka, *Working in Australia's Digital Games Industry: Consolidation Report*, ARC Centre of Excellence for Creative Industries and Innovation and Queensland University of Technology in partnership with the Games Developers' Association of Australia, (May 2011).

17 Stuart Cunningham and Peter Higgs, 'Creative Industries Mapping: Where Have We Come From, and Where Are We Going?' *Creative Industries Journal*, 1:1 (2008): 7–30; Stuart Cunningham and Peter Higgs, 'Measuring Creative Employment: Implications for Innovation Policy', *Innovation: Management, Policy and Practice*, 11:2 (2009): 190–200; Stuart Cunningham, 'Developments in Measuring the "Creative" Workforce', *Cultural Trends*, 20:1 (2011): 25–40.

18 Stuart Cunningham, 'The Creative Cities Discourse: Production and/or Consumption?' in *Cities, Cultural Policy and Governance, The Cultures and Globalization Series, Volume 5*, ed. Helmut K. Anheier and Yudhishthir Raj Isar (Thousand Oaks CA: Sage, 2012), 111–12.

19 Cameron, Verhoeven and Court, 'Above the Bottom Line', 100.

20 The ten producer roles in the questionnaire were: Associate Producer; Co-Producer; Executive Producer; Producer; Senior/Supervising Producer; Series Producer; Line Producer; Digital Producer; Recent Graduate; Other.

21 Hasan Bakhshi, Alan Freeman and Peter Higgs, *A Dynamic Mapping of the UK's Creative Industries* NESTA (December 2012).

22 Charles H. Davis reports that in the 'creative content and technical craft segments' of the screen industry in Canada (which comprise more than just production companies), 'more than 85 per cent' of the firms are microenterprises (Charles H. Davis, 'New Firms in the Screen-Based Media Industry: Startups, Self-Employment and Standing Reserve', in *Managing Media Work*, ed. Mark Deuze (Thousand Oaks, CA: Sage, 2011), 170). Mark Deuze notes that 'according to the Bureau of Labor Statistics of the US Department of Labor, in 2004 over four-fifths of the jobs in film and television were in establishments with twenty or more workers, even though most companies in the industry have fewer than five employees', Mark Deuze, *Media Work* (Cambridge: Polity Press, 2007), 176.

23 Davis, 'New Firms in the Screen-Based Media Industry', 168.

24 Only 53 per cent of all respondents answered this question.

25 Davis, 'New Firms in the Screen-Based Media Industry', 171.

26 Deuze, *Media Work*, 11.

27 See for example Caldwell, *Production Culture*, and Christopherson, 'Beyond the Self-Expressive Creative Worker', 73–95.

28 Deuze, *Media Work*, 23.

29 Deb Verhoeven and Allan Cameron, 'Above the Bottom Line: Analysing the Culture of Australian Screen Content Producers', *Lumina*, 6 (2011): 56–7.

30 See David Court and Simon Molloy, 'For Love and Money: Estimating the Value of Psychic Income in Australian Screen Production', *Lumina*, 10 (2012): 25–35.

31 Cameron, Verhoeven and Court, 'Above the Bottom Line', 57.

32 Australian Bureau of Statistics, *8679.0 – Television, Film and Video Production and Post-Production Services, Australia, 2006–07* (Canberra: ABS, 2008).

33 Australian Bureau of Statistics, *8515.0 – Digital Game Development Services, Australia, 2006–07* (Canberra: ABS, 2008).

34 Innovation and Business Skills Australia (IBSA), *Review of the Digital Games Development: Game Art, Animation and Programming* (December, 2009), 9. See also Haukka, *Working in Australia's Digital Games Industry*, 16.

Part Two

Media and Genre Contexts

8

The Producer in Animation: Creativity and Commerce from Bray Studios to Pixar

Donna Kornhaber

At the very beginning of Max and Dave Fleischer's first *Out of the Inkwell* cartoon, from 1919, Max appears on screen in a live-action sequence and begins to draw Koko the Clown, who slowly comes to life before the viewer's eyes. Such self-reflexive sequences were common to animated shorts of the era, offering a playful personalization of what was in reality an arduous and quasi-industrial production process. Yet, as Donald Crafton observes, there is something unusual about the Fleischers' particular variation: 'One must remember that Max Fleischer is only pretending to be the animator. In fact, he is the producer – a role nevertheless literalized by picturing himself "producing" Koko out of the inkwell. Dave is the actual animator, at least in the early films.'[1] That is not to say Dave was not featured in the short; one might even say he had the starring role. It was his likeness that served as the basis for Koko's character design, through the patented rotoscoping process that the Fleischers developed to draw animated characters over images of real bodies on live-action film stock. In essence, Max the producer was drawing his brother Dave the animator into existence. In Crafton's reading of the sequence, the opening is a statement on the nature of authorship itself in the animated medium, a meditation on the degree to which the animator must be entirely subsumed into the characters that he or she produces: 'Part of the animator's status as a privileged being begins to rub off on the drawings ... The "hand of the artist" disappears, its place now occupied by characters who become agents of his will and ideas and through which his presence is known.'[2] But what Crafton leaves out is the equally powerful statement made by Max's role in the short, the producer here literally taking on the role of artistic creator. In the absence of the animator himself, who is totally enveloped in the consuming processes of creating animated characters, it is the producer who assumes a place of authorship. Animation is here figured as something far more than what one might simply call a producer's medium; it is a medium in which the producer can actually become an artist.

The confusion of producer and animator depicted in the opening of *Out of the Inkwell* presents an early and powerful reflection on the unique conditions of production that would come to define animation as an artistic and commercial medium over the course of the twentieth century. Film animation, as it developed commercially in the United States, was profoundly and continually shaped by the need to successfully (and profitably) navigate a daunting set of production requirements, technological needs and logistical obstacles that together often conspired to place the producer in a central creative role. For despite the limitless imaginative possibilities of the medium itself – what Paul Wells calls the form's 'abnegation of all mental law' – animation as it has been practised by most commercial studios is also a particularly industrial form of artistry, one that must be coordinated as much as it must be created.[3] It is, in Tom Sito's memorable description, 'mass-produced magic, dreams by the yard'.[4] And that mass production is of a particularly complicated sort; it is what John Canemaker calls the 'tedious, stress-filled, spirit-draining, bone-crunching assembly-line procedures that are absolutely necessary to make cartoons come alive on the silver screen'.[5] Hundreds of visual technicians may be involved in the production of a hand-drawn animated picture, to say nothing of actors, composers, Foley artists and other non-visual contributors. Hence the small army of producing staff found on most animated films, ranging from line producers to production managers to executive producers – the 'walkaround boys' as some animators at Disney used to call them.[6]

In light of such conditions, Max Fleischer perhaps deserves his seat at the animator's table, for the act of creating a successful animated film in many cases has as much to do with administration as it does with artistry, the two sides of production often becoming inseparable. (As Sito puts it: 'To weld four hundred egos into a tool that creates art that looks like it was made by one person has little to do with the ability to draw'.)[7] Indeed, the names of the towering figures of American animation are often those of the medium's producers and animator-producers: John Randolph Bray, the Fleischers, Pat Sullivan, Paul Terry, Walter Lantz, Don Bluth, John Lasseter and, of course, Walt Disney. There is, to be sure, no shortage of luminary animator-directors, but even in many of these cases the names of their affiliated producers have entered into animation lore: Leon Schlesinger at Warner Bros., for instance, or Jeffrey Katzenberg at the later incarnation of Disney or at DreamWorks Animation. There is often in animation a uniquely intimate bond between producer and artist, and the history of American film animation is in many ways the history of this bond. The approaches, innovations and personalities of the medium's producers have been instrumental in shaping the greater directions and possibilities of the art.

4,000 drawings: Early production processes and the rise of the animation producer

If the management of the processes of artistic production can be considered part of the basic purview of the producer, then in many ways this figure stands at the very origin point of film animation in America. Questions of process were often a manifest part of the earliest animators' artistic products, with many animated shorts openly discussing or depicting the arduous task of creating an animated film. In the first film by comic strip artist and pioneering animator Windsor McCay, *Little Nemo* (1911), the process of animation is figured explicitly as a kind of physical challenge. In a live-action sequence that precedes the animated portion of the film, McCay accepts a challenge issued by his friends to 'make four thousand pen drawings that will move'. What follows is essentially an abbreviated documentary on the beginnings of animation production, with McCay drafting, arranging and photographing stacks upon stacks of drawings. Only at the end of this gargantuan process does the actual animated portion of the short begin, some seven minutes into a ten-minute film. The process of creating an animated film is depicted as a heroic act, an enormous undertaking for an artist to attempt and one that calls up tremendous reserves of artistic skill and physical perseverance. Film animation is figured essentially as an artisanal creation, a highly personal craft wherein the processes by which the final product is made are as much a part of the appeal and allure of the artistic work as the animated content itself.

McCay holds a seminal place in American animation as both a consummate draftsman and visionary fantasist, yet for all of his artistic influence he also represents a road untaken in the development of the animated medium. It is difficult to imagine animation in the artisanal tradition that McCay pioneered achieving any kind of large-scale commercial viability; his films are the solitary work of the single artist, requiring an excess of effort and a superabundance of time. They may portend, perhaps, a fine arts future for animation but ultimately they offer no model for rapid commercial production.[8] The origin point for what we might call the business of animation would instead fall to another early animator, a draftsman of only modest artistic talents but one whose technical and commercial vision would come to define the model by which most animation is still produced. Like McCay, John Randolph Bray began in the single-artist tradition, producing his earliest short, *The Artist's Dream* (1913), entirely on his own. But whereas McCay only sought distribution for his completed films, Bray attempted to develop a more stable business model by negotiating an advanced multi-film contract with Pathé Pictures. Even with the help of several assistants, it quickly became clear to Bray that he would not be able to meet Pathé's stringent demands; he managed to deliver only about half of the films required of him in the first year of his contract. Out of this desperation was essentially born the first animation studio, with Bray hiring other animators to help him fulfil the terms of the contract and in the process becoming the first animator-producer.

Bray's multi-animator studio would be enough to secure him a prominent place in the history of animation, perhaps alongside Canadian animator Raoul Barré, who was also developing a similar studio system around the same time. However, Bray ultimately proved to be a particularly far-sighted producer, refining his growing studio system in ways that would profoundly impact the industry as a whole. His goal, he later recounted, was 'to simplify and perfect the [animation] process, so that the cartoons could be supplied as a regular motion-picture feature – as *many* of them as the public might want'.[9] To this end, Bray confronted the issue of the artistic labour of animation head-on; his most important technical innovation, the development of cel animation, was in some sense a direct answer to the problem of the 4,000 drawings that McCay's *Little Nemo* seemed to valourize. By selectively using clear celluloid sheets instead of paper for certain drawings, Bray enabled his animators to reuse static images and overlay them to a film's dynamic images, saving them from the cripplingly labour-intensive work of redrawing every visual element in every frame.[10] But perhaps Bray's greatest innovation was the deliberate rationalization of his studio workplace, brainstormed after reading Frederick Winslow Taylor's *Principles of Scientific Management*. Rather than allow his animators to draw an entire frame of film on their own, Bray divided each frame into a series of components: character design, landscapes, clean-up, painting, photographing. Most importantly, he divided the actual process of animating character movement into two separate kinds of drawings: keyframes, representing the major sequential steps of an action, and in-betweens that filled in the remaining points in the sequence. These divisions had obvious industrial and commercial resonances for Bray: those artists who held the most important positions in the animation process were known as 'foremen' in his studio; those with less important positions, like the in-betweeners, were termed 'cheapmen'.

In a sense, Bray's legacy could not be more different from that of McCay. If the latter's films remain treasured art objects, remembrances of Bray are almost entirely centred on his process and technological innovations. Though he nurtured within his studio a number of figures who would go on to become major animators, including Max Fleischer, Paul Terry and Walter Lantz – foremen all – the actual artistic output of his production house is mostly forgotten. Thinking perhaps especially of Bray, McCay even once berated an assembly of fellow animators with the comment that 'Animation should be an art, that is how I conceived it. But as I see it, what you fellows have done with it is make it into a trade.'[11] Yet the distinction between artistry and industry is perhaps not so easily drawn. The processes and technologies that Bray pioneered would form the basis for almost all later production of hand-drawn animated shorts and features, with many of his techniques even being adapted to the age of computer animation. Bray's own work may be on no one's list of the century's best animated films, yet arguably nearly all the touchstones of animation history were made both logistically and technologically possible – and commercially viable – through his innovations.

The producer as author: The Fleischer brothers and Sullivan Studio

If there is an artistic side to Bray's commercial legacy, it is perhaps best understood through the case of the Fleischer brothers, both former Bray animators whose later work on series like *Betty Boop*, *Popeye* and *Superman* in the decades following Bray's ascendancy demonstrates the degree to which a producer's focus on technological and process innovation could also be directly harnessed to an animator's artistic ends. In its heyday during the 1930s, the Fleischer Studios, founded by the brothers as Out of the Inkwell Films in 1921, arguably came closest to rivalling Disney Studios for both market share and prestige. In contrast to Disney's focus on family-friendly entertainment, the Fleischers offered what Noell Evans calls an 'urbane sophistication', an embodiment of 'the flapper attitude, spirit, language, and music of the day'.[12] Fleischer cartoons were notable for their relatively frank references to sex, direct engagement with working-class characters and immigrant humour (all specialties of the Betty Boop cartoons); they also had a largely improvisatory approach to dialogue, as in the Popeye series. Leaving aesthetics aside, the work of the Fleischer Studios was also in many ways a continuation of Bray's business-minded approach to the medium. Beyond replicating the basic processes and labour division that they first learned at Bray, the Fleischer brothers, like Bray before them, deliberately placed technological innovation at the centre of their business. Among the original technical tools patented by Max Fleischer were a pre-Xerox technology for copying drawings from one cell to another, a machine called the Rotograph that allowed for the simulation of three-dimensional depth within the frame, and, most importantly, the rotoscope process, which allowed animators to draw directly onto live-action film strips and base their character design on actual human figures.

If the Fleischers were technical innovators, however, they were also, unlike Bray, animation artists first and foremost. Beyond collecting patent royalties as Bray had done, the brothers continually experimented with ways of using these tools to change and further develop the visual style of their cartoons. The Rotograph, for instance, was regularly used in the creation of the Popeye cartoons to add a new depth of space to the shorts – as well as a new source of visual gags as characters seemed to naturally disappear or hide behind objects in the frame while moving. Similarly, rotoscoping was used to develop the distinctively human character design of Koko the Clown and later became the central device in creating the aesthetic for the brothers' famous *Superman* series, which set new standards for stylized animated realism in the 1940s.[13] It is perhaps little wonder that Max, as producer, saw no contradiction in assuming the role of artist and creator in the live-action opening of *Out of the Inkwell*, as the technical experiments that he pioneered in the studio proved an integral part of the brothers' animation process.

This exalted view of the animation producer as essentially an artist in all but name can also be seen – though perhaps somewhat more sinisterly – in the history of Sullivan Studio, one of the Fleischer's early competitors and one of the leading animation studios of the 1920s. Pat Sullivan was a veteran of Bray's early counterpart, the Raoul Barré Studio, and, like the Fleischers, he was a figure who had some talent as an animator but ultimately chose to focus his career on producing, assembling a roster of artists to work underneath him while he focused on securing distribution deals and brainstorming new revenue streams. Yet, even as he mostly left drawing behind, Sullivan never abandoned the idea that he might still hold legitimate claim to artistic authorship of the works that his studio produced – a view that is most flagrantly evidenced in the circumstances surrounding the provenance of his studio's prize property, Felix the Cat. Felix, by far the most popular animated character of the 1920s and arguably one of the most popular animated creations of all time, was for all intents and purposes the work of Sullivan Studio animator Otto Messmer, who initially drew the character for a Paramount newsreel and who served as lead animator for all of the subsequent Felix shorts. Yet for over 50 years, from 1919 until 1975, Messmer's role in creating and animating Felix was essentially unknown; authorship was instead ascribed entirely to Sullivan on the basis of a carefully cultivated publicity campaign. Sullivan surely had a substantial role in promoting and developing Felix: he provided Messmer with a team of animators for the shorts, shrewdly acquired the rights to the character from Paramount, developed a series of profitable distribution deals for the films and orchestrated what was one of the industry's first and most successful merchandizing campaigns, cashing in on everything from Felix dolls to Felix sheet music. Yet the kind of authorship ascribed to Sullivan at the time was of a much more direct sort. It was Sullivan's name alone that appeared on the Felix film title cards, attributing to him full artistic responsibility. In promotional photographs, Sullivan even assumed Messmer's chair at the animator's desk to look like he was actually drawing Felix, with Messmer moving down to the seat next to him. When Sullivan negotiated a newspaper cartoon strip to tie into the Felix shorts, Messmer drew them and signed Sullivan's name.

The near-total erasure of Messmer from the story of Felix's creation can easily be viewed as an instance of overreach on Sullivan's part. Yet it also speaks to the particularly complicated relationship between producer and animator within the world of commercial animation. In Messmer's rather benign account of the situation, offered years later, 'He was the boss, the businessman. I was the foreman, the employee.'[14] For Messmer, in other words, Sullivan as studio head held ultimate claim to the products that his studio created. If it is an unusual way of looking at an act of artistic creation, it is also revelatory of the degree to which the industrialized nature of animation after Bray held distinct affinities to other forms of commercial production. Though he undoubtedly had the greatest claim to be considered Felix's true author, Messmer also seemed to recognize that he did not create Felix alone. Instead, he worked closely with a staff of other animators on every short, operating within a structure that Sullivan created and oversaw. If we might defend Messmer's position (and Sullivan's actions) at all, it is from the point of view that Felix was ultimately a collective product of a team of artists, the work of an entire company. From the perspective of Sullivan and Messmer alike, the producer ultimately held a kind of corporate authorship to those products.

The producer as artist: The development of Disney Studios

If the idea of collective authorship subsumed under the name and persona of one individual seems problematic in the case of Felix the Cat, it cannot be overlooked that this is not too far removed from the model on which the most famous of all animation studios openly operated for decades. In the popular imagination, the figure of Walt Disney can seem to hold an exceptional position in relation to other animation producers, but he is perhaps most productively understood in the specific context of his predecessors and competitors. The highly distinctive and extremely successful studio model that Disney developed to produce his animated films was born directly out of his problems in executing the same kind of basic studio model that Sullivan and the Fleischers were using, a model that had nearly driven Disney to bankruptcy over questions of artistic authorship not unlike those that bedevilled Messmer and Sullivan. The instigator of Disney's troubles was a figure named Charles Mintz, who aimed to turn the successful animation distribution business run by his wife into an animation studio in its own right. In a brazen bid to move from distribution to production, Mintz attempted in 1927 to essentially steal Disney's studio from him and make it his own, convincing almost the entire team of Disney animators to decamp for his newly formed production house and bring with them their most prominent animated character, Oswald the Lucky Rabbit. Beyond being a significant personal betrayal, the move forced Disney to confront the problems of authorship in the era of commercial animation. Oswald was Disney's star attraction at the time, and unlike Sullivan he could lay legitimate claim to having authored the character in every sense. Like Messmer, he had devised and originally animated the Oswald character; like Sullivan, he ran the studio that produced the Oswald shorts. Yet what Disney found in the face of Mintz's sabotage was that all such matters of authorship could be quickly rendered irrelevant. The rights to the Oswald character were owned by the end-distributor, Universal, and were easily transferred to Mintz. Whatever legitimate claims Disney had to the character, he had no power to exercise that authorship without the support of his animation staff. If the case of Sullivan and Felix showed that a producer could easily appropriate authorship from his animators within the Bray-style studio system, the case of Disney and Oswald showed that the animators could just as easily appropriate authorship from their producer.

The Disney Studios that was reborn in the wake of the Oswald experience – the studio of 1928–1966, equally famous to animation buffs and business school students – was essentially a reaction against the producing arrangements that had predominated in the animation industry through the 1920s, and all of the artistic works for which Disney is duly famous are products of this reorganization. The new arrangements that Disney instituted in his revised studio structure are, at their heart, a further extrapolation on the division of labour that Bray had first pioneered, aimed primarily at eliminating any artisanal traces that still remained within Bray's system. For although Bray and his successors at Fleischer and Sullivan had carefully subdivided the animation process itself, the total process of conceiving and creating an animated series still had an element of unfettered, single-author creativity. The Fleischer Studios, for instance, did not have a formal story department for nearly the first 15 years of its existence, instead allowing lead animators to create their own stories and experiment with new characters and scenarios. What Disney created instead was an organizational structure so complex and interdependent that it allowed for only one true creative imagination: that of the master producer, Disney himself. In what was arguably his most pivotal move, he created in 1931 an independent 'story department' separate from the studio's animation wing, compartmentalizing for the first time the tales that animated films would tell from the visual presentation of those stories. Within these two broad divisions, Disney further categorized his creative staff into a series of smaller subgroups. The story department could be regrouped into smaller subteams assigned to specific scenes within a film as needed, while the animation wing was organized into a vast array of segregated but interdependent functions, ranging from concept artists, who helped determine the overall visual style of a film, to 'inkers', who traced the images created by animators from paper onto cels, to 'line checkers', who examined the thickness of the inkers' lines for consistency. Through such divisions, Disney essentially devised a means to allow the production process to self-animate and self-correct: to run semiautonomously even without his constant direct input. Working with George Gallup and his Audience Research Institute, Disney pioneered the use of audience focus groups and animator-to-animator peer review sessions, so that pictures could be refined and corrected even without immediate input from himself or another supervisor. He even experimented with developing a numerical system that would compile information from these groups and allow him to personally monitor the progress of multiple projects with little more than a glance at the numbers.[15]

Ultimately, what is true in some degree for all commercial animation is true in the extreme for Disney: that the work of art in animation is almost entirely bound up in the technical and industrial structures put in place to enable its creation. The tremendous innovation and artistic success of the Disney Studios was always as much a matter of Disney's business savvy and aptitude for organizational design as it was a product of his creativity or that of his animators. The enormous undertaking, for instance, of producing the first feature-length animated film with *Snow White and the Seven Dwarfs* in 1937 – a feat involving over 500 artists producing some two-million individual illustrations – was made possible in large part through the careful subdivision and scalability of Disney's operation. Tellingly, when the Fleischer brothers, still working largely along a Bray-style production model, attempted their own feature film in response in 1939, the studio came close to insolvency. Likewise, the move to colour in 1932 that helped further define the Disney style of animation was in large part a commercial move, an attempt on Disney's part to differentiate his films and lockout competition through a two-year exclusive contract with Technicolor. Even the famous incorporation of sound in 1928 into Mickey Mouse's first short, *Steamboat Willie* – a huge commercial success that was instrumental in allowing Disney to rebuild and expand his studio after the disaster with Oswald – was born of a business calculation. Disney, ever the producer, created two half-finished versions of the short, one with sound and one without, and ran focus groups to determine which might be more popular, hanging the artistic direction of his career on a question of commercial success.

As is often the case with Disney, as with commercial animation more generally, the line between artistry and commerce can be difficult to define. For some, as in Richard Schickel's famous estimation, Disney's legacy is almost entirely that of a great businessman, a figure most notable for his 'economic success' and 'personal power' who, early in his career, 'ceased to make any claims as an artist'.[16] For an animator like Chuck Jones, however – a great admirer of Disney even if his own more cynical aesthetic seemed in many ways opposed to Disney's vision – it is wrong to think of Disney as more businessman than artist, more producer than animator. Disney, he claims, 'created a climate that enabled us all to exist … The things that happened at the Disney Studio were the backbone that upheld everybody else'.[17] In Jones' telling, Disney used his commercial sensibilities to artistically further the field, expanding the potential of the medium through new technical innovations and growing the audience for animation in the process. Or, put another way, Disney turned producing into a kind of artistic authorship in itself, making good on the premature claims of a figure like Sullivan and establishing a model whereby the producer might more truly assume the mantle of creative lead. As Stephen Cavalier observes,

> Disney's precise part in the making of his movies can seem mysterious; he stopped drawing early on in his career, so his role clearly wasn't that of an animator. He was not credited as a director or writer, and yet he received much more acclaim than the average producer. The truth is that Disney was all of those things, or at least he was guiding all of those activities, and more.[18]

Indeed, what is perhaps most remarkable about the output and operations of the Disney Studios is the degree to which for all the breadth of its staff and the depth of the individual talents assembled, the entirety of the studio seemed to be organized around executing Disney's personal vision. It is what Sito calls the 'one-artist, one-studio style', a system wherein the intensive subdivision of labour leaves only the figure at the top of the hierarchy with a clear vision of the total artistic picture.[19] It is something that Jones sensed intuitively during the four brief months he spent as a Disney animator. Frustrated at the segmentation and control that was the norm at Disney, Jones recalls confronting the famous studio head with the observation that 'There's only one job at this studio worth having: yours.'[20]

The producer as curator:
Leon Schlesinger and Warner Bros. Studios

It is telling, perhaps, that Jones should bristle under the system of organization at the Disney Studios, for the production scheme under which he created much of his best work could not have been more different from that which Disney devised. Even more to the point, the producer with whom Jones is most associated could perhaps not have been more opposed in temperament and outlook to Disney himself. If Leon Schlesinger holds an exalted place in the history of animation as the figure who created and oversaw the enormously influential Warner Bros. animation studio, that status sometimes seems almost accidental. Unlike most of the major animation producers before him, Schlesinger had no background in the medium when he started Warner Bros.' animation division in 1927. He was a businessman first and foremost: the owner of one of silent Hollywood's most successful title card companies and an entrepreneur with at least enough foresight to see that with the coming of sound he needed to identify a new revenue stream. A distant relative of the Warner brothers themselves and an important figure in the financing of *The Jazz Singer* (1927), he negotiated shortly after the premier of that film the rights to create within Warner Bros. a semiautonomous animation unit. It was by most accounts a financial move only, as Schlesinger seemed to hold no special love for the animated medium. In Jones' recollection, he was 'absolutely out for money, and he didn't care how he got it'.[21]

In contrast to a towering creative figure like Disney, Schlesinger seems easily dismissible as an artistic player in any real sense, little more than an unimaginative 'suit' who had only an incidental relationship to the actual works produced under his watch. Even as Warner Bros.' output came quickly to rival Disney's own work in popularity and esteem during the late 1930s and early 1940s, Schlesinger's actual role in that artistic success has tended to seem minimal. That is certainly the vision put forth by many of his own star employees, the legendary director-animators like Tex Avery, Chuck Jones, Bob Clampett, Frank Tashlin and Friz Freleng with whom he often had a tempestuous relationship. Jones would later describe Schlesinger as 'someone who can't write, draw, or laugh, and whose prime creative impulse is to say no' and regarded his main role in the artistic processes of the Warner Bros. studio simply as a figure who provided a kind of perverse motivation to the animators, 'someone to actively dislike'.[22] In his memoirs, Jones even recounts a scheme by which he and the other animators deliberately tried to keep their work and their working methods a secret from Schlesinger's production manager, Ray Katz, who would often patrol the studio hallways only to find the forewarned writers and animators engaged in any number of bizarre activities other than making animated films. Yet, what Jones and others have described as opposition and obfuscation – and what seems in contrast to the Disney model to be a case almost of gross professional negligence on Schlesinger's part – can also seem to have the greater contours of a deliberate commercial vision, a curatorial approach that stands in pointed contrast to the tightly controlled system that Disney set up. For despite Jones' picture of Schlesinger's general lack of involvement in the operations of his creative underlings, as a producer he in fact had a very direct role in monitoring all of his animators' final products. Schlesinger personally screened every short that his unit created to determine if it was worthy of release. ('Roll the garbage' was the phrase he used at the start of every screening; the friction between the producer and his animators seemed to run both ways.)[23] Yet, rarely would Schlesinger punish one of his director-animators even for a short that he disliked, usually only going so far as to issue a general warning.

For all of his gruffness and eccentricities, in other words, Schlesinger seemed to operate on a talent-driven model of production. It is telling that, for a figure who appeared on the surface to care little about the artists who worked under him or the work that they produced, Schlesinger managed to assemble at Warner Bros. a roster of animators that would become the stuff of legend, beginning with his first animator-directors Hugh Harman and Rudolf Ising and continuing through the era of Tex Avery and his 'Termite Terrace' unit. Having hired talented artists, Schlesinger proceeded to give them ample room to do the work they wanted – and, importantly, gave them ample room to fail. Even when he felt one of his directors had entirely missed the mark – most famously with Jones' highly stylized short *The Dover Boys* (1942), which Schlesinger detested but which would go on to be among Jones' most influential works – he still typically gave them the opportunity to fail again. Schlesinger threatened to fire Jones for *The Dover Boys* but ultimately declined to follow through, deciding in the end that he would be too difficult to replace. Once they were selected to be part of Schlesinger's elect, animators at Warner Bros. essentially had free rein to pursue their own individual visions and interests; only cost might bring them into irresolvable conflict with upper management, as most significant departures (Harman and Ising being the most famous examples) took place over financial disputes.

Ultimately, Schlesinger's is a producing approach that is imprinted on the work of the Warner Bros. animators just as much as Disney's production arrangements are marked on his creations. If the result of Disney's intensive control of the animation process was a powerfully self-consistent creative vision, Schlesinger's *laissez-faire* practices resulted in artistic innovations of a very different sort. As numerous commentators have observed, the great Warner Bros. cartoons of the 1930s and 1940s are as notable for their diverse styles and approaches as for their actual content. They are, in J. P. Telotte's description, 'untroubled by a single house aesthetic' and frequently set out to explore 'somewhat different visions of the house characters'.[24] Their diversity is, in a sense, Schlesinger's own creative mark. Coming from outside the industry, he rewrote the rules by which animation studios had operated since Bray, returning to something much closer to the artist-driven method that McCay had practised. Warner Bros. of course had all the usual divisions of labour of the modern animation production house; though the studio is associated with only a few select names of its major animator-directors, it employed some 200 artists overall. But the almost auteurist freedom that the top animator-directors had to shape their own projects was ultimately more artisanal than industrial. Whereas Disney practised a consolidation of artistic vision in the figure of the producer, Schlesinger redistributed the potential for such vision back to the animators themselves, creating within his studio what Giannalberto Bendazzi calls 'a republic of equals'.[25] For an animator like Jones, it was a frustrating but worthwhile arrangement: 'We were grossly underpaid', he later recalled, 'but we still did what we wanted to do.'[26]

To Pixar and beyond

By most accounts, the era of Disney and Warner Bros. represents a Golden Age of American film animation, both a consolidation of the experimentation of the 1910s and 1920s and a kind of pre-lapsarian moment before the demise of commercial short-form filmmaking and the rise of television serials in the 1960s. It also, importantly, represents a moment of consolidation in the processes of production by which animation might be made. Taken together, Disney and Schlesinger embody the extremes of commercial animation production during the twentieth century, exemplifying approaches centred on very different answers to the question of where the producer might stand in relation to creative authorship. Where new figures in commercial film animation have generated popular excitement in recent decades, it is often as much in connection to the ways in which they promise to revitalize or reinvent these basic modes of production as it is in connection to the actual animated films that they produce. Hence, for example, the enthusiasm that greeted former Disney animator Don Bluth in the 1980s on his quest to reinstitute and reinvigorate the kind of 'one-artist, one-studio style' of Disney's original vision during the founding of his own animation studio, Don Bluth Productions. Or, in a similar vein, the anticipation generated in the 1990s by news that super-producers Steven Spielberg, David Geffen and Jeffrey Katzenberg would found a studio to rival Disney and that spoke more to the aesthetic of individual animator-directors than to a controlling studio vision.

However, the most pervasive example of recent years may be that of John Lasseter, figured in much of the press around Pixar Animation Studios not just as a visionary animator but as veritably 'a latter-day Walt Disney', in the words of one *New York Times* profile.[27] It is a mystique that Lasseter himself, a former Disney employee and now Chief Creative Officer of Disney-Pixar since their 2006 merger, has at times sought explicitly to cultivate. Having first encountered computer animation in a Disney screening room while watching rushes of *Tron* in 1982, Lasseter has described his attraction to CGI technology specifically as a kind of fulfilment of Disney's own drive for technical and commercial innovation. 'I couldn't believe what I was seeing', he has said of his first encounter with computer animation. 'Walt Disney, his career, all his life, was striving to get more dimension in his animation … and I was standing there, looking at it, going, "This is what Walt was waiting for." '[28] To the extent that Pixar's films do evince a similar discipline of vision that was once connected to Disney's work, it is arguably in no small part for the similarity in production arrangements that Lasseter has cultivated in the studio he built. The degree of specialization required in a Pixar production is an extreme extrapolation even on the intensive subdivision that Disney first put in place. In addition to the standard divisions of background artists and layout specialists, concept artists and character modellers, the Pixar animation process includes specialists in character features such as hair and skin or visual features such as art research and lighting effects. True to Disney's vision of narrative and visual separation, writers and story creators at Pixar are even given access to their own separate facility, located some 50 miles away from the rest of the studio.

Yet, perhaps the most intriguing and most innovative aspect of Lasseter's approach to production has nothing to do with either computer pixels or campus layouts, nothing to do with the execution of his individual vision at all. In its intensive specialization and segmented production processes, Pixar seems to have all of the formal markings of Sito's 'one-artist, one-studio style', offering a twenty-first-century testament to the degree to which animation as a medium often still 'seems to need not merely a coordinating chief artist but a messianic father-genius'.[29] Yet, early in the studio's growth, Lasseter made the unusual decision to cede that 'messianic father-genius role' and to become something at least a little closer to a figure like Schlesinger operating inside a Disney apparatus. For an observer like Pixar's original CEO Steve Jobs (himself no stranger to the role of 'messianic father-genius'), Lasseter's decision to open the studio to other directors was pivotal in Pixar's ultimate success:

> John is brilliant in many ways. But the thing that most impresses me about him is that he realized right from the start that in addition to making his own films, he wanted to grow a generation of directors around him. He's hired well; he hired these young gems who've worked around him for a decade. And he has grown an entire team of creative leaders at the studio.[30]

The grooming of new directors from within a studio's ranks is certainly in itself nothing new; Disney did much the same in his era. But Lasseter has sought not only to cultivate new talent but to cultivate new visions, to open up Pixar to new artistic voices beyond his own. It is what Pixar director Andrew Stanton has called 'beta testing the studio'.[31] He explained, 'The studio definitely works but as we add every director, we're finding out what it is that makes Pixar work under these new and different circumstances. So with each director you find out what you need to do differently to capitalize on him or her'.[32] It is a movement perhaps best exemplified by the recruitment of Brad Bird, the independent animator-director (and former classmate of Lasseter's at CalArts) who was previously best known for *The Iron Giant* (1999), his animated adaptation of the Ted Hughes children's poem *The Iron Man* (1968) and whose two Pixar films, *The Incredibles* (2004) and *Ratatouille* (2007), have offered a new and often darker visual perspective and a more cynical take on the common Pixar tropes of family and friendship. He is, by some accounts, a figure distinctly apart from other directors in the Pixar stable, particularly in his interest in emulating the techniques of live-action, auteurist filmmaking in his animated work. As Lasseter recalls of their student days together, 'Brad would hang out all night ... talking about Scorsese and Spielberg and Coppola and how we could do what they did in animation'.[33] (It would be a lifelong interest that Bird both reversed and fulfilled in his turn to live-action filmmaking with *Mission Impossible: Ghost Protocol* (2011), bringing an animator's perspective to the action genre.) In terms of the visual contrast to Lasseter's own more classical filmmaking aesthetic, it is a little as though Chuck Jones were finally allowed to make a Disney film.

For all of the tremendous technical and creative innovation that Pixar has brought to contemporary animation, this decision to offer the studio's resources to animators other than Lasseter himself may seem far from the most profound. Yet in a medium where process and product are so intimately intertwined, the question of who sits atop the production studio hierarchy can be a substantial one. It can, in fact, be the most important question of all – the question of authorship itself, of what gets created and how. When Chuck Jones confronted Disney with his statement that 'There's only one job at this studio worth having: yours', Disney's reply was succinct: 'That job's taken'.[34] Lasseter has answered that same question quite differently, which may be his most important innovation yet.

Notes

1 Donald Crafton, *Before Mickey: The Animated Film, 1898–1928* (Chicago: University of Chicago Press, 1993), 298.

2 Crafton, *Before Mickey.*

3 Paul Wells, *Animation and America* (New Brunswick: Rutgers University Press, 2002), 55.

4 Tom Sito, *Drawing the Line: The Untold Story of the Animation Unions from Bosko to Bart Simpson* (Lexington: The University Press of Kentucky), 47.

5 John Canemaker, *Before the Animation Begins: The Art and Lives of Disney Inspirational Sketch Artists* (New York: Disney Enterprises, 1996), ix.

6 Sito, *Drawing the Line*, 33.

7 Sito, *Drawing the Line*, 52.

8 That is not to say that no animators since McCay have pursued the creation of single-artist animated films. Contemporary independent animator Bill Plympton has worked in this manner and is credited with being the only animator to ever complete a feature-length animated film on his own, drawing and colouring 30,000 cels for *The Tune* (1992).

9 Michael Barrier, *Hollywood Cartoons: American Animation in Its Golden Age* (Oxford: Oxford University Press, 1999), 12; original emphasis.

10 Bray developed cel animation around the same time as animator Earl Hurd, who pioneered a slightly more efficient version of the same process. Ever the businessman, Bray negotiated a patent trust with Hurd so as to pool the patent revenue from their techniques.

11 Stephen Cavalier, *The World History of Animation* (Berkeley: University of California Press, 2011), 64. Slightly different versions of the quote also appear in John Canemaker, *Windsor McCay: His Life and Art* (New York: Harry N. Abrams, 2005), 159 and in Sito, 390–91.

12 Noell K. Wolfgram Evans, *Animators of Film and Television: Nineteen Artists, Writers, Producers and Others* (Jefferson: McFarland and Company, 2011), 52, 53.

13 The rotoscope process had an especially far-reaching impact on the industry as a whole and became a widely used tool for creating animated human characters, put to use perhaps most famously by Disney in his first feature-length animation *Snow White and the Seven Dwarfs* (1937).

14 Crafton, *Before Mickey*, 321.

15 See Susan Ohmer, 'Laughter by Numbers: The Science of Comedy at the Walt Disney Studio', in *Funny Pictures: Animation and Comedy in Studio-Era Hollywood*, ed. Daniel Goldmark and Charlie Keil (Berkeley: University of California Press, 2011), 109–26.

16 Richard Schickel, *The Disney Version: The Life, Times, Art, and Commerce of Walt Disney* (New York: Simon and Schuster, 1985), 13.

17 Chuck Jones and Maureen Furniss, *Chuck Jones: Conversations* (Jackson: University Press of Mississippi, 2005), 69.

18 Cavalier, *The World History of Animation*, 79.

19 Sito, *Drawing the Line*, 51.

20 Maureen Furniss, Introduction to *Chuck Jones: Conversations* (Jackson: University Press of Mississippi, 2005), ix.

21 Jones and Furniss, *Chuck Jones: Conversations*, 24.

22 Chuck Jones, *Chuck Amuck: The Life and Times of an Animated Cartoonist* (New York: MacMillan, 1999), 94. Ultimately, the contempt in which the Warner Bros. animators held the relatively amiable Schlesinger would pale in comparison to their dislike for his truly humourless successor Edward Selzer, though he did take a similarly hands-off approach within the studio.

23 Jones and Furniss, *Chuck Jones: Conversations*, 163.

24 J. P. Telotte, *Animating Space: From Mickey to Wall-E* (Lexington: The University Press of Kentucky, 2010), 19–20.

25 Giannalberto Bendazzi, *Cartoons: One Hundred Years of Cinema Animation* (Bloomington: Indiana University Press, 1994), 94.

26 Jones and Furniss, *Chuck Jones: Conversations*, 24.

27 Laura M. Holson, 'He Runs that Mickey Mouse Outfit', *New York Times*, 4 March, 2007.

28 David A. Price, *The Pixar Touch: The Making of a Company* (New York: Random House, 2009), 52–53.

29 Sito, *Drawing the Line*, 49.

30 Karen Paik, *To Infinity and Beyond: The Story of Pixar Animation Studios* (San Francisco: Chronicle Books, 2007), 178.

31 Paik, *To Infinity and Beyond*, 224.

32 Paik, *To Infinity and Beyond*, 224.

33 Dave Gardetta, 'Mr. Indelible', *Los Angeles Magazine*, February 2005, 82.

34 Jones and Furniss, *Chuck Jones: Conversations*, ix.

9

'Trying to Ride a Naughty Horse': British Television Comedy Producers

Brett Mills and Sarah Ralph

When you have so many shows, I think at one point we had forty shows in production, and it was just so hard to be able to feel that any of them – any of your forty children if you like – were yours. It was like being in charge of a massive foster home.

Lucy Lumsden[1]

[E]ssentially – and I don't know whether this is unique to this business but – even as a company, the whole company is a freelancer. And we are an established indie now in London but ... Because it's project-based rather than career-based, there is no career. It's shows. And shows are therefore project-based ... It is a world in which all this could disappear.

Ash Atalla[2]

These opening quotations reveal some characteristic problems of being a producer within two distinctive areas of British television comedy production: comedy commissioning and development within a large broadcasting organization, and the independent production sector. Lucy Lumsden joined Sky as its first Head of Comedy in 2009, and has since commissioned the broadcaster's entire comedy slate from a standing start, including *Mount Pleasant* (Sky1/Sky Living, 2011–), *Stella* (Sky1, 2012–) and *Spy* (Sky1, 2011–). Prior to taking up the role at Sky, Lumsden had worked in comedy commissioning at the BBC for 11 years, and she thus has considerable experience within large broadcasters and her observation which begins this chapter underlines one of the problems of working within such an institutional context, whereby the job comes to be perceived as one solely about management. However, her use of the word 'children' also points to the close relationships producers have with the programmes they work on, and the desire to see each of them as individual and requiring care. Ash Atalla, by comparison, worked first as a freelance producer on a number of high-profile comedy series such as *The Office* (BBC2/1, 2001–2003) before setting up his own production company Roughcut TV in 2007. This company has gone on to produce comedy programmes for all the main UK broadcasters, including *Cuckoo* (BBC3, 2012–) and *Trollied* (Sky1, 2011–). His comments illustrate the precarious nature of operating in the independent production sector, where the freelance culture means considerable time and effort must be put into maintaining a steady flow of projects to ensure a company's survival. Drawing on statements such as this, this chapter will explore the diverse ways in which comedy producers working within different industry contexts negotiate the demands of their job, and endeavour to construct individual working practices that enable them to attain both 'creative autonomy'[3] and pleasure from their labour. It does so through detailed thematic analysis[4] of interviews undertaken with British television comedy producers conducted as part of two Arts and Humanities Research Council–funded research projects.[5] In foregrounding the statements of individual production professionals, it seeks to contribute to the growing body of work that employs empirical materials to explore conditions within the creative industries, particularly as work in this field has commonly been criticized for lacking such first-hand accounts.[6]

Close consideration of the working practices of television comedy producers feels long overdue. It is nearly two decades since Jeremy Tunstall's *Television Producers* gave attention to producers working within this 'genre-specific world'.[7] He identified two broad categories of comedy (mainstream TV comedy and alternative comedy) and consequently two distinct categories of comedy producer.[8] Painting two portraits (perhaps better termed as caricatures) of these, Tunstall describes mainstream comedy producers as being in their forties and, after attending drama school or working in theatre, having had a long career at a large terrestrial broadcaster before giving up their staff status. Typically, having worked for the corporation, they enthused about the BBC tradition of comedy and the broadcaster's facilities, and were *Daily Mail* readers. For Tunstall, alternative-comedy producers were usually younger than their mainstream counterparts, and had moved into BBC radio comedy straight from university. They were unlikely to have had an extended career with a large broadcasting organization and instead had experience working as a freelance producer or running an independent production company. They were also likely to read the *Independent*. Tunstall acknowledges that the boundaries of these groupings are constantly in flux, particularly with the tendency in comedy for the controversial, risky and eccentric to eventually be amalgamated into the mainstream. However, the rigid and formulaic construction of his classifications, particularly in terms of their biographical features, was simplistic at the time and even more inaccurate today. The individualized routes that our interviewees travelled to progress to their current position (including one participant who first began a career as a stockbroker) supports this critique. In exploring how the comedy producers we interviewed talk about the processes, conditions and demands of their role and how they go about managing them, this chapter also seeks to move beyond Tunstall's career-path determined categories and instead explore specific and particular circumstances within the context of an industry where producers can have staff status as a broadcaster, be managing director of their own independent company or work entirely freelance.

However, we would also like to point towards the methodological problems that arise when trying to make sense of the activities of producers, and the use of interviews in accessing such information. Exploring the motivations of producers – especially in a precarious labour market – seems key, as the production system is dependent upon such individuals continuing to accept that the 'spectre of unemployment' common in the creative industries is worth the excitement and joy an interesting project brings.[9] Yet producers are – like all workers – not very good at verbalizing their own skills and repeatedly deny their own abilities. Running through our interviews is reference to 'gut instinct' as the primary tool for deciding whether something is worth doing or not: Shane Allen refers to 'instinct and passion';[10] Jon Plowman worries that referring to 'gut instinct' makes him sound like 'some sort of haughty, whim-like despot';[11] Beryl Vertue is concerned that her 'gut instinct' will be lost if she ever worked in a large institution where 'you've got herds of people around you and bits of paper being flung down with the overnights [ratings] on';[12] and Atalla proclaims 'The instinct is so strong it's almost … religious [laughs]. It's almost like a fervour, at times.' But presenting 'gut instinct' as the main research finding resulting from talking to producers is not very productive or satisfying, and merely reinforces the idea that cultural labour is not as skilled as that necessary in other, more 'traditional' professions. Perhaps Tunstall's rather simplistic analysis resulted from a similar methodological problem, and this means it remains difficult to know how best to engage with television producers and explore their world. Indeed, many interviewees here seemed to express *pleasure* when they were probed on what was meant by 'gut instinct' and their failure to answer the question frustrated the interviewer. This may simply demonstrate that 'researcher-practitioner contacts are always marked by symbiotic tensions over authenticity and advantage'; and an interviewee's pleasure in being unable to give the interviewer what they want can be evidence of power structures at play.[13] When Atalla described the multiple activities his work required, and the wealth of people he had to engage with in order to carry it out, he compared it to 'trying to ride a naughty horse'. As researchers investigating producers, production and creative labour – and finding that the methods we employ only go so far in unearthing useful data – we suggest that producers are similarly 'naughty horses', and that analysis of what the interview material herein accepts that 'social presentation, self-concept and identity performance' are an intrinsic aspect of producers' behaviour.[14] Indeed, their success in the television industry might be a result of their ability to manifest that naughtiness in a manner conducive to media production.

'Another squeezed-out sausage': Management and industry

One of the interesting things about the producer role is that it requires those who fulfil it to negotiate creative activity with managerial work, and thus producers occupy multiple positions within hierarchical structures simultaneously. This necessarily impacts on how they do their job and how they are understood by their colleagues (indeed, it affects who might or might not see a producer they are working with as their colleague or not). Yet the producers we spoke to repeatedly insisted on having complex relationships towards ideas of management and, without fully removing themselves from such a sphere, consistently pointed towards other, higher levels of management as more accurately embodying the hierarchical structures that might affect the creative process.

For debates such as these about creativity, management and television production in Britain, comedy offers an interesting case study. Up until the 1980s the vast majority of television production occurred in-house, via the BBC or ITV. Yet the opening up of a television market in that decade, and the start of Channel 4, which broadcast programmes but did not make any, resulted in a significant demand for work produced by the independent sector.[15] The insistence that a significant proportion of British television production must occur outside the major broadcasters is enshrined in regulations, resulting in initiatives such as the BBC's 'Window of Creative Competition' (WoCC), which guarantees a minimum amount of programming commissioning and is open to both in-house and independent production.[16] The expansion of the independent sector happened at various rates for different kinds of programming, but one of the leaders was comedy, with many writers, producers and performers quickly setting up their own companies and selling programmes to the broadcasters.[17] There could be a number of reasons why comedy should be the genre that most quickly and effectively exploited this structural change, but perhaps one of the key reasons lies in the motivations and personalities of those individuals – including producers – that made up, and continue to make up, the workers in that field. It is too simple to make links between the anarchic and radical role often assigned to humour in society and the desire by such workers to be outside large, hierarchical systems.[18] That said, many interviewees insisted that their decision to work in smaller independent companies was one motivated by a feeling of a lack of fit with the large broadcasters. There is, then, a tension between the need to be part of larger productive networks already noted and the discomfort felt by being enveloped in a formalized network of too large a size.

The network that exists here is one predicated on comedy, rather than employer. For example, Allen feels that '[Y]ou've more in common with people across the industry and across other broadcasters, than you do with other parts of a broadcaster.' An interviewee such as Adam Tandy (who has worked on series such as *The Thick of It* [BBC Four/BBC Two, 2005–2012] and *A Touch of Cloth* [Sky One, 2012–]) is an interesting case in point, for he worked for many years as an employee for the BBC, but moved into freelance work and made clear he had no desire to move back to the former working relationship.[19] For Tandy – like many interviewees – such a freelance position offered multiple benefits. First, it meant that he could choose which projects to work on, and which people to work with, ensuring that he was only working on programmes that he felt an interest in and a commitment to. Second, he could manage the input that fed into a project by keeping a number of executives at the broadcaster's at arm's length, for he argues that his role is to maintain the integrity of an idea 'because actually, the best ideas are the ones that arrive fully-formed and know exactly what they are'. Finally, it meant he could control (up to a point) when to work and when not to, allowing a degree of flexibility that a permanent, employee status might not allow.

All of this is evidence of what Ross refers to as the ' "revolt against work" in the early 1970s', arising from workers in many industries realizing that ' "Jobs for life" was not a recipe for liberation, nor should it be.'[20] Or, as Tandy put it, outlining the rationale for his decision: 'You are more creatively free.' These responses mirror those found across the television industry where workers have consciously chosen to pursue freelance careers, as Storey *et al.* have shown.[21]

However, the worry about creative autonomy being compromised by large institutions was not confined to only those working within the freelance and independent sector; it troubled the minds of employees too. Lumsden outlined her working practice as: 'I try to work four days a week and that fifth day is when I do my thinking and my reading and take time.' What is noticeable here is that 'thinking' and 'reading' are not defined as 'work', which is what happens on the other four days of her week. This demonstrates how certain kinds of labour (especially those an individual takes pleasure in) are defined as something other than 'work'. Similarly, Plowman makes a distinction between the fun and interesting aspects of what he does – 'once I've read a script and think I quite like it then you start talking to people, you start talking to the writer and you start talking to other producers here' – and the institutional structures which he must negotiate and which are presumed to have no creative value – 'the boring system of how the BBC decides which programmes it makes'. Running through many of these comments were interviewees' displeasure at the institutions' failure to take advantage of the experience and expertise these producers felt they had built up and which were the reason they had been employed in the first place. So Allen, rather wearily, notes:

> Oh I don't want to sound arrogant in saying it but you think 'I've been producing and watching comedy like for 15, 20 years. It's my passion and I love it.' And sometimes some people may – from on high – like try and analyze comedy and try and give you a reason why they don't want to do it in a way that I don't think fully ... they don't have as much empathy for the genre as maybe they should.

That large, hierarchical managerial structures impinge upon creativity and innovation has been a recurring theme within analysis of the creative industries, with perhaps Adorno's being the most cited work outlining the negative social and political consequences that arise if culture, and those who work within it, are treated as commodities.[22] Or, to put it another way: 'And suddenly your amazing piece of creativity becomes commoditized and turned into just another squeezed-out sausage' (Tandy).

What is interesting here is the commonality of answers producers give no matter whether they are freelance or employed, and irrespective of the kinds of programming they work on. That some of the producers employed by the large broadcasting institutions might be precisely the people that those working in the independent sector see as stifling their creativity did not go unnoticed by the former. There is, running through these workers, a weary disdain for what is perceived as interference; and a vocalized fear of becoming institutionalized and therefore filling the roles they had spent much of their careers railing against. While it is likely that such mistrust of institutional systems is endemic in the television industry, there is a question as to whether it is particularly apparent in the comedy genre, considering the kinds of people that work in it. The producer, here, then, has an inherently contradictory role, repeatedly negotiating managerial aspects of the job with those felt to be more creative and which are enabled at least partly through that very managerial behaviour which is seen as so problematic.

'That's My Baby': The parent–child relationship and emotional labour

The quotation by Lucy Lumsden at the start of this chapter illustrates other conflicting responsibilities a producer within a broadcasting organization has to negotiate. They are required to manage an extremely large slate of programmes at different stages of development, and at the same time sustain a close, nurturing relationship with a show, and with the creative personnel working on it. Implied in Lumsden's comment is that having a 'close touch' with shows is not only held to be an essential aspect of the producer's job but is personally important to them in terms of the pleasures they get from their work. This principle can be found in various guises in the talk of all of the producers interviewed, but is particularly signalled by the repeated employment of analogies relating to 'children' and 'babies' to describe the personalized relationship they have with their shows. Allen refers to the common use in the industry of the phrase 'That's my baby' to describe the 'special, rare thing' of a project that has come to fruition. Likewise, Henry Normal, managing director of the independent television company Baby Cow Productions, speaks of enjoying a 'great sense of extended family' when working directly with fresh comic talent.[23] When Plowman was asked about the effect of having a new series he was responsible for criticized in the press or by audiences, he replied, with a degree of flippancy, 'I cry a lot.' However, when this response was probed he went on to account for the high level of personal investment he has in programmes, particularly those that he had fostered and developed from their earliest phases, and again this relationship was described as comparable to that of a parent protecting their child:

> A show that you've been the first person to read, that you really like, that you've managed to persuade some really good actors to be in because they really like it, that other people here [at the BBC] really like, and they like it enough to give you a million quid to make a series of six of them, it becomes your kids a bit, you know. If the audience then go, 'I'm sorry, I don't like your kids', you're going to defend it pretty hard.

Producers feel disappointment not only for themselves that a comedy has failed to achieve the success that was hoped for, but also for those creative practitioners that they have worked with during the course of its production. Vertue talks of the dual frustration of her personal responsibility for a project not being realized successfully, but also a keen sense of accountability:

> [Y]ou get very disappointed, because everyone's worked so hard. And I think it's quite annoying to think you must have got it wrong then. So I'm annoyed about it, really. 'So why's that gone wrong, then?' What is very annoying is if you knew what was wrong with it and still it somehow got away with you. And you do feel emotionally involved because by that time these are all people you've worked with before, and you've all put loads into it.

Significant here is Vertue's description of her feelings of emotional involvement with both the programme and its workers. Hesmondhalgh and Baker have noted that there is an obligation by those working within the creative industries to deal with the particular emotions that are generated during the course of their jobs.[24] This management of emotions, or 'emotional labour', applies to both the creative workers' own and those of others around them. 'Emotional labour', as defined by Arlie Hochschild, requires that the worker to 'induce or suppress feeling in order to sustain the outward countenance that produces the proper state of mind in others'.[25] Hesmondhalgh and Baker operationalize the concept in order to understand the experiences of young television researchers working on a talent show, demonstrating how emotional labour is at work in behaviours such as keeping an emotional distance from contestants, pretending to care about guests or trying not to care too much and having a sense of personal responsibility for a contestant's failure to proceed on the show. There is a clear sense in which a form of emotional labour is required by Plowman and Vertue in the situations they describe. They both must negotiate their own frustrations and disillusionment in the face of one of their 'kids' not proving popular, but also manage the disappointment of the creative personnel that they have employed on the project, maintaining the workers' motivation for any future projects that they may be involved in together. The act of suppressing emotional feelings in order to be able to continue to work efficiently is of particular importance to those producers who work in independent production companies. Ash Atalla describes how having a close relationship with a project that might not end up going into production is 'kind of tortuous actually' and that consequently, 'sometimes it's best not to think about which of those babies is going to make it'.

While a strong personal investment in a project can lead to frustration and disappointment, and necessitate acts of emotional labour in order to quash inevitable feelings of anxiety, such emotions are not only widely accepted as an aspect of the job of producer but their absence can prove troubling both professionally and personally. Lumsden explicitly ties just such a lack of feeling to her decision to move on from her role as controller of comedy commissioning at the BBC. Her account relates to an award ceremony she attended where a show she had commissioned (*Outnumbered* [BBC1, 2007–]) won a comedy award:

> I remember sort of feeling kind of strangely numb. And wondering 'God, this is how good this job gets.' It's really strange, this is a creative job and yet I'm not really

feeling anything. And I think it was just having... some people are really good at it, they can have the dispassionate view and really have a feeling that you love it all and that it doesn't really matter if one thing succeeds and one things fail, but it really did matter to me.

A producer, particularly one working within a large broadcaster, must therefore find a balance between two aspects of the job that are frequently in conflict, one of which depersonalizes production processes and concerns large-scale programme management, while the other is entirely dependent on such personalization and is indeed essential to the producer's professional and personal fulfilment.

'Stand next to someone more talented': Trust

In his large-scale, longitudinal survey of creative workers in the television industry in the mid-to-late 1990s, Richard Paterson found 'trust' to be a crucial quality in a creative environment. It was perceived to be important in relationships between cultural workers, but also between workers and their employers. In the precarious and uncertain culture of television production it can help bring 'temporary order to the incipient chaos'.[26] Paterson's respondents reported a propensity for people to work with those that they already knew and trusted within the industry. For producers, there is a tension between a need to manage market risk and a demand for fresh and inventive ideas that are ordinarily brought to the industry by new talent. An unproven writer or writing team, even with an innovative suggestion for a new comedy programme that the producer is inspired by, is inevitably a creative gamble. The risk is heightened further if the project is pitched with other creative personnel already attached that are also inexperienced, as Lumsden noted when speaking about developing new talent:

> I think where it struggles is when you've got new talent and possibly a newer indie, who are also kind of cutting their teeth. And it's just, you know, be sensible about it. Be sensible in *any* industry about who you stand next to. Stand next to someone more talented and more known to the industry than perhaps you are.

In order to manage the uncertainty of working with untested writers, Lumsden alludes to a preference for working with writers that are developing their project with an established independent production company and thus in 'the hands of the experts'. She cites recognized 'indies' who specialize in comedy such as Tiger Aspect, Hat Trick and Objective. Allen similarly talks of having being enthused by the talent of Kayvan Novak, creator of *Fonejacker* (E4, 2006–2008) and *Facejacker* (Channel 4, 2010–), when first reading material he had sent to Channel 4, and then 'putting him in touch with a production company to make that programme'. The implication, therefore, is that there is a concerted strategy by broadcaster commissioner-producers to negotiate two seemingly conflicting demands in their work – controlling commercial risk and producing innovative comedy – by regularly teaming new talent with established independent players that they know and trust. This supports Robins and Cornford's proposal that new kinds of 'tight–loose' relationships have been formed between the larger independent production companies and broadcasting organizations that are mutually beneficial.[27] The broadcaster gains confidence through the genre-specific programme-making expertise of the production company, while the arrangement also suits the ambitions of the 'super-indies' to develop their own empires through integration on their own terms.[28]

There are, nevertheless, always exceptions with regard to a producer's considered actions in managing risk through using experienced and trusted programme-makers. Sometimes pure gut instinct for a project works against the established ways of avoiding commercial failure. As is demonstrated here by Lumsden's account of her decision to commission comedy series *This Is Jinsy* (BBC Three/Sky Atlantic, 2010–):

> I say all of that and then I contradicted myself with *This Is Jinsy* which was really new. But, you know, it didn't land that confidently on Sky Atlantic on its first airing. But we've gone with it again because it's just so inventive and exciting and different and I think those boys are really talented and have something really interesting to say.

Having commissioned the show's original pilot for BBC Three, Lumsden picked up the show for a full series not long after her move to Sky and has kept faith with it by commissioning a second series even though its audience ratings were unexceptional. It is a case-in-point for a producer putting trust, not in the knowledge and expertise of others, but in their own intuitive feeling for innovation and talent. That such faith is an important motivator for producers is evidenced in Atalla's expression of the possible extreme measures required in order for a project he has trust in to get made: 'I'm determined to get it on TV. Might have to sell my house to do that.'

'Allowing them to play in the sandbox': The individual and the team

While the interview material drawn on here prioritizes individuals and their statements about their working practices, such labourers do, of course, spend much of their time working with others, and creative work is often understood as collaborative. For example, David Gauntlett places creativity in a broader context of 'making', and titles his book *Making Is Connecting* 'because through making things and sharing them in the world, we increase our engagement and connection with our social and physical environments'.[29] In a number of books, Richard Florida has explored the ways in which institutions and cities can be structured in order to foster creativity, and these hinge upon the assumption that such work relies on encouraging interactions between individuals.[30] In response to these ideas, policy and charity groups, such as Nesta,[31] argue that creative 'clusters' should be encouraged via the planning of cities and other infrastructures, making economic cases for investment that encourages human creative interaction.[32] While our interview schedule did not explicitly encourage participants to explore their working practices within such policy-infused and large-scale contexts, what recurs throughout the data is reference to working with other people, and the roles producers play in encouraging such interplay. In some senses, the job description of a television producer could simply be someone who finds ways for other people to work together productively. As freelance producer Tandy put it when asked to define his role:

> As a producer I think what you're doing is you're bringing everything to the party. And you're letting the people with the vision – it may be the same person – but the person you're allowing them to play in the sandbox, play with the train set, make the thing that works. And you marshal them and you advise them. But fundamentally you're there to keep the train on the tracks.

Tellingly, Tandy makes it clear that the 'people with the vision' does not include him, yet his role is enabling that vision to come to fruition. The idea that being a producer is about 'enabling' others recurs in the interviews, and the material suggests that the essential job requirement for being a producer is a talent as a facilitator in order for others to achieve their ambitions.

What this means is that the producer occupies a position in which he or she is both part of a team yet also outside of it. While clearly a productive and resourceful role, producers are not understood to be creative to the same extent as, for example, writers, actors and directors. Yet the producers here insisted their job *was* creative, even if it was so in a manner different to the conventional understandings of the concept. For Beryl Vertue, her creative work can be found in 'the whole business of trying to make something happen in the best possible way', and acknowledges that this can go wrong if 'you end up choosing dodgy people'. By this account, encouraging disparate people to work towards a mutual vision functions as creativity, and the interviewees pointedly avoid talking about their role as one of 'oversight' or 'management', which might be difficult to square with assumptions about creativity. For example, Vertue talks about how the hit sitcom *Men Behaving Badly* (ITV/BBC One, 1992–2008) came about, as she worked with Simon Nye – who had had the story published as a novel – and who had no experience of working for television:

> And so I asked to meet the writer, and discovered Simon had never written anything and worked in a bank. And said, 'Would you like to write a television series, based on this book?' [He said,] 'I've never written a television series.' So I said, 'Well, I'll help you as much as I can.' But then we broke the book down. Because you were teaching someone what you knew and they had never done it before.

By this account, Vertue can make a convincing claim to be the primary instigator behind the existence of *Men Behaving Badly* as a television series, and her ability to 'teach someone' how to go about writing for television demonstrates an authority and expertise central to her role. The decision to mentor Nye is both a managerial *and* creative one, whose product depends squarely on the interaction between multiple people which would not have happened if Vertue hadn't seen the possibility of an opportunity. Examining the American film and television production system, John Thornton Caldwell catalogues the ongoing personal and legal disputes concerning who is and is not creative (and, by extension, who is therefore the author of a media product). Despite the marketing desire to find *the* author of a television programme, Caldwell argues 'negotiated and collective authorship is an almost unavoidable and determining reality in contemporary film/television'.[33] The producers interviewed here consistently acknowledge the necessity of collaboration, and their role is to foster it.

Perhaps more significantly, these producers repeatedly point to the pleasure to be had in such collaboration, and it is the ability to work with other people – and, in many cases, to make them *better* – that appears to be a key inducement to working as a producer. For Allen joy is to be found in 'Evolving an idea and working closely with talent and with performers, that's the brilliant bit.' For Normal, there is pleasure in the 'camaraderie and helping' of newer, younger comics. That the interaction between producers and new writers changes over time as the process develops is acknowledged by Atalla, who states, 'And so you start off with, perhaps quite a pure relationship between yourself and a writer, and it gradually grows [...] So you gradually have gone from "this was just us" to other people.' Andy Hamilton (who has worked on series such as *Drop the Dead Donkey* [Channel 4, 1990–1998], *Bedtime* [BBC One, 2001–2003] and *Outnumbered* [BBC One, 2007–]) explains how it is via collaboration that experienced creative workers such as him continue to learn from the teams they are a part of:

> I like the collaborative process of making it. If you get a chance to make something and you're working with a crew and artists and an editor, I enjoy all of those things. I enjoy the writing phase, and then the execution of it, filming it, recording it, whatever, and then the editing, if it's a show that has editing, I enjoy that as well. Exploring the plasticity of what you've made. It's always interesting. It always throws up new things. Like anything, you know, experience only tells you so much, it doesn't tell you everything. You still find things out.

Clearly, here we see what Florida calls 'the passionate quest for experience' resulting in 'a creative life packed full of intense, high-quality multidimensional experiences', which is a mindset he argues defines those in the creative industries.[34] What our interviews with producers show is that this context is as vital for this group of workers as it is for others, suggesting that producers enter, and remain in the television comedy business for precisely the same reasons as other cultural workers. The particular set of skills necessary to be a good producer matter little; despite Tunstall's characterization of them as somehow distinct from others in the industry, the *motivation* for engaging in such labour accords with that of those with whom they collaborate.

'Remember … when you were 14 years old'

So, what does this analysis tell us about what it is to be a television comedy producer? How can these findings inform existing work, such as that produced by Tunstall two decades ago? Tunstall points towards the onset of a blurring of the 'traditional' roles that existed in television production for many years, and delineated positions such as the producer, the director and the writer. He prophesizes the increase in the number of people fulfilling multiple aspects of each of these positions, not least in response to the growth of the independent production sector, which itself responds to performers' desire to have more autonomy over their work.[35] In that sense, the model of 'the producer' needs to be updated, and what Tunstall refers to may be quite a different beast from what is being explored here. Indeed, as this chapter started by delineating two quite different types of producers (in-house and independent), it is clear that the role is a loosely defined one, which seems to respond to whatever demands are placed upon it. That said, all our respondents made a case for producing to be understood as a creative act, and it is this aspect that may be the most significant shift since Tunstall's analysis. If there was one ambition that united our interviewees it was that their labour remained creative and, as has been shown earlier, a number of them are willing to forego job security in order to ensure this is the case.

It is therefore worth acknowledging the pleasure to which these producers referred. For example, Tandy saw working on an interesting project as more valuable than taking a break, saying he'd agreed to be involved in a particular programme because 'This is worth not having any holiday.' Similarly, Lumsden recounts the joy that her work can bring:

[O]ne of the best moments when in an otherwise dull, neon-lit office, magic happens and you have this incredible performance in front of you and you can't stop laughing. And you walk away thinking, 'How can I not commission that? That was brilliant!'

Allen argues that the stage in your life when comedy matters the most is when you are a teenager, and therefore attempts to recreate that mindset, and has that aged audience in mind, when looking at projects. His advice is therefore to 'remember […] when you were 14 years old what you loved about comedy'.

That similar statements recurred across our interviews shows there are clear similarities in the roles and functions producers fulfil in the television comedy industry, no matter whether they are salaried or freelance, in-house or independent. Perhaps the key finding here is the recurring insistence on the part of our interviewees that their work is creative, even though it may wrongly be assumed to be primarily managerial: indeed, Tunstall's categories seem to foreground such managerial aspects. Being a producer is a constant negotiation between the bits of the job you are required to do, and those which you enjoy doing and which led you to working in the industry in the first place. As this book shows, academic work on media production has written producers consistently out of the creative process, yet exploration of the working practices of many within the television industry shows that producers engage in a wide range of creative activity. Thus, more work on the specific particularity of that creative labour – which is related to, but is not identical to, that of roles which are conventionally understood as creative, such as writers and directors – can contribute to a fuller understanding of the routes and processes by which the creative industries function and cultural texts such as television programmes come into being. The 'naughty horse' is a complex and vital role, and these interviews show that those who occupy it are acutely aware of that complexity, and the negotiations they must repeatedly carry out in order to succeed are a result of the job's multiple facets.

Notes

1 Lucy Lumsden, Interview with Sarah Ralph, 10 September 2012.
2 Ash Atalla, Interview with Sarah Ralph, 11 September, 2012.
3 David Hesmondhalgh, *The Cultural Industries*, 3rd edn. (London: Sage, 2013), 81.
4 The analytical framework used on our interview materials is an adaptation of an approach to discourse originally employed within the field of health psychology: Interpretative Phenomenological Analysis (IPA). The aim of IPA, according to Jonathan A. Smith who developed the approach, is to investigate in *detail* people's accounts of their individual experiences and explore how they make sense of their personal and social worlds. Rather than investigating broadly across groups and populations, IPA begins by making detailed and intensive examinations of individual cases, before building these into a more general, integrated analysis later in the research process. This allows the researcher to communicate an understanding of the significant generic themes of the analysis, but also to make more specific statements about individual participants. Though IPA procedures are detailed, the overall process provides a significant degree of flexibility that lends itself well to its application to the reflections of television comedy industry professionals and their 'worlds'. For a more detailed explanation of this analytical approach and its recommended stages of analysis see Jonathan A. Smith and Mike Osborn. 'Interpretative Phenomenological Analysis', in *Qualitative Psychology: A Practical Guide to Research Methods*, ed. Jonathan A. Smith (London: Sage, 2008), 53–80 and Carla Willig, *Introducing Qualitative Research in Psychology*, 2nd edn. (Maidenhead: Open University Press, 2008).
5 The first of these, 'Funny Business: Interviews with Members of the British Terrestrial Television Comedy Industry' (2005–2006), was conducted by Brett Mills at the University of Glamorgan. The present project, 'Make Me Laugh: Creativity in the British Television Comedy Industry' (2012–2014), is being led by Brett Mills, with Sarah Ralph as Research Associate, at the University of East Anglia (visit www.makemelaugh.org.uk).
6 Richard Paterson, 'The Contingencies of Creative Work in Television', *The Open Communication Journal*, 4 (2010): 1.
7 Jeremy Tunstall, *Television Producers* (London: Routledge, 1993), 2.
8 Tunstall, *Television Producers*, 128.
9 David John Lee, 'Precarious Creativity: Working Lives in the British Independent Televisions Production Industry' (PhD diss., Goldsmiths College, University of London, 2009), 156.

10   Shane Allen, Interview with Sarah Ralph, 27 September 2012. At the time of this interview Allen was the Head of Comedy at Channel 4 but had just been announced as the new BBC Head of Comedy, a role which he took up in December 2012.

11   Jon Plowman [then Head of BBC Comedy], Interview with Brett Mills, 8 June 2005.

12   Beryl Vertue, Interview with Brett Mills, 21 June 2005.

13   John Thornton Caldwell, *Production Culture: Industrial Reflexivity and Critical Practice in Film and Television* (Durham and London: Duke University Press, 2008), 2–3.

14   Tunstall, *Television Producers*, 236.

15   See, for example, the detailed account of the establishment and aims of Channel 4 in the opening chapter – 'The Birth of the Channel' – in Dorothy Hobson, *Channel 4: The Early Years and the Jeremy Isaacs Legacy* (London: I.B. Tauris, 2008): 1–21.

16   'The WoCC', BBC, accessed 15 January 2013, http://www.bbc.co.uk/commissioning/tv/how-we-work/the-wocc.shtml.

17   Brett Mills, *The Sitcom* (Edinburgh: Edinburgh University Press, 2009), 67.

18   For example, see Ron Jenkins, *Subversive Laughter: The Liberating Power of Comedy* (New York: Free Press, 1994); and Michael Billig, *Laughter and Ridicule: Towards a Social Critique of Humour* (London: Sage, 2005).

19   Adam Tandy, Interview with Brett Mills, 18 December 2012.

20   Andrew Ross, *Nice Work if You Can Get It: Life and Labor in Precarious Times* (New York: New York University Press, 2009), 5.

21   John Storey et al., 'Living with Enterprise in an Enterprise Economy: Freelance and Contract Workers in the Media', *Human Relations*, 58:8 (2005): 1033–54.

22   Theodor W. Adorno, *The Culture Industry: Selected Essays on Mass Culture* (London: Routledge, 2006).

23   Henry Normal, Interview with Brett Mills, 22 March, 2006.

24   David Hesmondhalgh and Sarah Baker, 'Creative Work and Emotional Labor in the Television Industry', *Theory, Culture and Society*, 25 (2008): 97–118 at 108.

25   As quoted in Hesmondhalgh and Baker, 'Creative Work and Emotional Labor in the Television Industry', 108.

26   Paterson, 'The Contingencies of Creative Work in Television', 5.

27   Kevin Robins and James Cornford, 'What Is "flexible" about Independent Producers?', *Screen*, 33:2 (Summer 1992): 196.

28   Robins and Cornford, 'What Is "flexible" about Independent Producers?', 197.

29   David Gauntlett, *Making Is Connecting: The Social Meaning of Creativity, from DIY and Knitting to YouTube and Web 2.0* (Cambridge: Polity, 2011), 3.

30   For example, see Richard Florida, *The Rise of the Creative Class* (New York: Basic Books, 2003) and *Cities and the Creative Class* (London: Routledge, 2004).

31   Formerly the National Endowment for Science, Technology and the Arts (NESTA), Nesta is an independent charity funding a wide range of research.

32   Caroline Chapain et al., *Creative Clusters and Innovation: Putting Creativity on the Map* (Nesta: London, 2010).

33   Caldwell, *Production Culture*, 199.

34   Richard Florida, 'The Experiential Life', in *Creative Industries*, ed. John Hartley (Oxford: Blackwell, 2005), 134.

35   Tunstall, *Television Producers*, 135–36.

10

Keith Griffiths' Poetics of Production

Sonia Friel

Keith Griffiths is commonly associated with the production of stop-motion animated films on account of his long-standing partnerships with Jan Švankmajer and the Quay brothers, which have arguably given rise to his most widely recognizable body of work and remain the chief focus of critical discussions. However, this narrow emphasis can be somewhat misleading. Over the course of a prolific career, Griffiths has catered for a remarkable multiplicity of media, distribution platforms and scales, ranging from low-budget television documentaries to feature films and international, multi-platform installations. Moreover, his selection of projects is not primarily based on a preference for a particular medium or genre, but on a deeply rooted identification with those who treat creative practice as an opportunity for pioneering discoveries and radical inventions. It is the renegade experimenters on the margins of any creative discipline that Griffiths consequently finds most inspiring, and in his hands the role of the producer is transformed into a passionate vocation to seek out '… outsiders, whether they are artists or film-makers' and to provide a space in which their experiments can thrive.[1]

This philosophy of cultivating invention presents numerous challenges during production and distribution. Since a considerable number of the artists and film-makers with whom Griffiths works rely on experimental or intuitive methods that are inherently unpredictable, their proposed projects take courage to pursue and are largely contingent upon adaptive, unfettered conditions of production. The oblique and unconventional pieces that frequently result from such methods also tend to appeal to a niche market – one that is often extremely passionate, but does not readily translate into sizeable financial returns.

For over 40 years, however, Griffiths has not only catered for such work, but has also made it profitable. Reflecting on this achievement, he notes:

> The reality is that we keep producing modest films and television programmes that are on the margins of the industry as a whole, but because we produce high quality imaginative work on schedule and on budget – we keep working.[2]

This winning combination of efficiency and high quality is particularly difficult given Griffiths' primary focus on catering for unpredictable creative methods; hence, he is careful to keep the scope of projects achievable, and leads tight-knit, efficient teams. His success also reflects the wealth of expertise within his enviably diverse network of industry professionals, scholars and artists, all of whom appreciate the potential of innovative creative practice, understand its target market and are similarly committed to providing for its unique and demanding requirements during production. With this solid infrastructure in place, working apart from mainstream production channels can become a considerable asset. Moreover, when coordinating distribution, Griffiths recognizes that 'a "niche" exhibition strategy for some films can create a "cultish" climate and that this, with good press and publicity, maximises audience potential'.[3] The works produced from this background consequently often extend beyond 'high quality' into the award-winning and the iconic, appealing to a wider audience than is usually the case for such apparently marginal material.[4]

Griffiths' long-term and successful commitment to nonconformist material has established him as something of a maverick within the independent film industry. He is a prominent figure at film festivals, approached regularly by funding boards and industry panels for consultancy and advisory positions.[5] Within critical and academic circles, however, his substantial contribution to contemporary film and media production remains virtually unexplored. While this dearth of critical analysis is unfortunately all too predictable – after all, he is not only a producer, but an independent, marginal producer – Griffiths also rarely puts himself in the spotlight. Although he is a highly opinionated and even formidable character in conversation, when discussion has turned to his own life and work he has sometimes seemed deliberately evasive; indeed, scarce few biographical details exist in the public domain and very little headway has been made into the rich interests and motivations that underlie Griffiths' production ethos.

This reluctance to either self-document or be documented stems, for the most part, from Griffiths' professional modesty; and perhaps also from his suspicion that others might pigeonhole and misrepresent his intentions in a bid to portray him as a neatly defined character or caricature. Yet the air of mystery that surrounds him also dovetails with his own creative interests as a director and writer. Griffiths is rather unusual in that he has directed documentaries and short films alongside his production career and has published a mixture of critical and semi-fictitious texts. These are often replete with word play, pseudo-histories and literary subterfuge, revealing a fascination with the ambiguous territory between truth and fiction, one that can even occasionally inspire Griffiths to merge the two when discussing his own life: ' "fictive", this is a word I like … It is a passion for me though [it] causes chaos with academic accuracy for sure.'[6]

Even though Griffiths' evasiveness and tendency to self-fictionalise make him a challenging research subject, numerous frank and in-depth discussions between him and this chapter's author have facilitated an understanding of his production ethos. Griffiths' lifelong commitment to innovative material is particularly significant; largely indebted to his earliest experiences of film-making and production, it has clear practical ramifications for the way in which he and his production teams have worked subsequently with artists and directors. Equally significant is Griffiths' interest in the tension he sees between 'reality' and 'magic', as it has shaped his criteria for selecting projects as well as his production methods. By considering these two areas in turn, this chapter hopes to reveal that they are not as distinct from one another as they initially appear, but rather contribute to a production approach that is more akin to a poetics of production than a pragmatic strategy. It then considers briefly their joint influence through an analysis of a selection of works that Griffiths has produced, demonstrating the benefits of his unconventional methodologies in a variety of contexts – from television documentaries in the early 1990s through to his most recent digital and curatorial projects.

Nurturing difference

On the wall of Keith Griffiths' office hangs a single, framed postcard of a 1965 work by the French Fluxus artist Ben Vautier. In bold, black-on-white Helvetica type it commands the viewer to IMAGINEZ AUTRE CHOSE – to imagine something different. This instruction has become something of a mantra for Griffiths during production, informing his selection of projects and encouraging him to always think outside the box. His firm conviction that innovative material has the potential to rupture the passive indifference that Robert Bresson once described as a 'school of inattention: people look without seeing, listen in without hearing',[7] has shaped significantly his own cultural interests and tastes, surfacing in his preference for the minority treasures of literature, film and art, and in the themes he explores creatively: even his politics are 'driven by the "imaginative and innovative", however one chooses to define that for oneself'.[8] It has also led Griffiths to campaign for the widespread consideration of 'something different' within art and film production as a whole. Many of his contributions to industry publications and discussions demand that the art and film industries cater for the diverse needs of unconventional work at every level, striving towards the innovative from the top down as well as the bottom up.

Griffiths' gravitation towards the 'different' was already apparent during his formative career. As a student at Leicester College of Art and the Royal College of Art, he met a 'fantastic diverse range of people'.[9] These included fellow RCA students Tony Scott, the Quays, Chris Springhall, Michael Whyte and Peter Leake. Griffiths worked enthusiastically with these peers on a similarly diverse range of cutting-edge creative projects alongside his studies.[10] After graduating from the RCA, Griffiths worked in regional arts associations and became increasingly involved in some of the more peripheral, radical groups of local independent film-makers that he and his colleagues were particularly keen to nurture.[11] Emerging as a prominent contributor to broader debates concerning independent and marginal film-making,[12] when Griffiths was appointed Deputy Head of Production to Peter Sainsbury at the BFI in 1976, his familiarity with the diverse requirements of these communities more than compensated for his relative lack of hands-on production experience. Here, once again, he was working with co-operatives and young film-makers fresh out of art school on 'low-budget films in a low-budget manner'.[13] Nevertheless, Griffiths was learning on the job – as indeed were some of the young directors working alongside him – and the rare freedom they were granted gave them the time and confidence to pursue many different options; he recalls countless meandering trips spent scanning the roads between London and Bristol for shooting locations during the filming of Chris Petit's *Radio On* (1979). In this respect, the five years that he spent at the BFI proved invaluable, as they alerted him to the benefits of a lateral and fairly ad-hoc approach, which, although it was not uniformly well received, seemed particularly well suited to those working in a more spontaneous, intuitive way.[14]

Griffiths' position at the BFI also gave him a unique perspective during a pivotal period within the history of British independent film-making. Throughout the 1970s, the Independent Film-makers' Association had campaigned for better funding and the more extensive distsribution of work made by the 'independents', chiefly in response to their lack of representation on the BBC. With the imminent arrival of Channel 4, their cause became more pressing. This was because even when an agreement had been reached that the new channel would fund independent content, opinions varied dramatically as to how best to meet its needs.[15]

In the midst of this volatile climate of debate, Griffiths' own response to this dilemma began to coalesce. In a polemical article published in *Broadcast* magazine in October 1979, he proposed a model for the new channel to consider that hinged on the concept of an 'experimental laboratory'.[16] Griffiths envisaged this laboratory as a dedicated environment in which independent film-makers could experiment with materials and techniques free from the constraints of creative briefs or deadlines. Despite this relative autonomy, however, its members would receive adequate industry funding and would see selections from their combined output aired on regular television slots. This approach was derived partly from his own experiences of production, but was also informed by a number of comparable initiatives that Griffiths had encountered during overseas research trips.[17] He was inspired particularly by the social potency of the heterogeneous, and at times contentious, material that such initiatives were introducing into mainstream distribution channels. Believing that 'the diversity and future of television could lie in nurturing this reservoir of ideas and talent', Channel 4 seemed to him to present a similar opportunity for television, and viewers' relationship with it, to be entirely transformed.[18]

Elements of this model were immediately reflected in Griffiths' own production ethos. Channel 4, which first broadcast on 2 November 1982, was obliged by statute to 'encourage innovation and experiment in the form and content of programmes'. With their newly founded independent production company Large Door Ltd. – a pun on Buñuel's surrealist masterwork *L'Age d'Or* (1930) – Griffiths, Simon Hartog and media academic John Ellis were quick to capitalize on this rare opportunity to introduce marginal work into the public domain. The three worked closely with a range of independent film-makers to produce a cinema review series for the new channel that discussed non-mainstream film-making industries and auteurs in a manner that frequently undercut the conventions of the genre.[19] In many respects, Large Door also set a precedent for Griffiths: the overwhelming majority of his subsequent projects have involved working within independent production companies that were cofounded with close acquaintances.[20] Here he has endeavoured to provide artists and film-makers with a 'studio space ... with a small 's' in the non-Hollywood way of using the term' – a similar laboratory-esque environment in which creative experimentation is prioritized above all else.[21]

Griffiths is particularly attuned to the negative impact that a script can have upon experimentation, noting that '[m]ost "screenplays" are written so that one reads the film, which for me is self-defeating and discourages the imaginative tensions and visual and sensory pleasures to be gained from the creative play of both ideas and material'.[22] Having the freedom to pursue creative play is equally important to many of the film-makers and artists with whom he has chosen to work. Rather than religiously adhering to a script, they develop their pieces organically through intuitive methods, encouraging chance discoveries or layering multiple sources of visual information and narrative to produce 'unscriptable' results. In these instances, a traditional production trajectory, which starts with a tightly honed script and privileges it throughout, is simply not appropriate. Hence, Griffiths is keen to ensure that artists are given the time and freedom to venture off-piste whenever necessary, not only by defending the decision of those who choose to work without a script, but also by creating production schedules with sufficient space and time for creative play.

The inherent unpredictability and risk of such experimental processes have made Griffiths extremely selective in his choice of projects. While his production career has certainly been wide ranging, it has also included long-term, prolific partnerships with a small group of directors: the Quay brothers, Jan Švankmajer, Chris Petit, Patrick Keiller, Iain Sinclair and Simon Pummell. His conscious decision to adopt a 'small artisan model' within each of his companies rather than that of a large, well-oiled production machine has the distinct advantage of ensuring that a close alliance is forged between an artist or film-maker and their production team.[23] On a practical level, this enables the latter to tailor their approach according to the needs of individual projects, or to adapt quickly in response to new creative directions. Crucially, it is also founded on an unwavering, reciprocal trust, thereby providing a sense of security during creative processes that can seem especially uncertain. Griffiths has likened this relationship to a marriage on the basis that it hinges upon this trust, and specifically upon a shared commitment to an original creative spark in which both parties passionately believe.[24] While the artist agrees not to compromise this core concept, Griffiths and his teams endeavour to protect it from any external pressures, not least those pushing for a more commercially attractive or palatable product.

Griffiths has referred to this core group as his 'family' on a number of occasions: 'The important thing was developing a very close family of film-makers with whom one identified, whose work one loved.'[25] When one considers the filmic work made by this group collectively, many resonances emerge that lend weight to this notion of a familial creative community, from shared themes (psychogeography or the esoteric, for example) to an especially fluid approach to form and narrative that embraces ambiguity, self-referentiality and intertextual polyphony.

Bearing in mind that these directors are all fans of one another's work, have often written about one another and (in the case of Chris Petit and Iain Sinclair) have worked on films together, it can be tempting to treat such similarities as evidence of a highly collaborative production environment. The conclusion that Griffiths exerts a great deal of control over the creative direction of projects can be similarly persuasive, particularly when one considers that his own films have explored similar themes, created similar ambiguities and even been made in direct response to works he has produced.[26]

Yet it is important to recognize that the directors mentioned here all maintain their independence, and have tended towards particular themes and techniques over the course of many years of creative practice. Although Griffiths' precise influence on projects is difficult to determine, it is also never something that he tries actively to assert: 'I have no idea how influential one is in shaping work ... But the form is in their hands.'[27] When discussing his role, Griffiths is consequently keen to distance himself from the creative process; he is wary of popular terms like 'Creative Producer' on the grounds that they ascribe too much significance to the creative impact of production.[28] By contrast, he emphasizes its predominantly pragmatic objectives:

> I think it is a producer's job to see the whole process of making a film right the way through – from development to reaching an audience. This inevitably means focusing clearly on what one is making and how one can exploit the rabbit holes that one can find, to bring imaginative work to the surface. This demands holding a watching brief over every element of production, distribution, promotion, press and marketing, and ensuring that the real experts in those particular fields understand the animal they will be handling and don't try to shape it into something it is not.[29]

This attitude reflects Griffiths' commitment to ensuring that directors are given the freedom and space to realize their work to its full potential. As such, Iain Sinclair's oft-repeated description of Griffiths as 'the great facilitator of contemporary British cinema'[30] seems particularly apt, capturing both his pragmatism and the influence he exerts at one remove. From his defence of innovative film-making on an industry-wide scale to his cultivation of small enclaves of experimentation within which it can thrive, Griffiths' chief function as a producer seems to be that of an enabler. However, the close relationships he has formed with his core group of collaborators and his deep emotional investment in creative concepts mean that in practice his involvement is not always so clearly defined. During production Griffiths frequently alternates between an objective, pragmatic stance and that of a creative sounding board. He therefore considers his role to be both that of 'an "enabler" and sometimes a "catalyst" '.[31]

Having established Griffiths' dedicated but largely passive role during the creative process, one might look to his selection of projects to explain the thematic and formal similarities that exist between many of the works that he produces. It is especially significant that Griffith's interest in innovative and experimental work is fuelled by a keen desire to explore a tension between magic and reality, and that this desire informs his selection of projects:

> The awareness of the importance of this tension between 'reality' and 'magic' and the experiences to be gained from walking between the two, lies at the heart of my personal choices in the production of films and programmes and of the collaborations that these inevitably involve.[32]

Indeed, this tension seems to underpin many of the recurring themes and formal approaches that surface in Griffiths-produced works; from the psychogeographical re-evaluation of a landscape to the representation of narrative as intertextual and ever evolving, the fixity of the division between reality and magic or truth and fiction is continually being tested. Although Griffiths is intentionally distanced from the creative development of projects he produces, by choosing almost exclusively to work with artists and film-makers who share his passions, his gathering together of like-minded artists becomes in itself an expression of his own creative tastes.

Experimental alchemy

In 1987, Griffiths visited an exhibition curated by his close acquaintance Jürgen Glaesemer that brought the crux of this relationship between magic and reality to his attention. In doing so it 'profoundly affected [his] way of thinking about the films and TV programmes that [he] was either making or producing'.[33] 'Die Gleichzeitigkeit des Anderen' ('The Presence of the Other') had an unusual premise.[34] Rather than focusing on a particular movement, genre or aesthetic, it aimed to reveal an invisible system of meaning within art – one that appealed to deeper, unconscious forms of perception rather than to the intellect or rational mind. As Griffiths explains:

> The theme of 'The Presence of the Other' prompted an examination of artists' work for their magical content. Not the informational content or other logically comprehensible elements in their work, but into the 'other', or that which is hidden behind the rationally understandable elements of art. This was an exploration of art which not only portrays the visible but, as a voyage into the interior, renders visible.[35]

For Griffiths, this distinction (a deliberate reference to Paul Klee's observation that 'Art does not reproduce the visible; rather it makes visible')[36] manifests itself in the complex relationship between an artwork and its artist or audience, given that an appreciation of any 'visible' qualities (its technical finesse or use of symbolism, for example) is often underscored by a subjective and largely intuitive emotional response. Crucially, Griffiths also recognized that Glaesemer's curatorial approach – especially his juxtaposition of exhibited pieces with a simultaneous programme of films, concerts, lectures and readings – created confrontations between diverse media forms that often revealed hidden resonances, enabling an artwork to transcend its visual and informational elements.

As film-maker-in-residence at the University of Salzburg (1991), Griffiths was able to investigate extensively themes and methods emerging from 'The Presence of the Other'.[37] Over the course of his residency, Griffiths conducted a series of workshops that demonstrated ways in which to access hidden resonances within and between materials. The first of these centred on research, specifically on the preliminary interpretation of source material that a film-maker must conduct prior to making, for example, a documentary. Arranging a selection of disparate images on a table, Griffiths explained the significance he personally attached to handling and physical manipulation:

> I think 'found material' connects with research. The programmes I make tend to be a simple montage of sounds and images, some of which I shoot myself and some of which are archive. There is nothing unique in this. But conceptually, I think that the heart of the process of production is a sort of surrealistic game – I believe quite profoundly that the traces of the subject are buried deep within the source material, and that it is only by handling the objects, looking at the images with which one is working over and over and by pursuing one's research obsessively, that any kind of subjective viewpoint can emerge.[38]

This coaxing out of latent 'traces of the subject' within materials recalls Glaesemer's curatorial approach and also sounds distinctly Heideggerian. As Griffiths considers it to be of the utmost importance that he is emotionally invested in his subject matter and creates pieces that are informed by his own subjective interpretation, this research stage is an absolutely integral element of his own creative practice.

In a second workshop, simply entitled 'The Presence', Griffiths presented a selection of materials in a manner that preserved the ambivalence between the visible and invisible, thereby encouraging the workshop's participants to engage with the materials in a similarly subjective manner. Abandoning the traditional workshop format, he created an immersive environment within the University's vaulted cellars that was inspired by the complex relationship between the sixteenth-century alchemists John Dee and Edward Kelley. Here, participants met with an eclectic mixture of objects, performances, music, projections and screenings that shifted 'from documentary to fiction, from the historical to the contemporary; combining found images with constructed and staged images and tableaux'.[39] Like Glaesemer, Griffiths hoped to shift emphasis away from logically comprehensible information, thereby allowing the 'ideas that are buried within the narrative' to surface.[40] He also demonstrated that such an approach does not preclude more obvious or 'visible' forms of narrative; the dialogue used in the installation accentuated its ambiguity as characters improvised, merged truth and fiction and spoke using fractured, oblique language. To make sense of this experience, participants had to engage imaginatively with the broad range of audio-visual materials, teasing out meaning by considering deeper, perhaps more primal impressions and instincts. Griffiths also encouraged them to use this subjective experience as the basis for their own video sketches, allowing them to put some of the techniques they had witnessed into practice.

It is particularly fitting that Griffiths chose to base this second workshop on alchemy. He has been interested in the subject since meeting Jan Švankmajer and discovering the history of Rudolfine Prague. In later years, he would share this passion with the author Angela Carter, with whom he enjoyed numerous long discussions on the subject and exchanged books.[41] In conversation, Griffiths also often uses alchemy as a metaphor for his belief that latent traces within materials can be revealed through the creation of ambiguity: a 'clash of disparate elements' that results in a process of 'transmutation'.[42] However, Griffiths admits he sometimes finds this method 'a bit pretentious … except as a "thinking process." '[43]

Griffiths particularly approves the multi-disciplinary quality of the writings of alchemists such as Dee and Kelley, which combined science, arts, technology and magic to reveal unexpected intersections. Similarly, the media historian Siegfried Zielinski is a great inspiration. His *Deep Time of the Media* calls for the creation of an 'alchemical laboratory' in which science, art and more 'primitive' magical beliefs are given equal footing.[44] Zielinski puts this approach into practice in his own writings and in his approach to research. *Deep Time of the Media* draws from an extensive range of historical, technological and scientific material to reveal correspondences between the most unlikely of people and materials.[45] Zielinksi has also formed 'alchemical' research environments in Salzburg, Cologne and Berlin in which, as Griffiths recalls, 'ideas and boffins and practitioners could contaminate each other'.[46] Both Zielinski and the alchemists of old offer precedents for a particular kind of creative research that Griffiths mirrors in his own practice, 'pursuing … research obsessively' and incorporating an unusually holistic range of content and materials.

Key methods for preserving a tension between the invisible and visible have consequently emerged from Griffiths' workshops and reflections, both with regard to his particular approach to research (which involves tactile manipulation and is multi-disciplinary and holistic) and to his presentation of found materials where collisions between diverse objects and media create ambiguities that invite subjective interpretations. These approaches are immediately discernable in Griffiths' working practices as a director. In his more overtly fictitious films, the deliberate ambiguity between realism and non-realism has often provided the basis for fantastical metanarratives, which experiment with form and text in a self-referential manner that borders on the paradoxical. This is particularly evident in two shorts made in collaboration with Ian Christie: a profile of the Chilean director Raúl Ruiz for *Visions* and the short film *The Land of Counterpane*.[47] When filming more conventional documentaries, the vast majority of which were made for the Channel 4 series *Visions*, *Eleventh Hour* and *Ghosts in the Machine*, Griffiths also elaborated on many of the methods he explored in his Salzburg workshops. During a trip that saw Griffiths simultaneously gathering content for his Ruiz film and a documentary on Len Lye, he adopted an approach that prefigured his suggestion to 'pursu[e] one's research obsessively'. He recalls: 'I travelled round the world twice in Lye's footsteps in order that I would understand him myself and that his hidden traces could seep into the film.'[48]

Although *Doodlin': Impressions of Len Lye* (1987) was ostensibly 'a simple montage of sounds and images', it created ambiguity between its informational content and its 'hidden traces'. As in 'The Presence', this was partly achieved through the juxtaposition of a wide range of material without a didactic, overarching narration, requiring the viewer to engage actively with the material on show. It also shifted between established documentary conventions and a more playful, self-referential perspective (with the frame widening to reveal a tape recorder playing an audio recording, for instance). The effect of this was to render the invisible visible. In so doing, Griffiths encouraged viewers to engage with the documentary content as found material, to discover 'hidden traces' of meaning, and, ultimately, to 'participate in the subjective' themselves.[49]

Production strategies

These creative methods might seem far removed from Griffiths' work as a producer. However, they are absolutely integral to his production approach. While it can be useful to think of Griffiths as being attracted by the innovative and the marginal, more specifically he seeks out those who, like himself, use unconventional methods in order to create a tension between the visible and invisible. This tension is consequently at the heart of Griffiths' choice of projects. Returning to alchemy, he elaborates:

> the transmutation of different elements is very important to me. At the heart of all the films [I am interested in] I think are people who manage to make magic out of disparate elements ... that tension between [magic and reality] is *the* critical element in many films. The very spirit of a film comes out through not being able to tie it down.[50]

Hence, in many of the works that Griffiths produces, we see creative methods that are very similar to those already discussed: found materials are manipulated in order to access hidden systems of meaning, and content is presented in a deeply ambiguous manner that encourages subjective interpretations. These methods are particularly visible in the works of stop-motion animators such as Švankmajer, the Quays and Simon Pummell, in which physical manipulation and a subjective engagement with found materials are integral. Švankmajer has described handling and animation as coercing the inner life out of objects.[51] He admits that when filming he ensures that he is 'with the topic 24 hours a day' so that his unconscious desires can infiltrate and inform his approach.[52] However, they are arguably just as influential to the other members of Griffiths' core group, who manipulate materials and conduct extensive research in other, more hidden, ways.

Such techniques were fundamental to Patrick Keiller during the filming and production of his Griffiths-produced Robinson trilogy: *London* (1994), *Robinson in Space* (1996) and *Robinson in Ruins* (2010). In the initial stages of filming for *London*,

Keiller made the radical decision to abandon his extensive script in favour of a much more spontaneous approach, which he would also adopt for the latter two films. Working from the second half of his original script, Keiller produced a rough outline and treatment of just a few pages before shooting a large amount of footage in an ad-hoc manner as he wandered through the streets of London.[53] Bringing all of this footage into the editing suite, he then developed it in a manner reminiscent of Griffiths' manipulation of found material, experimenting with countless configurations and edits before settling on a structure, and lastly a narrative, that best expressed the film's central ambivalences.

In all three films, these ambivalences hinge on the mysterious psychogeographer Robinson. Although 'the problem of England' that they explore seems to be seen through his eyes and understood through his words, Robinson himself is neither seen nor heard. Rather, he is simply the subject of anecdotes recalled by a reminiscing narrator, and as such is reduced to a third person character who could just as conceivably be factual or fictitious, contemporary or historical. Robinson consequently provides Keiller with a powerful framework upon which to construct similar ambiguities within his representation of the quotidian. This could be through the juxtaposition of gritty reality with an idealized vision of England: for Keiller, *London* 'is essentially a joke about a man who thinks he would be happier if London were more like Paris, or like he imagines Paris used to be'.[54] Or it can be achieved by revealing stratified histories and memories beneath the surface of familiar spaces. Keiller uses these ambiguities to address contemporary issues within a much broader context, with Robinson's astute observations forming the basis of polemic social critiques. Yet for Griffiths, the most intriguing aspect of these films is the resultant tension between truth and fiction, an uncompromising indefinability that keeps an audience guessing: 'The confusion over defining [*London*] as either "fiction" or "documentary" lies at the heart of its power'.[55]

Director Chris Petit has worked almost exclusively with Griffiths since the latter produced *Radio On* (1979) at the BFI. Since 1992, Griffiths has also produced a number of collaborations between Petit and the author Iain Sinclair. In a trilogy of fictive documentaries for Channel 4 that explored cultural memory and representation, *The Cardinal and the Corpse* (1992), *The Falconer* (1997) and *Asylum* (2000), the pair used methods reminiscent of those advocated by Griffiths (and indeed by Keiller) to create a tension between the visible and invisible. Petit and Sinclair initially collected a huge amount of found audio-visual material and filmed extensively and freely, without a script. This was a relentless, long-winded process that verged on the obsessive. For *The Falconer*, which centred on the author Peter Whitehead – an evasive figure whose conversations spanned an eclectic assortment of topics – the research process alone took over two years, ranging from falconry, Egyptology and shamanism, to covert black market deals in the Middle East.

Petit and Sinclair coaxed hidden resonances from within the material itself in post-production. In a comment that echoes Griffiths' workshop on manipulation, Sinclair recalls 'playing old footage, over and over, until a mythical structure declares itself'.[56] The pair considered this an approach opposite to the conventional presentation of 'indifferently faked reality as a form of documentary truth'.[57] By creating films that openly combined truth and fiction, they hoped to puncture the illusion of documentary realism to reveal an underlying system of meaning that was closer to the mythical, the pre-symbolic and arguably to Glaesemer's 'other'. In contrast to Keiller, whose Robinson trilogy had a cohesive narrative thread (albeit one riddled with ambiguity), Petit and Sinclair's radical, revisionist use of editing and post-production often saw narrative and visual content deliberately demolished. By the time *The Falconer* and *Asylum* were in production, new technologies were available that provided the directors with unprecedented opportunities for corroding form and content. Audio-visual material was densely layered and distorted, at times almost to the point of abstraction; Bruce Gilbert's dense soundscape of fragmented speech, noise and static further heightened the sensation of intertextual contamination.

With Petit now shooting digitally and Sinclair on 8 mm film, the pair also experimented with older technologies and equipment, introducing unpredictable visual disturbances into their footage by reshooting sections of film directly from monitor screens and projections onto video. These efforts to rupture form and defamiliarize content were echoed by the graphics and animations of digital artist David McKean, who would subsequently describe his involvement as that of an 'interventionist watching for established styles of visual language, [before] distorting or destroying them'.[58] A similar effect was achieved by the films' amalgamation of high and low visual culture, as filmed documentary footage was freely blended with text, surveillance video, still images, animation, photographs and digital graphics.

This extensive manipulation of materials resulted in palimpsestic and at times disorientating films in which the intangible and the unspoken was often more meaningful than any rationally intelligible content. It is precisely this interrelationship between direct and pre-symbolic forms of communication that has prompted Griffiths to compare them to speech, with another allusion to Paul Klee's observation:

> If one listens closely to the way we talk or chat to each other, the narrative fractures – yet we listen – make connections and the empty spaces between can become as important to our way of seeing and creating meaning as the flow of words themselves ... the flow and richness of the images and text themselves strive to render visible the invisible.[59]

Griffiths was particularly sympathetic to the production requirements of the projects discussed earlier because of his commitment to those who seek to 'imagine something different' and his first-hand experience of similar creative methods. The trusting relationships cultivated with Keiller, Petit and Sinclair allowed him to give the directors considerable freedom to experiment with materials, confident in the knowledge that they would preserve the integrity of their original creative vision. Griffiths recalls that during the editing of *Asylum*, for instance, he 'just let them get on with it – play'.[60] It is difficult to imagine how these pieces would have been achieved had Griffiths not allowed for an unusually long process of editing and post-production, had he insisted upon a script or had he prevented the film-makers from devoting long periods of time to the collection of found material.

Nevertheless, the majority of mainstream distribution channels have, until recently, been hostile to such a liberal approach. Over the years, Griffiths has taken particular umbrage against television commissioning editors who seek to create 'neatly defined spaces, with recognizable structure and perspective, with clear agendas and menus to address our modern times'.[61] In his experience, this preference for digestible, conformist material that caters to public demand has often been the norm rather than the exception, fuelling an insidious sanitization of mass media that endangers any 'uncomfortable pleasures that might dare to breed in the cracks of the pavements'.[62] Although most productions by Griffiths were made for British terrestrial television, getting them commissioned has often been an uphill struggle. Pitching 'uncomfortable pleasures' such as *The Cardinal and the Corpse* to television channels proved to be a Sisyphean task, with Griffiths only ultimately prevailing on account of his extensive industry experience, his proven track record of successful productions, and his emphatic conviction that Petit and Sinclair's central creative conceit was radical and worthwhile. Griffiths recalls that all three of the films in the trilogy were particularly hard sells, even by his standards.

The unconventional results produced by these directors' intuitive methods have also sometimes complicated their works' delivery to television, as they faced technical review regulations that insisted upon professional formats and high picture quality. For his BBC2 documentary *Death of a Bank Manager* (1995), Chris Petit opted to film with a Hi8 camera (a non-professional format) and included a scene from *Doctor Who* that he had deliberately degraded by transferring it onto VHS, prompting the BBC technical review of the film to raise concerns over the brightness of the Hi8 footage and over picture quality, noting that 'a perfectly good 16 mm print [of the *Doctor Who* clip] exists in the BBC library'.[63] Petit and Sinclair's trilogy encountered similar problems upon delivery to Channel 4. Even though Griffiths had made the commissioning editors aware that the films would be 'sort of home movies and would contain professional footage but also "amateur" material', their low resolution and distorted content resulted in a protracted battle with the channel's Technical Standards department. Such was the resistance to their work that Petit and Sinclair gave *Asylum* the sub-title 'The Last Commission'.[64]

It is not only Griffiths' television output that has met with resistance from those seeking to create 'neatly defined spaces' on feature film productions. Conforming to the prevalent assumption that a director will work from a finely honed script has been particularly problematic. When mute rushes of Keiller's *Robinson in Space* were screened to the BFI and BBC, a final script had yet to be written; instead, Keiller provided a few pages of explanatory material and improvised a running commentary in which he described his rationale for using certain locations and shots. This radically unconventional approach had the support of certain members of the audience, including the BFI's Head of Production Ben Gibson, who had seen it bear fruit on *London*. Yet, as Griffiths wryly noted in his production diary, others were less enthusiastic: 'The idea that the script for Scofield's narration will be written by Patrick after we have filmed and edited for some nine months and that we are shooting a feature length project based on a few pages, left some people more than a little perplexed'.[65]

Conclusion: New perimeters

With the widespread adoption of digital technologies and distribution channels, film is now digitized as standard and the elaborate manipulation of footage in post-production has become commonplace. This has had a knock-on effect on production conventions as a whole. As Griffiths notes in his article 'The Manipulated Image', 'live-action footage is now inevitably only the first phase of a production process ... What were once defined as "post" or "end" processes have been fundamentally shifted to the very heart of the production of motion picture images'.[66] In this respect, many of the creative methods that Petit, Sinclair and Keiller were using over a decade ago still seem remarkably contemporary and familiar; so, too, does Griffiths' willingness to cater for extended post-production processes. However, the 'digital turn' has also elicited dramatic changes in the areas that he and his core group of directors have been most interested in exploring creatively. The emergence of new technologies and distribution channels has radically redefined what is considered innovative, for instance, and has generated numerous new systems of meaning that impact upon the tension between the invisible and visible. Such changes have motivated Griffiths and his peers to continue to innovate and adapt, and together they have branched out into new territories, inspired by the potential of a world that, as Griffiths describes, 'provides almost infinite scope for manipulating the cinematic image ... can provide a new range of special effects to incorporate into otherwise conventional narratives and ... can produce new images for new types of narrative and for non- or partly narrative films'.[67]

Petit and Sinclair have used the phrase 'The Perimeter Fence' to evoke the borderlands of representation since 1996. This territory has remained their chief focus ever since. In a world that is increasingly dependent on digital environments and highly structured forms of expression, Petit consequently considers the modern-day Perimeter Fence 'the equivalent to an empty field in the internet ... Constantly busy, but with absolutely nothing to show'.[68] It is a point of access to an environment in which audio-visual material is being produced and interconnected at an exponential rate, but one that ultimately requires the intervention of users to be developed in meaningful, self-reflexive ways. It is the manner in which this material is mapped, negotiated and represented that becomes important. Petit has been keen to delve under the visible manifestations of cultural memory to reveal the invisible structures and networks that this content depends upon, and is shaped by. Since 2010, Petit has worked on a number of individual and collaborative pieces (often involving Sinclair) as part of an overarching project entitled 'Museum of Loneliness', which he considers a 'a non-institution dedicated to working in the gaps, and positioned at the opposite end of dot com. No website, no facebook, no twitter, MoL is essentially a parasite working through other bodies'.[69] These are works that frequently explore the underbelly of cultural memory: the overlooked, marginal, censored or lost. Like *The Falconer* or *Asylum*, they reveal self-reflexively the gaps of meaning within and between diverse cultural artefacts, yet they have also seen Petit move away from digital film-making towards more ephemeral and antiquated media forms.

A similar shift has occurred in Griffiths' recent production selections. In recognition of the fact that 'It's not only mixed economy but mixed formats that fit into the new world',[70] he has increasingly opted to produce interdisciplinary, multi-platform projects with his most recent production company, Illuminations Films. Some of these (like many of the works created for Petit's 'Museum of Loneliness') are low key and low budget, and Griffiths is keen to ensure that Illuminations retains its intimate, artisanal approach. Yet he is also interested in productions that merge 'the art world, cinema, publishing, all the cross-platforms that exist' on a much more ambitious scale.[71] Although these larger projects often necessitate the involvement of numerous organizations, funding bodies and co-producers, Illuminations continues to forge close working relationships with artists and film-makers while simultaneously sourcing appropriate co-production partnerships and executive producing. On Thai director Apichatpong Weerasethakul's 'Primitive' (2009), this resulted in formidable co-production partnerships.[72] These gave Weerasethakul the flexibility to straddle the art and film worlds, and to create work for a variety of distribution channels. The final project comprised a multi-screen installation that toured internationally, two short films, the Illuminations-produced Palme D'Or-winning feature film *Uncle Boonmee Who Can Recall His Past Lives* (2010) and an artist's book.

Although, as Griffiths observes, multi-platform projects such as 'Primitive' are particularly well suited to a new media world, they also fuel his enduring interest in the hidden systems of meaning that exist between diverse media forms; in this respect, the influence of 'The Presence of the Other' is still evident today. Even on single-platform projects, this interest has inspired production methodologies that are part curatorial. For the 2007 'New Crowned Hope Festival', Griffiths and Simon Field commissioned six feature films and one short from directors representing a variety of minor film industries and film-making styles. Even though this in itself was not unusual, by screening the works alongside one another at the festival and as a subsequent international touring programme, the pair hoped 'to keep all the films in conversation with each other', thereby bringing hidden correspondences to the fore. As Griffiths understands it, 'the idea of a programme of production that has also developed into a programme of distribution is very fertile ground'.[73] This bold re-evaluation of the perimeters of production reaped immediate dividends. Not only was Illuminations' contribution to the 'New Crowned Hope Festival' highly acclaimed by critics, but the 2008 Los Angeles Critics Awards also recognized it as a major achievement in contemporary world cinema

Reflecting on the contemporary media landscape, Siegfried Zielinski suggests that now, perhaps more than ever, artists require, 'places which offer hospitality to experimenters and experiments' that are established and defended by a 'generous host or patron, for whom artistic waste is not synonymous with failure but a sign of independence and strength'.[74] Griffiths has been precisely such a generous host throughout his career, providing a safe haven within which creative play is encouraged on the basis that, while some experiments may come to nothing, 'it is exactly in this very space and with this particular tension exactly that *invention* happens'.[75] His enduring quest for 'something different' has placed him on the outskirts of an industry that ultimately strives towards bigger-budget productions and highly efficient working practices. By continuing to battle against the current, towards the small scale or the unpredictable, Griffiths inevitably has been met with considerable resistance. Yet his pioneering instinct has also seen him embark on a lifelong, cumulative process of discovery – one that began with his engagement with the sociopolitical effects of innovative film, shifted towards the concept of an alchemical, experimental laboratory, and now finds him exploring new methods at the perimeters of production itself.

Acknowledgements

I should like to thank Keith Griffiths for his assistance during the preparation of this chapter and for supplying rare materials. I would also like to thank BFI Special Collections and Duncan Petrie, who jointly facilitated access to Griffiths' production diary of 1994–1995, excerpts of which are included in *Inside Stories: Diaries of British Film-Makers at Work*, ed. Duncan J. Petrie and Nick Pettigrew (London: British Film Institute, 1996).

Notes

1   Keith Griffiths, cited in Eric Pratter and Arnold Schnötzinger, 'Found Impressions: Storytelling as a Principle of the Documentary in the Work of Keith Griffiths', in *Keith Griffiths: The Presence*, ed. Siegfried Zielinski and Angela Huemer (Graz: Edition Blimp, n.d.), 76.

2   Keith Griffiths, unpublished production diary entry, 26 April 1995. Griffiths recognises this in part can be attributed to the fact that his early production career coincided with a unique couple of decades in terms of film culture and funding within the United Kingdom, during which public funding was available from organizations such as BFI, the ACGB, the BBC, C4 TV, and, in later years, the Lottery. This was a climate that was particularly hospitable to the up-and-coming artists and industry 'outsiders' that Griffiths found most compelling, enabling them to work on projects with their overheads covered, leaving a little extra for fees. Yet, even as these sources of funding have gradually dried up, Griffiths has continued to ensure that projects involving similarly peripheral artists are economically viable.

3   Keith Griffiths, unpublished production diary entry, 4 May 1995.

4   Peter Strickland's *Berberian Sound Studio* (2012), which was co-produced by Keith Griffiths and Warp X for the UK Film Council, Film4, and Hans Geißendörfer GmbH, was awarded four British Independent Film Awards and Critics' Circle Film Award for British Film of the Year in 2012.

5   Griffiths has been an advisor and consultant for the Munich Film Festival (1986–1988); a member of the Advisory Board of the Film and Video Umbrella (1990–1992); a member of the Independent Film Advisory Group of the National Lottery (1995–1996); on the Arts Council England Lottery Advisory Panel on Film (1996–2000); a member of the London Film Festival Industry Advisory Group

(2000–2010); Programme Consultant for the Locarno International Film Festival (2008–2010); and is currently on the CineMart International Advisory Board for the International Film Festival Rotterdam.

6   Keith Griffiths, e-mail to the author, 18 November 2012.

7   Robert Bresson, *Notes on the Cinematographer*, trans. Jonathan Griffin and with an introduction by J. M. G. Le Clézio (London and New York: Quartet Books, 1986), 99.

8   Keith Griffiths in interview with Marina Estela Graça, in *O Experimentalismo Na Produção de Documentos Animados: Simpósio Arte e Animação*, ed. Marina Estela Graça (Porto: Casa da Animação, 2004), 48.

9   Keith Griffiths interview, 'The Alchemy of Shadows: A Keith Griffiths Production', *Entropy*, 1: 6, *Waking Dreams: The Multiple Worlds of Independent Film* (Summer 1998), 13.

10   At the RCA these included a 'making-of' film about Peter Medak's adaptation of *A Day in the Death of Joe Egg* (1970), which Chris Springhall directed, Griffiths edited and Tony Scott worked on as Director of Photography, and the animated short *Mr Machine* (1971), which Griffiths co-directed with Peter Leake for Eduardo Paolozzi's 1971 Tate Gallery retrospective.

11   Griffiths spent three years (1973–1976) working at the Greater London Arts Association as Film and Video Officer alongside Simon Hartog after a brief stint as Film and Visual Arts Officer at Lincoln and South Humberside Arts (1972–1973). Hartog, who had been a founding member of the London Film-makers' Co-op in the 1960s, introduced Griffiths to highly politicized groups such as Cinema Action and Berwick Street Film Collective. He subsequently became close to a number of key figures within London's independent film-making scene including Ron Orders (Liberation Films), Ron Peck (founder of Four Corners Film) and Marc Karlin (Cinema Action and co-founder of Berwick Street Film Collective).

12   While working at the GLAA, Griffiths edited the quarterly journal *Film and Video Extra* and Martin Walsh's, *The Brechtian Aspect of Radical Cinema* (London: British Film Institute, 1981), published numerous articles on social and political film-making, organized an international conference on community media for the BFI and National Film Board of Canada ('Video Perspectives') and curated the season 'WNET 13: The TV Laboratory' for the National Film Theatre, London.

13   Griffiths produced five feature length films and numerous shorts for the BFI during this time, including Laura Mulvey and Peter Wollen's *Riddles of the Sphinx* (1977); The London Women's Film Group's *Rapunzel Let Down Your Hair* (1978); Phil Mulloy's *In the Forest* (1978); Chris Petit's *Radio On* (1979); Stephen and Timothy Quays' short *Nocturna Artificiala* (1979); and Richard Woolley's *Brothers and Sisters* (1981).

14   Griffiths resigned prior to the shoot of *An Unsuitable Job for a Woman* (dir. Chris Petit; 1982) after his 'non-professional, low budget methodology' resulted in clashes with the film's executive producer, Don Boyd; Keith Griffiths, e-mail to the author, 20 November 2012.

15   See, for instance, Clare Kitson, *British Animation: The Channel 4 Factor* (London: Parliament Hill, 2008).

16   Keith Griffiths, 'The Outer Limits', *Broadcast*, 1 October 1979. Griffiths discussed this article with Jeremy Isaacs (then Chairman of the BFI Production Board) in the late 70s; in 1981, Isaacs became the first Chief Executive of Channel 4.

17 These include San Francisco's KQED, Boston's WGBH, and especially David Loxton's New York TV Lab for channel WNET 13, where a creative 'laboratory' environment was used to generate a large amount of innovative material, from which selections were regularly televised.
18 Griffiths, 'The Outer Limits', 20–21.
19 *Visions*, Channel 4, November 1982–July 1985 (three series). For an insider's perspective see John Ellis, 'Visions: A Channel 4 Experiment 1982–5', in *Experimental British Television*, ed. Laura Mulvey and Jamie Sexton (Manchester and New York: Manchester University Press, 2007), 136–45.
20 As well as Large Door Ltd., Griffiths founded Koninck Studios with the Quay brothers in 1979. The studio expanded in the mid-1980s to incorporate Koninck International and Koninck Projects. He founded Illuminations Films with John Wyver as a sister company to the latter's Illuminations Television in 1996. In 2004, they were joined by ex-Director of the International Film Festival Rotterdam, Simon Field.
21 Keith Griffiths, e-mail to the author, 18 January 2013.
22 Keith Griffiths, 'Anxious Visions', *Vertigo* 1:4 (Winter 1994): 47–52 at 50.
23 Keith Griffiths, e-mail to the author, 18 January 2013.
24 Marina Estela Graça, 'Keith Griffiths Interview', 46.
25 'The Alchemy of Shadows: A Keith Griffiths Production', 15.
26 During the production of Chris Petit and Iain Sinclair's *Asylum* (2000), Griffiths anonymously published a parallel fictive piece that sees *The Falconer* (1997) rediscovered by 'Darke' (whom he modelled on the journalist Chris Darke) in a dystopian vision of post-millennial London. Anon. [Keith Griffiths, with illustrations by David McKean], 'The Entrapment', *COIL* 7, 15 September 1998, n.p.
27 Marina Estela Graça, 'Keith Griffiths Interview', 48.
28 Marina Estela Graça, 'Keith Griffiths Interview', 45.
29 Marina Estela Graça, 'Keith Griffiths Interview,' 45–46.
30 Iain Sinclair, *Lights Out for the Territory: 9 Excursions in the Secret History of London* (London: Granta Books, 1997), 308.
31 Keith Griffiths in Marina Estela Graça, 'Keith Griffiths Interview', 45.
32 Griffiths, 'Anxious Visions', 48.
33 Griffiths, 'Anxious Visions', 48.
34 'Die Gleichzeitigkeit des Anderen', Bern Kunstmuseum, 21 March–14 June 1987.
35 Griffiths, 'Anxious Visions,' 48.
36 Paul Klee, *Paul Klee: Creative Confession and Other Writings*, postscript by Matthew Gale (London: Tate Publishing, 2013), 1.
37 An edited collection of his research during this period was entitled *Keith Griffiths: The Presence* in homage to Glaesemer; see Siegfried Zielinski and Angela Huemer, eds., *Keith Griffiths: The Presence* (Graz: Edition Blimp, n.d.).
38 Pratter and Schnötzinger, 'Found Impressions: Storytelling as a Principle of the Documentary in the Work of Keith Griffiths', 76.
39 Keith Griffiths, cited in Alois Pluschkowitz, 'The Witches' Multiplication Table: A Workshop Report', in *Keith Griffiths: The Presence*, ed. Siegfried Zielinski and Angela Huemer (Graz: Edition Blimp, n.d.), 23.
40 Griffiths, cited in Pluschkowitz, 'The Witches' Multiplication Table'.
41 Griffiths, e-mail to the author 23 November 2012. Angela Carter gave Griffiths the first typed manuscript of her short story *The Curious Room* (or *Alice in Prague*),

which pays homage to John Dee, Rudolfine Prague and Švankmajer's feature film *Alice* (1988). When Griffiths tentatively asked Carter for her permission to develop the story into a film, she responded with a handwritten note that read 'I thought you would never ask!' Unfortunately, as funding for the film was never found, it 'sits in file for a rainy day'.

42 'The Alchemy of Shadows: A Keith Griffiths Production', 16.

43 Griffiths, e-mail to the author, 1 April 2013.

44 Siegfried Zielinski, *Deep Time of the Media: Toward an Archaeology of Hearing and Seeing by Technical Means* (Cambridge Massachusetts: MIT Press, 2006), 258.

45 Zielinski, *Deep Time of the Media*, 279. The two have been friends for many years; most recently, Griffiths contributed a fictive text to an edited collection published to mark Zielinski's 60th birthday ('Keith Griffiths, Ship in a Bottle', in *Objects of Knowledge, of Art and of Friendship: A Small Technical Encyclopaedia: For Siegfried Zielinski*, ed. David Link and Nils Röller (Leipzig: Institute for Book Art, 2011), 142–44. A video of Zielinski lecturing on alchemy featured in the Salzburg workshop 'The Presence'. *Deep Time of the Media* even sees Griffiths placed on a revised cartography for the 'anarchaelogy' of the media.

46 Griffiths, e-mail to the author, 2 April 2013.

47 'Screen Pioneers: No. 3: Raul Ruiz' [sic], *Visions*, Channel 4, 20 March 1985; 'Land of Counterpane', *Ghosts in the Machine II*, Channel 4, 31 May 1988. Griffiths considers these two shorts an important precursor to many of his later works because of their fictive narratives and playful subversion of content and form; Keith Griffiths in e-mails to the author on 18 November 2012 and 11 December 2012.

48 Pratter and Schnötzinger, 'Found Impressions: Storytelling as a Principle of the Documentary in the Work of Keith Griffiths', 77.

49 Pratter and Schnötzinger, 'Found Impressions'.

50 'The Alchemy of Shadows: A Keith Griffiths Production', 16; original emphasis.

51 Brigid Cherry, 'Dark Wonders and the Gothic Sensibility', *Kinoeye*, 2:1 (7 January 2002), at http://www.kinoeye.org/02/01/cherry01.php.

52 Jason Wood, 'A Quick Chat with Jan Svankmajer and Eva Svankmajerová' [sic], *kamera.co.uk*, n.d., at http://www.kamera.co.uk/interviews/svankmayer_svankmajerova.html.

53 Footage for *London* was filmed for at least two full days per week from the end of January 1992 until the middle of November 1992 on approximately 400 100ft rolls of film stock.

54 Patrick Keiller, cited in Edmund Hardy, 'A Quick Chat With Patrick Keiller', *kamera.co.uk*, n.d., http://www.kamera.co.uk/interviews/a_quick_chat_with_patrick_keiller.php.

55 Griffiths, 'Anxious Visions', 49.

56 Iain Sinclair in Paul A. Green, 'Asylum: The Last Commission', August 2000, http://www.culturecourt.com/Br.Paul/media/Asylum.html.

57 Sinclair, cited in Green, 'Asylum: The Last Commission', August 2000, http://www.culturecourt.com/Br.Paul/media/Asylum.html.

58 David McKean in interview with John Cranmer, 'A Bird's-Eye View', *Design Week*, 15 May 1998, 21.

59 Griffiths, 'Anxious Visions', 49.

60 Griffiths, e-mail to the author, 24 January 2013.

61   Griffiths, 'Anxious Visions', 49.
62   Keith Griffiths, 'Lost London and the Fight Against "Dentists"', *Film in Focus*, 4 April 2008, http://www.filminfocus.com/blog/lost_london_and_the_fight_against_dentists_.
63   Griffiths, unpublished production diary entry, 19 July 1995.
64   Griffiths, e-mail to the author, 24 January 2013.
65   Griffiths, unpublished production diary entry, 25 April 1995.
66   Keith Griffiths, 'The Manipulated Image', *Convergence: The International Journal of Research into New Media Technologies* 9:4 (December 2003): 18.
67   Griffiths, 'The Manipulated Image', 12.
68   Chris Petit, *Museum of Loneliness* [12' limited edition LP], Mordant Music, 2013.
69   Introduction to Petit's 'Museum of Loneliness', *Make mine a double* season at Curzon Cinemas.
70   Geoffrey Macnab, 'Mixing with Mavericks', *Screen International* (20 March 2009): 11.
71   Macnab, 'Mixing with Mavericks'.
72   Haus der Kunst, Munich, FACT, Liverpool and Animate Projects commissioned the project.
73   Geoffrey Macnab, 'Cinema's Tap in the Desert', *Sight & Sound*, 17:7 (July 2007): 38.
74   Zielinski, *Deep Time of the Media*, 279.
75   Griffiths, 'Anxious Visions', 50.

11

The American Independent Producer and the Film Value Chain

James Lyons

In August 2012 the Sundance Institute, the organization responsible for the Sundance Film Festival, made available on its official website a short film entitled 'The Creative Producer: The Unsung Hero of Indie Filmmaking'.[1] The opening section of the film had been digitally manipulated to simulate the poor playback quality of an old video tape, showing 'footage' from an early 1990s road movie in the style of Gregg Araki. It began with a bespectacled young man, sitting in the backseat of a car, opining pretentiously, 'I feel the only way to truly satisfy my urge to create an aesthetic world view is to become a cinematographer ... or a film critic.' His female companion, literally (and, we quickly comprehend, figuratively) in the driver's seat, responds, 'You guys are crazy, PRODUCING is where the *real* money is ... and the *power*', before revving the engine for clichéd dramatic emphasis. The archness continued in the ensuing section of the film, which consisted of unnamed individuals at a film industry gathering responding to the question 'So what do YOU think an indie producer does?' Alongside answers such as 'makes a movie happen' and 'producers do everything', one individual offered: 'Take credit for the works that more talented people made', before adding, somewhat sheepishly, 'but the producer *may* have helped make it happen, which is why they deserve a lot of credit'.

While such playful irreverence might be expected from Sundance's self-styled independent film, it was by no means the prevailing sentiment that it sought to convey. If the film admitted to the common perception that producers care mainly about money, power and taking credit, this was an impression that it, and the Creative Producing Initiative it was intended to support, was seeking patently to overturn. As its title indicates, the film was intended to *champion* the independent producer, and the majority of its running time consisted of insights from independent producers Lynette Howell, Heather Rae and Andrea Sperling on how they defined themselves as 'creative producers'. This emphasis on creativity, which was, in actuality, addressed rather loosely by the interviewees (Howell described it as 'giving someone else the tools to do what they do', while Rae emphasized developing 'trust'), reflected the fact that the film was timed to dovetail with two events in the Institute's Creative Producing Initiative, namely the Creative Producing Lab, and the Creative Producing Summit.

The Creative Producing Initiative, which offered 'a year-long fellowship programme for emerging producers', was a recent phenomenon, started in 2008, while the Creative Producing Summit replaced the Independent Producers Conference, which dated back to the late 1980s.[2] Reflecting a climate of increased financial uncertainty, 2008 was also the year that a number of Hollywood studios closed their specialty divisions. In an emerging era of digital distribution and exhibition, in which the capacity to successfully monetize films was far from assured, the apparent need for independent producers to 'get creative' was plain to see. This may account, at least in part, for numerous recent appearances by the adjective 'creative' in organs of the independent film sector, coupled invariably with the producer.[3]

Overall, the Sundance Institute's film was rather more successful in providing insight into individual producers' experiences, and persuading us of their specific commitment to supporting the craft of directors, than in offering a definitive sense of what independent producers *do*. This is perhaps not surprising: the sheer diversity of productions that, over the last two decades, have been released under the umbrella of the American independent film sector from multi-million dollar releases by well-resourced specialty film production and distribution companies such as Focus Features, Lionsgate or Sony Pictures Classics to micro-budget offerings from small-scale, unaffiliated outfits such as Film Science, Parts & Labor or Red Bucket Films certainly tests an individual's capacity to offer a succinct and all-encompassing description. On the other hand, one of the sector's lasting contributions to the profession of film production has been to prompt the Producers Guild of America (PGA) to formalize a definition of the producer's role to clarify disagreements over attribution. The remarkable success of Miramax's *Shakespeare in Love* at the 71st Academy Awards in 1999, where it won seven Oscars and was nominated for another six, was also notable for the sight of its five producers mounting the stage to accept the statue for best picture. In the wake of this event, the PGA formulated an arbitration process 'for determining "Produced by" credits for films and television series', adopted by the Academy in 2006 as the sole criterion for award nomination.

While some have questioned *Shakespeare in Love*'s legitimacy to be deemed properly 'independent' (Miramax had been bought by Disney in 1993), the complexity of financing arrangements for many films in the sector can certainly be said to have contributed to the escalating producer credits.[4] Harvey Weinstein, one of *Shakespeare in Love*'s honoured quintet, stated in relation to the film's controversy that 'we haven't paid enough attention to how much the role of producer has changed over the years. In the independent film world, making movies has become so complicated that it sometimes takes a village to get it done.'[5] From another perspective, Michael Cieply notes that 'new-wave producers argue that arbitrary definitions will inevitably break down as the lines between finance, marketing and production continue to blur', a statement that seems to fit the mode of operations of, to take two notable examples, prolific digital film-maker Joe Swanberg, and transmedia pioneer Lance Weiler.[6]

Understood in these terms, the PGA's attempt to circumscribe precisely producer definitions, and the contrary impulse of the Sundance Institute to argue for a more expansive and fluid description, can be seen as different responses to the same set of circumstances, driven by contrasting institutional imperatives. As with the 2003 screener debacle, which saw independent film producers, including Ted Hope, John Sloss and Christine Vachon, join forces with the Independent Feature Project/NY and IFP/LA to file a lawsuit against the MPAA for banning the distribution of awards screeners, an avowed anti-piracy measure was widely understood in the independent sector as an attempt to disadvantage independent producers. The interpenetration of studio and independent film operations has resulted in attempts to enact protectionist measures, in the process complicating the way that film scholarship has emphasized the discursive or predominantly textual nature of contemporary independence. If Yannis Tzioumakis is correct to suggest that 'the industrial background of a film has become gradually an irrelevant factor in its claim to independence', it is also true that the question of whether a film *looks* or *feels* independent can be of rather less significance than the challenge it may present to the delicate balance of stakeholder interests.[7] In the complicated and unstable economy of the sector, more often than not it is the producer who becomes the fulcrum around which 'getting' and 'taking' credit can (on occasion, as with *Shakespeare in Love*, quite literally) take centre stage.

One possible way to plot a route through the complex terrain of independent film production is to take a macro view, guided not by how an assortment of individual producers perceive their role, or perceive how their role is perceived, but by the analytic concept of the film value chain. Although relatively unfamiliar within humanities-based film scholarship, the value chain concept has been adapted by business, economics and marketing analysts to create a systematic overview of the film business model, and one in which questions of creativity, and creative power, can also be discerned. In the rest of this chapter I outline the potential of the film value chain concept in understanding the functions of the American independent film producer, serving as a helpful corrective to overly impressionistic conceptions of film-making in the sector and of the producer's role.

After working through some of the implications of the concept for a general understanding of independent producer operations, I use the case study of the Oscar-nominated feature film *Frozen River* (Courtney Hunt, 2007), as a way to illustrate the challenges and issues involved in applying the value chain model to an actual example. The fact that *Frozen River* has attracted high-profile plaudits for its producers makes it a particularly informative instance, one that offers a rich opportunity to analyse roles and functions and to interrogate the value chain model. Moreover, *Frozen River* was released towards the end of the 20-year expansion of the independent/specialty film sector, instigated by the tremendous commercial and critical success of *sex, lies and videotape* (1989) and consolidated spectacularly by *Pulp Fiction* (1995). This has been followed more recently by a period of significant retrenchment. As Alisa Perren notes, 'since 2008, a series of broader economic, technological, and cultural developments has contributed to the near collapse of the specialty sector', evident in the aforementioned folding of a number of the major studio's specialty divisions (Warner Independent Pictures and Picturehouse; Paramount Vantage; and Disney's sale of Miramax) and also the terminal decline of DVD sales and the dwindling of private investment in the sector.[8] While ostensibly an independent producers' success story, *Frozen River* in fact demonstrates many of the structural weaknesses in the model of independent film-making that has evolved since the 1980s, something which a precise analysis of its value chain, and the role afforded the producer, makes abundantly clear.

'We are all slashes – artists/entrepreneurs'[9]: The film value chain

The value chain concept was first outlined by Harvard Business School's Michael E. Porter in *Competitive Advantage* (1998), his landmark volume on business strategy, and used to 'disaggregate a firm into its strategically relevant activities', which are, as the term implies, linked to each other.[10] Jehoshua Eliashberg, Anita Elberse and Mark Leenders have applied Porter's value chain concept to an analysis of major studio operations, with film production, distribution and exhibition 'corresponding to the three key stages in the value chain for theatrical motion pictures that precede their "consumption" by movie-going audiences'.[11] They argue that

> Different types of entities and individuals participate in each stage of the value chain. The competitive landscape includes vertically integrated major studios, independent production companies, independent distributors, major national exhibition chains, and smaller regional exhibitors and art houses. Studios are often simultaneously engaged in four distinct functions: financing, producing, distributing, and advertising.[12]

Their analysis makes apparent the usefulness of applying the value chain concept to the interlinked stages of studio film production, and in identifying the role played by specific individuals within it. However, as Peter Bloore observes, operations in the independent film sector present additional complexity. Unlike a major studio that may perform most, if not all, of the aforementioned value chain activities 'in house', independent film productions rely on 'a chain of companies, businesses, and freelancers, all working on different elements of the production and exploitation process, and adding value in different ways along the chain'.[13] The importance of Bloore's own theorizing in relation to the value chain concept lies in the way that he has sought to devise a model that captures, as comprehensively as possible, operations in the independent sector, by which he means both European and American non-studio films. Of particular interest is the way that he outlines with precision the range of functions undertaken by producers within the sector, as set out in Figure 11.1.

Read from left to right, the diagram disaggregates stages of activity from development to consumption, extending existing conceptions of the value chain by specifying the number of links pertaining to operations in the independent sector, but also by positing a gradation of individuals specific to each stage, listed in approximate 'order of creative power and influence, with the most powerful at the top'.[14] In this context creativity is, as Angus Finney notes, 'far from being limited to ideas, creativity … is the axis around which all other filmmaking activity revolves'.[15] Bloore's model thus supplements existing frameworks by seeking to capture this notion of

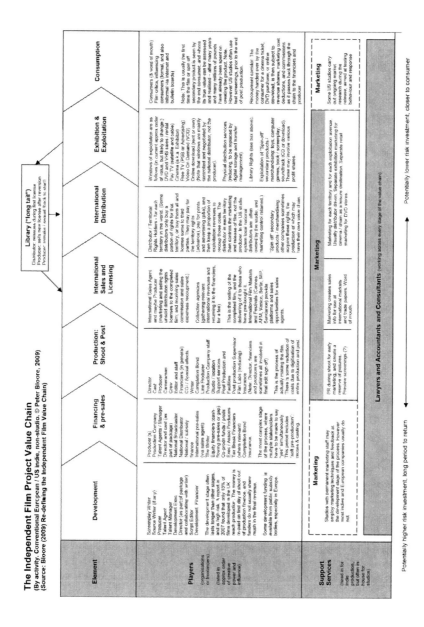

Figure 11.1 Peter Bloore's model of the independent film project value chain

creative influence, understood as playing such a significant role in the disintegrated value chain of the independent film sector.

It is perhaps worth noting the challenge this notion of creativity presents to the rather idealized image it still retains within humanities scholarship. Its use here reflects the growth of 'creative industries' discourse, and the study of the cultural economy across disciplines 'from cultural studies to economics, and from geography to policy studies to critical theory and sociology'.[16] As it pertains to the job of independent producer, 'creativity' applies the post-industrial worker's need to be 'flexible' and 'enterprising' to a nexus of entrepreneurial and artistic activities, which might range from the identifying and optioning of material, the contracting and managing of collaborators, through the arrangement of production finance to the positioning and marketing of the finished film. Moreover, the romantic image of independent film as privileging 'art' over 'commerce', which, as Geoff King points out, is firmly embedded in the 'particular cultural-taste formations' of the sector, is severely tested by the intensification of entrepreneurial expertise that this environment is understood to require, even as the implied artistry connoted by producer 'creativity' works to complicate that divide.[17]

Returning to the value chain, there are a number of things that are immediately striking about setting out the stages of film production in this way. For instance, given the extent to which scholarship and cinephilia maintain a strongly *auteurist* perspective on independent film, the diagram limits the director's input to three of the seven segments of the chain, but also expresses their relative degree of influence within those segments themselves. Predictably, production and post-production see directors occupy a leading position, but development and financing and pre-sales see them relegated below a number of other individuals, notably the producer (or producers), whose influence may also extend beyond post-production into international sales and licensing. Moreover, as value chain models do not graphically depict the duration of each segment, Bloore draws on Steven Blume's research on film revenue streams in order to offer a supplementary timescale diagram (Figure 11. 2) which suggest another way to conceive the relative contributions of director and producer.[18]

Taken together, the two diagrams offer a very useful overview of the process, making clear the extent to which a director-oriented focus may significantly under-represent the comparative length and value of other key functions to the overall process. Moreover, since the value chain offers a breakdown of functions, it can account for the fact that, especially in micro-budget productions, but also in instances where the director has the stature to initiate projects and attract financing (for instance P. T. Anderson, Richard Linklater or Jim Jarmusch), they may operate in several capacities. This seems an obvious point, but concentrating on directing as a function, rather than director as an entity, can be helpful in correcting the auteurist supposition that, on an independent film, the director does 'everything'.

Conversely, the idea forwarded in the Sundance Institute film that the producer does 'everything' is similarly questioned; there are a specifiable number of producer functions that any individual producer, or group of producers, may fulfil, given the nature of the film project in question. Bloore notes that a perceived weakness of the value chain in the independent film sector is the 'separation of the producer from the distribution and marketing process', which speaks to its inherent fragmentation.[19]

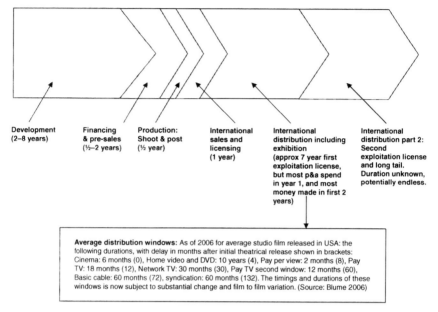

Development (2–8 years)

Financing & pre-sales (½–2 years)

Production: Shoot & post (½ year)

International sales and licensing (1 year)

International distribution including exhibition (approx 7 year first exploitation license, but most p&a spend in year 1, and most money made in first 2 years)

International distribution part 2: Second exploitation license and long tail. Duration unknown, potentially endless.

Average distribution windows: As of 2006 for average studio film released in USA: the following durations, with delay in months after initial theatrical release shown in brackets: Cinema: 6 months (0), Home video and DVD: 10 years (4), Pay per view: 2 months (8), Pay TV: 18 months (12), Network TV: 30 months (30), Pay TV second window: 12 months (60), Basic cable: 60 months (72), syndication: 60 months (132). The timings and durations of these windows is now subject to substantial change and film to film variation. (Source: Blume 2006)

Figure 11.2 Bloore's supplementary timescale diagram

Finney points out that consequently 'each element in the chain is heavily dependent on the next player/operator's partnership and co-operation in order to drive a project forward'.[20] One established approach to this issue of fragmentation is the strategy of nurturing lasting associations with financiers and distributors, or, on the other hand, with specific writers or directors. An example of the former would be Lawrence Bender Productions and Miramax, while James Schamus' (Focus Features) collaborations with Ang Lee, or Christine Vachon's (Killer Films) work with Todd Haynes, offer key instances of the latter. As Bloore suggests, the nurturing and maintaining of successful relationships such as these relies upon 'softer people skills', a less quantifiable, but vital producer attribute that the value chain concept fails to express.[21] A similar point could be made for the role played by reputation, or proven track record, or, what independent producer Hank Blumenthal refers to as the ability to sustain successfully the 'vision' of the film from development through post-production.[22] An additional factor missing from Bloore's value chain model in relation to the American independent sector is the contribution of advocacy, education and funding organizations such as the Sundance Institute, the IFP (Independent Film-maker Project) or Film Independent, in potentially adding value to a film project at several links in the chain, from development financing, pre-sales networking, post-production expertise to festival exhibition.

'Quite a Cinderella story'? *Frozen River* and the value chain[23]

An instructive example of how the value chain concept can be used to inform an understanding of independent film-making, and the roles undertaken by producers in that process, is *Frozen River*, the debut theatrical feature of director Courtney Hunt, produced by Heather Rae and Chip Hourihan. Released to widespread critical acclaim, and numerous award nominations, including Academy Award nominations in January 2009 for best actress (Melissa Leo) and best original screenplay (Hunt), *Frozen River* tells the story of Ray Eddy (Melissa Leo), a blue-collar working mother in Messena, New York, struggling to cope with the disappearance of Troy, her husband, days before Christmas, along with the money required to complete the purchase of a new 'double-wide' trailer. Desperation leads Ray to smuggle illegal immigrants across the nearby USA/Canadian border, through the local Mohawk reservation with the assistance of Lila Littlewolf (Misty Upham), a young Native American women. Ray is eventually arrested, but leaves Lila to buy a trailer and take care of her two sons with money from the smuggling.

One of the primary ways in which the film's remarkable success was widely recognized was through the approbation bestowed on its producers. In December 2008, *Frozen River* made the American Film Institute Awards list of the year's top ten movies, with Hourihan and Rae fêted alongside the producers of high-profile major studio releases such as *The Dark Knight*, *The Wrestler* and *Frost/Nixon*.[24] That month *Frozen River* won Best Feature at the Gotham Film Awards in New York, with Hourihan, Rae, and Hunt all taking to the stage to accept awards. *Frozen River* also obtained seven nominations for the 2009 Independent Spirit Awards, including Best Feature nominations for Hourihan and Rae, and eventually winning two awards – Best Female Lead for Melissa Leo, and the Piaget Producer's Award for Rae. The Piaget Award, one of three 'Filmmaker Grants' worth $25,000 bestowed at the Independent Spirit awards, is intended to honour 'emerging producers who, despite highly limited resources, demonstrate the creativity, tenacity and vision required to produce quality independent films'.[25] (What those nouns mean, precisely, is not defined by Piaget, but is axiomatic in relation to the awarded production). The in-depth interview with Rae for the Sundance Institute film, closely aligned to the film's own high profile success at the Sundance Film festival (where it won the Grand Jury Prize in 2008), make it a prominent example of the independent film producer's craft on behalf of the sector's most eminent institution. However, a close look at the film value chain of *Frozen River* makes apparent a rather more complicated process of assembly, and one in which the title and functions of producer did not always correspond.

Development

As is often the case, the development process for *Frozen River* was the lengthiest stage in the value chain, spanning some 12 years. The project started as a poem, written by Hunt, which evolved into a short film script, begun after she had graduated from Columbia University's Master of Fine Arts programme in 1994.[26] Hunt's thesis film, *Althea Faught* (1994), a Civil War drama, was screened at the Tribeca Film Center for industry professionals, and was subsequently picked up by the Public Broadcasting Service (PBS) for the *American Playhouse* series.[27] This is worth noting not only because it makes clear Hunt's high-calibre training and evident talent and ambition, but also her initial access to key institutions and individuals in the sector, including Columbia faculty members Ira Deutchman (producer and executive at Cinecom, Fine Line Features, Redeemable Features and Emerging Pictures), Richard Peña (director of programming at the Film Society of Lincoln Center, and the New York Film Festival) and James Schamus (producer and executive at Good Machine, and Focus Features).[28]

Both Peña and Schamus had key roles to play in *Frozen River's* development phase, albeit, in Schamus' case, rather serendipitously. The producer often brought his latest feature film up to Chatham, a town with a population of 4,000 in Columbia Country, New York (Schamus had a house in nearby Hillsdale) for the annual FilmColumbia film festival, that gave Hunt (also a nearby resident) the opportunity to meet Melissa Leo, star of Schamus' *21 Grams*, in 2003. The fact that FilmColumbia's executive director and co-programmer is film journalist and author Peter Biskind gives an indication of the pedigree, if not the profile, of the festival; an environment in which the kind of soft people skills to which Bloore refers were clearly usefully employed by Hunt. Leo agreed to act in Hunt's short film of *Frozen River*, alongside Misty Upham, a Native American actor who would also eventually co-star in the feature.

The completed short film version of *Frozen River* was accepted into the prestigious New York Film Festival in 2004. Hunt later stated that she 'wrote and thanked Richard Peña ... for putting the short in the festival. It was a huge boon for us because it helped us with fundraising with everything, really'.[29] Most immediately, it gave her the assurance to write a feature film screenplay, which was the basis for her entry into the IFP's 'Emerging Narrative' programme in September 2004. Part of its Independent Film Market (renamed Independent Film Week in 2008), the 'Emerging Narrative' programme is comprised of a series of meetings and networking events, with the objective to pair writers or writer/directors (submission to the programme is for script projects) with producers, and also with 'executives, and agents who can help take their projects – and careers – to the next level'.[30] As the IFP's programme makes evident, securing an experienced producer is vital, particularly for new directors and/ or writers who represent a high (often too high) risk for investors. Hunt noted that being a 'first time feature director – that's the hurdle'.[31] On this occasion, Hunt was not successful, and returned again with her script the following year. However, it is not unusual for projects to appear more than once – Hunt commented that the 'IFP kept opening doors for me based on the quality of my work and not on its marketability'. Once again she emerged without either a producer or financing in place.[32]

During this time Hunt successfully entered the short film of *Frozen River* into two further festivals, FilmColumbia in late October 2004, and the Los Angeles Film Festival in June 2005, both of which helped to build a profile for the project, but perhaps most significantly to enhance Hunt's status. As she commented, such profiling would 'show people who hadn't seen you direct that you *can* direct ... That's the main thing. I think that was instrumental in terms of getting people to fund the film'.[33] Hunt's attendance at FilmColumbia in October 2005 provided the crucial next stage. Independent producer Chip Hourihan, who was screening his film *Mind the Gap* (2004), read Hunt's feature-length screenplay, and was persuaded by her to help produce the project.³⁴ With Hourihan's participation secured, the project qualified for entry to two additional project development schemes in 2006, the Los Angeles Film Festival's 'Fast Track' Programme, and the IFP's 'No Borders' Programme. Using Hourihan's expertise, a budget was drawn up for the feature, which, along with an attached producer, is necessary to be eligible for entry to 'Fast Track', a three-day film financing and networking event. At this stage, fellow independent producer Heather Rae also joined the project – according to Melissa Leo, as a result of her meeting Rae at Sundance and asking her to read the screenplay.³⁵ That Leo performed this function illustrates her keen advocacy for a film that offered her a first leading role, but also the years of professional experience that informed her understanding of the exigencies of independent productions, stretching back to early 1990s films such as *Venice/Venice* (1992) and *Last Summer in the Hamptons* (1995). Rae, who is Cherokee, was director of the Native American Program for the Sundance Institute between 1995 and 2001, and Leo stated that the producer's ability to facilitate casting from Native American reservations made her particularly valuable to the project.³⁶ Hunt, Hourihan and Rae then entered *Frozen River* into 'No Borders', a co-production market (which offers access to selected agents, distribution companies, financiers and production companies), and is open to 'new projects in development represented by established producers'.³⁷ As before, despite winning out against stiff competition in order to have the opportunity to pitch the project to a wide-range of potential participants, *Frozen River* failed to find the necessary investment.

Financing and pre-sales

By 2006, despite gaining entry to some of the independent film sector's most competitive and coveted project development programmes and festivals, and securing the commitment of two experienced producers, Hunt's project had still failed to solicit financial backing. As Hunt stated, 'we went everywhere that we could go that we knew – production companies – and they passed and they passed and they passed. They liked it ... But they didn't really know "How do we sell this. How do we sell it?" '³⁸ Consequently, Hunt decided to look outside the film industry for financing. Hunt's husband, New York attorney Donald Harwood, drew up a prospectus for the Securities and Exchange Commission, and submitted it to potential investors.³⁹

They attracted five private financiers – Hunt commented, 'Donald used the same verbal advocacy skills he uses in appeals court to advocate for the film and to prove to investors that it was a worthwhile use of money' and secured half a million dollars.⁴⁰ The most notable investor was New York real estate developer Charles S. Cohen, a client of Harwood, who provided $340,000. Cohen, a multi-millionaire and avowed cinephile (he published the movie book *Trivia Mania* (1984) under the extraordinary pseudonym Xavier Einstein), had the honour of being described as 'sent from the angels' by the celebrated avant-garde film-maker Jonas Mekas, after he rehoused the evicted Film-Makers Cooperative in 2008 for a nominal $1 fee for five years.⁴¹ His investment in *Frozen River* was not simply largesse, however; Cohen subsequently formed the Cohen Media Group (CMG), a production and distribution company that afterwards began to operate in the specialty film sector. For instance, CMG bought Costa-Gavras' *Capital* (2012) before it premiered at that year's Toronto Film Festival.[42] Cohen's financial investment made him one of the film's executive producers, along with Harwood, and New York attorney Jay B. Itkowitz, Harwood's law partner, and a fellow investor. As executive producers, none of these three individuals exercised a direct input into the creative process, although Cohen has stated that he 'offered script suggestions', an intriguing prospect for which unfortunately there is no corroboration.[43] CMG subsequently used Cohen's investment in *Frozen River* to help build a profile for the company's activities, with its website advertising the film amongst those on its roster, and including links for its DVD purchase.

Production: Shoot and post

Frozen River was shot on location in Plattsburg, New York, in February and March 2007, over 24 days. As the title of the film rather implies, a frozen body of water was necessary to the production. Chip Hourihan noted, 'Our biggest problem, once the money was raised, was that almost the entire shoot was weather dependent – we needed an actual frozen river, or lake, on which to drive the car, or there was no point in shooting.'[44] An unexpected cold snap enabled filming, but meant only nine days for pre-production. As Hourihan makes clear, the fact that he had been so closely involved with the development of the film since 2005 meant this extremely limited amount of preparation time could suffice, otherwise 'it could have never come together that quickly'.[45] Similarly, Rae's aforementioned work in casting actors from a nearby reservation, and in brokering agreements over land access and permissions with the local Native population, was vital to a screenplay that depicted events and circumstances occurring partly on, and in the context of, reservation life and politics.

Hourihan served as line-producer during the shoot, supervising day-to-day scheduling and operations, with Rae overseeing location, cast and community liaison arrangements. Molly Conners was employed as co-producer, a role that encompassed responsibilities ranging from maintaining good relations between the crew and the local population to finding in the nearby vicinity 'a mean dog that would bark on cue' in time for the day's shooting schedule.[46] Melissa Leo, commenting on the exigencies of the production, was keen to point to the fundamental role of all three producers, stating, 'The trio … is a really good example of how the movie got made … It's a collaborative art, and that collaboration of our three producers was golden.'[47] This platitude was reiterated in several interviews, with the actress only once being sufficiently candid to admit that the collaboration might crucially have involved serving as on-set mediator between seasoned actress and novice feature director.[48]

As Bloore notes, it is at such a stage that the producers' 'leadership and negotiation qualities [are] most vital in ensuring that multiple stakeholders have to be made to say "yes".'[49] Hunt's status as a first-time feature director could be argued to have made the reliance upon such producer qualities especially important. However, this needs to be understood as distinct from the notion of creative control; the fact that the financing of the film came from investors who were separate from the producers was something that Hunt described with reference to the notion of creative autonomy. She observed, 'Because I didn't have any, sort of, all-controlling producer saying, 'OK, you're not going to do this and you can't do that', I did steer my own ship … Less strings attached, you know. The people that invested wanted to invest.'[50]

Unfortunately, that investment did not stretch to financing post-production, funds for which had to be collected independently once principal photography had finished. As Hunt stated, 'When we got home [with] the movie, we had no money, and then we had to raise money for the post.'[51] Neither of the producers was involved in overseeing post-production. Instead, it was cinematographer Reed Morano who supervised colour correction at OffHollywood digital (which oversaw post-production work on the film and took a co-production credit), and editing was completed by Kate Williams at the Edit Center in New York, where independent film-makers can get their films cut in exchange for allowing editing students to work on them.[52] Williams encouraged Hunt to submit a rough-cut of the completed film for entry to the Sundance Film Festival in time for the August 2007 deadline.[53] *Frozen River* was selected subsequently as one of 16 entries for the 2008 'dramatic competition' section at Sundance.

International sales and licensing

Speaking before *Frozen River*'s Sundance festival screening in January 2008, Hunt perhaps not surprisingly described her primary ambition as to 'sell the film and pay back my investors'.[54] Given her previous attempts to find financial backing within the industry, more unexpected was her success in doing so, and in advance of the film's much publicized Grand Jury Prize award. Hunt secured the services of William Morris Independent (WMI) sales agents Rena Ronson and Jerome Dubiz at Sundance, who sold the film to Tom Bernard and Michael Barker of Sony Pictures Classics (SPC), for a 'low to mid-six figures' sum, according to *Variety*.[55] The purchase gave the company distribution rights to North America, Latin America, Australia and New Zealand.[56] When Sundance juror Quentin Tarantino stood up to announce the Grand Jury Prize winner, and proclaimed *Frozen River* 'one of the most exciting thrillers I am going to see this year', the film was furnished with a superlative quotation for publicity and sales purposes. French production and distribution company Rezo Films quickly brokered a multi-territory pact with SPC for rights to countries including France, Benelux, Scandinavia, Portugal, India and South Africa.[57] Rezo added Spain, Switzerland and Poland after the film played at the San Sebastian Film Festival in September 2008.[58]

International distribution/exhibition and exploitation

Frozen River exemplified the independent value chain model in that distribution, exhibition and exploitation was controlled and organized by the distributors, rather than the director or producers. In its principal territory, North America, this was done by the aforementioned Sony Pictures Classics (SPC). Formed in 1992, and with a history of acquiring and distributing the work of acclaimed film-makers such as Atom Egoyan, Sally Potter and John Sayles, SPC had an impressive record in garnering Academy Award nominations for its films (well over 100 at the time of writing). These have become, as Geoff King and Michael Z. Newman note, an increasingly effective means of boosting the profiles, and thus the profits, of films in the specialty sector of the market.[59] SPC's co-president Michael Barker described *Frozen River* as 'a movie that is very high quality, but it's not a movie that's very obvious in how to sell, or how to market it [*sic*]'.[60] The latter statement echoed industry opinion on the project at the development stage. The company devised a release strategy geared towards attracting awards recognition, building from a limited August release on just seven screens, which was used to generate positive reviews – from Kenneth Turan in the *Los Angeles Times* to Andrew Sarris in the *New York Observer*, the film received overwhelmingly favourable notices – to push for a wider release (up to 96 screens by mid-September 2008).[61] This also enabled Sony to send Academy members Oscar screener DVDs of the film at the beginning of September, around a month before major studio DVDs would be distributed. As Barker commented, 'For the longest time, we're the only film that Academy members had in their hand to watch.'[62] Sony also geared the release of the *Frozen River* consumer DVD to the second week of February 2009, timed to coincide with the announcement of the Academy Award nominations, thereby boosting orders on the back of the favourable publicity. The company also generated dedicated pages and a press kit on its website in keeping with the promotional campaign devised for the film.

The positive publicity and award nominations for *Frozen River* also heightened the profile of producers Chip Hourihan and Heather Rae, who helped add value to the film through personal appearances at promotional events and awards ceremonies.[63] For instance, interviews given by Rae and coverage of her Piaget award win in the press appeared at the same time as the film's Oscar nominations, and were timed to coincide with its DVD release in February 2009 (details of domestic and overseas DVD sales are not available).[64] By mid-March 2009, the film had completed its 33-week theatrical run, with total domestic gross of $2,511,476. Worldwide theatrical receipts eventually reached $5,414,283, with the film also still playing on the festival circuit as late as April 2011, when it premiered at the Hong Kong film festival.[65]

Conclusion

Breaking *Frozen River* down into its constituent value chain segments enables a clearer sense of where and how its producers added value to the film. Given that the film's producers have been highly commended within the independent sector, with Rae in particular lauded for her 'creativity, tenacity, and vision', the value chain makes apparent the vital yet delimited scope of their input in the context of the overall process. Given that Hunt was a first-time feature director, and that the film was made very quickly with limited pre-production, the proficiency of the producers in coordinating activities in order to enable the shoot to take place as planned, and on schedule, was paramount.

Producer Michael Shamberg has stated that, 'Once you're shooting, it's largely the director's movie', which, when you are working with singular figures such as Steven Soderbergh or Oliver Stone, may well be the only acceptable arrangement.[66] Hunt was clearly directing *her* movie – neither producer had a direct financial stake in the film, or studio executives to report to, yet the on-location activities of the producers were extensive, and concentrated on allowing that to happen. Due recognition of those efforts in terms of industry award wins and nominations seems entirely warranted. On the other hand, neither producer had a role in procuring the necessary investment to make the film, or in arranging the eventual sale of the completed film to a distributor. Hunt, out of necessity, performed these 'producer functions' (the former in conjunction with her husband), stating that 'I realized that the industry was not going to help me make this film'.[67] She also drove the project forward at the development stage, casting lead actors, winning festival spots for her short film and eventually securing commitments from established independent producers as she moved towards 'soft' pre-production (location scouting and casting).

Hunt sought to progress her film's development through the independent sector's major pre-production events and programmes, a number of which required an experienced producer for eligibility. While the websites for the Los Angeles Film Festival's 'Fast Track', the IFP's 'Emerging Narrative' and 'No Borders' programmes have all been keen to cite *Frozen River* as a notable previous participant, predictably, none of them acknowledged the fact that the feature project failed to secure any investment whatsoever. Retrospectively, the film may well have benefited from the enhanced sector profile offered by its association with these programmes, adding value to its exploitation and exhibition efforts, but this rather pales in comparison with the concrete value of the initial production capital that was being sought.

With respect to the control of the film's distribution, exhibition and exploitation, *Frozen River* followed the sector norm in having a fragmented value chain, with producers and directors handing over control to Sony Pictures Classics. In so doing, the film acquired a new set of producers and executives adept at understanding the market conditions and timing release strategies to maximize awards exposure, with the hope of boosting the profiles, and thus the profits, of films in the specialty sector of the market.

Thus, in response to the question 'What does an indie producer do?' *Frozen River* provides a revealing answer, one that is in large part a consequence of the fragmentation of the film's value chain. Whereas a studio feature may be overseen by an individual producer from development through post-production and marketing, Hunt served as de facto producer on *Frozen River* at crucial moments, such as securing investment capital for production, and arranging the film's sale at Sundance. If not typical in its configuration (the specific mix of serendipity and expertise that secured its investment is anything but), then the diffusion of producer functions by an assortment of individuals along the value chain was nevertheless in keeping with the sector's norms.

Patrick Goldstein suggests that 'especially with independently financed films ... producer credits are a road map to how the movie got made'.[68] With regards to *Frozen River*, that map shows only part of the journey, and signposts some destinations – trips to the 'Fast Track', 'Emerging Narrative' and 'No Borders' programmes, while obscuring others – the extent of Hunt's own producerly 'creativity, tenacity, and vision', for instance, or the pivotal role of Charles S. Cohen. Given the applicability of this journey motif, it is fitting that the Sundance Institute's film on 'The Creative Producer' adopts the trope of the road movie. It is perhaps also unintentionally apt that it opts for simulating an early 1990s production, as the infrastructure of the independent film sector, and the fragmented value chain model it is built around, coalesced at this time. Much of Hunt's creativity was in negotiating and overcoming this fragmentation, and in ways that the scrutiny of producer credits simply fails to reveal. Indeed, it could be argued that one of the advantages of the film value chain model is that it clarifies these contours of producer creativity within the independent film sector.

Hunt would probably object to being termed a producer, and would instead describe her activities as the necessary work of an independent 'film-maker', a term adopted frequently in the sector; indeed, one of the most influential publications, the Independent Feature Project's quarterly magazine, is titled *Filmmaker*. But as a catchall term, it is obfuscatory, failing to delineate specific functions of value chain activity. Hunt's need to undertake such producerly activities are undoubtedly a *weakness* of the fragmented value chain model, and a symptom of the structure of the American independent film sector by the end of the 2000s, to a point at which, as Tino Balio points out, 'a theatrical release for almost any independent film could only be a dream'.[69] While some producers are clearly still engaged in every effort to make that dream a reality, changes already underway usher in alternative possibilities. Writing about what he terms 'on-demand culture', Chuck Tryon points to trends such as crowdfunding, video-on-demand (VOD) and transmedia as offering the chance to build 'the distribution platforms and cultiva[te] the engaged audiences that will foster a new movie culture'.[70] Finney, reflecting on the potential of such 'digitally-driven restructuring' of the film industry, looks optimistically to the resulting 'compression of the film value chain', as a distinct advantage for independent producers.[71] One of the challenges for scholars will be to try and understand how these developments may evolve the role of the independent film producer, and the range of value chain activities under his or her aegis.

Acknowledgements

I would like to thank Pamela Preston, unit production manager and production accountant of *Frozen River*, for her assistance with information for this chapter.

Notes

1   'The Creative Producer: The Unsung Hero of Indie Filmmaking', *Sundance Institute*, accessed 2 September 2012, http://www.sundance.org/video/the-creative-producer-the-unsung-hero-of-indie-filmmaking/.

2   Jeremy Kay, 'Sundance Institute Selects Five for Creative Producing Initiative', *Screen Daily*, 30 June 2008, accessed 4 September 2012, http://www.screendaily.com/sundance-institute-selects-five-for-creative-producing-initiative/4039650.

3   One recent example would be Peter Belsito, 'Women to Watch: Midge Sanford, Sarah Pillsbury – Sanford Pillsbury – Creative Producers', *indiewire*, 27 April 2011, accessed 28 April 2011, http://blogs.indiewire.com/sydneylevine/sanfordpillsbury_blog.

4   For a detailed discussion of Miramax, see Alisa Perren's *Indie, Inc.* (Austin: University of Texas Press, 2012).

5   Harvey Weinstein, 'The Producers', *Los Angeles Times*, 24 February 2007, accessed 12 August 2012, http://www.latimes.com/news/la-oe-weinstein24feb24,1,4605845.story.

6   Michael Cieply, 'Oscar Rules Regarding Producing Are Relaxed', *The New York Times*, 13 June 2007, accessed 12 August 2012, http://www.nytimes.com/2007/06/14/movies/14acad.html?pagewanted=print.

7   Yannis Tzioumakis, *American Independent Film* (Edinburgh: Edinburgh University Press, 2006), x.

8   Perren, *Indie, Inc.*, 231.

9   Ted Hope, 'Grasping the New Paradigm', podcast audio, *Screen Australia*, MP3, 29 August 2012, accessed 21 September 2012, http://screenaustralia.richmedia-server.com/sound/MultiPlatformStory/ScreenAustralia_MultiPlatformStory_TedHope_1_NewParadigm.mp3.

10 Michael E. Porter, *Competitive Advantage: Creating and Sustaining Superior Performance* (New York: The Free Press, 1998), 33.

11 Jehoshua Eliashberg, Anita Elberse and Mark A. A. M. Leenders, 'The Motion Picture Industry: Critical Issues in Practice, Current Research, and New Research Directions', *Marketing Science*, 25:6 (2006): 639.

12 Eliashberg, Elberse and Leenders, 'The Motion Picture Industry'.

13 Peter Bloore, 'Re-defining the Independent Film Value Chain', UK Film Council, 2009, accessed 14 January 2012, industry.bfi.org.uk/media/pdf/h/b/Film_Value_Chain_Paper.pdf.

14 Bloore, 'Re-defining the Independent Film Value Chain', 7.

15 Angus Finney, *The International Film Business* (London: Routledge, 2010), 158.

16 Terry Flew, *The Creative Industries: Culture and Policy* (London: SAGE, 2012), 2.

17 Geoff King, *Indiewood, USA* (London: I.B. Tauris, 2009), 14.

18 Steven Blum, 'The Revenue Streams: An Overview', *The Movie Business Book*, 3rd edn., ed. Jason E. Squire (New York: Simon and Schuster, 2006), 332–61.

19 Bloore, 'Re-defining the Independent Film Value Chain', 12.

20 Finney, *The International Film Business*, 12.

21 Bloore, 'Re-defining the Independent Film Value Chain', 14.

22 Hank Blumenthal, 'Guest Post: Hank Blumenthal "Towards an Aesthetics of Producing Indie Movies"', *Hope for Film*, 31 May 2011, accessed 21 September 2012, http://blogs.indiewire.com/tedhope/guest_post_hank_blumenthal_towards_an_aesthetics_of_producing_indie_movies.

23 Michael Barker, quoted in Nate Dimeo, '"Frozen River": A Study in Oscar Marketing', *NPR*, 9 February 2009, accessed 21 September 2012, http://www.npr.org/templates/story/story.php?storyId=100468824.

24 Tom O'Neil, 'American Film Institute Awards Hail Top 10 Best Movies of 2008', *Los Angeles Times*, 14 December 2008, accessed 12 November 2012, http://goldderby.latimes.com/awards_goldderby/2008/12/american-film-i.html.

25 'Grants and Awards', *Film Independent.org*, accessed 8 December 2012, http://www.filmindependent.org/labs-and-programs/grants-and-awards/. The award was bestowed on Rae not only for her production work on *Frozen River* but also on *Film Independent.org* (Russell Friendenberg, 2008).

26 Sasha Stone, 'Original Screenplay: Talking to Courtney Hunt', *Awards Daily*, 9 February 2009, accessed 12 September 2012, http://www.awardsdaily.com/blog/2009/02/09/original-screenplay-talking-to-courtney-hunt%E2%80%A8/.

27 'Film Division Students Score at Sundance Festival', *Columbia University Record*, 19:18, 25 February 1994, accessed 13 November 2012, http://www.columbia.edu/cu/record/archives/vol19/vol19_iss18/record1918.30.

28 Peña stepped down from both roles in 2012.

29 'Sundance Features: Courtney Hunt, *Frozen River*', *The Reeler*, 22 January 2008, accessed 4 September 2012, http://www.thereeler.com/sundance_features/courtney_hunt_frozen_river.php

30 'ifp faq', *ifp.org*, accessed 4 September 2012, http://www.ifp.org/programs/independent-film-week/project-forum-2/emerging-narrative/faq.

31 'Sundance Features: Courtney Hunt, *Frozen River*'.

32 Michael Jones, 'Indie org IFP gets Ready to "Howl"', *Variety*, 5 September 2008, accessed 13 November 2012, http://www.variety.com/article/VR1117991720?refcatid=3236.

33 'Sundance Features: Courtney Hunt, *Frozen River*'.

34 Sharon Abella, 'Interview with Chip Hourihan/Producer (along with Heather Rae) of *Frozen River*', 15 August 2010, accessed 12 November 2012, http://1worldcinema.com/tag/world-cinema-interview/page/3/.

35 Brad Balfour, 'Melissa Leo – Down by the *Frozen River*', *Pop Entertainment.com*, 7 February 2009, accessed 4 September 2012, http://www.popentertainment.com/melissaleo.htm.

36 Balfour, 'Melissa Leo – Down by the *Frozen River*'.

37 'ifp no borders international co-production market', *ifp.org*, accessed 8 December 2012, http://www.ifp.org/programs/independent-film-week/project-forum-2/no-borders-international-co-production-market/.

38 Stone, 'Original Screenplay'.

39 'Two Law School Alumni Create "Bracing" Film', *Northeastern University Graduate Studies*, 27 August 2008, accessed 4 September 2012, http://www.northeastern.edu/graduate/stories/?id=43

40 'Two Law School Alumni'.

41 Robin Menken, 'Looking Back at Counter Culture, Counter Cinema: An Avant-Garde Film Festival', *Cinema Without Borders*, 1 January 2011, accessed 12 September 2012, http://cinemawithoutborders.com/notebook/2420-looking-back-at-counter-culture-counter-cinema-an-avant-garde-film-festival.html.

42 Dave McNary, 'Cohen Media Group Acquires Costa-Gavras Thriller', *Variety*, 4 September 2012, accessed 5 September 2012, http://www.variety.com/article/VR1118058657.

43 Ryan Gierach, 'PDC Owner's Film Gets Two Oscar Nominations', *WEHONEWS*, 26 January 2009, accessed 5 September 2012, http://wehonews.com/z/wehonews/archive/page.php?articleID=3088.

44 Abella, 'Interview with Chip Hourihan'.

45 Abella, 'Interview with Chip Hourihan'.

46 Courtney Hunt and Heather Rae, 'Commentaries', *Frozen River* (Sony Pictures, 2009).
47 'New Directors/New Films – "Frozen River" – 26 March 2008', *The Film Panel Notetaker*, 27 March 2008, accessed 5 September 2012, http://thefilmpanelnotetaker. com/new-directorsnew-films-frozen-river-march-26-2008.
48 Thelma Adams, 'For Your Consideration: Melissa Leo for Best Actress in *Frozen River*', *Huffington Post*, 29 July 2008, accessed 5 September 2012, http://www. huffingtonpost.com/thelma-adams/for-your-consideration-me_b_115239.html.
49 Balfour, 'Melissa Leo'.
50 Bloore, 'Re-defining the Independent Film Value Chain', 9.
51 Stone, 'Original Screenplay'.
52 D. W. Hudson, 'Courtney Hunt: As a Director, You Have Five Minutes', *Greencine. com*, 10 February 2009, accessed 5 September 2012, http://www.greencine.com/ central/courtneyhunt?page=0%2C1.
53 '"Frozen River" – Editor Kate Williams Interviewed by Thelma Adams', *AFWJ.org*, 30 July 2008, accessed 12 September 2009, http://awfj.org/2008/07/30/frozen-river-editor-kate-williams-interviewed-by-thelma-adams/.
54 S. James Snyder, 'The Traffic Upstate is Just Brutal', *The L Magazine*, 16 July 2008, accessed 2 September 2012, http://www.thelmagazine.com/newyork/the-traffic-upstate-is-just-brutal/Content?oid=1140370.
55 'Sundance Features: Courtney Hunt'.
56 Sharon Swart and Michael Jones, 'Sony Pictures Classics Inks "River" ', 23 January 2008, accessed 12 September 2012, *Variety*, http://www.variety.com/article/ VR1117979543?refCatId=13.
57 John Hopewell, 'Rezo Reveals "Frozen River" Sales', *Variety*, 26 September 2008, accessed 29 November 2012, http://www.variety.com/article/ VR1117992978?refCatId=13.
58 Hopewell, 'Rezo Reveals "Frozen River" Sales'.
59 Geoff King, *Indiewood USA*; Michael Z. Newman, *Indie: An American Film Culture* (New York: Columbia University Press, 2011).
60 '"*Frozen River*": A Study in Oscar Marketing', Narrated by Melissa Block, 'All Things Considered', *NPR*, 9 February 2009, accessed 17 October 2012, http://www.npr.org/ templates/story/story.php?storyId=100468824.
61 '"*Frozen River*": A Study in Oscar Marketing'.
62 '"*Frozen River*": A Study in Oscar Marketing'.
63 Kiran Pahwa, 'Heather Rae at 2009 Film Independent Spirit Awards – Press Room', 24 February 2009, accessed 13 November 2012, *Top News.in*, http://www.topnews.in/ heather-rae-2009-film-independent-spirit-awards-press-room-2129960.
64 'Grants and Awards', *Film Independent.org*.
65 *Box Office Mojo*, http://boxofficemojo.com/movies/?page=weekly&id=frozenriver.htm.
66 Patrick Goldstein, 'The Unkindest Cut', *The Los Angeles Times*, 20 February 2007, accessed 4 June 2010, http://www.calendarlive.com/movies/cl-et-gold20feb20,0,7118982.story?coll=cl-movies.
67 '"Frozen River" – Courtney Hunt interviewed by Jennifer Merin', *AWFJ.org*, 30 July 2008, accessed 12 September 2012, http://awfj.org/2008/07/30/frozen-river-courtney-hunt-interviewed-by-jennifer-merin-exclusive/.
68 Goldstein, 'The Unkindest Cut'.
69 Tino Balio, *Hollywood in the New Millennium* (London: Palgrave MacMillan, 2013), 151.
70 Chuck Tryon, 'On-Demand Culture', *Filmmaker*, 21:2 (Winter 2013): 104–06.
71 Finney, *The International Film Business*, 209.

Part Three

National and Transnational Contexts

12

Lita Stantic: Auteur Producer/ Producer of Auteurs

Constanza Burucúa

Introduction

A trademark name and a well-respected producer, Lita Stantic should be acknowledged as one of the most influential voices in contemporary Argentine cinema. By looking at a trajectory that spans more than 40 years – which is still showing no signs of waning – this chapter aims to provide a comprehensive and critical account of the work and the legacy of a woman who has consciously and actively committed her life to producing, and in one single occasion directing, the kind of cinema that she believes in and that she repeatedly refers to as 'necessary': a cinema of untold stories, of alternative points of view, of defiant approaches to a continually changing reality.[1] Likewise, by looking at the history of Argentine cinema since the 1960s through the lens of a producer's oeuvre, this chapter intends to provide a different approach to that history. It will focus not only on the role played by this particular producer but also on the consequences and the impact that her choices and decisions have had in relation to how gender and generational conflicts and politics have played out and changed over time, both at a representational level and in terms of the dynamics of the industry itself.

To achieve this reorientation, the chapter will begin by discussing Stantic's background and her career. In the absence of an in-depth study concerned with her films as an organic body of work, it will review what has already been said about it within scholarly discourses by briefly examining what was privileged in previous accounts. It will then focus on the idea of the *auteur*-producer and discuss how pertinent such a descriptor would be in this particular case. Having been exposed to every 'new wave' in Argentine cinema since the late 1950s, and in most cases even participated in them as an active voice, it seems pertinent to inscribe Stantic's work in a wider Latin American tradition of socially committed cinema. Such contextualization will serve to analyse her key contributions in relation to the role and achievement of women in Argentine cinema and develop a consideration of the political dimension of her cinema. The focus throughout will be on the concrete aspects of her work as a producer, in order to define the role that Stantic has played in the formation and consolidation of the so-called New Argentine Cinema, a generational shift in film production, created by the country's economic debacle of 2001.

The making of a producer

Daughter of Slovenian immigrants, Stantic was born in Buenos Aires in 1942. From a very young age, she knew that she wanted to be a part of an industry that, by the late 1950s and early 1960s, was exclusively run by men. She first began a career in literature with the aim of becoming a film critic but, eager for more opportunities, she decided to take courses on scriptwriting and film-making with Simón Feldman, one of the leading figures of what was becoming to be known at the time as the *nueva ola* (new wave) of Argentine cinema. Feldman was one of the first film-makers to be able to combine his career with a commitment to educate new generations of future film-makers. After that, Stantic joined the *Asociación Cine Experimental* (Association of Experimental Cinema, ACE) where she was taught, among others, by Manuel Antín, another new wave *auteur*, who became a key figure in cultural policy making after the return of democracy in 1983. Antín founded, in 1991, one of the most successful film schools in Argentina and Latin America to date: *Fundación Universidad del Cine* (FUC). At ACE, Stantic first met Octavio Getino in a group of around 60 students, only 4 of whom were women. Always aware of the wider gender imbalance, Stantic became an active advocate for the presence and visibility of women in the industry (and beyond) by the late 1970s, when she began her collaborative work with María Luisa Bemberg.

By 1965, Stantic had also met Pablo Szir, another young film-maker who was her creative partner for a few years and the father of her only child. With Szir as director and Stantic as producer, they co-wrote and made a couple of short documentary films, *Diario de campamento* (*Diary of Camping*, 1965) and *El bombero está triste y llora* (*The Fireman Is Sad and Cries*, 1965), before joining the militant *Grupo Cine Liberación* (Group Cinema Liberation), led by Octavio Getino, Fernando Solanas and Gerardo Vallejo.[2] After the success of *The Hour of the Furnaces* (1968) at the 1968 edition of the Pesaro Film Festival, Solanas and Getino decided to extend the group to some 30 people with the aim of broadening the exhibition of their groundbreaking and, at the time, clandestine film. With Szir leading one of these groups equipped with a 16 mm projector, Stantic participated in many of the venues held in factories, private homes, union offices and lecture rooms. Today, she understands *Grupo Cine Liberación* less as a model of production than as a successful model of exhibition, a cinema through which people were enabled to get really close, not only physically but most importantly ideologically, to the then active urban guerrilla groups that were fighting in the name of a revolution that, in the wake of the 1959 Cuban revolution, seemed imminent in Latin America. Although today she opposes all sorts of violence, Stantic is still moved by the memory of those days when the idea of a more fair and equal world seemed attainable.

In 1973, while her relationship with Szir was dissolving, Stantic realized that the escalation in political violence in the country could only lead to more violence and so she decided to distance herself from militant cinema and politics. Before that moment, she produced Szir's *Los Velázquez* (1972), about a mythologized bandit who robbed the rich in order to help the peasants, who, in turn, persistently helped him to hide and escape from the police, until he was finally caught in an ambush in the late 1960s. The film was based on the novel *Isidro Velázquez: formas prerrevolucionarias de la violencia* (*Isidro Velázquez: Pre-Revolutionary Forms of Violence*) by Roberto Carri, who, like Szir, disappeared during the last military dictatorship. Carri's kidnapping and disappearance is referred to in his daughter Albertina's *Los rubios/The Blonds* (2003), a film that sparked one of the most heated debates about memory, trauma and filmic representation seen in Argentina since its release. Szir's disappearance was also dealt with in the only film that Stantic directed, *Un muro de silencio/A Wall of Silence* (1993). What is not part of the plot of her film, though, is the fact that the negative of their last collaboration, *Los Velázquez* disappeared along with Szir. The editor, who was working with the positive copy of the film at the time of the director's abduction, destroyed it out of fear. Always fantasizing about the possibility of recovering the film, yet aware of the improbability of this happening, Stantic still refuses to qualify *Los Velázquez* as a 'missing' (*desaparecido*) film. Cautious and respectful of the weight that the word carries with it, she deems it appropriate not to use it for anything other than people – she prefers to think about the film in terms of something that 'once existed but that is not there anymore'.[3]

Throughout the 1970s, Stantic put the organizational skills acquired during her years as a militant film-maker and producer in the 1960s, while a member of the *Grupo Cine Liberación*, at the service of the advertising industry. Unlike Fernando Solanas, who claims to have learnt everything from his years as a musician working in advertising,[4] Stantic openly declares that she did not learn anything from advertising: it was simply a job.[5] However, it is also true that it allowed her to stay active as a producer and to get acquainted with the people working in an industry that, throughout the 1970s, served as kind of refuge for many film-makers. During this period she became better known within the film industry and she acted as production manager in some of the very few good films released during a period dominated by censorship and mediocrity; among these was Lautaro Murúa's *La Raulito* (1975) and, at the peak of the military regime's power, the obliquely somber denunciation of corruption, *La parte del león/The Lion's Share* (Adolfo Aristarain, 1978). For Alejandro Doria's *La isla/The Island* (1979), Stantic became an executive producer and, together with the director, she founded her first production company, MBC Producciones, a short-lived partnership.

After the release of Doria's next film, *Los miedos/Fears* (1980), Stantic was approached by María Luisa Bemberg who, having penned the script of *Crónica de una señora/Chronicle of a Lady* (1971, Raúl de la Torre) and having directed only a couple of short films – *El mundo de la mujer* (*The Woman's World*, 1972) and *Juguetes* (*Toys*, 1978) – wanted to embark on a career as a film-maker and wanted

MBC Producciones to be in charge of the production of her project. Doria, like many others at the time, was wary of the idea of a female director who was also almost 60 years old and he refused to commit to producing her film. By contrast, Stantic, despite not being overly impressed by the script (she prefers the film to the book), felt that it was a risk worth taking.[6]

Thus, the partnership with Doria ended and a new company, GEA Cinematográfica S.A., was established. It was a courageous decision because, as Stantic puts it: 'The truth is that those ten years that I worked with María Luisa were very important to me, because it was really a challenge for two women to run their own film production company.'[7] Stantic had the know-how of the producer and Bemberg, coming from one of Argentina's wealthiest families, provided the initial capital required to set up the company. Together, they worked on five films: *Momentos/Moments* (1981), *Señora de nadie/Nobody's Wife* (1982), *Camila* (1984), *Miss Mary* (1986) and *Yo, la peor de todas/I, the Worst of All* (1990) (Figure 12.1).

Although best known as a director, Bemberg was also very much involved in questions concerning the production, as well as the distribution and even the exhibition, of her films. A very dialogical relationship, both creatively and in more practical terms, Stantic and Bemberg's partnership involved working together in almost every aspect of a film's production process from the development of the scripts – still to this day a key point for Stantic when the time comes to get involved with new projects. Their partnership involved decisions concerning the casting of the actors – also a central aspect in Stantic's more contemporary collaborations with directors such as Lucrecia Martel and Adrián Caetano – and the painstaking duties of accompanying a film in every stage after its commercial release, from the most modest suburban theatre to the festival circuit.

Camila was their third collaboration and the first film that they made as a co-production. The collaboration with Impala Producciones, a Spanish company, including the casting of the then very popular Spanish actor Imanol Arias in the role of Father Ladislao Gutierrez, proved successful at every level. The film became

Figure 12.1 Lita Stantic and Maria Louisa Bemberg in Venice. Courtesy of Lita Stantic

a box office hit and its critical acclaim brought not only an Oscar nomination for the film (in the Best Foreign Language Film category), but also international attention to Bemberg's work. Beyond the accolades, what all this meant was that from that point onwards, GEA Producciones was able to work with foreign partners. This also meant that both Bemberg's films and the one that Stantic directed a few years later would have respected international actors and actresses cast in the leading roles. This strategy, by increasing their films' visibility among international audiences, especially those of art-house circuits, also helped ensure the backing of international financiers and distributors. Thus, *Miss Mary* was a film co-produced with an American company (New World Pictures) and starred Julie Christie; and Bemberg and Stantic's last film together, *I, the Worst of All*, was co-produced with a French partner (ASSAI Communications) and starred the Spanish actress Assumpta Serna and French actress Dominique Sanda.

As noted by Elena Goity, the films produced by GEA Producciones, on the whole, are characterized by their coherence and continuity in terms of their ideology, their themes and subject matter and their production practices.[8] In retrospect, continuity and coherence are also trademarks of Stantic's overall career as a producer. This is the cultural capital that she now takes to every new project to which she commits, together with the knowledge acquired throughout the past three decades in terms of co-producing, financing and distribution strategies, skills that she first learnt during her years in partnership with Bemberg.

By the time Bemberg was working on her last film, *De eso no se habla/I Don't Want to Talk About It* (1993), an Argentine–Italian co-production starring Marcello Mastroianni, Stantic was working on her own film, *Un muro de silencio*, a film produced with the participation of the UK's Channel 4 and the *Instituto Mexicano de Cinematografía*. It was because of this autobiographical and highly self-reflexive film that Stantic first caught the attention of film historians and critics who, although they were keen to discuss Stantic as a director, inevitably also had to acknowledge her background as a producer whose personal and professional life had been intertwined with Argentine cinema, and history, since the 1960s.

Understanding Stantic's career

When Annette Kuhn and Susannah Radstone's edited volume *The Women's Companion to International Film* appeared in 1990, Lita Stantic's career already merited an entry.[9] Acknowledged by Ana María López as a successful executive producer who had been building up a solid body of work since the 1970s,[10] Stantic's visibility at that time was indissolubly linked to María Luisa Bemberg who, after the international success of her third film – *Camila* – and thanks to the work that the two women had been doing together as producing partners in terms of distribution, was becoming 'not only the first commercially successful Argentine female film director, but also one of the few Argentine directors whose films [were] regularly distributed internationally'.[11] What is remarkable about the references to Stantic in this publication is that her name is already associated with questions that relate her to both the international projection of Argentine cinema and to co-production, which, by the mid-1980s, was rapidly becoming the dominant mode of production, not only in Argentina but throughout Latin America.

As Octavio Getino explains, in the context of the Argentine film industry, co-production agreements flourished as a means to overcome the limitations of a shrinking internal market by finding alternative niches in other markets, mainly in European and Latin American countries.[12] According to Getino[13] and Marvin D'Lugo,[14] the figure of the film *auteur* as an intermediary became central in these new cultural and commercial ventures given that 'they negotiate their own political and artistic visions in accordance with the commercial demands of global film finance arrangements'.[15] It is in line with these ideas on authorship and co-production that Stantic's work becomes relevant in D'Lugo's reading. Thus, although he primarily focuses on her *auteur* status, he frames her work accurately in *Un muro de silencio* within a pre-existing and continuing career as a producer and he places her as a 'key figure in the territorialization of Argentine cinema … working beyond the alliances that have formed the usual male-dominated commercial patterns'.[16] D'Lugo further praises her for being both independent and creative, 'continually seeking to redefine the progressive political position of Latin American film as a critical intervention in regional cultural politics'.[17] In this manner, by noting Stantic's role not only as an intermediary between the local (artistic visions) and the global (cultural and commercial demands), but also as a dynamic voice in terms of gender politics within the film industry and as an active agent in the reconfiguration of a Latin American tradition of socially committed cinema, D'Lugo's piece showcases the main aspects highlighted by other scholars before him in relation to Stantic's work. Thus, in 'Breaching the Walls of Silence: Lita Stantic's *Un muro de silencio*',[18] John King described her as an 'ethical film-maker'.[19] He acknowledged both her partnership with Bemberg and Stantic's own capacity to gather talented female professionals involved in production, art direction and scriptwriting and her commitment to increasing the presence and the scope of women in the national film industry. Soon after King's piece appeared, Catherine Grant also analysed her work by focusing on *Un muro* in 'Camera solidaria',[20] an article that offered one of the earliest attempts to study, in relation to Argentine cinema, how the co-production model affected questions of authorship and representation by mostly addressing such issues from a feminist perspective.

As far as the reception of her work in the Argentine context goes, in 1994, right after the film's release, the first collection of essays entirely dedicated to post-dictatorship Argentine cinema appeared in *Cine Argentino en Democracia, 1983–1993* (*Argentine Cinema in Democracy, 1983–1993*).[21] Unsurprisingly, Stantic's name is a recurrent feature in it, but mainly because of her turn as a director, with *Un muro* unanimously credited for its courage in challenging the amnesty laws and the pardons promoted by the successive democratic governments, which were predicated on a supposed need to bring closure to the recent past and its traumatic legacy.[22] It is only in the more contemporary *Cien Años de Cine Argentino* (*One Hundred Years of Argentine Cinema*, 2012) that Stantic's work *as a producer* is fully recognized.[23] In this book, Fernando Martín Peña dedicates a section to the role of producers from the 1990s onwards, paying special attention to Stantic's body of work in terms of its coherence, arguing that Stantic's 'filmography does not seem arbitrary, for in every case it had the characteristics of personal expression'.[24] From this perspective, a body of work composed by films which become sites of personal expression – that of the directors but, also, of Stantic as their producer – it seems pertinent to begin focusing on questions concerned with the overall coherence of her work, which in turn will lead to a discussion of how appropriate the idea of an '*auteur* producer' would be if applied to Stantic. As anticipated in D'Lugo's arguments, in order to sustain the pertinence of such description, it becomes useful to begin by inscribing her career in the wider context of Latin American cinema and to relate her work to this cinema's political dimension, by paying particular attention to its gender politics and the role women play in it.

Lita Stantic: Coherence as trademark

With the publication in 1991 of 'An/Other View of New Latin American Cinema',[25] B. Ruby Rich challenged the by-then stagnant readings of this multifaceted and evolving movement, which in her view were approaches that were no longer capable of accounting either for the new kind of cinema that was being produced in the region or for anything that wouldn't somehow replicate the handful of films acknowledged as the movement's canonical texts. While updating the scope of both the New Latin American Cinema and its historiographies, Rich identified a shift taking place within Latin American cinema that she described as a 'move from exteriority to interiority'.[26] Accordingly, she argued that the films being produced in the politically and socially changing landscape of Latin America during the 1980s were closer to the chronicle than to the epic and that, rather than being explicitly political, these films offered a new form of looking inward that was implicitly political. This manifested itself through equivalent transformations in their cinematic and aesthetic practices. Still a cinema of the dispossessed, in Rich's argument, it was not surprising, though, that '[s]uch a shift has also, not coincidentally, opened up the field to women'.[27] She demonstrates this point by turning her analysis to the films of some of the most notable women film-makers active in Latin America during those years, Bemberg among them. In a similar argument, when referring to their ten-year-long collaboration with the director, Stantic says: 'We were opening windows'.[28] Thus, although she credits the figure of the director as the main creative force behind a film, it is not to please anybody but out of conviction: 'The mother of the film is the director'.[29] The use of 'we' in this context fairly summarizes the dialogical nature and the dynamic of her partnership with Bemberg.

Similarly, Stantic is correct to argue that Argentina has today an unusually high number of active women film-makers and that Bemberg 'was a pioneer in that respect, since many young women who are directors today, began to fantasize about becoming a film-maker when they saw *Camila*.[30] Like every other Bemberg film, *Camila* is as much about the main character as it is about Bemberg herself, and, eventually, about Stantic as well. In her own words: 'María Luisa always wrote the same story: a woman that rebels and who does not want to be told what she has to do or who she has to be. She wants to live her own story.'[31] (It is worth noting here that in Spanish, history and story are the same word: *historia*.) This was precisely the ethos that guided them when they decided to join forces in order to make films and when, together with photographer Sara Facio and other women working in the film sector,[32] they established '*La Mujer y el Cine*' (*Woman and Cinema*) in 1988.

This civic association was created with the mandate to stimulate women to exercise leading roles within the film industry and to promote their presence in the medium given that, in their understanding, the women's gaze and their different points of view were meant to enrich and widen everybody's world. In 2008, marking the occasion of the association's twentieth anniversary, their press release read: '[t]wenty years ago … we envisaged that together we could and because we could, we had to work for gender equity in the field of cinematographic expression; [we were] aware that it was also a means to fight for the consolidation of democracy'.[33] The alignment of their militancy, as women clamouring for a more equitable industry in gender terms, with the socially and politically deeper process of re-democratization taking place in Argentina after 1983, speaks to the persistence of the idea of a socially committed cinema, a cinema that ultimately cannot help but be political.

Thus, as Stantic explains, whenever she decides to produce a film directed by a woman, the decision to embark on such projects does not necessarily stem from the fact that the script is written by a woman but, mostly, from her impression that they advance a novel, and generally defiant, take on a particular issue, that they will become what she identifies as 'necessary' films. It is precisely this understanding of a film being socially necessary that summarizes her ethical commitment to both cinema and reality and that, although evolving, guided her work as a producer since the time when she was one of the very few women in the ranks of *Grupo Cine Liberación*.

However, it would be misleading and incorrect to think that this principle applies exclusively to Stantic's interest in women directors such as Lucrecia Martel, Paz Encina (*Hamaca paraguaya/Paraguayan Hammock*, 2006), Lucía Cedrón (*Cordero de Dios/Lamb of God*, 2008) and, more recently, María Florencia Alvarez (*Habi, la extranjera/Habi, the Foreigner*, 2013). In Stantic's own words: 'It's not that I say, "If it's a woman, I would prefer it"; I receive projects from women that I find more appealing than the ones I receive from men … but there's no calculation.'[34] As demonstrated by her support to the early projects of Pablo Trapero, Adrián Caetano and Diego Lerman, the coherence of her choices, as well as her acute sense of 'necessity' – a film that is needed – is not restricted to her commitment to a feminist film practice. It is therefore in terms of the ideological coherence of her films that we can think about Stantic as an *auteur* producer. At the same time, at this point in her career, this coherence has become part of the cultural capital that she brings into the new projects that she embarks on, transforming her into a producer who, beyond and ahead of trends, has acquired the rare ability of turning film-makers into *auteurs*.

Auteur producer/producer of *auteurs*

It is when looking at Stantic's body of work in retrospect and in the wider context of the Argentine film industry and culture that this consistency becomes manifest. In 1994, with the passing of new legislation concerning the audio-visual sector (law 24.377), fundamental changes were introduced in the national film industry. Among the most significant ones was a new raft of incentives for television networks and multimedia conglomerates to participate both in the exhibition and the production of nationally produced films. Thus, a new type of cinema began to be shaped by these new actors who, in Gustavo Aprea's words, 'only conceive projects that match the "rules" of spectacle and that imitate the Hollywood model'.[35] One such project was *Sol de otoño/Autumn Sun* (Eduardo Mignogna, 2006), a box office success about an elderly couple, starring the very well established Norma Aleandro and Federico Luppi. Although her company did not participate in the financing of the film, Stantic was its executive producer. However, Stantic, whose work had never been about passing circumstances, refused to conform to this type of opportunist cinema.[36] She embarked on the production of a string of documentaries – some of them for television, one directed by Martel (*Las dependencias*, 1999) – therefore reconnecting again with the kind of inquisitive cinema to which she had been historically inclined. Attentive and receptive to the aesthetic and thematic explorations of a new brood of film-makers whose projects were not viable either within the parameters of the traditional model of co-production or within those of the newly TV-funded model of film production, Stantic also found herself attracted to a handful of projects that, as already noted, were going to become spearhead texts of the phenomenon known as New Argentine Cinema.

Lita Stantic became a 'significant presence'[37] in the configuration of this new cinema, as noted not only by Peña but also by Andrés Di Tella,[38] a protagonist himself of the then ongoing changes within the national film culture from his position as the first director of the *Buenos Aires Festival Internacional de Cine Independiente* (BAFICI) created in 1999 and a launching platform for many of these up-and-coming directors. Of course, there was no calculated premeditation in her decisions at the time, as she points out:

> It's not that at any point I thought: 'the new generation is coming and this is what I'm going to do', it was not like that; I received a book that I liked that was *La ciénaga* and more or less at the same time, [Pablo] Trapero showed up with a film that he had already shot and I liked it.[39]

Thus, between 1999 and 2002, Stantic collaborated with Trapero on the completion of *Mundo Grúa/Crane World* (1999), another film that she thought 'was necessary'.[40] She then produced Martel's first feature-length film, and participated as associate producer on *Bolivia* (Caetano, 2001) and *Tan de repente/Suddenly* (Lerman, 2002). Although all of these films were very different in terms of scale, style and thematic concerns, both critics and audiences soon acknowledged them as representative of a generational break with the existing cinema: what these directors (together with others, such as

Daniel Burman, Lisandro Alonso, Albertina Carri, Martin Rejtman, to name a few) wanted to say, how they wanted to communicate it and who they were addressing, had changed significantly.

Of course, it was not just the films that had changed, since the viability of this new cinema, in terms of production, depended as well on the introduction of some innovative strategies. The production process was 'segmented' with different sources of funding generated along the way for the stages of script writing, shooting, editing and distributing a work.[41] Sources of finance were diversified, including the participation of international bodies such as Programa Ibermedia (a consortium with funding from Spain, Portugal and most of the Spanish and Portuguese speaking countries in Latin America), the Hubert Bals Fund (Holland), the Sundance Institute (USA) and Fonds Sud Cinéma (France), all of which, as Aprea notes, 'support projects not as much on the basis of profitability but by valuing originality'.[42] Similarly, the growing presence of local investors such as educational institutions (Antín's FUC being the most prominent one) and independent production companies, such as Stantic's and a handful of new ones, set up by some of these recently established film-makers and film professionals interested in producing both their own projects and those to which they feel attracted, have been key elements in getting the films made.[43]

Stantic's work as a producer

It is in relation to this reconfigured landscape of the film sector that we have to look at the concrete aspects of Stantic's work as a producer in order to appreciate the overall imprint of her trajectory within the national film industry. Like Martel, and Bemberg before her, who both gave Stantic the script of their films, or like Trapero, who showed her the first rough cut of *Mundo Grúa*, it is now customary for Stantic to be approached by film-makers and scriptwriters with their projects. The decision to commit or not to a particular one has less to do with any kind of marketing assessment than with a shared horizon of interests. Once this is established, the work or, as she puts it, the 'association' between the producer and the director, begins.[44]

It is Stantic's job to ensure the commercial viability of the project and to reach the right sources of financing throughout the different stages of the production process. Having begun to co-produce films in the mid-1980s, her strategy consists in finding the right match for each project. In that sense, she does not necessarily work by default with the same local or international companies. Besides the almost ubiquitous presence of the state-run *Instituto Nacional de Cine y Artes Audiovisuales* (National Institute of Cinema and Audiovisual Arts, INCAA), there are partnerships with local financiers as well as with international companies (mostly Spanish and French, although the participation of regional investors from Brazil and Chile in her latest projects is worth noting) or financing bodies, such as Programa Ibermedia and the Hubert Bals Fund, which mostly support projects in the pre-production stages and, in the case of the former, also occasionally with their distribution, as with Martel's second film, *La niña santa/The Holy Girl* (2004) (Figure 12.2).

Figure 12.2 Lita Stantic, Pedro Almodóvar and Lucrecia Martel. Courtesy of Lita Stantic

The first stage of production concerns polishing the scripts, a task that Stantic gets involved with at a creative level, discussing with the film-makers the successive versions of the screenplay. She also, when relevant, directs them to the right forums of discussion, including, for example, the Sundance Institute, where Martel got the opportunity to work further on the script of *La ciénaga* before production actually began.

At this point, Stantic accompanies the film-maker during the shooting, suggesting re-takes when necessary and, in her words, trying to 'watch the film from the outside in order to be able to suggest things that the directors may accept or not'.[45] This dialogue, or exchange of opinions, continues during the editing process, in which it is customary for the producer to participate actively in the decisions about the cuts. However, Stantic makes it a point of honour never to take the final cut: 'Why would I do it? Would I fight with the director and fire him or her? It would be absurd.'[46] Finally, since the international success of *Camila*, Stantic has cultivated methodically a solid network of regional and international distributors. But, because of the nature of the projects that she has engaged with since *Mundo Grúa* – non-commodified and not necessarily easily palatable visions of mostly local situations or conditions – the attention that her films have received outside Argentina varies. So, for example, Martel's films get a wider international theatrical release than the *opere prime* of Paz Encina (*Hamaca Paraguaya/Paraguayan Hammock*, 2006) or Lucía Cedrón (*Cordero de Dios/Lamb of God*, 2008). Despite this, and very much in tune with a growing tendency worldwide, in the distribution of her films there is an increasing complexity in making deals about the rights and profits that will accrue from sales in different formats, including DVD and cable television and, perhaps more importantly, all those other emerging formats that fall under the 'all media' category, such as video on demand.

Conclusion

In Stantic's experiential understanding of cinema, in the way that she has lived it throughout her professional career since she joined the militant *Grupo Cine Liberación*, a film is 'necessary' when it raises the questions that it has to raise and when that need finds its way to communicate itself while making the most (creatively, expressively) of the available resources. Very much in tune with Julio García Espinosa's conception of *Por un cine imperfecto*/'For an imperfect cinema',[47] – one of the paradigm texts of the New Latin American Cinema – such a comprehension of what cinema should be and how it should be done has been adhered to systematically by Stantic as a producer. Hence, if there is a coherence that traverses her work, this has been determined by her long-standing commitment to a certain type of socially committed cinema, by her curiosity about novel and challenging discourses on the real and by the leaning towards plural and inclusive film practices, all of which make her consistently receptive to the concerns and the interests of new voices. It is because of this consistency that like-minded film-makers seek her out to produce their films. This core principle ensures that she remains current and easily able to engage in creative dialogue with seemingly disparate directors.

It is in this sense, then, that we should consider Stantic's authorial status as the consequence of the overall coherence of her career while at the same time being traceable in each film produced. Similarly, it can be further argued that, at this point in her career, the association of her name with a project leads to an almost automatic acknowledgement of its director as an *auteur*. It is as if, by mere association, Stantic confers this status on any director. As a result, the *auteur* producer has become, in several cases, the producer of *auteurs*. The examples of Martel, Trapero and Caetano, preceded by Bemberg and even Doria, demonstrate this point; the early careers of directors such as Cedrón and Encina were certainly launched on this premise.

A promoter of a tradition of Latin American cinema that heralded its practice as an act of responsible citizenship, Lita Stantic has gained the respect of both the industry and the public opinion thanks to the solid consistency of her work – an asset that she brings to every new project in which she ventures. The history of the Argentine film industry, and that of the wider national film culture, its inflections, its dialogue with Latin America and with the rest of the world, could be viewed in the light of her body of work: for more than 40 years, she has traversed this industry actively, wisely and strategically, refusing to accommodate or to engage in any kind of crass commodification, either for national or for international audiences. She has remained committed to the perpetual need for a cinema that will address critically Argentine history, society and culture.

Notes

1　Many ideas and references in this chapter are taken from two recorded interviews by the author with Lita Stantic in Buenos Aires in April 2012.

2　Interview with the author.

3   Interview with the author.

4   In an interview by the author with Fernando 'Pino' Solanas, at the University of
    Western Ontario in February 2011.

5   Interview with the author.

6   Interview with the author.

7   Interview with the author.

8   Elena Goity, 'Las Realizadoras Del Period', in *Cine Argentino en Democracia
    1983/1993*, ed. Claudio España (Buenos Aires Fondo Nacional de las Artes, 1994),
    272–83.

9   Annette Kuhn and Susannah Radstone (eds.), *The Women's Companion to
    International Film* (London: Virago Press, 1990).

10 Ana María López, 'Stantic, Lita', in *The Women's Companion to International Film*, ed.
    Annette Kuhn and Susannah Radstone (London: Virago Press, 1990), 383–84.

11 Ana María López, 'Bemberg, María Luisa', in *The Women's Companion to
    International Film*, ed. Annette Kuhn and Susannah Radstone (London: Virago Press,
    1990), 39–40.

12 Octavio Getino, *Industrias del Audiovisual Argentino en el Mercado Internacional*
    (Buenos Aires: Ediciones Ciccus, 2009), 49.

13 Getino, *Industrias del Audiovisual Argentino en el Mercado Internacional*, 83.

14 Marvin D'Lugo, 'Authorship, Globalization, and the New Identity of Latin American
    Cinema: From the Mexican "ranchera" to Argentinean "exile"', in *Rethinking Third
    Cinema*, ed. Anthony Guneratne and Wimal Dissanayake (New York and London:
    Routledge, 2003), 103–25.

15 D'Lugo, 'Authorship, Globalization, and the New Identity of Latin American Cinema',
    107.

16 D'Lugo, 'Authorship, Globalization, and the New Identity of Latin American Cinema',
    116.

17 D'Lugo, 'Authorship, Globalization, and the New Identity of Latin American Cinema'.

18 John King, 'Breaching the Walls of Silence: Lita Stantic's *Un muro de silencio*', *Revista
    Canadiense de Estudios Hispánicos*, XX/1 (1995): 43–53.

19 King, 'Breaching the Walls of Silence', 50.

20 Catherine Grant, 'Camera Solidaria', *Screen*, 38:4 (1997): 311–28.

21 Claudio España (ed.), *Cine Argentino en Democracia 1983/1993* (Buenos Aires: Fondo
    Nacional de las Artes, 1994).

22 I am referring here to the *Ley de Punto Final/Law of Full Stop* (1986), the *Ley de
    Obediencia Debida/Law of Due Obedience* (1987), both passed during the presidency
    of Raúl Alfonsín, and to a series of pardons decreed by President Carlos Menem
    between 1989 and 1990.

23 Fernando Martín Peña, *Cien Años de Cine Argentino* (Buenos Aires: Editorial Biblos,
    2012).

24 Martín Peña, *Cien Años de Cine Argentino*, 239.

25 B. Ruby Rich, 'An/Other View of New Latin American Cinema', in *New Latin
    American Cinema, Volume One: Theory, Practices, and Transcontinental Articulations*,
    ed. Michael T. Martin (Detroit: Wayne State University Press, 1997), 273–97.
    Originally published in *Iris*, 23 (Summer 1991).

26 Ruby Rich, 'An/Other View of New Latin American Cinema', 281.

27 Ruby Rich, 'An/Other View of New Latin American Cinema', 281.

28 Interview with the author.

29 Interview with the author.

30 Interview with the author.

31 Interview with the author.

32 Apart from Bemberg, Stantic and Facio, the other founding members of 'La Mujer y el Cine' were Beatriz Villalba Welsh, Susana Lopez Merino, Gabriela Massuh and Marta Bianchi.

33 '20 años de La Mujer y el Cine', accessed 8 January 2013, http://www.lamujeryelcine. com.ar/main.php?seccion=3&sub=32.

34 Interview with the author.

35 Gustavo Aprea, *Cine y Políticas en Argentina* (Buenos Aires: Universidad Nacional de General Sarmiento and Biblioteca Nacional, 2008), 23.

36 Peña, *Cien Años*, 240.

37 Peña, *Cien Años*, 240.

38 Andrés Di Tella, 'Recuerdos Del Nuevo Cine Argentino', in *Hacer Cine Producción Audiovisual en América Latina*, ed. Eduardo Russo (Buenos Aires: Editorial Paidós, 2008), 247.

39 Interview with the author.

40 Interview with the author.

41 Jens Andermann, *New Argentine Cinema* (London and New York: I. B. Tauris, 2012), 9.

42 Gustavo Aprea, *Cine y Políticas en Argentina*, 23.

43 Andermann, *New Argentine Cinema*, 9.

44 Interview with the author.

45 Interview with the author.

46 Interview with the author.

47 Julio García Espinoza, 'For an Imperfect Cinema', in *Twenty-five Years of the New Latin American Cinema*, ed. Michael Chanan (London: BFI Publishing and Channel 4, 1983), 28–33. Originally published in *Cine Cubano* 66/67 (1970).

13

Beyond National Humiliation:
Han Sanping and China's Post-Olympics
Historical Event Blockbusters[1]

A. T. McKenna

The notion of the producer as conduit, intermediary, mediator, nurturer and showman resonates throughout production studies. Han Sanping is all of these things; but he also comes from a family of revolutionaries and was army-trained during the Cultural Revolution. Han is the most powerful man in Chinese cinema. If you want to film in China, you must go through Han. If you want your film released in China, you must go through Han. With Hollywood scrambling for a slice of the vast Chinese market, this makes Han one of the most powerful men in the movie world.

Han was promoted to CEO of China Film Group (CFG) in 2007, and appears as a quasi-autonomous senior Party official-cum-movie mogul. He has producer credits on over 600 movies and is regularly dubbed the Godfather of modern Chinese cinema. Robert Cain, a China-based American producer, said of him: 'If you took Jack Valenti, Lew Wasserman and Steven Spielberg and rolled them into one you'd begin to get an idea of Han's power and influence in China.'[2]

China Film Group was formed in 1999 under the State Administration of Radio, Film and Television (SARFT) as a conglomeration of eight media entities. It has interests in production, exhibition, distribution, importing, exporting and television. It is vertically, horizontally and politically integrated, and is by far the most powerful company in Chinese cinema. Han occasionally announces that the CFG will be floated on the stock exchange,[3] but it remains a state-owned enterprise.[4]

Upon leaving the army in the 1970s, Han worked as a lighting technician at Emei film studios before entering the Beijing Film Academy in 1983. He became deputy director, then director of the Beijing Film Studio in the 1990s, before becoming general manager of the CFG. On being promoted to CEO he pugnaciously predicted that box office revenues in China would rise from $350 million in 2006 to $1.3 billion in 2011.[5] In 2011, the figures read over $2 billion.[6]

This chapter examines the historical event blockbusters produced by Han following the 2008 Beijing Olympic Games. *City of Life and Death* (Lu Chuan, 2009), *The Founding of a Republic* (Han Sanping and Huang Jianxin, 2009) and *Beginning of the Great Revival* (Han Sanping and Huang Jianxin, 2011) are blockbuster movies that depict and commemorate famous events from recent Chinese history. They have all been described as, or as variants of, *zhuxuanlu* films. *Zhuxuanlu, leitmotif* or main melody, is a style of state-backed propaganda film that proliferated in the People's Republic in the years following the Tiananmen Square massacre; they are made to convey official orthodoxy or philosophy to the audience. For the post-Olympics historical event blockbusters the main melody is said to be rooted in Hu Jintao's theory of 'harmonious society'.[7] But the problem with a melody is that if you are listening for it, you will hear it, especially one as cinematically ubiquitous as 'harmonious society', and even more so with the CFG, which is the exclusive producer of the state's mid-budget *zhuxuanlu* films. However, to describe these films as *zhuxuanlu* is, while not inaccurate, a little reductive because it overemphasizes pedagogic intent at the expense of commercial and cultural contexts.

The emergence of a cinema of consensus, especially following a national tumult, is not unusual, and 2008 was a tumultuous year for the People's Republic. In May, the devastating Sichuan earthquake killed nearly 70,000 people; also, unrest in Tibet made headlines in the West, leading to the disruption of the worldwide Olympic torch relay by demonstrators. The Games themselves were brilliantly orchestrated and a public relations success for China. The propaganda surrounding the Olympic celebrations, however, drew criticism for presenting a sanitized view of Chinese history, and an uncomplicated vision of national unity and international benevolence.[8] Arguably, Western sensitivities were heightened, given that the Games took place during the unfolding financial crisis, which accentuated China's status as an economic powerhouse.

Eric Rentschler's work on the German mainstream cinema which emerged after the fall of the Berlin Wall is particularly instructive here.[9] This is especially true because in both cases the domestic cinema of consensus superseded an influential and internationally renowned art-cinema movement: New German Cinema and The Sixth Generation of Chinese Directors, respectively. However, looking beyond the enormous political and industrial institutions that dominate cinema production and consumption in China, and using a very powerful, influential and visionary producer as a vantage point, helps to provide a more nuanced understanding of Chinese blockbuster cinema and its portrayal of national histories.

In China, as elsewhere, historical education has its roots in the school system, and the Century of National Humiliation plays a key role.[10] This concept seeped into cinema with the spectacularization of Chinese slaughter, suffering and victimhood in mawkish 1990s blockbusters such as *Don't Cry Nanjing* (Wu Ziniu, 1995) and *The Opium War* (Xie Jin, 1997). Han's blockbusters, by contrast, are less exhibitionistically masochistic and bring a level of sophistication, and sometimes humour, to a genre which had been forbiddingly austere, rendering them more accessible by commercializing the Party line. Han has taken national humiliation history and refashioned it cinematically, providing objective interpretations of national tragedies, injecting a touch of camp into national icons, and adding blockbuster razzamatazz to revolution. Such irreverence is not unproblematic. Sebastian Veg argues that incorporating parody into state-controlled cinema invests Han's films with a specious artistic legitimacy.[11] However, the move beyond top-down propaganda and national humiliation narratives, and the concurrent embrace of grass-roots populism and blockbuster eventism, reveals a great deal about China's booming film industry. More importantly for this volume, it also reveals the power of the producer in revising and re-negotiating national memory.

In the late 1990s, Han was instrumental in the development of the Chinese event movie, using his connections and negotiating skills to guide Feng Xiaogang's *The Dream Factory* through the censorious bureaucracy of Chinese officialdom before releasing it to coincide with the 1998 New Year celebrations.[12] Subsequently, Feng Xiaogang's 'New Year Comedies' became a staple for the next few years.[13] For Han, hype, showmanship and eventism are essential for powering a booming film industry in a country awash with piracy:

> You have to let audiences see in films what they can't see on TV and on their mobile phones. If it's all hand-made noodle – a few yuan under Lijiao bridge but a hundred yuan in a five-star hotel, what are people buying? They're buying service. Chinese people don't like service ... [but] these habits are changing slowly, especially in the young.[14]

As already mentioned, engaging with and nurturing a young audience is a key concern for Han. This is not merely a commercial matter; it also speaks to the patriotic edification of China's youth. In 2007, Han controversially began casting a television adaptation of Cao Xueqin's much cherished novel *Dream of Red Mansions* with an *X Factor*-style televised audition and selection process in order to encourage young people to 'pay more attention to China's ancient literature and culture'.[15] The casting of the CFG's production of *Red Cliff Part One* and *Part Two* (John Woo, 2008/2009), meanwhile, prompted fevered speculation and controversy among China's young netizens about who should, or should not, be cast in John Woo's star-studded rendering of one of the most famous battles in Chinese history. The first part of this vast patriotic epic was released into the atmosphere of excitement and expectation that accompanied the run-up to the Beijing Olympics and became China's highest-grossing film, breaking the record held for ten years by *Titanic* (James Cameron, 1997).

Red Cliff and subsequent blockbusters have also been able to capitalize on China's massive cinema-building programme which has provided more outlets for the concurrent increase in film production, counterweighting the 'lopsided industry strong in production but weak in exhibition' observed by Yingjin Zhang.[16] Moreover, although Han advocates risk-taking to maximize profits, these risks are tempered by political, monopolist and protectionist measures.[17] The Chinese industry enforces a quota system on foreign films and operates Domestic Film Protection Months, or blackout periods, usually around national holidays, when foreign film screenings are restricted.[18] Moreover, the CFG, or its myriad subsidiaries, partners and associates, has control or influence over imports, exhibition and distribution of all movies in China.

Han is a Chinese mogul with Hollywood characteristics. He is a sound, Mao-quoting Party Man with all the ebullient immodesty of the Great American Showmen:

> I am Han Sanping, what can I say? Chairman Mao once said 'cadres are a decisive factor, once a political line has been established'. Applying this to an enterprise, you can say that its success is directly related to its high-level leaders ... of course I have been the decisive factor and I don't think I need to play this down.[19]

As George Custen observes, Hollywood's Great Man view of history was created by Great Men – the powerful producers and moguls of the studio system.[20] Similarly, Han's market-orientated revisionism combines populism and prestige, while also departing from accepted formulae. In his historical event blockbusters we see former enemies of China treated sympathetically, if not rehabilitated, and the creation myths of the PRC injected with camp and infused with consumerist glamour in a timely break from narratives of national humiliation.

The hot potato

Of the films discussed in this chapter, perhaps the best known in the West is *City of Life and Death* (aka. *Nanjing! Nanjing!*, 2009), Lu Chuan's film about the 1937 Nanjing Massacre (colloquially known as The Rape of Nanking), in which an estimated 300,000 Chinese civilians were killed by the invading Japanese forces. It is a totemic event in Chinese history, with a complex historiography. Barely discussed during the Mao-era, the massacre is now a cornerstone of the patriotic education programme in the Chinese school system and the centrepiece of China's national humiliation narrative.[21] It has been depicted on film, in China and elsewhere, many times.[22] Indeed, Han, alongside Zhou Li, co-directed the 1988 film, *Sanctuary*, set during the Nanjing siege, so it can safely be assumed that the event holds a certain amount of resonance for him, especially since his film pre-dates the current Chinese preoccupation with the massacre.

City of Life and Death is the most challenging of the films discussed in this chapter and almost certainly could not have been made without the involvement of Han and the CFG, whose power and influence can help to smooth diplomatic, bureaucratic and censorship obstacles. However, the controversies caused by the film not only highlight Han's willingness to support challenging work from young film-makers, but also the compromises and restrictions of the state's film-making system, of which Han is very much a part.

Lu Chuan's monochrome rendering of the massacre is powerful and harrowing and, most controversially, challenges the popular Chinese understanding of brutal and remorseless Japanese aggressors by showing the vulnerable human face of their soldiers. *City of Life and Death* is by far the most objective film yet made about the massacre and has caused considerable controversy in China, with Lu Chuan reportedly receiving death threats.[23] It also caused some dispute among commentators and scholars of Chinese cinema and culture. Shelly Kraicer, in a polemical intervention, draws on 'harmonious society' rhetoric to identify the film as 'post-*zhuxuanlu* cinema [in which] crude propaganda ... is out; tolerant recognition of the potential humanity of even so-called enemies ... is in'.[24] Tony Rayns disagrees, arguing that *City of Life and Death* is 'a corrective' to earlier depictions, which 'wallowed in victimhood'.[25] For Damien Kinney, meanwhile, *City of Life and Death* 'offers the most daring picture of moral complexity, but it is nonetheless constrained by contemporary Chinese nationalist rhetoric and politics'.[26] Discussion of the industrial background and the nature of Han's involvement can help to untangle some of these debates.

Having finished his previous film, *Kekexili: Mountain Patrol* (2004), Lu began planning *City of Life and Death* but abandoned the project because of its expense and political sensitivity.[27] *Kekexili*'s awards for Best Film and Best Cinematography at the 2004 Taiwan Golden Horse Festival, however, saw the project revived. Initial funding for *City of Life and Death* came from Megamedia, with more funding from friends and the film's producer, Tan Hong. Early pre-production stages were undertaken without a certificate from SARFT, which is a requirement for making a film in China. Funding problems and bureaucratic niggles were smoothed over thanks to the involvement of Han and the CFG.[28]

The CFG was looking to fund a film to mark the 70th anniversary of the Nanjing Massacre. There were four other projects in contention for the CFG's funding and, according to Han, 'We could only afford to make one film on the Nanjing Massacre. Lu Chuan tried to persuade me and influence me again and again, and eventually he did.'[29] Lu has also spoken of Han's keenness to support young film-makers.[30] He called Han a 'superfan of my films'.[31] Lu has worked with Han as Director of the Creative Centre of the CFG since its inception, and the CFG part-funded *Kekexili* and Lu's first film, *The Missing Gun* (2002). Significantly, Lu's graduate thesis, about Francis Ford Coppola, was entitled *The Author in the System*, and Lu has said: 'From the very beginning, I have decided that I am to be an author working within the system.'[32] As the director of the most controversial Chinese film of recent years, Lu is no renegade or dissident, but a mainstream film-maker with commercial instincts. Indeed, domestic political soundness and international prestige is a rare combination for a Chinese film-maker, leaving Lu ideally placed to reinterpret the massacre in an aesthetically engaging and broadly politically correct manner.

City of Life and Death was completed and released in 2009, missing the Nanjing Massacre's 70th anniversary by two years. It was a large-scale and complex project that Lu spent two years researching, but delays from censorship bodies are almost inevitable for film-making in China and Lu spent 'seven or eight months' awaiting script approval before he could begin shooting.[33] Shooting took place between October 2007 and June 2008,[34] followed by more censorship negotiations. The film's release was preceded by a huge marketing campaign and much media interest, and Lu's sensitive portrayal of the Japanese soldiers was a prominent topic in pre-release publicity and interviews.[35]

Despite the sympathetic depiction of Japanese soldiers being a selling point, upon its release in China many called for *City of Life and Death* to be withdrawn from cinemas, but pressure was abated by support from Li Changchun, the Chinese Communist Party's (CCP) propaganda chief.[36] There are conflicting reports about whether the film was designated as one of the ten films to commemorate the 60th anniversary of the PRC – the *New York Times* says it was chosen;[37] *Cinema Without Borders* claims it was 'shut out'.[38] Such is the capriciousness of Chinese censorship, however, that both may have been true at different times. The following year it was nominated in various categories at the Hundred Flowers (*Huabiao*) Awards, organized by SARFT, only to have the nominations cancelled a week before the ceremony.[39] Also, in 2010, the CFG withdrew the film from Palm Springs Film Festival in protest at the screening of *The Sun Behind the Clouds: Tibet's Struggle for Freedom* (Ritu Sarin, Tenzing Sonam, 2010), a documentary about the Dalai Lama.[40] For the 2011 Oscars, *City of Life and Death* was not put forward as China's entry for the Best Foreign Film Academy Award for apparently 'political reasons'.[41] A frustrated National Geographic, that had distributed *Kekexili*, pulled out of a North American distribution deal after 'China Film Group's demands grew in complexity and restrictiveness'.[42] Eventually, it was distributed in English-speaking territories by Kino.

At the very least, such controversies significantly undermine assertions that *City of Life and Death* is a *zhuxuanlu* or even post-*zhuxuanlu* film. Indeed, the confused and contradictory ways in which the film was handled is revealing and facilitates an understanding of Han's power and influence. Han's support can, and does, provide up-and-coming directors with access to budgets and political clout. However, even though this support resulted in a remarkably objective view of the Nanjing Massacre, Han is no cheerleader for free speech and his sponsorship of young film-makers is subject to wider political and industrial concerns.

The restrictions of the system and the specific restrictions on blockbusters are also exposed. *City of Life and Death* stands at a curious intersection here. At the 2009 Shanghai Film Festival, in response to fellow panellist Wang Xiaoshuai's criticism of Chinese cinema's increasing blockbuster mentality, Lu argued that blockbusters could be both popular and critically lauded.[43] Yet it is precisely the combination of critical value and popular appeal that has proved problematic. Blockbuster films, given their popularity and, therefore, societal influence, are problematic in a society for which propaganda is so important, particularly when they provide historical revisionism, nuancing or correctives.

City of Life and Death was both timely and opportune. Its objectivity and eschewal of the more hackneyed tropes that defined previous Nanjing films brought both critical acclaim and marketplace distinction.[44] It was released at a time of comparative openness in the PRC, and the controversy it caused was arguably less than it might have been. Ill feeling towards Japan regarding her behaviour during the war, which had led to riots in 2005, was not so pronounced; the ongoing dispute over the Diaoyu/Senkaku Islands was momentarily in remission, and China looked certain to overtake Japan as the region's biggest economy. Moreover, the post-Olympics national feel-good factor should be taken into account, as should the fact that the PRC was approaching its 60th birthday, as explored in the next section.

The de-reification of Chairman Mao

Chris Berry has provided a useful distinction between the giant film, which follows the 'main melody' and the Chinese blockbuster, which is 'less serious and lacking in pedagogical purpose'.[45] He cites *The Opium War* as the film that synthesized the two forms: a blockbuster film with a serious representation of a historical event, and an event film in numerous ways. It was the most expensive Chinese film made up to that time, and was widely publicized. In addition, it depicted and commemorated a historical event, and was released against the backdrop of another historical event – the handover of Hong Kong, which had become a British colony following the First Opium War and the 1842 Nanjing Treaty. It also had a seriousness of tone that was off-putting to Chinese audiences.[46] Furthermore, the giant film faded as, following the phenomenal success of *Hero* (Zhang Yimou) in 2002, the blockbuster rose.

In October 2008, Han received an 'order' from SARFT 'to shoot an all-encompassing, solid, documentary-coloured film that positively represents the establishment of the new China'.[47] In the afterglow of the Olympic Games, and in an industrial context much healthier than that of 1997, Han sought to synthesize the giant film and the blockbuster once again. *The Founding of a Republic* was released as part of the celebrations commemorating the 60th anniversary of the People's Republic, and it is important to emphasize the word *part*. Blockbusters, almost by definition, are accompanied by a publicity circus in which the film is integrated. In addition, the time of release may seek to capitalize on another celebration: summer, Christmas, New Year or the Olympics, for example. In the case of *The Founding of a Republic*, the film and its release were integrated into a national celebration, one that included a military parade, a grand pageant, a gala, massive media coverage and a flood of memorabilia. The historical moment and cultural context of the film's release undoubtedly shaped the film itself, and it is important to bear this in mind in any analysis.

The Founding of a Republic tells the story of the Chinese Civil War from the end of the Second World War until 1949 when Mao Zedong's victorious Communists formed the People's Republic. Its release, on almost every screen in mainland China, was preceded by a massive marketing campaign and coincided with National Day, 1 October, which saw the televised celebrations from Tiananmen Square in Beijing. It also acted as something of a counterpoint to the impressively regimented ceremonies by providing a star-studded, accessible and rather amiable rendering of a bloody chapter of Chinese history.

The Founding of a Republic is a multi-director effort, with Han and Huang Jianxin on primary director duties; Chen Kaige, Feng Xiaogang and Peter Chan are 'guest directors'; and Lu Chuan is assistant director. In keeping with the 'harmonious society' melody, but still startling on first viewing, is the sympathetic depiction of the *Kuomintang* and also Chiang Kai-Shek, presented as a noble but misguided patriot who exiles himself for the sake of China's unity. Mao, meanwhile, is wise, jolly and sagacious.

Mao's image, as many commentators have noted, was conspicuously absent from the Beijing Olympic Games. 'Mao Zedong long ago disappeared from foreign propaganda efforts', writes Anne-Marie Brady, 'and these days is only selectively used in domestic propaganda'.[48] Mao's reintroduction into state propaganda via *The Founding of a Republic* is not the Mao of old whose likeness is carved in looming stone in Peoples' Squares throughout China. Mao, like so many icons of popular culture, needed reinventing or, perhaps, de-inventing. The Mao of *The Founding of a Republic* is not the unobstructed focal point as in statues or Tiananmen Square's 'Maoseleum', but rather nestled among hundreds of Chinese stars who obscure as much as illuminate.

If a producer has the resources, then saturating a movie with stars can be a good option.[49] It can add prestige, box office appeal, ensure funding, attract distributors and create publicity during production as various stars sign up to a project, and Han has claimed starry epics such as *Around the World in 80 Days* (Michael Anderson, 1956) and *Birth of a Nation* (D. W. Griffith, 1915) as influences on his movie.[50] With *The Founding of a Republic*, Han certainly had the resources and the influence; moreover, most of the Chinese A-listers who flit in and out of the movie donated their services for free. The stars, it seems, were attracted by the idea of patriotic commemoration, not a big-bucks pay day. In this sense, Han was less of a mega-mogul doling out huge cheques, and more of a Bob Geldof figure who, as in Band Aid's charity single, assembled, organized and orchestrated a huge roster of stars and celebrities for a worthy cause. For such a star-filled blockbuster, it cost a mere 30 million yuan (around $4.4 million).

According to Han, he was responding to the urgency of the government's request, having been given less than a year to pull the project together and release it in time for the 60th anniversary celebrations. 'Casting stars who have personal charisma and superb acting skills', said Han, 'were the only choice to finish the project in such a short time'.[51] He also noted that bankable stars would increase audience appeal, particularly among the young.[52] For Huang Jianxin, the stars were not only attracted by the opportunity to appear in China's anniversary film, but also by the 'power of the China Film Group and the personal charm of Han'.[53] Terence Chang joked, referring to Han by nickname, 'Everyone has to show their respect if Grandpa San asks.'[54]

With so much talent attracted to the project, most of the leading roles were played by respected and recognizable stars and actors. Most of the megastars, it should be noted, play only fleeting roles. Zhang Ziyi has a couple of lines, as does Jet Li, and one could be forgiven for not noticing the well-known faces of countless others, whose appearances often provoke an after-the-fact double-take: 'Was that Jackie Chan?' Many of the stars only turned up on set for a couple of hours, filmed their part in one take, and then went on their way.[55] Thus, the audience is provided with a roll-call of Chinese notables, something conducive to the interactivity of spot-the-star games for an audience. *The Founding of a Republic* presents a simmering stockpot of celebrity, with stars popping on the surface before disappearing completely, setting the story of Mao's victory within a sort of cinema of distractions. It is more a film of famous faces than a film of history.[56]

In her work on *Hero*, Sabrina Yu has highlighted the embrace of camp as a viewing strategy among young Chinese audiences, who gather to laugh at its anachronistic language, overwrought melodrama and po-faced seriousness.[57] By the same token, there is plenty in *The Founding of a Republic* to keep the young and savvy viewer distracted from the main story. Along with the conveyer belt of stars, there are scenes of Mao frolicking in fields with his nieces, a meeting held in the dark because the austere Mao wants to save the candle, slow-motion scenes with saturated colour of triumphant arrivals and stirring speeches, and deliberately nit-picky scenes featuring debates about what should be the People's Republic's Anthem, and what design the flag should be (Figure 13.1).

Just as the Beijing Opening Ceremony sought to emphasize continuity, so the Mao of *The Founding of a Republic* is a figure onto which continuity of culture is projected. This version of Mao, a lynchpin of Chinese continuity, is made even more apparent thanks to the appearance of Zhang Ziyi. Late in the film, as the victorious Communists begin to busy themselves with the business of government, Mao has his photograph taken with a group of beaming women activists, a nod to Mao's famous dictum: 'Women hold up half the sky.' One of the women questions the leadership's choice of flag design for the People's Republic. Mao listens patiently to her concerns, and seeks the opinion of another activist, Gong Peng, who says she prefers the five-star design (the current PRC flag); at this point Madame Sun Yat-Sen intervenes and agrees with Gong, saying that the design symbolizes class harmony. That Gong, a briefly featured fictional character, is played by Zhang Ziyi adds an interesting frisson, with Mao acting as conduit from China's past glory to future prosperity.

Xu Qing plays Sun Yat-Sen's widow, Chiang Kai Shek's sister-in-law, a member of the powerful Soong family and future honourary president of the PRC; Zhang Ziyi nominally plays Gong Peng, but she really plays Zhang Ziyi, superstar; Tang Guoqiang is Mao, but he is also Tang Guoqiang the famous Mao impersonator, impersonating Mao. The scene functions as far more than a star cameo and rendering of Mao's sagacity. It reaches into the past, to Sun Yat Sen, the father of modern China, and to the film's present, to Chiang Kai-Shek, the vanquished but noble foe; it reaches to the audience's present, to the relatively new cultural phenomenon of the Mao impersonator,

Figure 13.1 Camp Chairman: The Great Helmsman frolics in a flowery field with his nieces. Mao is played by Tang Guoqiang, China's foremost Mao impersonator

and to the new Mao, a de-invented, de-reified, pop-culture icon who reflects China's aspirations as opposed to defining them. Zhang Ziyi, meanwhile, sprinkles stardust on the chairman. The audience is treated to one of cinema's most smouldering beauties girlishly proclaiming, with bright eyes and sunshine smile, 'Chairman Mao, looking at this flag makes one feel enthusiastic' in a scene made all the more striking by her cleverly uncharacteristic hairdo, which facilitates one of the film's most successful 'ooh look!' double-takes (Figure 13.2).

The star performers, then, have textual meaning and ideological resonance beyond the cameo. Moreover, by accentuating the artifice of the text, they connect the viewer to the context, to the holiday mood of the national celebration of which the film is a part; not for nothing did Han call the film 'a birthday gift'.[58] This means that *The Founding of a Republic* has a curious bifocality. Shelly Kraicer has expressed admiration for its kitschy approach, writing, 'It's not history, nor does it pretend to be. The film treats its audience to a series of knowing winks, a delightful conspiracy of consensual entertainment'.[59] Others, meanwhile, express deep concern at Han's campy sugaring of the propaganda pill.[60] One should, however, remember its blockbuster context.

Julian Stringer has observed that 'a fine line has always separated the public's willingness to be seduced by the values of public showmanship from its impulse to recoil in the face of vulgar exhibitionism'.[61] In this case, such tensions take on a political dimension. There is a temptation to leap conceitedly to the moral high ground when faced with a blockbuster rendering of a national creation myth, or appear archly knowing when batting away ethical concerns as naïve or unsophisticated. However, blockbuster aesthetics do not only generate binary either/or responses, they also exploit the tension between, and capitalize on the pseudo-empowerment of the viewer accepting the invitation to indulge in a particular viewing strategy, such as camp or irony, which superficially subverts the text. *The Founding of a Republic*, as noted, caters directly to viewer savvy.

Blockbusters not only try to create consensus through populism, but also capitalize on consensus through eventism. *The Founding of a Republic* was released on the nation's birthday against the backdrop of a booming economy. It was preceded

Figure 13.2 Zhang Ziyi (centre) and a Women's Delegation charm Chairman Mao (Tang Guoqiang) into changing the design of the PRC flag in *The Founding of a Republic* (2009)

by a successful Olympics and a devastating earthquake. It speaks directly, then, to the cinemas of consensus of post-War America, post-Wall Germany and post-9/11 Hollywood blockbusters. With its facile pomposity and invitation to kitschy interactivity, it is more anthem than *leitmotif*.

There is a strutting confidence to *The Founding of a Republic* which situates it at a time in the Chinese film industry when confidence was in no short supply, thanks to films such as *Red Cliff*. In *The Founding of a Republic*, the spectacularization of Chinese victimhood, which marked films such as *The Opium War* or *Don't Cry Nanjing*, is replaced with a series of negotiations that result in a consensus; indeed, there is little indication as to *why* a revolution was necessary. Moreover, from the notoriously high-risk world of the blockbuster, and from a man who has cited risk-taking as integral to success, comes a blockbuster that owes so much to the protectionist strategies which provide saturation releasing, elimination of competition and free stars, all within the context of national celebration.

Communists in the marketplace

Han had said that should *The Founding of a Republic* be a success, the formula could be repeated in future 'tribute films'.[62] Once again sharing the director's chair with Huang Jianxin, his crowd-pleasing strategy was repeated in 2011 with *Beginning of the Great Revival*, released to commemorate the 90th anniversary of the founding of the CCP. Han has always been a strong advocate of attracting younger audiences, and *Beginning of the Great Revival*, even more than the other films discussed here, goes to great lengths to appeal to the young. The film is dominated by younger stars, alongside elder statesmen such as Chow Yun Fat and John Woo, and Han who makes a fleeting appearance as a photographer. Pragmatically recognizing the appeal of celebrity over history, Han told a reporter, 'The first step is to draw attention. After that, people may find that they have the patience to follow the plot of the film.'[63] In the main, the cast is united in youth and beauty: the young Mao and Zhou Enlai are played by the dashing Liu Ye and Chen Kun, while Li Qin plays Yang Kaihui, Mao's second wife, and Fan Bingbing an improbably beautiful Empress Dowager Cixi.

With its bigger budget and higher production values evident on the sumptuous screen, the stars' youthful good looks are complemented by the handsome sets, dapper costumes and lush photography. The youthful viewpoint is further emphasized by a young team of scriptwriters, all aged 'around 30'.[64] Camp elements, it should be noted, are toned down. In addition, there is a lot of smiling in *The Founding of a Republic*, but *Beginning of the Great Revival* is filled with furrowed young brows, its youthful earnestness appearing as *Das Kapital* channelled through *Dawson's Creek*.

Beginning of the Great Revival tells the story of the founding of the CCP and its historical roots in post-Imperial China and the May Fourth Movement (1919), when students and intellectuals protested the handing over of various Chinese territories, former German concessions, to Japan following the Versailles Peace Treaty. It is considerably more 'revolutionary' than *The Founding of a Republic*. The youth of the actors not only reflects the age of their characters, but also the vigour they bring to debates, and the idealism with which they pursue their goals. Karl Marx's theories are referenced approvingly and extensively; the Russian revolution is portrayed as a victory for hope; class struggle, notably absent from *The Founding of a Republic*, features strongly in dialogue if not in action; and Communism is depicted as modern and for the young.

Sebastian Veg has noted the rise in traditional red propaganda that provided the cultural context of *Beginning of the Great Revival*'s release.[65] The production context, however, is equally important. Like its predecessor, it is routinely dubbed a 'propaganda film', particularly in the West, but it would be rather more accurate to call it a propaganda *production*. The film itself is a tale of uncomplicated idealism and, as Veg has observed, de-politicized red nostalgia.[66] But the context is one of professional manoeuvring and aspirational motifs. Its depiction of a nascent band of revolutionary heartthrobs, dreamboats and babes emerges from a production context dominated by market economics and the Party.

An article in the *China Daily* repeatedly references the 'market-oriented' model followed by *Beginning of the Great Revival*. In the spirit of the market, says the article, the hundred-odd stars were paid, as opposed to donating their services, though only a small 'symbolic' amount. Indeed, in contrast to the scuttlebutt surrounding *The Founding of a Republic*, the article downplays the patriotic motivations for those appearing in *Beginning of the Great Revival*, instead, noting the 'scramble for parts because appearing in an epic red-themed film shows they are well-connected and popular', quoting an unnamed source as saying that Chow Yun-Fat 'values the enormous mainland market that director Han Sanping can reach'.[67] The modern market economy, as demonstrated by the production, incorporates some very Chinese characteristics: *guanxi* and *mianzi* – well connectedness and 'face'.

To be well connected, anointed by Han, is a theme that runs through the production, most starkly in the uncasting of Tang Wei. Tang played Tao Ye, an early girlfriend of Mao, but her part was cut before release. Tang had been banned from making films in mainland China following her sex scenes in *Lust, Caution* (Ang Lee, 2007). Her casting in *Beginning of the Great Revival* was seen as an acknowledgement of her 'return to official favour'.[68] Her excision from the film was an indication of a judgement reversed.[69]

The issue of status is one of great importance for the film's subject matter. The film ends with a handful of revolutionaries convening the CCP's first meeting, then the closing intertitle tells us of the power and wealth the CCP has brought to the nation. Just as being cast in Han's epics can increase the status of a star, so membership of the Communist Party is a requirement for anyone who wishes to progress in public service or state-run enterprise. The film portrays the idealism of youth, but the young people it seeks to appeal to know full well the effect Party membership, or lack thereof, can have on their aspirations.

Along with Tang Wei, another striking absence is Lu Xun. As a key figure in the May Fourth Movement, Lu Xun is a giant of modern Chinese literature. Although he never joined the Party, his work was beloved by Mao and the Communists, and Lu Xun Park in Shanghai contains a museum devoted to his memory. His writings lambast Chinese docility and his stories were, until recently, a stalwart of the school curriculum. As Julia Lovell has observed:

> in 2007 the beginnings of a Lu Xun withdrawal from textbooks began, partly to make way for escapist kung fu texts. Perhaps the intention was to vary the literary diet of the young; or perhaps to redirect their impressionable young minds from Lu Xun's dark introspection towards a more exuberant self-confidence. Perhaps it was also an attempt to discourage the youth of today from Lu Xun's inconveniently critical habits.[70]

Lovell's speculation seems remarkably prescient when applied to *Beginning of the Great Revival*, which moves away from the introspection of the victim, and embraces self-confidence, escapism and youthful exuberance.

Lu Xun was an abrasive critic of Confucianism and, while a film about the May Fourth Movement that did not feature condemnations of Confucius would be historically unthinkable, the condemnations in *Beginning of the Great Revival* are rather moderated. The film's wise elders do not contradict, but do temper, zealous proclamations, which are presented as understandable, but youthful, exuberance. This is clearly a nod to Confucius' recent rehabilitation but it is also, perhaps, a recognition that untempered exuberance and critical habits among the young have, in recent history, resulted in the brutal hooliganism of the Red Guards and the 1989 Tiananmen Square protests.

The production contexts of *Beginning of the Great Revival* speak of political positioning, industrial intrigue and aspirational materialism. John Woo was the first star cast. Woo had left China for Hong Kong with his family shortly after the revolution and he is not considered to be sympathetic to Communism. His 'homecoming' for *Red Cliff*, along with his favourable reports of the creative freedom he was allowed in China was a political coup for China's industry.[71] Referring to his scenes not making the final cut of *The Founding of a Republic*, Han told Woo at a press conference: 'I will get mad at anybody who tries to cut your part again this time.'[72] Liu Ye plays Mao. Liu had been recommended by Lu Chuan, and brought both indie and mainstream credibility with him. He was also a politically correct choice, having never played a traitor or been connected to scandal, unlike Tang Wei.[73] Li Qin, as Yang Kaihui, represents a people's choice, previously having been popularly approved by telephone-vote for a role in *The Dream of the Red Mansions* (2010). The star-spotting game of *The Founding of a Republic*, then, acquires an air of political enquiry: who's in, who's out, and why? Tang Wei's removal generated much speculation, and the absence of Lu Xun, so recently valourized in classrooms, cannot have gone unnoticed (Figure 13.3).

There are conflicting accounts of *Beginning of the Great Revival*'s success, with some reports of box office figures being artificially inflated by tactics ranging from free tickets to fraud.[75] However, it seems safe to say that it did not match *The Founding of a Republic*'s success. The China of 2011 was a rather different place to the China of 2009, with rising food prices, regional unrest and increased Internet censorship. The main

Figure 13.3 The changing face of Mao, here played by Liu Ye[74]

difference in the context of the films' releases, however, was the absence of the post-Olympic glow. As noted, cinemas of consensus capitalize on times of natural consensus and, Olympics aside, commemorating the founding of a Party does not really compare with the national creation myth of the previous film.

However, one must not underestimate the effect of the film's production context and its jarring contradictions had on its intended audience. *Beginning of the Great Revival*'s poor revolutionaries are played by beautiful stars who, gorgeously dressed, were chauffeured to the glitzy publicity functions in luxury cars provided by the film's American sponsor, Cadillac.[76] Han's highly publicized plucking of young stars for inclusion in his project, and de-selection of the troublesome, effectively fetishizes official approval in a tribute to an organization that can massively help or hinder the life chances of the viewer.

Conclusion: Holiday homework

Emile Yueh-yu Yeh and Darrell William Davis argue that the CFG's blockbusters not only glorify the People's Republic, but also that their inevitable success, thanks to protectionist measures, erroneously indicates that the people have expressed their approval through the market. The nationalist blockbuster and the market, they argue, are 'mutually reinforcing'.[77] However, the CFG's 2010 New Year blockbuster, *Confucius* (Hu Mei), provoked a backlash against protectionism. The hugely popular *Avatar* (James Cameron, 2009), now China's most successful film, was withdrawn from screens in its 2D version to make way for *Confucius*, and netizens called for a boycott of China's holiday film as a protest against 'official manoeuvring'.[78] The following year, *Beginning of the Great Revival* ousted *Kung Fu Panda 2* (Jennifer Yuh, 2011), and delayed the release of *Harry Potter and the Deathly Hallows: Part 2* (David Yates, 2011), no doubt causing similar frustrations.

There are signs that China's historical event blockbuster is an exhausted cycle, as the Han-produced *Back to 1942* (Feng Xiaogang, 2012) and *The Last Supper* (Lu

Chuan, 2012) have underperformed financially. Moreover, one can ascribe some of the success of *City of Life and Death* and *The Founding of a Republic* to novelty, the novelty of an objective viewpoint and camp propaganda, respectively. Monopolist measures do not fully counter novelties wearing off and cycles playing out. The didacticism of earlier main melody films is certainly diluted by Han's approach, but the cumulative effect of the cycle may have led to genre fatigue, especially as the films can seem like homework during the holidays. More recently, romantic comedies such as *Finding Mr Right* (Xue Xiaolu, 2013), notably starring Tang Wei, have proved hugely successful at the Chinese box office. Robert Cain has cited the phenomenal surprise success of the comedy *Lost in Thailand* (Xu Zheng, 2012) as a reaction against cinematic historical worthiness.[79] Also, Han has recently complained that Chinese cinema lacks heroes.[80] With the decline of the historical epic, this problem is being addressed through co-productions with projects such as Stan Lee's Chinese superhero *The Annihilator*, to be produced by National Film Capital and Lee's POW! Entertainment.

Han is a Chinese mogul with Hollywood characteristics, so it can be useful to look back to the Hollywood studio era for precedent. In 1936, Paramount Pictures, recently saved from bankruptcy, contracted Joseph Kennedy to conduct an audit of the company. He concluded that there was too much 'business interference' and that the studio should appoint a movie man, a showman, as president. Barney Balaban was appointed and remained at the helm for 30 years.[81] Similarly, in the Chinese cinema of the 1990s, there was too much government interference, too much censorship. Han is not a man who opposes censorship, and clearly believes in cinema's role in state propaganda, but he also understands how to work within these restrictions and, as a trusted Party Man, how to negotiate. His historical event blockbusters demonstrate a move beyond hectoring national humiliation narratives towards audience-centred cinema, showmanship and eventist ballyhoo. The current cycle may have played out, but it was an important one that introduced a certain amount of malleability into China's relationship with its reified history.

Acknowledgements

A version of this chapter was presented at the symposium, 'The Creation and Circulation of Chinese Identities Through Cinema', organized by the Chinese Film Forum in Manchester, January 2013. I would like to thank the organizers, Felicia Chan and Andy Willis, and to all those who offered advice on my chapter.

Notes

[NB: All web resources accessed between January and March 2013].

1   It is customary in China to place the family name before the given name (Han Sanping, not Sanping Han), and I have adopted this form throughout, except where

the person is better known in a different form (e.g. Jet Li, John Woo). I have adopted *pinyin* Romanization throughout (Mao Zedong, not Mao Tse-Tung), unless the person is better known in a different, or Westernized, form (e.g. Chiang Kai-Shek, Chow Yun-Fat).

2   Robert Cain, 'China Film Personality: Han Sanping', *China Film Biz*, 7 March 2012, http://chinafilmbiz.com/2012/03/07/china-film-personality-han-sanping/.

3   Patrick Frater, 'China Film Group Sets Plan For IPO', *Variety*, 18 September 2007, http://www.variety.com/article/VR1117972249/; Jonathan Landrath, 'Chinese Movie Mogul Promises New Party Leaders Will Open Market to Hollywood', *Asia Society*, 2 November 2012, http://asiasociety.org/blog/asia/chinese-movie-mogul-promises-new-party-leaders-will-open-market-hollywood.

4   For an excellent industrial analysis of the China Film Group up to 2007, see Emile Yueh-yu Yeh and Darrell William Davis, 'Re-nationalizing China's Film Industry: Case Study of China Film Group and Film Marketization', *Journal of Chinese Cinemas*, 2:1 (May 2008): 37–51.

5   Frater, 'China Film Group Sets Plan For IPO'.

6   Clifford Noonan, 'China's 2011 Box Office Take Tops $2 Billion', *Variety*, 10 January 2012, http://www.variety.com/article/VR1118048424/.

7   Anon. 'Building Harmonious Society Crucial For China's Progress: Hu', *People's Daily*, 27 June 2005, http://english.peopledaily.com.cn/200506/27/eng20050627_192495.html.

8   Geremie R. Barmé, 'China's Flat Earth: History and 8 August 2008', *The China Quarterly*, (March 2009): 64–86; Anne-Marie Brady, 'The Beijing Olympics as a Campaign of Mass Distraction', *The China Quarterly*, (March 2009): 1–24; James Liebold, 'The Beijing Olympics and China's Conflicted National Form', *The China Journal*, 63 (January 2010): 1–24.

9   Eric Rentschler, 'From New German Cinema to the Post-Wall Cinema of Consensus', in *Cinema and Nation*, ed. Mette Hjort and Scott Mackenzie (London: Routledge, 2000), 260–78.

10   Zheng Wang, *Never Forget National Humiliation: Historical Memory in Chinese Politics and Foreign Relations* (New York: Columbia University Press, 2012).

11   Sebastian Veg, 'Propaganda and Pastiche: Visions of Mao in *Founding of a Republic*, *The Beginning of the Great Revival* and *Let the Bullets Fly*', *China Perspectives* (2012/2): 51.

12   Jason McGrath, *Postsocialist Modernity: Chinese Cinema, Literature and Criticism in the Market Age* (Stanford: Stanford University Press, 2008), 174–76.

13   Shuyu Kong, 'Genre Film, Media Corporations and the Commercialization of the Chinese Film Industry: The Case of "New Year Comedies"', in *Futures of Chinese Cinema: Technologies and Temporalities in Chinese Screen Cultures*, ed. Olivia Khoo and Sean Metzger (Bristol: Intellect Books, 2009), 147–68.

14   'What Makes the Most Profit? Risk Does', China Film Group CEO Interview with *Southern Weekly*, Danwei, 28 September 2009, http://www.danwei.org/film/what_makes_the_most_profit_ris.php.

15   Zan Jifang, 'A Mansion Makeover', *Beijing Review*, 8 February 2007, 44.

16   Yingjin Zhang, 'Chinese Cinema in the New Century: Prospects and Problems', *World Literature Today*, (July–August 2007): 36.

17   'What Makes the Most Profit? Risk Does'.

18 In 2001, upon China's accession to the World Trade Organization, China's import quota was doubled from ten to twenty. In 2011 that number was raised to 34, 14 of which must be in IMAX or 3D.

19 'What Make the Most Profit? Risk Does'.

20 George F. Custen, *Bio/Pics: How Hollywood Constructed Public History* (New York: Rutgers University Press, 1992), 18–22.

21 Damien Kinney, 'Rediscovering a Massacre: The Filmic Legacy of Iris Chang's *The Rape of Nanking*', *Continuum: Journal of Media and Cultural Studies*, 26:1 (February 2012): 12.

22 See Damien Kinney, 'Rediscovering a Massacre', 11–23; Michael Berry, *A History of Pain: Trauma in Modern Chinese Literature and Film* (New York: Columbia University Press, 2010), 108–36; A. T. McKenna, 'Screening the Others of Nanjing', in *China and the West: Encounters with the Other in Culture, Arts, Politics and Everyday Life*, ed. Lili Hernandez (Newcastle-on-Tyne: Cambridge Scholars Press, 2012), 61–72; Anon., '10 Movies About the Nanjing Massacre', *China Daily*, 16 December 2011, http://www.chinadaily.com.cn/cndy/2011-12/16/content_14274011.htm.

23 Edward Wong, 'Showing the Glimmer Amid the Atrocities of War', *New York Times*, 22 May 2009, http://www.nytimes.com/2009/05/23/world/asia/23luchuan.html?pagewanted=1&hp&_r=0.

24 Shelly Kraicer, 'A Matter of Life and Death: Lu Chuan and Post-Zhuxuanlu Cinema', *cinemascope*, 41 (2013), http://cinema-scope.com/features/features-a-matter-of-life-and-death-lu-chuan-and-post-zhuxuanlu-cinema-by-shelly-kraicer/.

25 Tony Rayns, 'Review of *City of Life and Death*', *Sight and Sound*, 20:5 (May 2010): 58.

26 Kinney, 'Rediscovering a Massacre: The Filmic Legacy of Iris Chang's *The Rape of Nanking*', 20.

27 Debra Kaufman, 'Behind the Lens: *City of Life and Death*', *Creative Cow Magazine* (2011), http://magazine.creativecow.net/article/city-of-life-and-death.

28 Anon., 'Lu Chuan Secures Investment for "Nanking" Film', *CRIEnglish.com*, 26 June 2007, http://english.cri.cn/3086/2007/06/26/1261@242425.htm.

29 Anon., *City of Life and Death* Press Kit.

30 Tang Yuankai, 'Searching for Truth: Interview with Lu Chuan', *Beijing Review*, 28 May 2009, 20.

31 Anon., *City of Life and Death* Press Kit.

32 Clarence Tsui, 'Director Lu Chuan Retells China's History in *The Last Supper*', *Hollywood Reporter*, 3 January 2013, http://www.hollywoodreporter.com/news/director-lu-chuan-retells-chinas-408067.

33 Martin Guttridge, 'Telling Truths: Interview with Lu Chuan', *International Life*, http://www.internationallife.tv/city-of-life-and-death.

34 Kaufman, 'Behind the Lens: *City of Life and Death*'.

35 Liu Wei, 'The Human Touch', *China Daily*, 14 April 2009, http://www.chinadaily.com.cn/cndy/2009-04/14/content_7673929.htm.

36 Wong, 'Showing the Glimmer Amid the Atrocities of War'.

37 Wong, 'Showing the Glimmer Amid the Atrocities of War'.

38 Robin Menken, '*City of Life and Death* wins CWB's Bridging the Borders as one of the Best Films of the Decade', *Cinema Without Borders*, 16 June 2011, http://

cinemawithoutborders.com/news-issues/2660-city-of-life-and-death-wins-cwb-s-bridging-the-borders-award.html.

39   Anon., '*City of Life and Death*: *Hollywood Reporter* Interview with Lu Chuan', *Haunted Screens*, 6 October 2009, http://joyceanashawati.wordpress. com/2009/10/06/a-city-of-life-and-death-chuan-lu-2009/.

40   Edward Wyatt, 'China and Tibet Skirmish at a Film Festival', *New York Times*, 8 January 2010, http://www.nytimes.com/2010/01/09/movies/09film.html?_r=0.

41   Steve Pond, 'A Week before Deadline, Oscar Foreign-Language Race Takes Shape', *Reuters*, 24 September 2011, http://www.reuters.com/article/2011/09/24/idUS291389151820110924; NB. The PRC's 2011 Oscar entry was another Nanjing drama, *Flowers of War* (Zhang Yimou, 2011), starring Christian Bale. This film is notably more lachrymose that *City of Life and Death*, and rather more in keeping with the National Humiliation narrative.

42   Anon., *City of Life and Death* Press Kit.

43   Xiao Dao, 'Director in Despair', *China Daily*, 18 June 2009, http://www.chinadaily. com.cn/cndy/2009-06/18/content_8295846.htm.

44   McKenna, 'Screening the Others of Nanjing', 71.

45   Chris Berry, 'What's Big About the Big Film? De-Westernizing the Blockbuster in Korea and China', in *Movie Blockbusters*, ed. Julian Stringer (London and New York: Routledge, 2003), 223.

46   Berry, 'What's Big about the Big Film? De-Westernizing the Blockbuster in Korea and China', 226.

47   Veg, 'Propaganda and Pastiche', 44.

48   Brady, 'The Beijing Olympics as a Campaign of Mass Distraction', 10.

49   A. T. McKenna, 'Joseph E. Levine and *A Bridge Too Far*: A Producer's Labour of Love', *Historical Journal of Film, Radio and Television*, 31:2 (2013): 211–27.

50   Anon., 'CPC Film Eyes Box-Office Record', *China Daily*, 15 June, 2011, http://www. chinadaily.com.cn/china/2011-06/15/content_12706549.htm.

51   Tang Yuankai, 'A Mainstream Historical Epic', *Beijing Review*, 8 October 2009, 40.

52   Yuankai, 'A Mainstream Historical Epic'.

53   Liu Wei, 'Star Attraction', *China Daily*, 2 September 2009, http://www.chinadaily.com. cn/showbiz/2009-09/02/content_8644781_2.htm.

54   Min Lee, 'China Injects Star-Power Into Anniversary Film', *Seattle Times*, 2 September 2009, http://seattletimes.com/html/nationworld/2009793243_apasmovchinablockbusterpropaganda.html.

55   Peter Foster, 'Epic Film *The Founding of a Republic* Marks 60 Years of Chinese Communism', *The Telegraph*, 17 September 2009, http://www.telegraph.co.uk/culture/film/film-news/6197946/Epic-film-The-Founding-of-a-Republic-marks-60-years-of-Chinese-Communism.html.

56   Many thanks to Tianqi Yu of University of Nottingham in Ningbo, China, for suggesting the phrase 'film of famous faces'.

57   Sabrina Yu, 'Camp Pleasure in an Era of Chinese Blockbusters: Internet Reception of *Hero* in Mainland China', in *Global Chinese Cinema: The Culture and Politics of 'Hero'*, ed. Gary Rawnsley and Ming-Yeh Rawnsley (London: Routledge, 2010), 135–51.

58   Anon., 'All-Star Epic for the 60th Anniversary of PRC to Premiere Next Week', *China.org.cn*, 8 September 2009, http://www.china.org.cn/culture/2009-09/09/content_18490136.htm.

59 Kraicer, 'A Matter of Life and Death'.
60 Tony Rayns, 'Letter to the Editor', *cinemascope* no. 42, http://cinema-scope.com/
    columns/columns-letter-to-the-editor/; Yih-Jye Hwang and Florian Schneider,
    'Performance, Meaning and Ideology in the Making of Legitimacy: The Celebrations
    of the People's Republic of China's Sixty-Year Anniversary', *The China Review*, 11:1
    (Spring 2011): 43–49; Veg, 'Propaganda and Pastiche', 41–53.
61 Julian Stringer, 'Introduction', *Movie Blockbusters*, 7.
62 Tang Yuankai, 'A Mainstream Historical Epic', *Beijing Review*, 8 October 2009, 41.
63 Anon., '"Red" TV Dramas Arouse Patriotism in China's Younger
    Generation', *People's Daily Online*, 21 July 2011, http://english.people.com.
    cn/90001/90776/90882/7446955.html.
64 Liu Wei, 'New Film to Celebrate Founding of the Party', *China Daily*, 4 April 2010,
    http://www.chinadaily.com.cn/entertainment/2010-04/29/content_9790014.htm.
65 Veg, 'Propaganda and Pastiche', 48–50.
66 Veg, 'Propaganda and Pastiche', 43.
67 Anon., 'CPC Film Eyes Box-Office Record', *China Daily*, 15 June 2011, http://www.
    chinadaily.com.cn/china/2011-06/15/content_12706549.htm.
68 Patrick Frater, 'Tang Wei Invited Back to Party', *Film Business Asia*, 3 September 2010,
    http://www.filmbiz.asia/news/tang-wei-invited-back-to-party.
69 Jing Gao, '*Lust, Caution* Actress Tang Wei Ousted from Propaganda Film', *Ministry
    of Tofu*, 12 May 2011, http://www.ministryoftofu.com/2011/05/lust-caution-actress-
    tang-wei-ousted-from-propaganda-film/.
70 Julia Lovell, 'Introduction, Lu Xun', *The Real Story of Ah-Q and Other Tales of
    China: The Complete Fiction of Lu Xun*, trans. Julia Lovell (London: Penguin
    Classics, 2009), xxxv.
71 Roger Clarke, 'Impossible Mission', *Sight and Sound*, 19:7 (July 2009): 11.
72 Anon. 'John Woo Signs On to Act in CPC Anniversary Film', *China.org.cn*, 29 July
    2010, http://www.china.org.cn/arts/2010-07/29/content_20597760.htm.
73 Liu Wei, 'The Reel Mao', *China Daily*, 25 May 2011, http://www.chinadaily.com.cn/
    cndy/2011-05/25/content_12573124.htm.
74 In earlier times, an actor playing Mao Zedong would have his entire family
    investigated for any hint of political incorrectness. Though a politically sound
    choice, Liu Ye made his reputation by taking on challenging roles in indie movies
    and brought extra-textual credibility with him. Having played a gay man in *Lan Yu*
    (Stanley Kwan, 2001) and a *Kuomintang* soldier in *City of Life and Death*, he now
    occupies a judge's chair on *China's Got Talent*.
75 Xiyun Yang, 'People, You Will See This Film. Right Now!', *New York Times*,
    24 June 2011, http://www.nytimes.com/2011/06/25/movies/chinese-get-
    viewers-to-propaganda-film-beyond-the-great-revival.html?_r=0; Peter Ford,
    'How to Ensure a Movie Becomes a Success in China? Trickery', *Christian
    Science Monitor*, 11 July 2011, http://www.csmonitor.com/World/Global-
    News/2011/0711/How-to-ensure-a-movie-becomes-a-blockbuster-in-China
    Trickery?cmpid=ema:nws:World%20Daily%2007112011&cmpid=ema:nws:NzI5N
    jYzNTI3NwS2.
76 Cadillac is owned by General Motors, which had been bailed out by the American
    taxpayer in 2009. Cadillac's sponsorship of *Beginning of the Great Revival* led to
    some concern in the United States that the American taxpayer was indirectly
    funding Communist propaganda in China. Kerry Picket, 'GM Sponsors and

Celebrates Soon to Be Released Chi-Com Propaganda Film', *Washington Times*, 17 May 2011, http://www.washingtontimes.com/blog/watercooler/2011/may/17/gm-sponsors-and-celebrates-soon-be-released-chi-co/.

77   Yueh-yu Yeh and Davis, 'Re-nationalizing China's Film Industry', 48.

78   Raymond Zhou, 'Confucius Loses His Way', *China Daily*, 29 January 2010, http://www.chinadaily.com.cn/life/2010-01/29/content_9396402.htm.

79   Robert Cain, 'How China's Three Stooges Out-Grossed *Titanic*; *Lost in Thailand* Reaches 1 Billion RMB Box Office in 19 Days', *China Film Biz*, 2 January 2013, http://chinafilmbiz.com/2013/01/02/how-chinas-three-stooges-out-grossed-titanic-lost-in-thailand-reaches-1-billion-rmb-box-office-in-19-days/.

80   Chen Chenchen, 'Can Domestic Film Industry Be Saved By Heroes?', *Global Times*, 5 January 2013, http://www.globaltimes.cn/DesktopModules/DnnForge%20-%20 NewsArticles/Print.aspx?tabid=99&tabmoduleid=94&articleId=753709&moduleId= 405&PortalID=0.

81   Rosten, *Hollywood: The Movie Colony, The Movie Makers*, 253–54; Bernard F. Dick, *Engulfed: The Death of Paramount Pictures and the Birth of Corporate Hollywood* (Lexington: University Press of Kentucky, 2001), 21.

14

The Producer and Belgian Cinema(s): The Case of Jean (and Jan) Van Raemdonck

Gertjan Willems

Introduction

Jean or Jan Van Raemdonck (29 October 1922–7 November 2010) was without doubt one of the most important and prolific film and television producers within the history of the Belgian audio-visual industry. Producing his first art documentaries around 1950, Van Raemdonck switched to fiction at the end of the 1960s and quickly became the personification of the production company Art et Cinéma, better known under its Dutch name Kunst en Kino. Van Raemdonck is widely acknowledged for bringing professionalism into the then largely artisanal Belgian film industry, which, for a long time, was conspicuous for the absence of people whose sole or main activity was producing films.[1] When examining Van Raemdonck's career, it should be noted that Belgium is divided linguistically between the Dutch-speaking Flanders in the north and the French-speaking Wallonia in the south. Because of the existence of these two major language communities, the unitary Belgian state changed into a federal state throughout the second half of the twentieth century. Accordingly, Belgium's film production, as well as its broader film culture, was generally divided along linguistic lines. However, Van Raemdonck remained engaged in both Dutch and French-language productions. Therefore, his career is to a large extent marked by a navigation of the specific Belgian linguistic and cultural terrain. At the same time, Van Raemdonck was a pioneer in setting up co-productions and giving a transnational dimension to the Belgian audio-visual industry.

Typical of the general lack of scholarly attention for producers, the figure of Van Raemdonck, despite an acknowledgement of his importance, has hitherto received very little attention within studies of Belgian cinema and television. This chapter addresses this shortcoming by examining Van Raemdonck's role as a producer within the specific national, subnational and transnational complexities of the Belgian audio-visual context. Evolving around the tension between cultural and commercial aspects, particular attention is given to Van Raemdonck's most significant production output, his Flemish pastoral feature films and their relation to the Flemish film production policy process. Even though the importance of systematic support mechanisms for the actual production of many film projects (particularly in Europe) has only increased since its introduction during the 1950s and 1960s, close attention to this policy factor remains very rare within film studies. Furthermore, by examining Van Raemdonck's business acumen, this chapter also pays attention to his level of creative authority and his essential role in professionalizing the Belgian audio-visual industry.

This study relies primarily upon original archival material. Sadly enough, the company records of Kunst en Kino were largely destroyed when they were turned over to the Belgian production company Eyeworks, which bought all the rights for Kunst en Kino productions. Only the documents assigning copyright have been retained. This places serious limitations on this study, but I have tried to compensate for these by relying extensively on other archives, among which the most important ones were the archives of the Flemish government's film department and the Flemish public broadcaster VRT.[2] Furthermore, the large amount of documentation found in these archives was complemented by interviews with directors, producers and policy makers who have had significant professional contacts with Van Raemdonck. All quotations from archive materials and interviews have been translated from Dutch or French into English by the author.

From Jean to Jan

Jean Van Raemdonck took his first professional steps in the Belgian film industry as the executive of the not-for-profit association Cinéma Inter-Entreprises, which was founded in 1948. According to its statutes, the aim of the association was to produce and distribute scientific, technological and educational films, particularly in industrial circles, which quickly led to a merger with the Belgian National Institute for Scientific Cinema.[3] In the meantime, Van Raemdonck's brother-in-law, the multi-talented artist and critic Paul Haesaerts, had collaborated with the acclaimed Belgian film-maker Henri Storck on Haesaerts' first art documentary *Rubens*. After Haesaerts' positive experience with Rubens – according to Richard Barsam 'among the first great postwar films on art'– Haesaerts founded the appropriately named production company Art et Cinéma to develop further his art documentary activities.[4] Soon after its establishment, in 1949, Van Raemdonck became the head of production of his brother-in-law's company (Figure 14.1).[5]

Throughout the 1950s and 1960s, Van Raemdonck produced more than 30 films on art subjects, nearly all of them directed and scripted by Paul Haesaerts. With films about various artists and art movements – the most famous one being probably *Visit to Picasso* (*Visite à Picasso*, 1949, Paul Haesaerts) – Van Raemdonck helped to establish an internationally renowned so-called 'Belgian tradition' in the genre of art documentaries. Besides Haesaerts and Storck, this included film-makers such as Charles Dekeukeleire, André Cauvin and Luc de Heusch.[6] Van Raemdonck's productions in this tradition were also 'Belgian' in the sense that they were financially backed by a mixture of francophone and Dutch-language financiers, which resulted in art documentaries in Dutch, French and sometimes both languages.

Figure 14.1 Portrait of Jean/Jan Van Raemdonck. Photograph by J. Pol Payen. Courtesy of the Royal Film Archive in Brussels

During the second half of the 1960s, Haesaerts, and with him the art documentary activities of Art et Cinéma, started to retreat into the background. Van Raemdonck quickly came to prominence and set the company's course definitively towards fiction. During the 1970s and 1980s, Van Raemdonck produced 12 feature films (two were productions in which he acted as co-producer) and several television series. The majority of these productions were in Dutch, whereas his often relatively low-profile television films and series from the 1990s were mostly in French. This production output made him one of the most prolific film and television producers in Belgium and is quite remarkable because its small domestic market makes it almost impossible for a professionally made Belgian feature film to be profitable. Obviously, this has always been a major obstacle in raising the necessary finance, which has led to a lack of continuous production in the Belgian film industry.[7] Van Raemdonck's solution for this problem, in line with his consumer-minded approach in choosing his projects, was deceptively simple:

> The private sector is only looking for profit. You should propose good deals, pay back the money and guarantee some profit: this way, you inspire confidence in financial circles. Until now, I never had any problems with that. It doesn't matter if it is about film, the steel industry or other branches, you should just show that you have an interesting proposal.[8]

Van Raemdonck's greatest strength as a producer was indeed in attracting funding for his projects. All of the interviewees agreed that Van Raemdonck was a very successful lobbyist, who would typically settle his affairs during informal dinners. Van

Raemdonck's good nose for finding investors was clear from the earliest stage of his production career. The financial structure of the art documentaries of Art et Cinéma was already marked by a variety of sources, such as arbitrary government grants or commissions by public institutions and (often) Belgian public television, but also private investments by independent wealthy art lovers. When he turned to fiction, Van Raemdonck optimized this craft of pitching projects and attracting various sorts of funding.

For Van Raemdonck, the most important and perhaps even the only selection criterion in searching for possible investors was their ability to provide financial or logistical support, regardless of their linguistic, cultural or (sub)national background. Being born in a French-speaking upper-class family in the Flemish city of Ghent, Van Raemdonck indeed appeared to be in a good position to exploit both linguistic communities in Belgium. As a former staff member of the government's film department recalls: 'He lobbied wherever he could find money. Some people blamed him for this, as they remained faithful to Flanders, while Van Raemdonck also raised francophone money.'[9] Indeed, seen within the context of the Belgian community difficulties, and especially the issue of Flemish emancipation at the time, this was not as evident as it may sound. The establishment of an official autonomous Flemish film support system in 1964 had been the result of a struggle against Belgian unitary initiatives regarding film. Until the 1980s, co-operations with the francophone community were largely out of the question for many key figures within Flemish film circles. Moreover, according to the director Roland Verhavert, Van Raemdonck was often considered 'completely "un-Flemish". He was from a French-speaking bourgeois family and entirely oriented towards the French market and culture. He didn't know anything about Flanders. As the wind changed, "Jean" became "Jan". He did his best, but he was never able to speak Dutch fluently.'[10]

Van Raemdonck did indeed make serious efforts to familiarize himself with the Flemish, Dutch-speaking culture. As a symbolic action, he always used the name 'Jan', the Flemish equivalent to the French 'Jean', in his contacts with Dutch-speaking persons or institutions, as language was often a very sensitive issue in those days. Similarly, as part of his strategy to convince possible investors, he translated the company's name 'Art et Cinéma' into 'Kunst en Kino', while maintaining the original French nomenclature with his francophone contacts. As Verhavert further explains, this 'Flemish turn' had a pragmatic motivation: 'At the time, there was a trend of "pro-Flemishness". There was a Flemish emancipation in the cultural field and Van Raemdonck knew that there was more to gain on that track than on the francophone one.'[11]

Mira, or the start of the Flemish pastoral film genre

In a similar pragmatic vein, Van Raemdonck's turn to fiction was inspired by the newly introduced government funding possibilities during the 1960s.[12] Because of the emerging institutionalization of the Flemish cultural and political emancipation at the time, selective, cultural film support in Belgium was devolved to the regions.

From their inception, support mechanisms became vital for nearly all Belgian film productions up until the present day. In the case of Van Raemdonck, the Flemish film production policy was of particular importance because, although outnumbered by his francophone productions, the majority of his most significant productions were Flemish.[13] This was mainly due to the huge success of Van Raemdonck's very first feature film, *Mira* (1971), a milestone in the film history of Flanders and more generally of Belgium and the Low Countries (Figure 14.2).[14]

Van Raemdonck had become involved in this Flemish-Dutch co-production via the film's screenwriter, the prominent Flemish literary figure of Hugo Claus, who had shortly before collaborated with Art et Cinéma on Paul Haesaerts' art documentary *Bruegel* (1969). Claus also engaged his friend and by then already established Dutch film-maker Fons Rademakers to direct and co-produce the film. The initiative for *Mira*, however, came from the BRT, the Dutch-language division of the Belgian public television, which commissioned a film adaptation of Stijn Streuvels' 1927 novel *The Decline of the Waterhoek* (*De Teleurgang van den Waterhoek*) to celebrate the hundredth anniversary of the Flemish pastoral writer in 1971.[15] Focusing upon an early twentieth-century rural community and its resistance against the construction of a new bridge, *Mira* tells a classic story about the conflict between tradition and modernity. At the same time, the film refers to the flourishing hippie culture at the time of the film's production by focusing on the liberal and 'free love' attitude of its title character, played the Dutch actress Willeke Van Ammelrooy.[16]

Apart from being selected for the official competition of the 1971 Cannes film festival, *Mira* proved to be an immense popular domestic success, largely as a consequence of the voluptuous presence of Van Ammelrooy. *Mira*'s success story heralded the 'pastoral film trend' in Kunst en Kino's production output. *The Conscript* (*De Loteling*, 1973, Roland Verhavert), *Pallieter* (1975, Roland Verhavert), *Flaxfield* (*De Vlaschaard*, 1983, Jan Gruyaert), *The Lion of Flanders* (*De Leeuw van Vlaanderen*, 1984, Hugo Claus) and

Figure 14.2 Mira (Willeke van Ammelrooy) experiencing a romantic moment with her uncle Lander (Jan Decleir) in *Mira* (1971). Courtesy of the Royal Film Archive in Brussels

The Van Paemel Family (*Het Gezin Van Paemel*, 1987, Paul Cammermans) illustrate that Van Raemdonck was keen on reaping the commercial benefits of the '*Mira* formula'. Apart from displaying some female nudity, this involved the adaptation of a work from the 'heimat strand' of the Flemish literary patrimony, resulting in period dramas focusing on the rural working class during the late nineteenth or early twentieth century (with the exception of *The Lion of Flanders*, a medieval spectacle film).[17]

When looking at Van Raemdonck's production output throughout the 1970s, 1980s and 1990s, it is striking that his other, non-pastoral productions were also nearly all rooted in the Flemish, francophone Belgian or the French literary (or broader cultural) patrimony. This literary motif in Van Raemdonck's production choices had a dual motivation. On the one hand, Van Raemdonck came from a high culture milieu and was an art admirer who believed that the quality and reputation of a given literary work would affect the quality of its cinematic adaptation. On the other hand, as his activities as a small-scale art-dealer indicate, Van Raemdonck was also very interested in the commercial value of cultural products. This was translated into a preference not only for respectable, but also widely known and successful literary works as the starting point for his productions. The combination of the cultural value of a work and the commercial lure of a presold title is exemplified by Van Raemdonck's choice to adapt Hugo Claus' 1983 novel *The Sorrow of Belgium*, which was immediately regarded as a masterpiece and quickly became a bestseller.[18] In an interview during the shooting of the television series, Van Raemdonck explained that at the time when the novel was released, 'I hadn't read it, but I was already thinking about an adaptation. Later on, the success of the book confirmed my idea.'[19]

In this respect, it should be noted that due to his francophone background and in spite of his efforts to catch up with Flemish culture, Van Raemdonck's affinities with Flemish literature were fairly limited. Consequently, the commercial attractiveness of a literary work frequently appeared to be decisive in his production choices. This is clearly illustrated by the case of *Pallieter* (1975). Its director, Roland Verhavert, recalled that after the success of *The Conscript* in 1973, 'Van Raemdonck asked me: what is the most popular book from Flemish literature? I said: that must be *Pallieter*. Fine, then we will adapt *Pallieter*, he said! So that was clearly from a commercial point of view.'[20] At the same time, Verhavert also stressed the fact that in spite of Van Raemdonck's consumer-minded attitude, he would never make straightforward crowd-pleasing films of any kind, but instead considered the cultural respectability of his productions to be essential for attracting a large audience.

As the pastoral films were among the most popular and prestigious film productions in Flanders, they dominated the outlook of Flemish cinema during the 1970s and 1980s.[21] Although there was often a considerable amount of praise for certain artistic qualities of these films, they have also been criticized for their romantic, nostalgic and conservative character. Sharing affinities with the British 'heritage films' and the German-language 'heimat films', it is not surprising that the pastoral films of Kunst en Kino have been interpreted in terms of Flemish nation-building.[22] For Van Raemdonck, however, these issues seemed to be of minor importance. The pastoral film genre was in the first place a vehicle that succeeded in the difficult task of attracting large domestic audiences, which in turn was the mechanism that attracted funding: these pastoral films secured the largest sums from Flemish film support during the 1970s and 1980s.

Attracting Flemish film support

Under the Flemish film support system – introduced in 1964 and a classic example of a 'soft, culture-orientated subsidy system' – film-makers could apply for a grant to a politically appointed 'Selection Commission for Cultural Films'.[23] This film commission subsequently gave detailed, but non-binding, recommendations to the Minister of Culture, who eventually took the final decision as to whether the grant should be awarded. Although the relevant minister was ultimately the most powerful actor, the commission's recommendations were usually followed, which made the film commission a key agent within the film policy process. It has often been stated that Flemish film policy in this period tried to stimulate films that could contribute to the construction of a Flemish national identity and therefore preferred period film based on classics from Flemish literature, such as Kunst en Kino's pastoral films.[24] When examining the film support process for these pastoral films, however, it seems that the correlation between pastoral films, Flemish ideological objectives and the allocation of official film support was much more complex than is often assumed. Furthermore, a detailed historical account of the Flemish film support process behind Kunst en Kino's pastoral films provides insight into several essential aspects of Van Raemdonck's fund-raising and production practices.

Because of the success of *Mira*, Van Raemdonck's relationship with the different Flemish film policy actors started in a very favourable way. *Mira* was appreciated not only for its popular success but also because it was the first film that was able to reimburse a part of the acquired financial support: a special loan that in practice mostly functioned as a subsidy. According to a former staff member of the government's film department, this inspired political confidence in the capabilities of Flemish films, which resulted in an increase of the annual film grant.[25] *Mira* also provided Van Raemdonck with a privileged position in his dealings with the film commission. In a commission meeting two months after the film's premier, it was stated that 'The Commission pays tribute to the production of *Mira* and agrees that the producer takes priority for approved projects.'[26]

Accordingly, the positive support recommendation for *The Conscript* was largely based on the precedent of *Mira*. After the film's completion, however, the commission criticized *The Conscript*'s 'folkloristic character', which was also discerned in *Mira*.[27] The commission members expressed a hostile attitude towards pastoral films based on a specific strand of the Flemish literary patrimony and portraying a nostalgic and romantic image of Flanders. Therefore, the commission had 'serious reservations about the adaptation of *Pallieter* by Verhavert', Kunst en Kino's next pastoral film project in line.[28]

The public approval for *Mira* and *The Conscript* notwithstanding, the film commission thus rejected the similar pastoral film project *Pallieter*. In response, Van Raemdonck promised in a letter to the commission 'to approach *Pallieter* from an expressionist standpoint, different from *Mira* and *The Conscript*'.[29] As a proof of his sincerity, he engaged the prominent Flemish writer Hugo Claus to revise the screenplay, which motivated the commission to invite the film-makers for a hearing. Besides repeating his willingness to meet the commission's concerns about *Pallieter*'s folkloristic character, Van Raemdonck also tried to anticipate the commission members' literary attitude and their insistence on fidelity by arguing that 'the film will restore the book in its original form'.[30] Furthermore, in his attempt to convince the commission, Van Raemdonck exerted all his commercially persuasive talents. For example, he promised that if *Pallieter* got supported, he would 'ensure the promotion and distribution of two or more films of young film-makers, as if they were my own productions'.[31] Moreover, according to Verhavert, Van Raemdonck also actively lobbied the Minister of Culture Jos Chabert, who subsequently would have put pressure on certain commission members to give a positive recommendation.[32] Whatever the truth of the matter, by April 1974, a majority of the commission members were prepared to vote in favour of *Pallieter*. After viewing the completed film in November 1975, however, the commission members declared unanimously that they were disappointed in this film, which, in spite of Van Raemdonck's promises, in their view again displayed 'an outdated folklore'.[33]

Van Raemdonck's next literary adaptation project was consequently immediately rejected. In its advice to the minister, the Film Commission argued that the project was 'submitted by Kunst en Kino, which has always asked and received large amounts for very conformist projects'.[34] As a result, Van Raemdonck did not produce any pastoral films during the second half of the 1970s. Instead, he focused on projects that succeeded in attracting government support, such as the Dutch co-production *Doctor Vlimmen* (1977), the television series *Rubens* (1977) and the stage adaptation *Friday* (1980). When, at the end of the 1970s, the composition of the Film Commission was renewed, Van Raemdonck again applied with a pastoral film project, *Flaxfield*. Notwithstanding the fact that the new commission members shared the same concerns as their predecessors regarding 'folkloristic' and romantic pastoral productions, Van Raemdonck again succeeded in convincing the commission by playing up the artistic merits of the director Jan Gruyaert, who had realized the unconventional film *Enclosure* (*In Kluis*) in 1978. The commission thus gave a positive recommendation 'on the condition that the director's maximal artistic freedom is ensured, in order to avoid the realization of a traditional heimat film'.[35] As with *The Conscript* and *Pallieter*, however, the Film Commission was disappointed after viewing the completed film, expressing the view that 'its fear (…) has come true: this film belongs to the package of traditional Flemish heimat films'.[36]

When analysing the support recommendations for these pastoral films, it should be taken into consideration that the Film Commission was not indifferent to the public appeal of these films, always an important argument in justifying the expenditure of public money. As the above examples indicate, however, the progress of the film support process was often disadvantaged because of the fact that these film projects were adaptations of the Flemish literary patrimony portraying a nostalgic Flemish national identity. The acquisition of government funding was in the first place indebted to Van Raemdonck's perseverance and strategic skills. As noted before, his intensive lobby activities were of great importance in this respect. Several of the interviewees indicated that Van Raemdonck did not only actively lobby the commission members individually, but also the relevant ministers and other political agents. According to Verhavert, Van Raemdonck 'didn't worry about these matters. He said, "I'm going to the minister", and then he did go to the minister'.[37] This may explain why the 1984 film and television series *The Lion of Flanders* was supported fully by both the Christian Democratic Minister of Culture Rika De Backer and her Liberal successor Karel Poma, in spite of the overtly negative evaluation by the Film Commission. In line with its attitude towards the previous pastoral film projects, the Film Commission found it simply impossible that 'half of the yearly budget would be spent on such a disputable prestige project'.[38]

Transnational opportunities

Although Van Raemdonck was one of the most successful producers in attracting funding, he was confronted with the problem of a small home market. Therefore, he did not limit his fund-raising activities to national and regional sources, but quickly discovered transnational production opportunities, mostly along linguistic lines. Within the context of the small Belgian – let alone the Flemish or the francophone Belgian – film industry, Van Raemdonck saw the co-production structure (as well as collaborations with broadcasting companies) as a necessity which he was eager to make into a virtue.

As far as Van Raemdonck's Dutch-language film projects are concerned, it is notable that four of his six pastoral films were co-productions with the Netherlands. In the case of *Mira*, this was due to the involvement of the production company of the film's Dutch director Fons Rademakers. The co-production structure of *The Lion of Flanders* was the result of this production being set up in association with the Flemish public broadcaster BRT as both a film and a four-episode television series. As was frequently the case for prestigious television series, a Dutch television broadcaster (in this case the KRO) was approached to join the project. For *Pallieter* and *Flaxfield*, Van Raemdonck found a suitable production partner in the figure of Gerrit Visscher, who was first a producer for the Dutch Cinécentrum and later founded his own company CinéVista. These collaborations were based on the principle of reciprocity. In return for Visscher's participation in *Pallieter* and *Flaxfield*, Van Raemdonck acted as a co-producer for the Dutch literary adaptations *Doctor Vlimmen* (*Dokter Vlimmen*, 1978, Guido Pieters) and *Stronghold* (*Wildschut*, 1985, Bobby Eerhart). Van Raemdonck's frequent collaboration with Visscher even culminated in the founding of the joint venture TFPA, a Dutch company mainly focusing on television productions.

For Art et Cinéma's francophone productions, the co-production structure was even more intensive, probably because of the greater linguistic opportunities, particularly with France. Van Raemdonck's only two francophone feature films, *The Red Room* (*La Chambre Rouge*, 1972) and *Isabelle and Lust* (*Isabelle Devant le Désir*, 1975), both erotic adaptations of francophone Belgian literature and directed by Jean-Pierre Berckmans, were co-productions with France. Going further down the erotic track was *The Secrets of Love* (1986, Harry Kümel), a compilation of three short costume films based on stories by the classic French writers Marguerite de Navarre, Nicolas-Edme Rétif and Guy de Maupassant. Although it was a co-production with the Netherlands (via Gerrit Visscher's company CinéVista), *The Secrets of Love* was post-synchronized in English, and subsequently in French, as the three short films were integrated in the French erotic *Série Rose* television series. Even Van Raemdonck's very first fiction project, the eight-episode youth series *The Treasure of the Castle with No Name* (*Les Galapiats*, 1969, Pierre Gaspard-Huit), about the adventures of a group of teenagers at a summer camp in the Belgian Ardennes, was already financed by a transnational consortium of francophone television broadcasters, with the RTB (the French-language division of the Belgian public broadcaster) as the driving force.

Notwithstanding the considerable success of this series in various countries, Van Raemdonck would only return to francophone television production in 1987 as the instigator of another transnational television series *The Simenon Hour* (*L'Heure Simenon*), based on various works of the famous francophone Belgian writer Georges Simenon. This series was set up by Van Raemdonck, in close collaboration with the Dutch public broadcaster KRO, as a major European co-production, involving German, Swiss and Austrian television broadcasters. This series should be seen in the context of the arrival of European co-production incentives during the 1980s. According to Van Raemdonck, there was a multiplication of funding possibilities, and he was convinced that the future of Belgian film and television production lay in increasing European collaboration.[39]

In the same vein, Van Raemdonck set up the television series *The Sorrow of Belgium* (*Het Verdriet van België*, 1995, Claude Goretta), which was co-produced by Belgian, Dutch, French, German, Portuguese, Finnish and Swedish broadcasters or production companies. *The Sorrow of Belgium* proved to be his last great production. In spite of several prestigious and often quite successful productions during the 1980s, Van Raemdonck was not able to continue Kunst en Kino's true heydays of the 1970s and had to deal with dwindling public interest. From 1987 on, when *The Van Paemel Family* did not have the box-office success of his previous pastoral films, Van Raemdonck turned solely to often relatively low-profile television productions, almost all of them set up as co-productions between Belgian, Dutch and/or French television broadcasting companies.

Professionalizing the industry

Van Raemdonck's previously mentioned insistence on 'respectable' productions aimed at a wide audience was not only translated into high quality requirements for the final film text, but also into the prerequisite of using the highest professional standards during the production and distribution process. In this respect, Van Raemdonck is widely acknowledged for his legacy in professionalizing the Belgian and particularly the Flemish film industry. After his death in 2010, one newspaper obituary stated, 'He was the very first real film producer. Jan took the world of Flemish filmmaking out of amateurish spheres and made it a real professional sector.'[40] This should be seen within the context of the small and underdeveloped Belgian audio-visual industry of the 1960s and 1970s. Contrary to the common practices of most other Belgian production companies, Kunst en Kino guaranteed a solid production dossier, a sufficient number of people on the set, the use of professional equipment and so on. Moreover, Van Raemdonck was regularly praised for his serious contracts with his cast and crew, which always got paid on time and for the correct number of hours worked.[41]

When the Dutch producer Gerrit Visscher started to collaborate with Van Raemdonck, he was surprised by the fact that 'everything was always very formal. There were no loose agreements, everything would be written down on paper.'[42] Correspondingly, a former staff member of the government's film department recalls how it was a pleasure to work with Van Raemdonck: 'I never had to send him a reminder, he was always on time with administrative affairs... Van Raemdonck was the only producer who openly showed his contracts.'[43] Notwithstanding his reputation as a playboy with a passion for women, horses and fine dining, Van Raemdonck was extremely committed and disciplined when it came to business.[44] This was also manifested in his engagement in several associations and commissions to defend the interests of the Flemish and Belgian audio-visual production industry.[45] Van Raemdonck wanted to improve the working conditions and to increase the continuity in film production, because according to him, 'you can't build a genuine film industry on exceptions', thereby referring to the average of only three to five released Flemish films per year from the 1950s until the 1990s.[46]

Another important aspect of Van Raemdonck's professionalism was the attention he paid to a well thought-out promotion and distribution strategy for his productions, which went much further than maintaining good relations with the press, distribution and exploitation sectors. This was very rare for Belgian film productions at the time and should be taken into consideration when examining the popular success of many of his films, as well as their prominence in discussion of Belgian cinema. In particular, the prestigious pastoral films were often transformed into omnipresent multimedia events, with *The Lion of Flanders* as a culmination point. Depicting the so-called Battle of the Golden Spurs of 1302, whereby the county of Flanders defeated the king of France, *The Lion of Flanders* was based on Hendrik Conscience's famous 1838 novel of the same name, a landmark of the Flemish movement's cultural and mythological repertory. For Van Raemdonck, however, the source novel in the first place functioned as a well-known vehicle to produce the first historical spectacle production of the Low Countries. The screenwriter and the director of *The Lion of Flanders* was Hugo Claus, arguably the most important Flemish literary figure of the second half of the twentieth century and a recurrent name in Kunst en Kino productions, both as a director, a screenwriter and an adapted author. Van Raemdonck liked to work with Claus not only because he saw him as a guarantee of quality, but also because his name ensured extra public attention. Nevertheless, due to various factors, the public success of the production fell drastically short of expectations, thereby showing that the promotional effort is merely one factor in the complex process of a film's success. However, heavily criticized for its overtly Flemish nationalist character, *The Lion of Flanders* is now considered as one of the most prestigious flops in Flemish film history.[47]

Creative authority

Van Raemdonck's professionalism also implied clear rules, including a strict production hierarchy in which he was pulling the strings. Even before becoming officially the general manager after Haesaerts' death in 1974, Van Raemdonck was already the personification of the company. As one commentator remarked after his death in 2010: 'Kunst en Kino … was Jan Van Raemdonck and Jan Van Raemdonck was Kunst en Kino.'[48] Indeed, despite the fact that Kunst en Kino would become one of the most prolific and professional film and television production companies in Belgium during the 1970s and 1980s, it always bore similarities to a one-man business. This should of course be seen within the context of the small and for a long time very artisanal Belgian film industry (which is therefore sometimes called a film *sector* rather than an *industry*), but it also indicates Van Raemdonck's level of personal involvement in his productions and how he was determined to keep everything under control. According to several interviewees, this was also reflected in an authoritarian relation with his few permanent employees.

Van Raemdonck's commitment towards nearly all of his productions raises questions about his creative authority over the final film and television texts. Particularly for his pastoral film productions, this issue is all the more interesting because these films, described by Philip Mosley as 'respectable auteurist adaptations', are generally approached from a director's perspective.[49] This was also true in their reception when released, which explains why Van Raemdonck was (and is) not a household name. Gerrit Visscher explains that 'This was the spirit of the times. The creative role of the director was emphasized and what the producer did was the business part, a whole other story. While the reality was totally different!'[50]

Van Raemdonck's involvement in his productions indeed went much further than merely raising the necessary funds and following up the project to assure it would not exceed its budget (over which he was indeed meticulously strict as well). For one thing, he was a producer who (mostly) chose his own projects, rather than realizing the ideas of others. This was quite exceptional in the Belgian film production context, where the director of a film often also acted as his own producer.[51] Therefore, Frédéric Sojcher refers to Van Raemdonck as a producer 'à l'américaine', pointing at the fact that apart from deciding over the film subject, the producer also chose the director, the screenwriter, the actors, the DOP, the editor and other key roles.[52]

This bringing together of cast and crew was a very creative act on its own. Van Raemdonck had a film in mind and subsequently looked for the right people who could bring the project as close as possible to his ideal. The fact that Van Raemdonck was interested in the creative process of films was also manifested in the realization of the erotic short film *The Jewels* (*Les Bijoux*, 1986, based on the poem of the same name from Charles Baudelaire's *Les Fleurs du Mal*), his only directing adventure. Furthermore, Van Raemdonck was not afraid to exert pressure when the vision of one of the crew members did not match his own. This could eventually lead to the replacement of the person in question, as was the case with the initial director of *Stronghold* (1985).[53] This qualifies Van Raemdonck's claim that after finding the right people, 'One should leave absolute freedom to the artists.'[54] Indeed, on another occasion, Van Raemdonck explained his involvement in his film productions as follows: 'In a company, you also don't give carte blanche to the engineers, do you?'[55]

In this respect, Van Raemdonck remembers how, after the shooting of *The Sorrow of Belgium*, the series' director Claude Goretta said to him: 'You are a very difficult man. But, I've made so many films, and I should say you are also the producer with the greatest commitment.'[56] The director Roland Verhavert claims that this was precisely one of the reasons why he stopped collaborating with Van Raemdonck after 1977: 'He wanted to set his stamp too much on the film ... Although I could do a lot, and I see them as my films, I could not continue like that.'[57] It should be noted, however, that Van Raemdonck's influence in the shooting of a film was still relatively limited compared to his involvement in the editing stage. He frequently stated explicitly that he intervened 'when there are problems with the film's clearness or its length', which points again to his consumer-minded attitude.[58] This way, he retained the authority to make the final decisions about any production.

Conclusion

Throughout his career as a producer, comprising an impressive amount of art documentaries, short films, television films, television series and feature films, Van Raemdonck almost single-handedly turned Kunst en Kino into one of the largest and most professional production companies in Belgium. In his drive for the highest possible technical standards, a maximum appropriation of both public and private funds, solid production dossiers, serious contracts, big promotion and distribution efforts and a ceaseless engagement in various professional audio-visual associations, he made an important contribution to the professionalization of the Belgian and especially the Flemish audio-visual industry. Furthermore, Van Raemdonck's professionalism was translated in a personal and somewhat authoritarian commitment to almost all of Kunst en Kino's productions (hitherto usually examined from a director-centred approach), which had important implications for the creative authority over the final audio-visual texts.

Van Raemdonck's greatest professional talent was probably his ability to attract various sorts of funding. In this respect, Van Raemdonck was among the first Belgian producers who structurally implemented the system of co-productions in his production activities. This transnational attitude went hand in hand with Van Raemdonck's rootedness in the specificities of the Belgian national film and television production context. Running parallel with political and institutional evolutions in Belgium, Van Raemdonck started his career in the 'Belgian tradition' of art documentaries, but switched in the late 1960s to the separate production of francophone and Dutch-language fictional content. These productions were largely divided along linguistic lines, both culturally and in terms of funding.

During Kunst en Kino's heydays in the 1970s and 1980s, Van Raemdonck's prestigious feature films determined the outlook of Flemish cinema. The bulk of these films constituted a relatively coherent group of pastoral period films based on Flemish literary classics, which deserve credit for succeeding in the difficult task of attracting large domestic audiences. While these films can be placed within a conservative and romantic pro-Flemish ideological discourse, Van Raemdonck considered them primarily as culturally respectable and commercially attractive productions. The funding for these films was in the first place provided by the official Flemish film support mechanism. Contrary to common assumptions, however, this did not happen without resistance. When examining why several of Van Raemdonck's projects received government support in spite of the film commission's objections, the perseverance and strategic skills of Van Raemdonck should be taken into account.

Archives consulted

Documentation and Information Centre for the Press (DOCIP), Brussels (Belgium)
Flemish Audiovisual Fund (VAF), Brussels (Belgium)
Media Department of the Flemish Government, Archives of Fonds Film in Vlaanderen, Brussels (Belgium)
Royal Belgian Film Archive, Brussels (Belgium)
State Archives, Archives of Media and Film 2004, Beveren (Belgium)
Study and Documentation Centre Hugo Claus, Antwerp (Belgium)

Notes

1   The lack of professional producers in the Belgian film industry is explained in more detail in Francis Bolen, 'De Quelques Producteurs, des Vrais', *Ciné-Dossiers*, 62 (1977): 1–8. See also Philip Mosley, *Split Screen: Belgian Cinema and Cultural Identity* (New York: State University of New York Press, 2001), 105.
2   A list of all the archives consulted was given at the end of the chapter. Abbreviations used in the footnotes to refer to the explicit use of this archival material are: AMF 2004 (Archives of Media and Film 2004), SAB (State Archives in Beveren) and SCF (Selection Commission for Cultural Films).

3   Francis Bolen, 'Un Producteur: Jean Van Raemdonck', *Ciné-Dossiers*, 70 (1978): 11.

4   Richard Meran Barsam, *Nonfiction Film: A Critical History* (Bloomington: Indiana University Press, 1992), 260.

5   Bolen, 'De Quelques Producteurs', 2.

6   Barsam, *Nonfiction Film*, 258.

7   Mosley, *Split Screen*, 3.

8   Jean-Pierre Wauters, 'Jan Van Raemdonck: Alles Loopt Gesmeerd …', *Film en Televisie*, 209 (1974): 18.

9   Bert Podevijn, Interviewed by the author, Ghent, 4 February 2013.

10 Roland Verhavert, Interviewed by the author, Torhout, 5 February 2013.

11 Verhavert, Interviewed by the author.

12 Bolen, 'Un Producteur', 11.

13 Flemish film policy considered films as 'Flemish' when the major production company was situated in Flanders. For a company like Kunst en Kino, based in the bilingual Belgian capital of Brussels and thus officially belonging to both the Flemish and the French Community, the language of the production was decisive, as well as the number of Flemings occupying key functions in cast and crew and the 'Flemishness' of a film's subject.

14 Ernest Mathijs, *The Cinema of the Low Countries* (London: Wallflower Press, 2004).

15 Erik Martens, 'Mira', in *The Cinema of the Low Countries*, ed. Mathijs, 89.

16 Marcel Janssens, 'De Verfilming Van *De Teleurgang Van De Waterhoek*', in *De Huid Van Mira*, ed. Piet Thomas (Tielt: Lannoo, 1998), 74.

17 Martens, 'Mira', 88.

18 Elke Brems, 'The Genealogical Novel as a Way of Defining and/or Deconstructing Cultural Identity: Flemish Fiction since 1970', *Memory Studies*, 5: 1 (2012): 78–79.

19 Liliana Casagrande, 'In het boek niet verder geraakt dan bladzijde 2', *Het Belang van Limburg*, 23 August 1993, 7.

20 Verhavert, Interviewed by the author.

21 Wim De Poorter, 'From Y Manana to Manneken Pis. Thirty years of Flemish Filmmaking', in *The Low Countries. Arts and Society in Flanders and the Netherlands: A Yearbook 1997–1998* (Rekkem: Stichting Ons Erfdeel, 1998), 141.

22 Andrew Higson, 'Re-Presenting the National Past: Nostalgia and Pastiche in the Heritage Film', in *Fires Were Started: British Cinema and Thatcherism*, ed. Lester D. Friedman (London: Wallflower Press, 2006). Elizabeth Boa and Rachel Palfreyman, *Heimat: A German Dream. Regional Loyalties and National Identity in German Culture 1890–1990* (Oxford: Oxford University Press, 2000).

23 Angus Finney, 'Support Mechanisms across Europe', in *The European Cinema Reader*, ed. Catherine Fowler (London and New York: Routledge, 2002), 212–22, at 214.

24 Alexander Dhoest, *De Verbeelde Gemeenschap: 50 Jaar Vlaamse Tv-Fictie en de Constructie van een Nationale Identiteit* (Leuven: Universitaire Pers Leuven, 2004), 143; Jan-Pieter Everaerts, *Film in België: Een Permanente Revolte* (Brussel: Mediadoc, 2000), 245.

25 Bert Podevijn in: Freddy Sartor, 'Vlaams filmproducent Jan Van Raemdonck', *Filmmagie*, 610 (2010): 22.

26 SAB, AMF 2004, nr. 8, SCF meeting, 6 May 1971.

27 SAB, AMF 2004, nr. 10, SCF meeting, 21 December 1973.

28 SAB, AMF 2004, nr. 10, SCF meeting.

29 SAB, AMF 2004, nr. 175, letter from Van Raemdonck to the SCF, 25 January 1974.

30 SAB, AMF 2004, nr. 11, SCF meeting, 5 April 1974.
31 SAB, AMF 2004, nr. 175, letter from Kunst en Kino to the SCF, 21 January 1974.
32 Verhavert, Interviewed by the author.
33 SAB, AMF 2004, nr. 12, SCF meeting, 18 November 1975.
34 SAB, AMF 2004, nr. 14, SCF meeting, 6 May 1977.
35 SAB, AMF 2004, nr. 18, SCF meeting, 20 November 1981.
36 SAB, AMF 2004, nr. 20, SCF meeting, 13 January 1983.
37 Verhavert, Interviewed by the author.
38 SAB, AMF 2004, nr. 18, SCF meeting, 6 February 1981.
39 'Une Production Belge D'ensemble De Plus En Plus Qualitative', *Moniteur du Film en Belgique – Filmwijzer in België*, 100 (1991): 15–17; Victor Henning and Andre Alpar, 'Public Aid Mechanisms in Feature Film Production: The EU Media Plus Programme', *Media, Culture & Society*, 27: 2 (2005): 232–34.
40 Jacques Dubrulle, quoted in: Erik De Troyer, 'Jan veranderde Vlaamse filmwereld', *Het Laatste Nieuws*, 9 November 2010, 19.
41 Sartor, 'Vlaams filmproducent Jan Van Raemdonck', 22.
42 Gerrit Visscher, Interviewed by the author, Huizen, 25 March 2013.
43 Bert Podevijn, Interviewed by the author, Ghent, 4 February 2013.
44 Bolen, 'De Quelques Producteurs', 4.
45 Wauters, 'Jan Van Raemdonck', 18.
46 Jan Van Raemdonck quoted in: 'Une Production Belge', 17.
47 Everaerts, *Film in België*, 66.
48 Sartor, 'Vlaams filmproducent Jan Van Raemdonck', 22.
49 Mosley, *Split Screen*, 173.
50 Visscher, Interviewed by the author.
51 'Une Production Belge', 15.
52 Frédéric Sojcher, *La Kermesse Héroïque du Cinéma Belge: Le Miroir Déformant des Identités Culturelles (1965–1988)* (Paris: L'Harmattan, 1999), 297.
53 Visscher, Interviewed by the author.
54 Corinne Le Brun, 'L'avis Des Producteurs', *Cinéma Belge* 60 (1983): 34.
55 Marie Mandy, 'Leeuw van Vlaanderen', *Le Journal du Festival Blad*, 19 January 1984, 54.
56 Jan Van Raemdonck, Interviewed by Erik Martens, Brussels, 2003.
57 Verhavert, Interviewed by the author.
58 Mandy, 'Leeuw van Vlaanderen', 54.

15

Post-Imperial Co-Producers:
Emile Sherman, Iain Canning and
Contemporary Anglo-Australian Cinema

Christopher Meir

The runaway success of *The King's Speech* (Tom Hooper, 2010), which culminated with the Best Picture Oscar at the 2011 Academy Awards, was hailed by many as the latest revival of British cinema and another triumph of the heritage genre that continues to be the nation's most popular media export. But when producers Emile Sherman, Iain Canning and Gareth Unwin took to the stage that night in Los Angeles to accept their Oscars, their combined presence was also a reminder of the film's transnational roots as a production based in the film cultures and industries of Britain and its former colony Australia. To make this, in some senses quintessentially 'British' film, Unwin's British-based Bedlam Productions had teamed with Sherman and Canning's See-Saw Films, a company which divides its offices between London and Sydney. The producers had assembled a cast and crew of mainly British and Australian talent to tell a story that depicted the heroic actions of Australian Lionel Logue (Geoffrey Rush) in coming to the aid of the newly crowned King George VI (Colin Firth), helping the monarch to overcome a speech impediment that, within the film's logic at least, hampered his ability to lead the nation and Empire in the face of the threat posed by the rising tide of Nazism. Logue was able to do this not only because of his medical skill, the film suggests, but also because of his freedom as an Australian to defy the conventions of the British social order, a freedom that allowed him to address the King as an equal, winning the respect of the ruler in the process.

With such a production background, its intercultural thematic content and its exceedingly high international profile, *The King's Speech* can be seen as the most successful cinematic venture to date between Britain and Australia, but it is far from being the first or last of such collaborations. Indeed, at the core of the making and marketing of the film are two producers whose oeuvres are testaments to the vitality of the British-Australian cinematic network. Canning and Sherman founded See-Saw Films shortly before the making of *The King's Speech* and with a number of successful projects since, as well as a number of projects preceding their partnership, the two have thus far made careers out of demonstrating the continuing richness of the British-Australian cultural/industrial nexus. The chapter will argue that exploring the work of See-Saw, as well as, to a lesser extent, the respective oeuvres of Sherman and Canning before forming the company, can help to illuminate the larger cinematic relationship that exists between Britain and Australia. That such a network can exist at all is in some ways a testament to the skill and industry of producers such as Canning and Sherman as well as contemporaries whose oeuvres are also shaped by this transnational connection between Australia and Britain (some of whom will also be discussed later). After all, unlike more widely discussed transnational networks, such as those of Latin America, Europe or East Asia, the Anglo-Australian does not have geography on its side. Thousands of miles and many time zones separate Australia and Britain, making travel and communication more difficult and costly than in continental cinemas. Given the logistical challenges posed by this geographic reality, the work of the producer becomes more and more important to ensuring films get made and out to audiences (Figure 15.1).

However, See-Saw does not make a worthwhile object of study just because of the company's track record in making critically and commercially successful films across such a great geographical expanse. After all, Canning and Sherman are not the first producers to work across these lines and are instead the latest in a long line of film-makers to have done so. British and Australian cinemas have deep historical ties at numerous levels, ties that both mirror and are symptomatic of the larger historical relationship that exists between the nations themselves. This of course is a history that includes a long imperial relationship that eventually gave way to 'Commonwealth' and Dominion, and which has continued on a trajectory that has steadily seen Australia move away from the United Kingdom politically while economic and cultural bonds have remained very strong, even if those bonds have undergone distinct changes over time. Scrutinizing the role of the producer helps us to better understand cultural and industrial aspects of film cultures, and what will become apparent in this chapter is

Figure 15.1 Colin Firth as King George VI and Geoffrey Rush as Lionel Logue in *The King's Speech* (2010)

that such aspects of film cultures can help us to understand much larger historical connections between nations. As we will see, See-Saw is a company that occupies a particular and significant position within the continuum of Anglo-Australian cinematic relations, one which is apparent at the levels of industrial practices as well as in some cases the cultural and aesthetic contents of their projects. Crucially, it is also a position that is arguably reflective of the current state of relations between the countries themselves, at least within the larger context of the relationships between the former members of the British Empire.

In this chapter, I will first provide an account of the larger tradition of British-Australian cinema, sketching out its contours, changes and developments up to the present day. I will then detail the careers of Sherman and Canning before the founding of See-Saw, pointing out the ways in which their experiences would eventually help determine the transnational practices of the company. This will be followed by an overview of the work of the company itself, focusing on the obvious debt these works owe to their origins in British-Australian cinema. I will then argue that See-Saw's work and, crucially, their working methods show significant departures from the tendencies apparent in previous British-Australian film-making, departures which are indicative of the growth and development of the network as a whole as well as the evolving relationship between Britain and Australia as political and economic partners in a post-imperial world. Before doing any of this, however, we must begin with the emerging fields of cinematic transnationalism and film and history, the two areas in which this research has the most import, and the role that the producer plays in the debates within these fields.

Critical transnationalism, film and history and the producer

As was discussed in the Introduction, the producer has been curiously absent from critical discourses on national and transnational cinemas, but the problems in the field of cinematic transnationalism go beyond overlooking the producer. As several critics, including most prominently Mette Hjort and Will Higbee and Song Hwee Lim, have argued, a serious problem within the field has been its collective lack of critical rigour and historical specificity.[1] In place of the rather amorphously defined and uncritically celebratory transnationalism that the field currently practises, these critics have called for a greater concern with assessing the ideological natures of specific manifestations of transnationalism. Higbee and Lim note that transnationalism has become exclusively focused solely on geographically determined networks; transnationalism in their view has essentially become a synonym for regionalism.[2] In her attempt to provide a typology of different kinds of transnational encounters between film-makers, Hjort has also provided useful categories for this study, particularly those of 'epiphanic' and 'affinitive' transnationalism, each being a category in which film-makers take advantage of larger historical and cultural connections between national cultures.[3] While I will not be arguing that See-Saw's films fit directly into these categories, I will nevertheless be adopting her general idea that some forms of transnational film practice are built upon larger cultural and historical commonalities and that assessing power dynamics inherent in these encounters is a vital part of the critical project of transnational film theory.

Given that the specific relationship in this case is one related to Britain's imperial past, this chapter will hope to show that analysis of the producer in transnational contexts can provide a new way to examine the relationship between film and history. Film and history has heretofore been a paradigm which either examines texts that are historical representations, scrutinizing them in relation to the interpretations of the past that they claim to represent, or which historicizes media texts regardless of their narrative content in relation to the larger contexts of when the film was made and released, in so doing analysing what the text in question demonstrates about that context and vice versa. As can be appreciated from my opening discussion of *The King's Speech*, such methods can be usefully applied to See-Saw's films at a thematic level and we will discuss some of them in precisely such terms later in the chapter. But contexts of production and circulation can themselves be reflective of these cultural and historical affinities, even if the thematic content of specific films does not lend itself to the reading strategies that critics in the field of film and history tend to favour. In addition to the specific argument regarding Australian and British cinematic relations that this chapter will seek to articulate, it thus also hopes to have import for the ways in which transnationalism and film and history conceive of their objects of study and will seek to argue that the producer should be central in both fields. Before attempting to use these producers to mount such an argument about the resonances that producers can have, however, we will begin with an overview of Anglo-Australian cinematic relations, a context that is vital for understanding the significance of See-Saw's work.

From Dominion to 'de-Dominionizing':
The Anglo-Australian cinematic relationship up to 1981

Since the earliest days of film-going in Australia in the 1890s, British colonial interests have shaped Australian film culture as well as Australian films, even if, as many historians point out, the American film industry has had the most influence on Australian filmgoers.[4] After Hollywood films, British films have long dominated the country's box office, regularly ranking second in terms of ticket sales for films by national origin. Such a position puts British films well ahead of the local product, as with rare exceptions (particularly in the 1980s) they have far outgrossed indigenous films at the box office.[5] Besides this industrial domination, there has been a particular and consistent interest in British culture even within indigenously produced films. At the level of thematic content, Australian films before the Second World War, particularly those of popular director-producer Charles Chauvel, often featured a sense of national identity that was at best deferential to Britishness and at worst saw Australian identity as part of a larger imperial identity that aspired to being British.[6]

With the coming of the Second World War and the related transition between Empire and 'Commonwealth', Anglo-Australian relations underwent a significant change, as did cinematic relations between the two countries. The year 1942 saw the adoption of the Statute of Westminster by the Australian parliament, an act which enshrined Australian independence within the Commonwealth, a form of independence with remaining ties of loyalty and cooperation that is typified by the continued support of Australia for the Allied war effort. From the British perspective, the movement towards Commonwealth was one that was equally geopolitical – an attempt to hold on to the influence that came with imperial power – and economic – an attempt to avoid the costs of ruling an empire, while still maintaining access to markets for its exports.[7] Film played its parts in both of these ambitions, with distributors such as British Empire Films seeking to market British films in all corners of the changing Empire along with attempts to enshrine exemptions for British films within the Quota Act of 1927, which allowed for British films to be considered 'homegrown' products throughout the Empire.[8]

Such a backdrop underpinned what is the most frequently discussed moment in Anglo-Australian film history, Michael Balcon's attempts to form a subsidiary of Ealing Studios in Australia. Beginning in the mid-1940s with the making of *The Overlanders* (Harry Watt, 1946) and continuing with later films including *Bitter Springs* (Ralph Smart, 1950) and *Eureka Stockade* (Harry Watt, 1949), Balcon sought to make films in Australia using British capital. In so doing, Balcon was banking on the nation's (to British eyes at least) exotic landscapes as a unique setting for Western-style adventure films, with the plan more or less being to market the films to both countries. In this business model, Australia was anticipated to be a site of both cheap production and willing audiences. The venture would ultimately prove to be unsuccessful as films subsequent to *The Overlanders* failed to find audiences in either country. As Peter Limbrick notes, many have seen this failure as indicative of a larger shift in Australian culture away from British influence and towards that of the United States. But this reasoning is flawed, says Limbrick, as Hollywood had already long dominated the Australian box office and controlled the country's distribution infrastructure to boot.[9] The British share of that market would not be enough to sustain a fully developed industry and Balcon's experiment was thus miscalculated as was the larger British idea of cultural domination of its colonies. The failure of this venture would keep Balcon from attempting to establish similar Ealing offices in Canada and South Africa.[10]

Even if Balcon's experiment with film-making in Australia demonstrated that Britain could not easily dominate its former colonies through the mechanisms and ideologies of the Commonwealth, the films themselves and their subsequent reception do show that deeper cultural affinities were still viable as material for film-making. This is particularly the case with *The Overlanders*, which was at least in part intended as state propaganda drawing attention to and valorizing Australia's contribution to the British war effort. Jonathan Rayner has described the ways in which the film's heroes, particularly Dan (Chips Rafferty), are 'as stereotypically British as [they are] Australian'.[11] Rayner also argues that the film's construction of Australianness 'is restricted by the stipulations of membership in the Commonwealth'.[12] Deane Williams likewise argues that the film is a document of neither British nor Australian film history, but instead a composite text that reflects the nations' shared histories.[13] The cultural affinities and familiarity underpinning the films are such that the Ealing films are held to contrast sharply with the more exploitive wave of Australian-set American films of the 1950s, films such as *The Sundowners* (Fred Zinnemann, 1960), which also use the country as an exotic setting, but which also evince little to no understanding of Australian culture.[14]

Whereas films such as *The Overlanders* portrayed Australia as a proud Dominion nation within the Commonwealth, film-making in the 'Australian new wave' of the 1970s and 1980s would reflect very critically on the shared history of the two nations. Thomas O'Regan has described a 'de-dominionizing' tendency in films such as *Breaker Morant* (Bruce Beresford, 1980) and *Gallipoli* (Peter Weir, 1981), which depict the suffering of Australian soldiers at the hands of an uncaring British military elite in the Boer War and the First World War, respectively.[15] For O'Regan, such revaluations of imperial history were part and parcel of Australian new wave's interrogation of Australian identity, one in which British heritage was just one aspect of that identity and a deeply problematic one at that. These films were successful at home in Australia and, significantly (and ironically), in Britain as well.[16] Their production, unlike the Ealing films, was wholly Australian, without any significant creative contributions from British film-makers or actors. On the British side, interest in Australia was apparent in the decades via wholly British funded 'creative runaway' films such as *Walkabout* (Nicholas Roeg, 1971) and *Ned Kelly* (Tony Richardson, 1974), which used the nation as a backdrop for mythical explorations of youthful coming of age and rebellion. Such estrangement at the levels of true industrial collaboration and thematic content can be usefully contextualized within the distance growing between the two nations at a political level as the Commonwealth 'family' zeitgeist of the immediate post-war period gave way to a growing sense of the anachronism of the institution of the Commonwealth, an alienation that was typified by Britain's turn to Europe as its primary trading partner with the joining of the Common Market in 1973. At the same time, however, it was also apparent that even if this institution was a neo-colonial throwback, the affinities between the countries were still relevant at least at the level of film content. Such affinities can be seen in British and Australian television productions in the 1970s, which did, unlike British and Australian cinema, see extensive Anglo-Australian co-production, much of which was historically themed.[17] It would be some time, however, until film producers collaborated in this way.

Emile Sherman, Iain Canning and See-Saw Films

For reasons that will become apparent, I will for now suspend the discussion of British-Australian cinematic relations to turn to an account of the careers of Emile Sherman and Iain Canning, careers which, I will argue, are emblematic of the changing relationship between film-makers in the two nations. Emile Sherman's career in cinema began with a highly personal project, *Uncle Chatzkel* (Rod Freedman, 2000), a documentary about Sherman's long-lost uncle who had stayed behind in Lithuania when the rest of the family emigrated to South Africa. Up to this point Sherman had little interest in working in cinema.[18] But after the experience of working on the film, he would go on to produce the now forgotten low-budget indie film *Sample People* (Clinton Smith, 2000), which starred pop music icon Kylie Minogue. This was followed by a series of stints as executive and associate producers on bigger budget films including a spoof version of the Ned Kelly story *Ned* (Abe Forsyth, 2003) and the internationally acclaimed *Rabbit Proof Fence* (Phillip Noyce, 2002). These films were stepping stones for a run of moderately budgeted indie films on which Sherman acted as producer, films that included Australian genre films such as *The Night We Called It a Day* (Paul Goldman, 2003). Sherman has described this phase of his career as one in which he struggled to find his voice as a producer and during which he made the mistake of chasing audiences rather than trusting his own taste and judgement.[19] As he learned to do this more and more, Sherman went on to produce a number of internationally successful art films, including *Candy* (Neil Armfield, 2006), which starred Heath Ledger, and *Disgrace* (Steve Jacobs, 2008) a film based on J. M. Coetzee's Booker Prize–winning South African novel. Other films preceding the formation of See-Saw included art films such as *Opal's Dream* (Peter Cattaneo, 2006) and *$9.99* (Tatia Rosenthal, 2008) as well as a number of other works.

A key aspect of Sherman's film-making for our purposes that was established during this period was his ability to work across national lines. Several of his films from this period were co-productions, including films made with partners in the United Kingdom (*The Night We Called It a Day, Opal Dream* and *The Oyster Farmer* [Anna Reeves, 2004]), Israel (*$9.99*) and South Africa (*Disgrace*). Such was Sherman's savvy with international co-production that two of his films – *$9.99* and *Disgrace* – would actually reshape Australia's national co-production policy, with the former being the catalyst (and to date sole beneficiary) of the bilateral co-production treaty between Israel and Australia, while the latter helped to pave the way for a similar treaty being signed between Australia and South Africa. For many of these projects, as well as his indigenous Australian films, Sherman was able to win support from public funding agencies and public service broadcasters, including Screen Australia, various state film companies and BBC Films, amongst others. Sherman's use of transnational production techniques went beyond simply utilizing production networks and accessing public funding. Films such as *Rabbit Proof Fence* and *Uncle Chatzkel* were not co-productions but nevertheless featured numerous transnational elements. The latter film involved location shooting in Lithuania and a screenplay that engaged with themes of diaspora. *Rabbit-Proof Fence* dealt with Britain and Australia's shared history and, like many of his films with See-Saw, also featured important creative contributions from figures such as Kenneth Branagh and veteran British producer Jeremy Thomas, who acted as an executive producer on the film.

At the time that he founded See-Saw along with Emile Sherman, Iain Canning was less experienced as a producer of feature films. Indeed, his debut film with a full producer credit was *The King's Speech*, See-Saw's first venture. Despite this relative inexperience as a full producer, Canning had worked on a number of films as an executive or associate producer. Significantly, his first credit in this regard was as an associate producer on *Candy*, on which he worked with Sherman. This was followed by two stints as executive producer, one each on *Control* (Anton Corbijn, 2007) and *Hunger* (Steve McQueen, 2008). The connections Canning forged while making these films would prove very significant to See-Saw's film-making, but it was his work on Australian films such as *Candy* and the animated feature *Mary and Max* (Adam Elliot, 2009) that more closely anticipated his partnership with Sherman. Crucially, before moving into film production, Canning was a key figure at sales companies Renaissance Films and Becker International. As we will see, it is this familiarity with the landscape of international sales and distribution, his working relationships with auteur directors and his ability to work between Australia and the United Kingdom that would become invaluable in the development of See-Saw Films.

See-Saw Films was incorporated in early 2008 and almost immediately began work on *The King's Speech*, which Sherman and Canning saw as the ideal project with which to launch the company.[20] Both producers have spoken about the theme of the clash of cultures between Australians and the British as being a prime reason for making this the first See-Saw film.[21] However, the Anglo-Australian dimensions of the film go much deeper than just this narrative premise. Besides these on-screen thematic resonances of familiar cultural difference and shared history, a combination of Australian and British influences can be seen across the making of the film. The film was directed by Tom Hooper, who has an Australian mother and a British father, and who has spoken of the Anglo-Australian themes appealing to him on a personal level.[22] The cast includes many actors of the British 'quality' tradition such as Colin Firth, Michael Gambon and Helena Bonham Carter, but also Australians Geoffrey Rush (himself something of an antipodean 'quality' actor) and Guy Pearce, who was somewhat unexpectedly cast as Edward VIII.

While *The King's Speech* was not an 'official' (i.e. treaty sanctioned) British-Australian co-production, See-Saw's next project would be. *Oranges and Sunshine* (Jim Loach, 2010) – which was developed by producer Camilla Bray at the UK-based production outfit Sixteen Films – was made within the requirements of the Australia-UK co-production treaty and therefore, like Sherman's *Opal Dream* before it, benefited from the treaty's provisions of eligibility for tax relief and production subsidies in both countries. Making the film in such a way allowed See-Saw to garner funding from a number of public film bodies in Australia, such as Screen Australia and Screen New South Wales, while also working with Sixteen Films and BBC Films in the United Kingdom. This complex financial arrangement, which also included other partners from both countries, was complemented by scripting, casting and a creative team that all reflected the film's Anglo-Australian production context. The film's plot concerns a British social worker, Margaret Humphreys (Emily Watson), working in the 1980s, who uncovers a series of 'adoptions' that were actually arranged by the Home Office as *de facto* deportations of children from troubled homes in England to state institutions in Australia. The film then goes on to trace Humphreys' attempts to assist victims of this practice, a process that involves several trips between England and Australia as she tracks down long-lost relatives, informs 'orphans' of their actual histories and in other ways attempts to heal symbolically the wounds of imperial history. To tell this story, Canning, Sherman and Bray brought together an English director (Jim Loach), English actors (e.g. Watson and Aisling Loftus) and Australian actors, including Hugo Weaving, whose career has crossed Anglo-Australian lines many times, and character actor David Wenham.

See-Saw's next two projects were somewhat anomalous within the context of the company's typical Anglo-Australian working methods. *The Kings of Mykonos* (Peter Andrikis, 2010) was a low-brow comedy devised as a star vehicle for comedian Nick Giannopoulous and aimed squarely at Australian audiences. *Shame* (Steve McQueen, 2011) was the next project from See-Saw, in many ways a continuation of sorts from Canning's work before See-Saw. Alone amongst their oeuvre to date, *Shame* is a film without any Australian content or creative contribution. The film is instead directed and co-written by Steve McQueen, a then emerging British auteur director (with whom Canning had worked on *Hunger*), featuring two stars of contemporary British cinema (Michael Fassbender and Carey Mulligan) and was set and shot wholly in New York City. The film was also funded in part by public bodies such as the UK Film Council and public service broadcaster Channel 4. While at a narrative level one cannot point to *Shame* as a film that embodies the cultural connections between Australia and Britain in the ways that *The King's Speech* and *Oranges and Sunshine* do, nevertheless it is an example of the ways in which the Anglo-Australian production axis was able to support and sustain auteur art-house cinema, a mode of cinema that has long depended on co-production networks for its existence.

Auteur cinema is the mould into which See-Saw's two latest productions fit. The first of these is *Dead Europe* (Tony Krawitz, 2012), a British-Australian-Greek 'co-venture', which is concerned with Isaac (Ewen Leslie), an Australian of Greek parentage who returns to Greece to scatter his late father's ashes. In the course of doing this, Isaac learns of a curse placed upon his family in their village. Investigating this curse and solving the mystery of a young Jewish boy that seems to be haunting him leads Isaac across Europe, with location shoots for the film in Greece, Hungary and France. In some ways, *Dead Europe* can be considered as a darker version of *The Kings of Mykonos* as both films use the Australian-Greek production axis to tell a story about diaspora, but the key difference for our concerns is that this film also uses British finance and creative contributions, with Sherman and Canning taking producing credits on the film along with Australian producer Liz Watts. Even if the film does not have any British narrative content to speak of, it does manage to use its British connections as a way into European production networks, where the filmmakers were able to partner with production firms in Greece and Hungary, in effect taking advantage of Britain's Southern European peripheries.

The mix of auteurist generic forms and lateral access to regional partnerships were also important parts of the industrial formula for *Top of the Lake* (Jane Campion, 2013), the latest project released by See-Saw and its first foray into television drama serials. Sherman and Canning took executive producer credits on this project

(Philippa Campbell is credited as producer), credits which reflect their influence on the project in that executive producers are typically the most influential production figures on television series.[23] Jane Campion is an Australasian auteur writer-director who needs little introduction in discussions of Australian or New Zealand cinema, but she is also someone who should be familiar to those interested in Anglo-Australian cinematic relations. Although she has benefited from continental European financial support for her films as well as audience interest in countries such as France and Italy, an aspect of her film-making that is too seldom discussed is her dependence on British production resources and audiences throughout her career. Before her international breakthrough with *The Piano* (an Australian, New Zealand and French co-venture), Channel 4 backed her television series-cum-feature film *An Angel at My Table* (1990). After *The Piano* (1993), the British division of European conglomerate Polygram invested in *The Portrait of a Lady* (1996). *In the Cut* (2003) received funding from Pathé Pictures, which in turn was receiving funding from the UK Film Council under the Lottery franchise scheme. Her most recent feature film, *Bright Star* (2009) was officially registered as a UK-Australia co-production and received funding from BBC Films and the UK Film Council in addition to support from a number of Australian institutions including the Australian Film Funding Corporation and Screen Australia.[24]

Besides Campion herself (a New Zealand native and Australian citizen), the creative team for *Top of the Lake* had a mix of largely Australian and British talent, including Australian screenwriter Gerard Lee and actor David Wenham and experienced Scottish character actor Peter Mullan. Significantly, few New Zealanders besides Campion were involved in the project, the other major exception being actress Jacqueline Joe, who plays Tui, the girl who is missing for most of the series and therefore seldom on screen. The other New Zealanders cast in the series played minor roles with little dialogue or development as characters. The absence of any major creative contribution from New Zealand echoes the peripheral status the country has in the project, just as the casting of famous American actors (Elizabeth Moss and Holly Hunter) speaks of the power that the US market wields in the decision-making process for Anglophone media production.[25]

From domination to cooperation: See-Saw Films and contemporary Anglo-Australian cinema

Having examined See-Saw's production output in some detail, we can now return to the relationships between Britain and Australia's film cultures. Since the early 1980s, this relationship has undergone significant change and See-Saw's oeuvre as a production company has been shaped by these changes while also typifying them in a number of ways. These shifts are mainly to be found in the attempts to facilitate greater co-production activity between the two nations at the level of international film policy. The two nations entered into a formal co-production treaty in 1990, but two officially sanctioned co-productions (i.e. those which qualify for production incentives in both countries simultaneously) actually precede the treaty. These were made in 1986 and 1987 under the auspices of a one-off memorandum of understanding between the two countries.²⁶ In the latest official figures, since 1990, a total of 39 official British-Australian co-productions have been completed, 22 of which were feature films. Amongst Australia's co-production partners, this makes the United Kingdom its second most prolific partner, rivalled only by Canada, from which 42 co-productions have been developed.²⁷ Even in comparison to their counterparts in Canada, UK producers have made many more features. The Canadian treaty has thus far produced mainly animation, television series and documentaries, producing only seven features so far, one of which (*Map of the Human Heart*, Vincent Ward, 1991) was a multi-lateral co-production with Britain's Channel 4 and other partners. High profile British-Australian co-productions include the works of auteur directors such as the aforementioned Jane Campion, Vincent Ward and Gillian Armstrong as well as films such as *Sirens* (John Duigan, 1993), which starred Hugh Grant and was a sleeper box office success in both countries, and the Nick Cave-scripted bushranger film *The Proposition* (John Hillcoat, 2006). Excluding the United States, Britain has thus been Australia's most important partner for film production, with Australia occupying a similar position within British film policy where the treaty with Australia is one of its longest-standing pacts and one of its most productive.

Such 'official' co-production comes in addition to the substantial amount of informal collaboration and production that goes on between film-makers in the two countries, including See-Saw's co-ventures and films that were technically officially registered as either British (e.g. *The King's Speech* and *Shame*) or Australian (e.g. the forthcoming *Tracks* [John Curran, 2013]). Moreover, besides See-Saw, production companies such as Pictures in Paradise, founded by former Palace Pictures executive Chris Brown, and Warp X, a subsidiary of Britain's Warp Films run by Australian producer Anna McLeish, are also products of British-Australian industrial collaboration. In the case of Pictures in Paradise, Brown emigrated to Australia from the United Kingdom and has maintained his personal contacts in Britain and has utilized these to benefit from co-production incentives in some cases (e.g. *The Proposition*). In the case of Warp X, the company was started as a way of 'licensing' Warp's 'brand' of film-making for Australian projects that would ideally travel along the same distribution routes as Warp hits such as the works of Shane Meadows or *Submarine* (Richard Ayoade, 2010). McLeish learned of the potency of this brand first-hand during her time at distributor Madman Entertainment, which has so far handled all of Warp's films in Australia, which, like many British films, sell well in the Australian market.²⁸

Links to distribution companies in Australia is something that See-Saw shares with Warp X. Since the launch of the company, See-Saw has had a close relationship with Transmission Films in Australia, so close that both Canning and Sherman were for a time on the board of directors and Transmission refers to See-Saw as its 'sister company' and has acted as distributor for all of the company's films in Australia besides *Oranges and Sunshine*.²⁹ See-Saw also had a 'first-look' agreement with Momentum Films in the United Kingdom, an arrangement that combined with the Transmission deal helped to ensure distribution in these two lucrative markets. This also requires, of course, that the films be marketable in both countries, adding a distinctly bi-cultural commercial pressure to the company's film-making, but one that is arguably not all that onerous given the cultural affinities and mutual box office interest between the two nations, for not only have British films long been successful in Australia, but Australian films have also had disproportionate international success in the British market.[30] Besides providing access to these two specific markets, the distribution relationships that See-Saw established from the outset have also helped to facilitate access to the world's most lucrative box office, that of North America.[31]

Not only has this provided the company with market access for its products, it has also ensured that the money made on its films and television programmes actually ends up in the hands of the producers. As is widely known in the film business and within media industry studies scholarship, distribution is the most lucrative part of the industry and much of the profits reaped by distributors come from the exploitive relationships that they form with producers, particularly independent producers.[32] By being directly involved in the distribution of its works in Australia and closely involved with British distribution, See-Saw is in a position to protect its own interests and to profit from their successes, at least in its core markets. Moreover, the ownership position Canning and Sherman have in Transmission allows them to profit from the distribution of other films (essentially, their competition) in Australia. Such positioning thus makes See-Saw a more stable and well-resourced production house than many of its rival independent producers.

An additional innovative manoeuvre that has helped to buttress See-Saw's financial position has been the founding of subsidiary Fulcrum Media Finance. This company specializes in lending money to Australian film-makers, effectively 'cash-flowing' the 'producer's offset', a subsidy offered by Screen Australia after the completion of eligible projects, as well as similar tax credits in the United Kingdom and New Zealand.[33] Fulcrum has 'lent' money to See-Saw on several occasions when the company was planning to seek reimbursement from the offset, essentially guaranteeing the company cash flow during production. Fulcrum also lends money to independent producers across the British-Australasian production axis, producers who are ostensibly See-Saw's competitors, once again enhancing the stability of the overall firm. With its interests in production finance and distribution, two aspects of the industry that typically do not see direct involvement from producers, See-Saw is an independent company that has used the detailed knowledge of the industrial landscapes of both countries (and New Zealand) to create a more profitable and therefore stable and productive independent company in an industry that is usually prone to the instability of 'boom and bust' economics that tend to affect the independent end of the global film industry more severely than the established majors.

In terms of its business model, working methods and corporate organization, See-Saw is thus a company that fits very comfortably within the larger context of Anglo-Australian cinematic cooperation. Indeed the company, with its culturally symmetrical approach to production and distribution, embodies this cooperative zeitgeist perfectly. This larger cooperative context extends beyond cinema and encompasses much trade activity and policy between the two nations, activity that is itself built on historical and cultural affinities. But the affinities and symmetries are not just to be found in the industrial contexts of See-Saw's films. At thematic levels, these films also often engage with British and Australian cultural and historical links. As previously discussed, *The King's Speech* can be seen as allegory of Australian service to the Crown in the fight against Nazism. If O'Regan sees Australian films of the 1970s as manifesting a 'de-dominionizing' tendency, then we can see *The King's Speech* as reversing this tendency, effectively 're-dominionizing' Australia in relation to Britain. This tendency can usefully be understood in relation to the persistence of Australia's allegiance to the British monarchy, in spite of calls for Republicanism, a persistence that manifested itself in the last referendum on the issue in 1999 when the monarchy was upheld by a ten-point margin.

Similarly, *Oranges and Sunshine* can be usefully contextualized within interpretations of imperial history. This film, which Screen Australia described as a 'natural fit' for co-production between the two nations[34] deals with the traumatic aspects of that history by focusing on the true-life forced deportation of British children to Australia in the 1960s where many of them fell victim to physical and sexual abuse at the hands of their adopted families. While at first glance, this would seem to be a film that reflects critically on Britain's influence on Australia, by virtue of its sympathetic English protagonist who acts as a healer of the broken spirits of the victims of these policies, the film is actually an apology of sorts along with an assurance that Britain cares about atoning for the sins of the past. It also helps that the film is itself set in the past (the 1980s), allowing for a double distancing of its events from present-day audiences, a tactic that is common in co-productions, allowing all audiences to lament the injustices portrayed in the film while not offending any national audiences in the present.[35] As already discussed, other See-Saw films depict this relationship in less direct, and indeed less textual, ways, but one way or another, the company's works are in different ways reflective of industrial and cultural connections between Australia and the United Kingdom (Figure 15.2).

Figure 15.2 *Oranges and Sunshine* (2010) as 'natural fit' UK-Australia co-production: Margaret Humphreys (Emily Watson) heals post-imperial wounds by comforting abuse victim Jack (Hugo Weaving)

Anglo-Australian cinema and the Commonwealth

Those connections have clearly changed and evolved greatly over the last century, even if interesting parallels remain. As O'Regan pointed out in the mid-1990s, the move towards formal co-production policy with Canada and the United Kingdom at least merits some comparison to the 'Commonwealth' industrial sphere that was hoped for in the 1950s, one which would have included the Dominion nations of Australia, South Africa, New Zealand and Canada along with the United Kingdom itself.[36] Such an economic group, it was hoped, would rival American economic and cultural power. Eerily similar rhetoric can be found in contemporary film policy, including Screen Australia's co-production reports, which speak of the need to pool resources to combat the industrial dominance of Hollywood.[37] Such a rhetorical change comes as financing options for non-Hollywood film become increasingly rare and co-production of whatever kind has become a necessity for many independent film-makers. Within such a context, film policy amongst these Commonwealth nations has the overarching goal of pooling the resources of the nations to create a network of support to their audio-visual industries.

These networks have changed and grown in many ways in recent years. The networks are now larger than simply the Dominion nations of the former Empire. Britain's partners now also include India and Jamaica, a concession at least in the case of the former that it is an emerging economic superpower, as well as European nations and, more recently, Brazil, Morocco and China. Australia, for its part, has a variety of partners, including China and a number of European partners. Despite these expansions of their respective networks to non-Commonwealth countries, it is still the Commonwealth nations that end up being the primary partners in terms of co-production activity, a fact that can be attributed to shared cultures as much as they can to deep economic bonds, bonds which are themselves historically determined as much as they are by ethnic and linguistic ties, ties which are themselves yet further legacies of the colonial project.

Another key change that has occurred in last 30 years has been a shift in the power dynamics within Britain's partnerships with its former colonies. As can be seen in the oeuvre of See-Saw Films, there has been a marked progression from the neo-imperialist days of Ealing's experiments in making films in Australia. As opposed to Balcon's visions of exploiting Australia, we have in See-Saw a company more committed to collaboration, with input from each side of the world being more or less weighted equally, a reflection of not only the historically specific affinities between Australia and Britain but also industrial affinities in that both are largely white, English-speaking and relatively wealthy nations. A similar progression can be seen from the anti-British thematic trend of the 1970s and 1980s to an implicitly caring and cooperative view of British-Australian relations in Canning and Sherman's films together. How this compares to analogous industrial and cultural cooperative enterprises amongst other Commonwealth nations cannot be addressed here, but nonetheless remains a vital question. For now however, we can conclude this chapter by returning to the role of the producer in accounts of cinematic transnationalism.

Conclusions: Producers and transnational film networks

I hope to have shown that between Australia and Britain exists a media network which is neither united by geography nor centred around America, even if distribution in the United States remains a lucrative goal for many of the works produced within that network. This network is both very old and very active, even if its output is not on the scale of that of other, more widely discussed networks. Moreover, it is one that has changed in significant ways over the course of its existence, and See-Saw Films, this chapter's case study, embodies many of the latest changes in the dynamics of that network. By surveying a transnational network such as this, we have a context within which to appreciate the creative labour of the producers working within that network, labour which balances cultural and commercial aspects of film-making. As can be seen throughout this book, the producer's role in selecting projects that will meet the needs of target markets, assembling a creative team that is suited to the material and ensuring that they bring the film together in the appropriate fashion for the target market make him or her indispensable to discussions of creativity generally.

However, the producer is even more significant to understanding national and transnational media ecologies. Producers in national contexts must negotiate the demands of marketing films in those contexts, while understanding and working within and benefiting from policy frameworks, knowing the pools of talent which exist both within and without the nation and then of course knowing where to find funding in any given context. For producers in transnational contexts, these difficulties are multiplied considerably, particularly when, as in the case of See-Saw, those difficulties include vast geographic distances. Surviving within such complex work environments is laudable; thriving in them as See-Saw has done thus far is the mark of a truly talented and innovative production enterprise. Moreover, understanding their working methods not only helps appreciate their skills as producers but also allows us to better understand the overall network. Such a point is vital for this book as it is yet another reminder of the need of film historians to pay closer attention to producers.

This chapter has also sought to demonstrate the historiographical weighting that must be given to the producer in critical analyses of transnational networks. As can be seen from this discussion of Sherman and Canning (which has also touched on Balcon and Chauvel), focusing on the producer can help us to appreciate the larger trajectory of the historical relationships that exist between a former colonial power and its former subjects. The question remains, however, as to why we should explore these relationships through the work of the film producer. What is apparent through this study of British-Australian cinematic relations is that the dynamics of a relationship such as this include historical, cultural and industrial dimensions. Within the divisions of labour that exist in media production, it is only the producer who must deal with all of these in one form or another. By exploring the work of See-Saw during its relatively brief but so far successful run, we are able to witness the contours and intricacies of that network in ways that examining the careers of stars or directors could not come close to achieving. For this reason, if we want to explore the relationship between media and history in the multifaceted ways in which this chapter has sought to illuminate the relationship between Australia and Britain, it is to the producer that we must turn.

Notes

1   Mette Hjort, 'On the Plurality of Cinematic Transnationalism', in *World Cinemas, Transnational Perspectives*, ed. Nataša Ďuričová and Kathleen Newman (London: Taylor & Francis, 2010), 12–33. Will Higbee and Song Hwee Lim, 'Concepts of Transnational Cinema: Towards a Critical Transnationalism in Film Studies', *Transnational Cinemas*, 1:1 (2010): 7–22.

2   Higbee and Lim, 'Concepts of Transnational Cinema', 9.

3   Hjort, 'On the Plurality of Cinematic Transnationalism', 16–18.

4   See for example, Peter Limbrick, 'The Australian Western, or a Settler Colonial Cinema Par Excellence', *Cinema Journal*, 46:4 (Summer 2007): 84.

5   Tom O'Regan, *Australian National Cinema* (London: Routledge, 1996), 78.

6   O'Regan, *Australian National Cinema*, 312.

7   Lee Grieveson, 'Introduction', in *Film and the End of Empire*, ed. Lee Grieveson and Colin MacCabe (London: BFI Publishing, 2011), 3.

8   For more on the absurdity of this Act's provisions in relation to the Empire, see Priya Jaikumar's, *Cinema at the End of Empire: A Politics of Transition in Britain and India* (Durham: Duke University Press, 2006), 41–63.

9   Limbrick, 'The Australian Western', 83–84.

10 Limbrick, 'The Australian Western', 82.

11 Jonathan Rayner, *Contemporary Australian Cinema: An Introduction* (Manchester: Manchester University Press, 2000), 11.

12 Rayner, *Contemporary Australian Cinema*, 12.

13 Deane Williams, 'The Overlanders: Between Nations', *Studies in Australasian Cinema*, 1:1 (January 2007): 79–89.

14 Rayner, *Contemporary Australian Cinema*, 11. See also Brian McFarlane and Geoff Mayer, *New Australian Cinema: Sources and Parallels in British and American Film* (Cambridge: Cambridge University Press, 1992), 2.

15 O'Regan, *Australian National Cinema*, 314.

16 Official figures do not exist, but on its website, Screen Australia anecdotally reports that *Gallipoli* for instance topped the UK box office for a week upon its release in the country in 1981. See http://www.screenaustralia.gov.au/research/statistics/mrboxuk.aspx, accessed 19 August 2013.

17 O'Regan, *Australian National Cinema*, 95.

18 Centre for Screen Business, 'Interview with Emile Sherman', accessed 19 August 2013, http://csb.aftrs.edu.au/2012/04/17/emile-sherman/.

19 Emile Sherman, Interview with the author, 11 April 2013.

20 Canning has said that See-Saw was incorporated in February of 2008 and the partners agreed to make *The King's Speech* in March of that year. See Watershed.com, 'BAFTA Preview: *The King's Speech* Q&A', accessed 19 August 2013, http://www.watershed.co.uk/dshed/bafta-preview-kings-speech-iain-canning-and-gareth-unwin/.

21   Canning notes this in Watershed.com, 'BAFTA Preview: *The King's Speech Q&A*'. Sherman has seconded this point several times. See for example AFTRS Centre for Screen Business, 'Emile Sherman Interview', http://csb.aftrs.edu.au/2012/04/17/emile-sherman/ (accessed 19 August 2013).

22   Quoted in *The King's Speech: An Inspirational Story of an Unlikely Friendship*, featurette included on the US DVD release of *The King's Speech*.

23   Emile Sherman, Interview with the author, 11 April 2013.

24   The film also received funding from a French partner (Pathé Renn), but the film was not registered as a French-Australian co-production despite there being a treaty in place between France and Australia.

25   The casting of Moss in particular was controversial for reasons related to national identity. The Australian Broadcasting Company had originally signed on as a backer for the project, but only on the condition that an Australian or New Zealander actress be cast in the lead role of Robin. When Moss was cast, a move that was interpreted as an attempt to cash in on Moss' fame in North America stemming from her role in the popular television drama *Mad Men*, the ABC pulled out of the project.

26   Screen Australia, *Friends With Benefits: A Report on Australia's International Co-Production Program* (Government of Australia, 2012), 27. The films in question were *The First Kangaroos* (Frank Cvitanovic, 1988) and *The Four Minute Mile* (Jim Goddard, 1988).

27   Screen Australia, *Friends With Benefits*, 6.

28   Anna McLeish, Interview with the author, 12 November 2012.

29   This has typically been done through Paramount Pictures International, the Australian distributor owned and operated by Paramount. Transmission has a close relationship with PPI and regularly outsources the distribution of major releases to the American company in order to benefit from the scale of the American company in terms of distribution within Australia.

30   O'Regan, *Australian National Cinema*, 82–83. It should be noted too that not all of See-Saw's films have been distributed in the United Kingdom by Momentum. *The Kings of Mykonos* did not receive a British release at all and *Oranges and Sunshine* was distributed by Icon Entertainment.

31   Emile Sherman, Interview with the author, 11 April 2013.

32   For just one of many accounts of such relationships, see Janet Wasko, *How Hollywood Works* (London: Sage, 2003), 59–103.

33   These are the UK Tax Credit and awards from the New Zealand Screen Production Investment Fund. See AFTRS Centre for Screen Business, 'Emile Sherman Interview'.

34   Screen Australia, *Friends With Benefits*, 4.

35   Barbara Selznick, *Global Television: Co-Producing Culture* (Philadelphia: Temple University Press, 2008), 33.

36   O'Regan, *Australian National Cinema*, 74.

37   Screen Australia, *Friends With Benefits*, 3.

Index

Note: The letter 'n' following locators refers to notes

0 1341 1661941 9

CPSIA information can be obtained at www.ICGtesting.com
Printed in the USA
LVOW10s1238240616

493984LV00012B/113/P

9 781501 317774